Older Persons and the Law

AF736948

This book explores the law and legal system's impact on older persons. As well as describing the current law primarily in England and in Wales, it highlights the pivotal role that elder law lawyers play in using law to challenge and combat ageism. Important questions are raised about whether the law perpetuates ageism and whether the current working of the law effectively challenges discrimination, abuse, and social exclusion faced by older persons.

Elder law lawyers have an essential role in advocating for the rights of older persons. The book focuses on the need to uphold and respect the human rights of older persons, emphasising their dignity, autonomy, and right to inclusion. It examines key topics such as human rights in the context of ageing, the provision of social care, discrimination, decision-making capacities, mental health, and abuse and neglect. It also offers insights into the notion of personal liberty concerning older persons and whether existing safeguards are sufficient.

The international dimensions of elder law are discussed, highlighting the range of initiatives led by the United Nations and efforts by non-governmental organisations and regional bodies. These initiatives aim to confront and diminish ageism on both international and domestic fronts, emphasising the need for a concerted effort to enforce the rights of older persons across different cultures and legal systems.

This book will interest researchers, students, and practitioners specialising in family and social welfare law, elder law, human rights law, and discrimination law.

John Williams is Emeritus Professor at Aberystwyth University in Wales. He researches topics related to older persons and the law, including human rights, social care, capacity, abuse and neglect, care home design, relationships, and older prisoners. He has spoken at many conferences, appeared on TV and radio to discuss elder abuse, and advised governments and other bodies. John was an expert member of the panel investigating abuse in a care home, for the Commissioner for Older People in Northern Ireland. He works with several charities. John lives with his wife and assorted animals in the middle of a sheep farm in mid-Wales.

Older Persons and the Law

John Williams

Routledge
Taylor & Francis Group
LONDON AND NEW YORK

Designed cover image: Getty Images

First published 2025
by Routledge
4 Park Square, Milton Park, Abingdon, Oxon OX14 4RN

and by Routledge
605 Third Avenue, New York, NY 10158

Routledge is an imprint of the Taylor & Francis Group, an informa business

© 2025 John Williams

The right of John Williams to be identified as author of this work has been asserted in accordance with sections 77 and 78 of the Copyright, Designs and Patents Act 1988.

All rights reserved. No part of this book may be reprinted or reproduced or utilised in any form or by any electronic, mechanical, or other means, now known or hereafter invented, including photocopying and recording, or in any information storage or retrieval system, without permission in writing from the publishers.

Trademark notice: Product or corporate names may be trademarks or registered trademarks, and are used only for identification and explanation without intent to infringe.

British Library Cataloguing-in-Publication Data
A catalogue record for this book is available from the British Library

ISBN: 978-0-415-45421-6 (hbk)
ISBN: 978-1-85941-922-9 (pbk)
ISBN: 978-0-203-79805-8 (ebk)

DOI: 10.4324/9780203798058

Typeset in Times New Roman
by Deanta Global Publishing Services, Chennai, India

This book is dedicated to Mum and Dad, who were sadly deprived of the joy of togetherness in later life.

Contents

Preface

In writing this book, I have benefitted from the support I received during my career in the Department of Law and Criminology at Aberystwyth University in Wales. The students I had the pleasure of teaching were challenging and engaging. Throughout my career, I also had the opportunity to meet many social care and healthcare practitioners. I gained valuable insights from their practical experiences, which extended my thinking and reading beyond the confines of academia.

The support I received from many colleagues at Aberystwyth enabled me to assume the role of head of the department while continuing my teaching and research. I am grateful to all of them, although space prevents me from mentioning each one. However, I would like to acknowledge a few. First, my friend and coffee-drinking buddy, Chris Harding, always took the time to read and provide insightful feedback on my work, even though it was outside his area of research. He was generous with his time not only for me but also for other colleagues in Aberystwyth and beyond, as well as undergraduate and postgraduate students. His untimely passing was a loss to academia and the numerous people worldwide who valued his friendship, humour, and wisdom. He is missed as a wonderful colleague and a great friend.

It was an enjoyable and rewarding experience working with Alan Clarke, Sarah Wydall, and the team establishing the Dewis Choice Project at Aberystwyth. Dewis Choice has an excellent reputation for supporting older persons who have experienced domestic abuse, making a real and tangible difference in their lives. This project was a testament to the power of cross-disciplinary collaboration and the potential for real-world application of research. We always resolved disciplinary differences with good humour and robust discussion.

My long-time friends and colleagues, Diane Rowland, Uta Kohl, Ann Sherlock, Richard Ireland, and Ryszard Piotrowicz, have always supported and encouraged me. I am also grateful to have collaborated with Gwyneth Roberts and Aled Griffiths from Bangor University on older persons and the law.

Working with Eric Drogin, a forensic and clinical psychologist who holds faculty appointments with Harvard Medical School and is the Chair of the American Bar Association's Commission on Law and Aging, has given me valuable insight into ageing in America, particularly mental health. I thank him for all his support and the opportunity to contribute to Harvard's Program in Psychiatry and Law and address the ABA's Senior Lawyers Division.

Throughout the years, I have been involved with many third-sector organisations focusing on ageing, mental health, advice, advocacy, and domestic abuse. Witnessing firsthand the difficulties and suffering endured by many in society provides compelling evidence of the necessity for change.

Finally, I want to express my deep appreciation to my wife and best friend, Carol. Words are inadequate to express the value of her unwavering support. In a literal sense, this book would not have been completed without her!

Y Gors,
Aberystwyth,
Cymru.
Ionawr 2025.

Table of cases

Domestic Courts

A County Council v MS, 2014 WL 1219394, 60.
A Local Authority v AK [2012] 11 WLUK 947.
A Local Authority v DL [2012] EWCA Civ 253, [2013] Fam 1.
Re SA (Vulnerable adult with capacity: marriage) [2005] EWHC 2942 (Fam), [2006] 1 FLR 867.
DL Local Authority [2011] EWHC 1022 (Fam), [2012] 1 FLR 1119.
A Local Authority v EBY and Others [2023] EWHC 2494 (Fam), [2023] 10 WLUK 66).
A Local Authority v GP (Capacity: Care, Support and Education) [2020] EWCOP 56 | [2020] 9 WLUK 449.
A Local Authority v H (by her litigation friend the Official Solicitor), [2023] EWCOP 4, 192 BMLR 1.
A Local Authority v JB [2012] UKSC 52, [2013] 1 AC 484.
A Local Authority v KK and Others [2020] EWCOP 68 | [2020] 12 WLUK 355.
A Primary Care Trust v LDV (by her litigation friend the Official Solicitor), [2013] EWHC 272 (Fam), 2013] 2 WLUK 453.
ABB v Milton Keynes Council [2011] EWHC 2745 (QB); [2012] 1 F.L.R. 1157.
AC (Capacity: Hoarding: Best Interests), Re [2022] EWCOP 39; [2022] 8 WLUK 222.
Airedale National Health Service Trust v Bland [1993] AC 789. [1997] ELR 66.
AK (Adult Patient) (Medical Treatment: Consent), Re [2000] 8 WLUK 112, [2001] 1 FLR 129.
Ali v Birmingham City Council [2010] UKSC 8, [2010] 2 AC 39.
AM v South London & Maudsley NHS Foundation Trust [2013] UKUT 365 (AAC), [2013] 8 WLUK 60.
An NHS Foundation Trust v Amira (by her litigation friend, the Official Solicitor) [2023] EWCOP 25, [2023] 6 WLUK 145, [35].
An NHS Trust and another v WA and another [2020] EWCOP 37.
Attorney General ex rel Tilley v London Borough of Wandsworth [1981] 1 All ER 1162.
Azancot, Re (2009) COP 27/5/09.
B (Consent to Treatment: Capacity), Re [2002] EWHC 429 (Fam), [2002] 2 All E.R. 449.

Bank of Scotland Plc v AB Employment Appeal Tribunal, 2020 WL 00999593 and 2021] EWCA Civ 345,| [2021] 3 WLUK 205.
Begum v Tower Hamlets LBC [2003] UKHL 5, [2003] 2 AC 430.
Bolam v Friern Hospital Management Committee [1957] 1 WLR 583.
Bolitho v City and Hackney Health Authority - [1997] 4 All ER 771.
Brown v Parole Board for Scotland [2017] UKSC 69, [2018] AC 1.
C (adult: refusal of medical treatment), Re [1994] 1 All ER 819.
Callin, Heather and Ward v Leonard Cheshire [2002] EWCA Civ 366, [2002] 2 All E.R. 936.
Cambridge University Hospitals NHS Foundation Trust v AH [2021] EWCOP 64, [2021] 12 WLUK 175.
CC v KK [2012] EWHC 2136 (COP); [2012] 7 WLUK 861, 69.
Cheshire West and Chester Council v P [2014] UKSC 19, [2014] AC 896.
Cheshire West and Chester Council v PWK [2019] EWCOP 57.
Chesterfield Royal Hospital NHS Foundation Trust v TS [2021] EWCOP 41; [2021] 6 WLUK 284.
Collis, Re (unreported) 27 October 2010.
CtHR A v X [2012] EWHC 2400 (COP); [2012] 7 WLUK 953, 41.
D, Re (statutory will) [2010] EWHC 2159 (Ch), [2012] Ch 57.
De Freitas v Permanent Secretary of Ministry of Agriculture, Fisheries, Lands and Housing [1999] 1 AC 69.
Deceasedumbrella.com Ltd (formerly trading as Racs Collective Ltd), Re [2021] 11 WLUK 389.
Devon Partnership NHS Trust v Secretary of State for Health and Social Care [2021] EWHC 101 (Admin), [2021] 1 W.L.R. 2945.
DMM, Re [2017] EWCOP 32, [2017] 7 WLUK 588.
DP v Hillingdon LBC [2020] EWCOP 45, (2021) 180 BMLR 179.
E v Hammersmith and Fulham LBC [2021] EWCOP 7, [2021] 1 WLUK 304.
Edwards (deceased), Re [2007] EWHC 1119 (Ch), [2007] 5 WLUK 72.
F (Adult: Court's Jurisdiction), Re 2001] Fam 38, 54.
Gillick v West Norfolk & Wisbech Area Health Authority [1986] AC 112.
Hammond v Osborn [2002] EWCA Civ 885, 2002 WL 1310756.
Harrow LBC v Qazi [2003] UKHL 43, [2004] 1 A.C. 983.
Havering London Borough Council v AEL [2021] EWCOP 9 [48], [2021] 1 WLUK 375.
HE v A Hospital NHS Trust2003] 2 FLR 408, [2003] 2 F.L.R. 408.
IH (Observance of Muslim Practice), Re [2017] EWCOP 9; [2017] All ER (D) 61 (Jun).
(A Child) (Care Proceedings: Placement Outside Jurisdiction) Re, [2017] 4 W.L.R. 99, [2017] 2 WLUK 622, [57].
Islington LBC v EF [2022] EWHC 803 (Fam), [2022] 3 WLUK 548.
JE v DE and Surrey County Council [2006] EWHC 3459 (Fam), [2007] 2 F.L.R. 1150.
K v A Local Authority [2012] EWCA Civ 79, [2012] 1 FCR 441.
Kent CC v P [2022] EWCOP 3, [2022] 2 WLUK 59.

KM [2007] EWHC 2003 (Fam), [2009] 1 FLR 443, [121]–[124].
L v J [2010] EWHC 2665 (Fam), [2010] 9 WLUK 378.
Liverpool City Council v CMW [2021] EWCOP 50; [2021] 7 WLUK 644.
Local Authority X v MM (by the Official Solicitor) and KM [2007] EWHC 2003 (Fam), [2009] 1 FLR 443.
London Borough of Haringey v R (by his litigation friend, the Official Solicitor) and Others [2016] EWCOP 12, [2016] All ER (D) 78.
M (vulnerable adult) (testamentary capacity), Re [2009] EWHC 2525 (Fam) 35.
M, ITW v Z, Re [2009] EWHC 2525 (Fam); [2011] 1 WLR 344, 32.
Malette v. Shulman (Ont. C.A.), 1990 CanLII 6868 (ON CA).
MB, Re (Caesarean section) [1997] 2 F.L.R 426.
McCulloch v Forth Valley Health Board [2023] UKSC 26, [2023] 3 WLR 321.
Midland Bank v Shepherd [1988] 3 All ER 17.
Mohammed v Secretary of State for Defence2017] UKSC 2, | [2017] AC 821.
Montgomery v Lanarkshire Health Board [2015] UKSC 11, [2015] AC 1430.
NHS Trust v L [2012] EWHC 2741 (COP), [2012] 8 WLUK 345.
P (by his litigation friend the Official Solicitor) v Cheshire West and Chester Council and Another; P and Q (by their litigation friend the Official Solicitor) v Surrey County Council [2014] UKSC 19, [37]; [2014] AC 986.
PC v City of York Council [2013] EWCA Civ 478, [2014] Fam 10.
PH v A Local Authority [2011] EWHC 1704 (Fam), [2011] 6 WLUK 749.
PH v Betsi Cadwaladr University Health Board [2022] EWCOP 16, (2022) 186 BMLR 148.
Public Guardian v RI [2022] EWCOP 22, [2022] 6 WLUK 23.
PW (Jehovah's Witness: Validity of Advance Decision), Re [2021] EWCOP 52, [2021] 9 WLUK 212.
QJ v Local Authority [2020] EWCOP 7, [2020] 1 WLUK 374.
R (Brown) v Secretary of State for Work and Pensions [2008] EWHC 3158 (Admin), [2008] 12 WLUK 546.
R (Davey) v Oxfordshire CC [2017] EWCA Civ 1308; [2017] 9 WLUK 7.
R (JF) v The London Borough of Merton [2017] EWHC 1519 (Admin); [2017] 6 WLUK 674.
R (on the application of C) v A Local Authority [2011] EWHC 1539 (Admin), [2011] All ER (D) 171 (Jun); Havering London Borough Council v LD [2010] 6 WLUK 641.
R (on the application of Dowsett) v Secretary of State for Justice [2013] EWHC 687 (Admin), [2013] 3 WLUK 773.
R (on the application of Jenkins) v HM Coroner for Portsmouth and South East Hampshire [2009] EWHC 3229 (Admin), [2009] All ER (D) 103 (Dec).
R (on the application of JG) v Southwark LBC [2020] EWHC 1989 (Admin).
R (on the application of McDonald) v Royal Borough of Kensington and Chelsea [2011] UKSC 33, [2011] 4 All ER 881.
R (on the application of P) v London Borough of Newham [2001] EWHC Admin 589; (2001) 4 CCL Rep 48.

R (on the application of Raja and another (by their mother and litigation friend)) v Redbridge London Borough Council [2020] EWHC 1456 (Admin), [2020] PTSR 2129.
R (Sessay) v South London and Maudsley NHS Foundation Trust [2011] EWHC 2617 (QB; [2012] Q.B. 760.
R (Worcestershire County Council) v SSHSC [2023] UKSC 31, [2023] 1 W.L.R. 2790.
R v Bournewood Community and Mental Health NHS Trust, ex parte L (Secretary of State for Health intervening) [1998] 2 WLR 764. [1999] 1 AC 458.
R v Broadcasting Standards Commission ex p BBC [2000] EWCA Civ 116, [2000] 3 All ER 989.
R v East Sussex County Council ex parte Ward (2000) 3 CCL Rep 132.
R v Instan [1893] 1 QB 450 [1957] 1 WLR 583 (QBD) (584).
R v Port of London Authority, ex parte Kynoch Ltd [1919] 1 KB 176, CA, Bankes LJ.
R v R [1992] 1 AC 599.
R v Stone [1977] 2 All ER 341.
R. (on the application of Conway) v Secretary of State for Justice [2018] EWCA Civ 1431, [2020] QB 1.
R. (on the application of Ferreira) v HM Senior Coroner for Inner South London [2017] EWCA Civ 31, [2018] Q.B. 487.
R. (on the application of H) v Mental Health Review Tribunal for North and East London Region [2001] EWCA Civ 415, 61 BMLR 163.
R. (on the application of JG) v Southwark LBC [2020] EWHC 1989 (Admin) | [2020] 7 WLUK 355.
R. v Barnet LBC Ex p. Shah [1983] 2 AC 309.
R. v Islington LBC Ex p. Rixon [1996] 3 WLUK 251.
Rabone v Pennine Care NHS Trust [2012] UKSC 2, [2012] 2 AC 72.
RB Greenwich v CDM [2019] EWCOP 32; [2019] 4 W.L.R. 130.
Regina (E) v Islington London Borough Council [2017] EWHC 1440 (Admin), [2018] P.T.S.R. 349.
Royal Bank of Scotland PLC v Etridge (No.2) [2001] UKHL 44, [2002] 2 AC 773.
R v Bristol City Council, ex parte Penfold (1998) 1CCL Rep 315.
S v Birmingham Women's And Children's NHS Trust [2022] EWCOP 10; [2023] 1 F.L.R. 458, 58.
Savage v South Essex Partnership NHS Foundation Trust [2008] UKHL 74, [2009] 1 A.C. 6.
SB (A Patient) (Capacity to Consent to Termination), Re [2013] EWHC 1417 (COP),[2013] 3 F.C.R. 384.
SB, Re [2015] EWCOP 7, [2015] 2 WLUK 399.
Schrader v Schrader [2013] EWHC 466 (Ch), [2013] 3 WLUK 258.
Sheldrake v DPP [2004] UKHL 43, [2003] 1 AC 681, 707.
Sidaway v Bethlem Hospital [1985] AC 871, [1990] 2 AC 1.
Southend-on-Sea BC v Meyers [2019] EWHC 399 (Fam), (2019) 168 B.M.L.R. 91.

Southwark London Borough v KA and Others (Capacity to Marry) [2016] EWCOP 20, [2016] 3 WLUK 657.
SR, Re [2018] EWCOP 36, [2018] 6 WLUK 685.
St George's Healthcare NHS Trust v S (No.1) [1998] 3 All E.R. 673.
St George's Healthcare NHS Trust v S [1998] 3 WLR 936.
Staffordshire CC v K [2016] EWCA Civ 1317, [2017] Fam 278.
Staffordshire County Council v SRK (by his litigation friend SK), RK, Irwin Mitchell Trust Corporation, The Secretary of State for Justice [2016] EWCA Civ 1317, [2017] Fam. 278.
T (Adult: Refusal of Treatment), Re [1993] Fam 95, 102.
The Public Guardian v DA and Others [2018] EWCOP 26, [2018] EWCOP 26.
Tracy v Cambridge University Hospital NHS Trust [2014] EWCA Civ 822, [2015] Q.B. 543.
UR v Derby City Council [2021] EWCOP 10, [2021] 1 WLUK 399.
Uratemp Ventures Ltd v Collins [2001] UKHL 43, [2002] 1 AC 301.
Various Lasting Powers of Attorney, Re [2019] EWCOP 40, [2020] 3 All E.R. 879.
Watt v ABC [2016] EWCOP 2532, [2017] 4 W.L.R. 24.
Williams (Deceased) [2022, Re] EWHC 1334 (Ch), [2022] 5 WLUK 527.
Wingrove v Wingrove (1885) 11 PD 81.
Winspear v City Hospitals Sunderland NHS Foundation Trust [2015] EWHC 3250 (QB); [2016] Q.B. 691.
X (Deprivation of Liberty), Re [2014] EWCOP 25, [2015] 1 W.L.R. 2454.
X (Deprivation of Liberty), Re [2015] EWCA Civ 599, [2016] 1 W.L.R. 227.
X LBC v MR [2022] EWCOP 1, [2022] 1 WLUK 248.
YL v Birmingham City Council [2007] UKHL 27, [2008] 1 AC 95.
ZH v Commissioner of the Police for the Metropolis [2013] EWCA Civ 69; [2013] 1 W.L.R. 3021.

European Court of Human Rights

A v United Kingdom App no 100/1997/884/1096 (ECtHR, 23 September 1998).
A-MV v Finland, App no 53251/13 (ECtHR, 23 March 2017).
AN v Lithuania App no 37553/05 (ECtHR, 15 October 2015).
Ashingdane v United Kingdom App no 8225/78 (ECtHR, 28 May 1985).
Austin v United Kingdom App no 39692/09 (ECtHR, 14 September 2011).
Bărbulescu V. Romania App no 61496/08 (ECtHR, 5 September 2017) [71].
British Gurkha Welfare Society and Others v. the United Kingdom App no 44818/11 (ECtHR, 15 September 2016).
Buck v Germany App no 41604/98 (ECtHR, 28 July 2005).
Buckley v United Kingdom, Merits, App no 20348/92 (ECtHR, 29 September 1996).
Carvalho Pinto de Sousa Morais v Portugal App no 17484/15 (ECtHR, 25 July 2017).
Centre for Legal Resources on behalf of Valentin Câmpeanu v. Romania App no. 47848/08 (ECtHR, 17 July 2014).

Dodov v. Bulgaria App no. 59548/00 (ECHR, 17 January 2008).
Doorson v The Netherlands 54/1994/501/503.
Fernandes de Oliveira v. Portugal App no 78103/14 ECtHR, 31 January 2019) [124].
HL v United Kingdom App no 45508/99 (ECtHR, 5 October 2004).
Hristozov and Others v. Bulgaria App nos 47039/11 and 358/12 (ECtHR, 15 February 2018).
Ilnseher v. Germany App nos 10211/12 and 27505/14 (ECtHR, 2 February 2017).
J.D. and A v. the United Kingdom App nos 32949/17 and 34614/17 (ECtHR, 24 October 2019).
Jarrand v France App no 56138/16 (ECtHR 9 March 2022) [75].
Lingens v Austria App no 9815/82 (ECtHR, 8 July 1986).
M v Ukraine App no 2452/04 (ECtHR, 19 April 2012).
MC and AC v Romania App no 12060/12107 (ECtHR, 12 April 2016) [107].
Mc Donald App no. 4241/12 (ECtHR 20 May 2014) [47].
Mitovi v. the Former Yugoslav Republic of Macedonia App no. 53565/13 (ECtHR, 16 July 2015).
N. V. Romania (no. 2) App no 38048/18 (ECtHR, 16 November 2021).
Oberschlick v Austria App no 20834/92 (ECtHR, 1 July 1997) [60].
Observer and Guardian v United Kingdom, App no 13585/88 (ECtHR, 26 November 1991) [71].
Osman v United Kingdom App no 87/1997/871/1083 (ECtHR, 28 October 1998).
Pretty v United Kingdom App no. 2346/02 (ECtHR 29 April 2002) [65].
Pretty v. the United Kingdom App no 2346/02 (ECtHR, 29 April 2002).
Ribbitsch v Austria App no 18896/91 (ECtHR, 4 December 1995).
Schwizgebel v. Switzerland App no 25762/07 (ECtHR, 10 June 2010).
Selahattin Demirtaş v. Turkey App nos 14305/17 (ECtHR, 22 December 2020).
Silver v United Kingdom App no 5947/72 (ECtHR, 25 March 1983).
Soering v. The United Kingdom, App No. 14038/88, 7 July 1989.
Stanev v Bulgaria App no 36760/06 (ECtHR, 17 January 2012) and DD v Lithuania App no 13469/06 (ECtHR, 9 July 2012).
Stanev v Bulgaria App no 36760/06 (ECtHR, 17 January 2012).
Stanev v. Bulgaria, App no 36760/06 (ECtHR 17 January 2012).
Storck v. Germany App no 61603/00 (ECtHR, 16 September 2005).
Sunday Times v United Kingdom App no 6538/74 (ECtHR, 26 April 1979).
Tanko v Finland App no 23634/94 (ECtHR, 2 December 2008); Herczegfalvy v Austria App no 10533/83 (ECtHR, 24 September 1992).
Terna v. Italy App no 21052/18 (ECtHR, 14 April 2021).
Verein Klima Seniorinnen Schweiz and Others v SwitzerlandApp no 53600/20 (ECtHR, 9 April 2024).
Winterwerp v. the Netherlands App no 6301/73 (ECtHR, 24 October 1979).
X v United Kingdom App no 7215/75 (ECtHR 5, November 1981).
Young, James and Webster v United Kingdom App no 7601/76; 7806/77 (ECtHR, 13 August 1981) 63.

Table of legislation

Adult Support and Protection (Scotland) Act 2007.
Adults with Incapacity (Scotland) Act 2000.
Care Act 2014.
Children Act 1989.
Commissioner for Older People (Wales) Act 2006.
Community Care (Direct Payments) Act 1996.
Coronavirus Act 2020.
Coroners and Justice Act 2009.
Crime and Security Act 2010.
Domestic Abuse Act 2021.
Enduring Power of Attorney Act 1985.
Equality Act 2010.
Family Law Act 1996.
Government of Wales Act 2006.
Health and Social Care Act 2008.
Health and Social Care Act 2022.
Homicide Act 1957.
Housing Act 1996.
Human Rights Act 1998.
Local Authority Social Services Act 1970.
Mental Capacity (Amendment) Act 2019.
Mental Capacity Act (Northern Ireland) 2016.
Mental Capacity Act 2005.
Mental Health Act 1959.
Mental Health Act 1983.
Mental Health Act 2007.
National Assistance (Amendment) Act 1951.
National Assistance Act 1948.
National Health Service and Community Care Act 1990.
Offences Against the Person Act 1861.
Old Age Pensions Act 1908.
Older Americans Act 1965.
Powers of Attorney Act 2023.
Public Interest Disclosure Act 1998.

Serious Crime Act 2015.
Social Services and Well-being (Wales) Act 2014.
Stalking Protection Act 2019.
Suicide Act 1961.
Violence Against Women, Domestic Abuse and Sexual Violence (Wales) Act 2015.
Wales Act 2017.
Well-being of Future Generations (Wales) Act 2015.
Widows, Orphans and Old Age Contributory Pensions Act 1936.
Youth Justice and Criminal Evidence Act 1999.

Introduction

One thing we all have in common is that we are getting older, and there is nothing we can do to prevent this. However, some consequences of ageing can be mitigated, and the cosmetic industry has capitalised on this. Anti-ageing medicine is another area of growth. In some instances, medicine can effectively address conditions common in older age; others are the modern-day equivalent of the cure-all elixir promised by nineteenth-century snake oil salesmen. It is estimated that the value of the anti-ageing global market will rise from US$76.6 billion to US$93.1 billion by 2027.[1] However, it is essential to be aware of the potential pitfalls of the anti-ageing industry, such as unrealistic beauty standards and the constant pressure to look young. Cindy Joseph challenged the term 'anti-ageing,' much preferring the term 'pro-ageing.' Unusually, she started a career in modelling at the age of forty-nine and continued until a week before her death at the age of sixty-seven. She commented that she did not fit the status quo of the modelling world – 'I was 49 years old – I was under 5-foot-8, my hair was gray. Hello! I had crow's feet.' She modelled for Olay, Elizabeth Arden, Anthropologie, and Ann Taylor in her fifties and sixties. She challenged the common assumption in the fashion industry, and beyond, that our value goes down as we age.[2] As she said, 'aging is just another word for living.' Society holds mixed views on ageing and older persons. Ageism is prevalent in the media, public service, industry, commerce, employment, and social and health care, as discussed in the following chapters. More generally, older persons experience ageism in their daily interactions with others. They may be patronised, subject to name-calling, or assumed to be past it. Ageism is endemic, and its existence must be recognised and challenged.

Law is essential in any society. It governs human behaviour; without it, society would most likely descend into chaos. Law helps ensure rights, justice, and fairness. In some instances, the law may help change behaviour, leading to a change in attitudes. Elder law is a sub-discipline within law. An ageing population means that consideration has to be given to the relationship between older persons and the

1 D Petruzzi, 'Value of the global anti-aging market 2021–2027' (25 June 2024) <https://www.statista.com/statistics/509679/value-of-the-global-anti-aging-market/> accessed 28 September 2024.

2 DE Slotnik, 'Cindy Joseph, a model who embraced her age, is dead at 67' *New York Times* (New York, 25 July 2018).

DOI: 10.4324/9780203798058-1

law. Some laws are designed specifically for older persons, but these are relatively few. However, other areas of law will include older persons, but not exclusively. How does the law work for older persons? Is it a force for tackling or enabling ageism? To what extent do policymakers and lawmakers consider the interests of older persons when developing new laws? Do those responsible for implementing and enforcing the law ensure that older persons are not denied justice and are treated fairly? These are some of the issues that confront the elder law lawyer.

This book discusses some critical areas of elder law. However, it is not a comprehensive coverage. Wherever there is law, it is probably safe to assume that there is at least something of interest for scholars and practitioners of elder law. Space prevents detailed discussion, but the following are some examples not directly covered. Older persons, as well as being victims, may be perpetrators of crime. Are they treated fairly in the criminal justice system, particularly in prisons? Climate change has profound implications for older persons. The People's Climate Vote survey found that 78% of the people in the United Kingdom who are over sixty believe a climate emergency exists.[3] Many older persons are concerned about the future and how climate change will impact the lives of their children, grandchildren, and themselves. Climate change will directly impact many older persons globally. Older persons also have much to contribute to developing climate law and policy.

Place and space are another area of interest. One example is the need for lawyers to link with architects and designers to ensure that the design of facilities for older persons is human rights compliant. Does the design promote autonomy, dignity, and private life, or is it designed from the perspective of the building's owner? For example, does care home design support older residents in enjoying family life and intimate relationships?[4] At the community level, the Age-Friendly Communities initiative is dedicated to creating environments that support populations as they age and allow them to lead fulfilling lives. They enable older persons to remain in their communities, engage in activities, and contribute to their local areas as part of the global movement spearheaded by the World Health Organisation. The UK Network of Age-Friendly Communities brings together over seventy-five locations committed to enhancing services and infrastructure for older persons.[5] It supports healthy and active ageing and helps older persons contribute to and remain in their communities. Age-friendly communities are founded on human rights and equality laws. Nobody should be excluded from their community because they are older.

Technology can significantly improve the health and well-being of older persons. Remote health monitoring, online consultations, and connectivity with family, friends, and support groups are just a few examples. Similarly, artificial

3 UNPD, 'The peoples' climate vote 2024' (20 June 2024) <https://www.undp.org/publications/peoples-climate-vote-2024> - accessed 28 September 2024.

4 J Williams, 'Care homes and communities: A human rights approach to age-friendliness' in Gardiner GM and E O'Brien Webb (eds) *The Age-friendly Lens* (Routledge, 2023) 107.

5 Centre for Ageing Better, 'UK network of age-friendly communities' <https://ageing-better.org.uk/uk-network-age-friendly-communities> - accessed 28 September 2024.

intelligence (AI) technology can enhance the lives of older persons in their homes through applications such as health monitoring, home automation, cognitive stimulation, companionship, and emergency response. However, using AI and other technologies raises concerns such as privacy issues, reduced human interaction, ethical dilemmas, lack of personalised solutions, technological barriers, and potential errors. Addressing these challenges is crucial to ensure the legal, ethical, and potentially beneficial use of AI in the care of older persons and to realise the potential of technology to improve their lives.

The above illustrates that Elder Law has a far greater reach than wills, property transfers, and inheritance planning. What follows concentrates on a selection of the laws in England and in Wales, although there are references to other jurisdictions in the United Kingdom and beyond. The ninth edition of Encyclopaedia Britannica famously included in its index, 'WALES. See ENGLAND.' Although both nations are currently part of a unified jurisdiction, 'See England' no longer describes the contents of many areas of law, particularly health and social care. The Wales Acts of 1535 and 1542 annexed Wales to the Kingdom of England. However, in the 20th century, there was a gradual movement towards acknowledging Wales as a nation. In 1951, the government appointed a junior Home Office Minister of Welsh Affairs, later becoming a Minister of State. After the 1964 UK election, the Labour Government established the Secretary of State for Wales post and created the Welsh Office to implement Westminster Government policies in Wales. Fast forward to 1979, a referendum rejected devolution by a significant majority, but the issue resurfaced, leading to renewed calls for a Welsh democratic institution. Support for devolution increased during the 1980s and 1990s. In May 1997, the new Labour Government's manifesto included commitments to hold referendums on creating devolved administrations in Wales and Scotland. A Welsh referendum in 1997 resulted in a slight majority favouring devolution. This led to the Government of Wales Act 1998, establishing the National Assembly for Wales. The Act granted the National Assembly the power to make secondary legislation in those areas that were explicitly devolved. It met for the first time on 12 May 1999. In March 2011, Wales voted to grant full primary law-making powers to the National Assembly, with 63.5% support. In 2015, the United Kingdom Government published Powers for a Purpose, laying the groundwork for reserved power rather than the devolved powers model; the National Assembly would have the power to legislate on any subject not explicitly reserved to the Westminster Parliament.[6] The Wales Act 2017 made the National Assembly a permanent part of the UK constitution and changed its powers to the reserved powers model. It included giving the National Assembly the authority to choose its name and the voting system for its members. The National Assembly became the Senedd Cymru (Welsh Parliament) under the Senedd and Elections (Wales) Act 2020, gaining more legislative powers.

6 HM Government, 'Powers for a purpose: Towards a lasting devolution settlement for Wales' (Cm 9020, 2015).

In those areas within the devolution settlement for Wales, there is scope for Wales to adopt a different approach from England. This is particularly the case for social care and health. Rhodri Morgan, the First Minister of Wales from 2000 to 2009, used the term 'clear red water' or 'dŵr coch clir' to describe Wales' strategy of distancing itself from policy development in England.[7] The gap is apparent in some aspects of social care and health but less so in others. However, the divergence is such that 'for Wales see England' is not good enough. Differences need to be identified, and each can learn from the others. This is a potential strength of the devolved structure in the United Kingdom.

The subjects covered in this book reflect to some extent personal choices, although I hope they address some of the main areas of concern for older people. Chapter 1 is a general discussion that seeks to scope the subject matter of elder law. It emphasises the important role that elder law lawyers can play in eradicating ageism. Human rights are discussed in Chapter 2. In many ways human rights are central to ensuring that law and policy work for older people. Understanding mental capacity is essential to protect those older persons who, for many reasons, have limited capacity. The Mental Capacity Act 2005 is discussed in Chapter 3. The autonomy of older persons must be respected and, in particular, their right to decide. Chapter 4 looks at decision-making, particularly how people can plan for a possible loss of capacity and the role of the Court of Protection. A major challenge facing governments in England and in Wales is developing a sustainable and effective social care system. Despite reform in 2014, much remains to be done. Social care is discussed in Chapter 5. It is a sad reflection on society that many older persons experience abuse and neglect; the settings are many, and the perpetrators may be known to the older person or be strangers. England and Wales made some progress towards establishing an effective adult safeguarding law, but as with social care, more needs to be done. Abuse and neglect are covered in Chapter 6. Liberty is an essential human right, and older persons are as entitled to enjoy it as any other generation. However, there may be circumstances where it is necessary to deprive an older person of their liberty under the Mental Health Act 1983 or the Mental Capacity Act 2005. Both include considerable powers to deprive people of their liberty. Chapter 7 discusses this legislation and questions whether it remains fit for purpose. Finally, Chapter 8 looks at the international aspect of elder law and some initiatives by the United Nations and NGOs to address ageism at an international and regional level.

While this book focuses on older persons, it is not intended to minimise the significant challenges and hardships faced by other age groups. Children and young people have suffered hardships due to the effects of austerity on education and social care. Adults, particularly those with disabilities, experience discrimination and a loss of welfare support. Poverty, inadequate housing, food insecurity, and

7 See J Osmond, 'Making the "red water" really clear' (Institute of Welsh Affairs, 2010) <https://www.iwa.wales/agenda/2010/07/making-the-red-water-really-clear/> - accessed 28 September 2024.

isolation are widespread across all age groups. Those in the media and politics who aim to fuel intergenerational conflict have their reasons for doing so – shame on them. The reality is that, in many respects, different generations share everyday experiences and struggles, many of which can be more effectively addressed together.

1 Older persons and the law

Introduction

The former Lord Chief Justice of England and Wales, Lord Judge, in a speech at the 2012 Lord Mayor's banquet, related the story of his daughter returning to the United Kingdom after living in Lake Malawi. As she had not been a resident of the United Kingdom for the previous two years, her father agreed to be a guarantor for her mortgage application. Despite his judicial salary and pension entitlements, he was ineligible to be a guarantor at seventy-one because he was too old.[1] Evelyn Jones was a resident of a care home in Gwent, one of six care homes investigated by the police following cases of horrendous abuse of older residents. Her granddaughter said of Evelyn's pressure sores,

> It looked like a really bad burn. It was black, blue and sort of festering around the edges. She had two holes in the coccyx area, like a two-pence piece. But it was so badly infected that I could see the bones of her back penetrating through these holes. The pain and suffering she must have gone through to be in that state doesn't bear thinking about.[2]

These two examples represent extremes of the ageism spectrum of attitudes and behaviours. Whereas one is a tale to tell in an after-dinner speech, albeit not without consequences, the other is a harrowing account of deliberate ill-treatment and neglect. Both are rooted in the belief that older persons are different and less worthy of respect.

Robert Butler coined the term ageism in 1969. He was writing about opposition by residents of the affluent Washington community of Chevy Chase towards a proposed accommodation development for disadvantaged older persons. The residents were angered by, amongst other things, the inclusion of a swimming pool as

1 Lord Judge of Draycote, 'Lord Mayor's Banquet' (*Judicial Office Communications Team*, 11 July 2012) <https://www.judiciary.uk/wp-content/uploads/JCO/Documents/Speeches/lcj-speech-lord-mayors-banquet-2012.pdf> – accessed 28 September 2024.

2 BBC Wales News, 'Operation Jasmine inquiry: Justice demanded over homes neglect' (2013) <http://www.bbc.co.uk/news/uk-wales-22761073> – accessed 28 September 2024.

DOI: 10.4324/9780203798058-2

'these people' were not accustomed to luxury. There were class and colour issues, but ageism was a driving factor in their campaign.[3] Butler later defined ageism as,

> a process of systematic stereotyping or discrimination against people because they are old, just as racism and sexism accomplish with skin colour and gender. Ageism allows the younger generations to see older people as different from themselves; thus, they subtly cease to identify with their elders as human beings.[4]

Younger persons also experience age-based assumptions and attitudes, but for present purposes, the focus is on older persons. Ageism is destructive in many ways. Marques et al. categorised it as other-directed and self-directed.[5] The quality of interaction with older persons and the portrayal of older persons in media and culture influences other-directed ageism. Self-directed ageism is strongly influenced by older people's perceptions of their health and the ageing process. Over a lifetime, exposure to negative attitudes about ageing can make removing these thoughts and feelings challenging in later life. Women are more likely to be fearful of their own older age. The internalisation of negative societal views on older age is a significant cause of self-directed ageism, as is the direct experience of age discrimination. This may be exacerbated by poor quality of life.[6] These negative self-perceptions can contribute to increased frailty in older persons. Frailty perpetuates self-directed ageism, further diminishing the quality of life. This highlights the importance of interventions to break this cycle, as feelings of frailty can lead to a sense of inadequacy and irrelevance, thus affecting well-being.[7] The effects of ageism are well documented, and its negative impact on the mental and physical health of older persons should not be underestimated. The consequences can be severe, including depression, anxiety, stress, low self-esteem and confidence, and a feeling of being undervalued and incapable. This can lead to exclusion, isolation, and a reduced sense of belonging and purpose, harming overall life satisfaction. Moreover, chronic diseases and decreased well-being are possible consequences of ageism. However, the effects of ageism can be mitigated through positive perceptions of ageing, social support, and resilience.[8]

Ageist thinking is a pervasive problem affecting, for example, healthcare, media, arts, and science. Older patients may receive inappropriate medical care due

3 RN Butler, 'Age-ism: Another form of bigotry' (1969) *The Gerontologist* 9(4) Part 1) 243.

4 RN Butler, *Why survive? Being old in America* (Harper and Row, 1975).

5 S Marques, J Mariano, J Mendonça, et al., 'Determinants of ageism against older adults: A systematic review' (2020) *International Journal of Environmental Research and Public Health* 17(7) 2560.

6 M Ishikawa, 'Internalization of negative societal views on old age into self-perceptions of aging: Exploring factors associated with self-directed ageism' (2023) *Frontiers in Sociology* 8.

7 P Vanleerberghe, C Claes, J Campens, et al., 'The mediating role of self-directed ageism on frailty and quality of life in community-dwelling older people' (2024) *Discover Social Science and Health* 4(1) 1.

8 H Kang and H Kim, 'Ageism and psychological well-being among older adults: A systematic review' (2022) *Gerontology and Geriatric Medicine* 8, 1.

to assumptions that they may not tolerate specific treatments. Underrepresentation in clinical trials is also an issue for older persons, although age caps may depend upon the condition being trialled and the funder. Admittedly, clinical trials involving older persons face many problems, such as cognitive impairment, polypharmacy, comorbidities, and age-related bias. These issues may make collecting data on the safety and efficacy of treatments difficult. Nevertheless, tailored recruitment strategies, flexible trial designs, and inclusive approaches are needed to ensure clinical research adequately addresses the needs and characteristics of older persons. Ageism in media coverage is seen in the portrayal of older persons and the language used. Older persons are often depicted as frail, helpless, or dependent, supporting negative stereotypes about ageing. This reinforces ageist beliefs and negativity. Ageism in the arts manifests in limited opportunities for older artists to use their talents and stereotypical portrayals of ageing in artistic works. Additionally, older performers can be overlooked for roles and opportunities based solely on age, disregarding their skill and experience. Ageism in science can negatively affect researchers, study participants, and the scientific community. Older researchers may face challenges securing research funding and experience limited career opportunities due to age-related policies and practices.[9]

Employment provides countless examples of ageism. BBC Countryfile presenter Miriam O'Reilly, who at the age of fifty-three, was dropped from the programme as part of a campaign designed to appeal to a younger audience. A tribunal held that appealing to a younger audience was a legitimate aim, but dismissal on the grounds of age was not a proportionate way of achieving that aim. O'Reilly won her case against the BBC. In another case before a tribunal, a manager had asked about an older worker who had forgotten something in the following way – 'Is it Alzheimer's again?' Another employee was known as 'Dementia Debbie'. The manager dismissed this as a joke – routine office banter. Thankfully, the Tribunal did not see any humour in this demeaning behaviour. The employer had engaged in 'humiliating, degrading and offensive remarks.'[10] Unfortunately, the instances reaching tribunals are the tip of the iceberg. Much ageism remains hidden in the workplace. Inclusive and respectful language within the workplace and elsewhere will help combat ageism and create a more age-friendly society.

9 See, for example, D Nguyen, G Mika, and A Ninh, 'Age-based exclusions in clinical trials: A review and new perspectives' (2022) *Contemporary Clinical Trials* 114, 106683; A Shaw, 'Past it at 40? Artists fight "culture of ageism" in the art world' *The Art Newspaper* (London, 31 January 2022); Centre for Ageing Better, 'How the media fuels negative views about older people and ageing' (18 April 2023) <https://ageing-better.org.uk/blogs/how-media-fuels-negative-views-about-older-people-and-ageing> – accessed 28 September 2024; L Aronson, *Elderhood: Redefining aging, transforming medicine, reimagining life* (Bloomsbury Publishing USA, 2019).

10 M Baska, 'Worker asked if she had Alzheimer's by manager wins age discrimination case' (*People Management*, 27 November 2020) <https://www.peoplemanagement.co.uk/article/1747131/worker-asked-alzheimers-manager-wins-age-discrimination-case>. – accessed 28 September 2024.

The COVID-19 pandemic highlighted the prevalence of ageism in the working of governments and public services. During the pandemic's early stages, older age became a factor in triaging patients' access to critical care. The Clinical Frailty Scale was used to triage older patients but not younger persons with long-term disabilities. A general practitioner in Maesteg sent letters to patients with severe health conditions asking them to complete a do not attempt cardiopulmonary resuscitation form, contrary to the General Medical Council's guidelines and the Court of Appeal's decision in Tracy v Cambridge University Hospital NHS Trust.[11] COVID-19 is discussed in Chapter 2.

Older age, whatever that may be, is something that people often wish to avoid discussing. It may be a realisation of mortality or a fear of senescence that makes people shy away from discussing ageing and may prevent them from planning to ensure the best possible older age. Seeing ageing as a proxy of our future selves leads to othering older persons; they are not 'us.' Myths about older age abound. They include all older persons being the same, unsound body equals unsound mind, old dogs cannot learn new tricks, and all older persons are depressed and understandably so.[12] Kirkwood takes a more positive view of ageing in his 2001 Reith Lecture. He recognises that we are living longer and implores us not to let age get in the way 'of celebrating all persons on this earth as true equals.'[13] The law plays a role in tackling ageism and promoting a positive view of ageing; it impacts older persons in diverse ways. So, how does it work (or not work) for them?

Defining older age

What is older age? A significant milestone in identifying older persons as a group was the Old Age Pensions Act 1908, which introduced a non-contributory means-tested pension for those over seventy of five shilling a week and seven shillings and sixpence for married couples. The introduction of a State pension was a significant and welcome step. However, as Thane points out,

> the pensions paid at a fixed age contributed to the construction of old people as a new and increasingly dominant (though never uncontested) cultural stereotype, the 'old age pensioner,' who was represented as a dependent rather than a contributing member of society once pensionable age was reached, in contrast to older assumptions that people aged and became dependent, if at all, at variable ages.[14]

11 *Tracy v Cambridge University Hospital NHS Trust* [2014] EWCA Civ 822, [2015] Q.B. 543; Matha Bushby 'Welsh surgery apologises over "do not resuscitate" instruction' *Guardian* (London, 31 March 2020).

12 DH Powell, *The Nine Myths of Aging: Maximizing the Quality of Later Life* (WH Freeman, 1998).

13 T Kirkwood, *The End of Age* (Profile Books, 2001).

14 P Thane, *Old age in English history: Past experiences, present issues* (OUP, 2000), 236.

This stereotype is embedded in our culture in the idea of the old age pensioner, a term still used today despite the recent changes to the retirement age; it is rightly resented.[15] It is visually encapsulated in the 'SLOW Elderly people' road sign. Individual attributes were no longer the deciding factor in identifying needs; society assumed that chronological age was now the defining factor.[16]

The search for a definition of older age has a long pedigree. Thomas Paine argued that at sixty, our labours should be over 'and it is painful to see older age working itself to death.'[17] Today, people over sixty remain employed, often out of financial necessity but also out of choice. Almost a third are still employed, and 40% are working full-time.[18] Rigid and all-embracing definitions should be avoided. This is so for all age groups. The House of Lords recognised in the Gillick case that the age of consent of sixteen years was too rigid and could prevent children under that age from seeking contraception advice.[19] It is also the case that there is no single age at which a younger person can undertake certain activities. For example, at fourteen, a young person can take part in a public performance abroad with a justices licence; they cannot enter a contract until eighteen other than for necessities; at the age of twelve, any new passport must be signed by them and not a parent; at the age of fourteen years they are responsible for wearing a seatbelt; a child under the age of ten cannot commit a criminal offence; and at the age of eighteen, a young person is old enough to get a tattoo.[20] This random list shows that a single-age and rigid approach does not work for younger persons; the same is true for older persons. Much as lawyers like definability, rigid definitions can lead to ageist assumptions and a cohort of persons (possibly over a fifty-year lifespan) singled out as different from the rest. For example, as of the 13 February 2025, Ethel May Caterham was the oldest living person in the United Kingdom and Europe. On that date, she was 115 years and 176 days old and is the last surviving person born during the reign of Edward VII.[21] Older persons are treated as one homogeneous group, and this ignores culture, ethnicity, gender, and sexuality. It also ignores health status, education, wealth, and lifestyle differences. Some older persons may

15 K Hazell, 'Over 65s prefer "Grey Panthers" over "Old-age Pensioner"' (*HuffPost*, 30 July 2012).

16 See D Collins, 'The introduction of old age pensions in Great Britain' (1965) *Historical Journal*, 8(2), 246, 247.

17 T Paine, *Basic writings of Thomas Paine: Common sense, rights of man, age of reason* (Willey, 1942).

18 C Canocchi, 'Almost a third of over 60s still in work – and 40% of those are working full-time' (*This Is Money*, 15 October 2016) <https://www.thisismoney.co.uk/money/pensions/article-3838417/Almost-60s-work-40-working-time.html> – accessed 28 September 2024.

19 *Gillick v West Norfolk & Wisbech Area Health Authority* [1986] AC 112.

20 *At what age can I...* (Law Stuff, undated) <https://lawstuff.org.uk/at-what-age-can-i/>– accessed 28 September 2024.

21 Gereontology Research Group, 'World supercentenarian rankings list' (2024) <https://www.grg-supercentenarians.org/world-supercentenarian-rankings-list/> – accessed 28 September 2024.

remain in employment, while others have retired. However defined, older persons are a heterogeneous group.[22]

Does this mean that a search for a definition is so fraught with danger that it should be abandoned? Doing so would risk making older persons invisible in policy and legal discourse. It does, however, suggest caution by recognising, as has been done in the case of the age of consent, that a rigid definition can create artificial boundaries and place persons in categories which attract stereotyping. Care must be taken not to read too much into chronological ages chosen for administrative or political purposes. For example, the changes to the State pension eligibility age are based on something other than a rational definition of older age. They are founded on what the government thinks it can or wants to afford. It is necessary to identify, albeit with less than complete certainty, older persons. For example, does consumer rights law work well for older persons? Are older persons subject to discrimination in employment or access to services? Is the healthcare provided to older persons of an equal standard to that for younger persons? In answering these questions, a rigid definition is often unnecessary. The United Nations considers that older age probably begins at sixty in most developed countries, though that is not a strict rule.[23] Sixty is inappropriate for countries where life expectancy falls below that age; life expectancy at birth in seven countries is below sixty and below sixty-five in thirty countries.[24]

Some argue that older age should commence at seventy-five rather than sixty to sixty-five. Based on their research in Tokyo, Orimo et al. point to improvements in physical activity and functional independence and argue that 'we should change the definition of older to those over seventy-five.'[25] However, only some enjoy such benefits in later life. For example, Age UK estimates that the number of persons claiming State pensions who are living in poverty is over two million, with Black and Asian older persons most at risk.[26] Sanderson challenges the conventional view of older age, arguing that it ignores increasing life expectancy and that the characteristics of persons at each age are changing. He advocates using measures based on prospective age whereby persons are categorised as 'old' when they

22 A-M Cotter, (2016) *Just a number: An international legal analysis on age discrimination* (Routledge, 2016) 25.

23 See, for example, UNHCR, *Emergency Handbook: Older persons* (UNHCR, 2020). <https://emergency.unhcr.org/protection/persons-risk/older-persons> – accessed 28 September 2024.

24 World Health Organisation, *Life expectancy at birth (years)* (Global Health Observatory, 2020) <https://www.who.int/data/gho/data/indicators/indicator-details/GHO/life-expectancy-at-birth-(years)> – accessed 28 September 2024.

25 H OrimoIto, T Suzuki, A Araki, et al., 'Reviewing the definition of "elderly"' (2006) *Geriatrics & Gerontology International* 6(3), 149, 157.

26 Age UK, 'Number of pensioners living in poverty tops two million, with Black and Asian older people most at risk' (2021) <https://www.ageuk.org.uk/latest-press/articles/2021/number-of-pensioners-living-in-poverty-tops-two-million/#:~:text=The%20over-85s%2C%20renters%2C%20and%20single%2C%20female%20pensioners%2C%20are,the%20UK%20now%20stands%20at%202.1%20million.%20%5Biii%5D> – accessed 28 September 2024.

have an average of fifteen more years to live.[27] This accommodates the differences in life expectancy between countries. However, it does support a homogenous view of older persons, given its reliance on average remaining life expectancy. From the perspective of policy development and reform within England and Wales, there are variations in life expectancy. In Wales, for example, life expectancy for a man at age sixty-five is 16.8 years in Merthyr Tydfil and 19.1 years in Ynys Môn. In England, the life expectancy for a woman at age sixty-five is 23 years in Ryedale and 19.2 years in Salford.[28]

There are only two legal definitions of older persons in the United Kingdom. Section 24(2) Commissioner for Older People (Wales) Act 2006 defines an 'older person' as a person aged sixty or over. The equivalent legislation in Northern Ireland adopts a slightly different approach. Usually, an older person means sixty or over; however, if the Commissioner believes that a matter raises a question of principle affecting persons aged fifty or over, the Commissioner may direct that 'older person' means a person aged fifty or over concerning that matter.[29] The extended definition is used rarely.

Devoting too much energy to finding a precise definition is wasteful. Whether a person is older often depends on why the question is being asked. Furthermore, applying the label 'older person' does not assume sameness amongst those to whom it is applied. Putting too much energy into finding rigid definitions should be avoided, and instead, the focus should be on why we want to know – and whether we need to know. Upon reaching 'older age,' a person does not lose their multifaceted identity and have it replaced by a single homogenous one-dimensional personality defined only by chronological age. Older persons should not be stereotyped but seen as a diverse group with wide-ranging backgrounds and experiences. When developing laws and policies for older persons, it is necessary to recognise the diversity of this large cohort. Intersectionality is the recognition that social differences such as age, gender, class, sexual orientation, and ethnicity collectively impact the experiences of individuals and groups, leading to complex social standings and issues. In addition to these, geographic location, resources, and health status are important. These are not always factored into ageing research. Westwood et al. identified research gaps in understanding the different health experiences of older LGBT+ subgroups when considering intersecting social differences. They argue that purposive sampling in research could yield better insights into the diversity and intersectionality within the LGBT+ community. Targeting health interventions towards specific subgroups within the LGBT+ community can be helpful for policymakers, commissioners, and providers. It is essential to acknowledge that the

27 W Sanderson, 'What is old age?' (*World Economic Forum*, 21 April 2015) <https://www.weforum.org/agenda/2015/04/what-is-old-age/>– accessed 28 September 2024.

28 Office for National Statistics, *Life expectancy for local areas of the UK: Between 2001 to 2003 and 2018 to 2020* (ONS, 2020) <https://www.ons.gov.uk/peoplepopulationandcommunity/healthandsocialcare/healthandlifeexpectancies/bulletins/lifeexpectancyforlocalareasoftheuk/between2001to2003and2018to2020#life-expectancy-at-local-level.>. - accessed 28 Sepember 2024.

29 Sections.25(1) and (2) Commissioner for Older People Act (Northern Ireland) 2011.

health experiences and needs of older LGBT+ people are complex and can only be fully understood by taking into account all aspects of their identities and lives.[30]

For argument's sake, sixty to sixty-five is a pragmatic starting point for older age, but with the caveat that different contexts may result in adopting higher or lower ages. For example, prisoners age ten years faster than non-prisoners. Poor living conditions, lack of access to appropriate medical and social care and unhealthy diet accelerate the ageing process and for this reason the Prison Inspectorate use fifty as the benchmark for older age.

The demographics

The Census 2021 confirmed that the population of England and Wales is ageing; the population aged sixty-five and above rose from 9.2 million in 2011 to over 11 million in 2021. The proportion of people in this age group has increased from 16.4% to 18.6%. These numbers are projected to continue growing.[31] The growth in the number of persons living longer presents challenges, but must not be treated as a problem. Expressions such as 'demographic timebomb' or the 'burdens' arising from an ageing population are ageist as they make assumptions about longer-lived persons. Writing in 2002, Mullan concludes,

> There is no demographic timebomb. The anxiety about ageing that has become almost endemic in the 1990s is misplaced. It is certainly exaggerated. Sometimes commentators with particular obsessions or vested interests have manipulated it.[32]

These words ring true today. Kirkwood has an optimistic vision of older age and provides reasons for rethinking it; he challenges people's preconceived ideas about older persons.[33]

One common view is that older persons are an economic burden on society. The Office for National Statistics publishes data on what is referred to as the old-age dependency ratio (OADR). The calculation is the number of persons of State pension age per 1,000 working-age people. In 2024 the ratio was 297.46:1000; by 2041, it is projected to be 370.08:1000. OADR is a crude and outdated approach that fails to portray economic dependency accurately. It assumes that once the pension age is reached, a person automatically becomes dependent and a non-contributor to the economy. Abolishing the compulsory retirement age of sixty-five means

30 S Westwood, P Willis, J Fish, et al., 'Older LGBT+ health inequalities in the UK: Setting a research agenda' (2020) *J Epidemiol Community Health*, 74(5) 408.

31 Office for National Statistics, 'Population and household estimates, England and Wales: Census 2021' (Census 2021, 2 November 2022) <https://www.ons.gov.uk/peoplepopulationandcommunity/populationandmigration/populationestimates/bulletins/populationandhouseholdestimatesenglandandwales/census2021unroundeddata> – accessed 28 September 2024.

32 P Mullan, *The imaginary time bomb* (I B Tauris, 2002) 215.

33 T Kirkwood (n 13) 10.

more people continue working into their late sixties and beyond.[34] Some people in retirement enjoy excellent private pensions and remain financially independent. OADR fails to consider underemployment and economic inactivity amongst those below retirement age. Policymakers must also consider the impact of migration. Alternative measures are needed to ensure that planning for an ageing population is based on reliable data.[35] One such measure is the Active Dependency Measure (ADR). The ADR calculates the number of economically active people against economically inactive people. This approach is not foolproof; economic activity does not always equate with financial independence.[36]

Any measure used to meet the needs of an ageing population must not buy into the older age equals dependency mantra. Older persons continue to contribute to society, either directly or indirectly. For example, they may remain employed and help fill the gaps in the labour markets following the end of free movement. Concerns exist over the loss of older workers from the workforce and the inability of employers to replace them. The TUC estimates that the number of people between fifty and sixty-five who were not actively looking for work rose by over 200,000 between the third quarters of 2019 and 2021. It argues for significant changes in the work environment to preserve their skills and experience.[37] Older persons also provide free childcare, enabling parents to be economically active. In addition, many older persons care for other adults, thus protecting social and healthcare budgets. The 2021 Census found that older persons in England and Wales provided the highest hours of unpaid care; this involves fifty hours or more per week.[38]

Elder law

Tully argues that the roots of elder law can be traced back to 1965 when the Older Americans Act and Social Security Amendments were introduced. To meet the medical needs of older persons, Medicare was introduced. At the same time, Medicaid provided long-term care benefits to those with chronic or custodial needs

34 Employment Equality (Repeal of Retirement Age Provisions) Regulations 2011, SI 2011/1069.

35 C Harasty, and M Ostermeier, 'Population ageing: Alternative measures of dependency and implications for the future of work' (2020) International Labour Organization Working Paper – Issue 5 <https://www.ilo.org/sites/default/files/wcmsp5/groups/public/@ed_emp/documents/publication/wcms_747257.pdf> – accessed 28 September 2024.

36 Office for National Statistics, 'Living longer and old-age dependency – what does the future hold?' (2019) <https://www.ons.gov.uk/peoplepopulationandcommunity/birthsdeathsandmarriages/ageing/articles/livinglongerandoldagedependencywhatdoesthefuturehold/2019-06-24> – accessed 28 September 2024.

37 Trades Union Congress, *Older workers after the pandemic: creating an inclusive labour market* (2022) <https://www.tuc.org.uk/research-analysis/reports/older-workers-after-pandemic-creating-inclusive-labour-market> – accessed 28 September 2024.

38 Office for National Statistics, 'Unpaid care by age, sex and deprivation, England and Wales: Census 2021' (ONS, 2023) <https://www.ons.gov.uk/peoplepopulationandcommunity/healthandsocialcare/socialcare/articles/unpaidcarebyagesexanddeprivationenglandandwales/latest#unpaid-care-by-age-sex-and-geography-2021> – accessed 28 September 2024.

if the financial criteria were met. Two distinct systems for financing care were established – one for older persons of all financial backgrounds and the other for those financially disadvantaged.[39] Over the past thirty or so years, awareness and interest have grown in elder law, the law of older persons, senior law, and variations thereof. Unfortunately, terms such as 'the elderly client' or 'old age law' are also used. For this book, elder law is adopted. Academics and practitioners share this growth in interest in the law and older persons. Academic interest is driven by the need to support practitioners and demonstrate a commitment to ensure that older persons are not invisible in legal research and teaching. Research activity feeds into policy-making by national governments and international bodies. In training future generations of lawyers, Kohn and Spurgeon discuss the American experience and identify challenges for law schools.

> If U.S. law schools are to help prepare law students and the legal system to meet the challenges posed by an ageing population, law schools must make quality elder law education and knowledge a priority today.[40]

This challenge is shared by law schools across the four nations of the United Kingdom. Practitioners have traditionally confined their interests to wills, probate, and property matters. More recently, advice on mental capacity, abuse and neglect, and challenging public authority provision of health and social care have been added to the practitioner's offering.

What does elder law involve? As with any sub-discipline of law, it is not self-contained and embraces other parts of the discipline, such as medical law, negligence, public law, and criminal law. Indeed, as with the development of medical law and ethics, its origins are based on bringing together other sub-disciplines of law with a new focus. A fragmented approach involving different areas of law is less effective than the umbrella of elder law. Grubb points out that the more medical issues were litigated, the more lawyers and others recognised medical law and ethics as a separate sub-discipline.[41] Elder law has had a similar journey. Researching elder law also embraces the range of approaches legal scholars adopt beyond the traditional but valuable doctrinal approach. Socio-legal, feminist, critical legal studies, comparative, contextual, historical, and jurisprudential approaches are all at the disposal of the elder law lawyer.

The traditional boundaries of sub-disciplines in law may not permit the interests and needs of older persons to be addressed. Cahn et al. raised this point in their work on family law in America. They argue that it is essential that family law addresses the needs of families throughout their entire lifespan rather than focusing on the

39 BA Tully, 'The Growth and Business of Elder Law' (2020) *ACTEC LJ*, 46, 113; see also Chappel J, Golden Years (1st edn., Basic Books 2024).

40 N Kohn, and E Spurgeon, 'Elder Law Teaching and Scholarship: An Empirical Analysis of an Evolving Field' (2010) *Journal of Legal Education* 59, 414, 431.

41 A Grubb, 'The emergence and rise of medical law and ethics' (1987) *Modern Law Review* 50(2) 241, 267.

needs of younger persons. This means considering all family members' needs, regardless of age or life stage. Tailoring family relationships for older persons is complex. It addresses diverse preferences, varying expectations, complicated family dynamics, financial considerations, health and caregiving needs, and legal barriers. These challenges arise from the limited options and default rules provided by family law, the need for recognition of alternative family forms, the cost and complexity of legal processes, and assumptions about the needs of older persons. Family law must adapt to the changing demographics and needs of older persons. Reforms include broadening family types, shifting the focus away from marriage, and supporting caregiving. The goal is to prioritise autonomy and equity.[42]

As with all law, elder law should be studied within a broader societal context.[43] It must also be seen from an interdisciplinary perspective. Nissani reminds us that despite concentrating on one domain of human experience, disciplines are only 'comparatively self-contained.'[44] Bradney's pejorative title, 'Law as a Parasitic Discipline,' hides his message that law can be a focal point for other disciplines and sub-disciplines.[45] Elder law is no exception. Frolik puts it like this,

> Although the study of cases remains an aspect of an elder law course, it is heavily supplemented by readings, including materials from nonlegal disciplines. This cross-disciplinary approach finds favor with many academics who feel constricted by examining society solely through the legal lens. Whether by training or experience, they have come to appreciate that law operates in a world of larger, competing values that do not reveal themselves to a myopic legal view. Elder law is one route out of sterile legalism into the richness of public policy choices which balance multiple interests, limited resources, finite choices, and uncertain outcomes.[46]

Elder law lawyers should collaborate with other disciplines. Criminology, medicine, dentistry, sociology, nursing, and social policy are prime candidates. There needs to be a greater connection between elder law and gerontology. Less obvious ones include architecture, environmental studies, policing studies, and design.[47]

42 N Cahn, C Huntington, and ES Scott, 'Family law for the one-hundred-year life' (2023) *Yale LJ*, 132, 1691.

43 R Cotterrell, *Law's community : Legal theory in sociological perspective* (Clarendon Press, 1996) 381.

44 M Nissani, 'Fruits, salads, and smoothies: A working definition of interdisciplinarity' (1995) *The Journal of Educational Thought* 121-28.

45 A Bradney, 'Law as a parasitic discipline' (1998) *Journal of Law and Society* 25(1) 71, 84.

46 LA Frolik, 'The developing field of elder law redux: Ten years after' (2002) *Elder Law Journal* 10, 1.

47 N Kohn, M Brown, and I Doron, 'Building bridges between gerontology and elder law' (2019) Gerontology, *65*(1), 98; J Williams, 'Care home design and human rights' (2011) *Elder Law Journal* 1(4), 395; T Lorenc, M Petticrew, M Whitehead, et al. 'Environmental interventions to reduce fear of crime: Systematic review of effectiveness' (2013) *Systematic Reviews* 2, 1.

Other disciplines must embrace elder law lawyers and regard them as something other than providing legal advice for a research project.

The substance of elder law teaching and research can be categorised as the law *of* older persons and the law *and* older persons.

The law of older persons

Some laws apply exclusively to specific age groups. For example, children have laws that apply to them, although they often impose duties and responsibilities on parents and public authorities. The same is valid to a limited extent for older persons. For example, the law on eligibility for a State retirement pension applies to older persons. Although 'Old Age' was last used in the title of pension legislation in the Widows', Orphans' and Old Age Contributory Pensions Act, 1936, retirement pension law applies to older persons. However, it is of great interest to other age cohorts, particularly people nearing the age of entitlement, but as argued above, pension eligibility should not be used to define older persons. Another area of law focused on older persons is the Welsh and Northern Irish legislation establishing the two Older People's Commissioners. Interestingly, in the consultation exercise on the case for a Commissioner, the Equality Commission for Northern Ireland had reservations about somebody who is well, working, and willing to be active but has reached the age of sixty being included within the remit. The Equality Commission argued that it seemed to 'fly in the face of much contemporary experience.'[48]

Should there be more laws designed exclusively for older persons? In America, many states have laws protecting older persons or elders from abuse or neglect. California has enacted the Penal Code § 368 PC – California Elder Abuse Criminal Law, which makes elder abuse a misdemeanour or a felony. The victim must be sixty-five or older.[49] Other American states adopt a more comprehensive approach, and the laws include all adults who are vulnerable rather than being confined to older persons. In England and Wales, some argue in favour of adding older age as a personal characteristic in hate crimes. Older persons are relatively vulnerable to crime, and hate crime laws may provide greater protection given the psychological distress caused by age-motivated offences.[50] Bows adopts a cautious approach. Whilst recognising older persons are invisible victims of crime, she identifies risks in introducing age as a personal characteristic. She concludes,

> (A)lthough there may be some symbolic advantages to specifically criminalising elder abuse, there are considerable risks associated with introducing

48 Equality Commission for Northern Ireland, 'Response to OFMdFM consultation on a commissioner for older people in Northern Ireland' (January 2009) <https://www.equalityni.org/ECNI/media/ECNI/Consultation%20Responses/2009/OFMDFMCOPconsultationFinal2009.pdf?ext=.pdf>, para 3.10.

49 PR Greenwood, 'The criminal justice response to elder abuse' (2020) *Elder Abuse* 241-56.

50 S Goosey, 'Ageism as a hate crime: The case for extending aggravated offences to protect age groups' (2021) *Oxford Journal of Legal Studies* 41(3) 612.

> laws which separate older people from other groups and contribute to ageist attitudes and stereotypes about older people and result in paternalistic approaches that limit, rather than enhance, older people's rights.[51]

Treating older persons as a particular group risks inadvertent ageism and reinforces the stereotypical view of them being different. The critical issue is to ask why the existing criminal law does not adequately protect older persons. What is wrong with the criminal justice system and the adult safeguarding procedures that marginalise older victims of crime and abuse? Putting those right will better protect older persons than a bespoke law that can be perceived as paternalistic and is often difficult to enforce. A similar argument arises concerning the proposed UN Convention on the Rights of Older People.[52] Does this buy into the older-persons-are-different agenda? International instruments protecting human rights, such as the Universal Declaration of Human Rights and the European Convention on Human Rights, include older persons. Is ensuring these work for older persons the goal rather than compartmentalising the rights to be enjoyed?[53] Chapters 2 and 8 discuss this issue.

The law and older persons

The second category of elder law is the law and older persons. How does the general law work for and affect older persons? For example, does social care law work in the same way for older persons as for other age groups? Is medical law applied equally across different age groups? Is the Human Rights Act 1998 applied fairly to all ages? Studying how the law generally works for older persons is central to elder law. Arguably, it is the dominant component. Is there something in our justice system that consciously or unconsciously discriminates against older persons, rendering them semi-visible or, in some cases, invisible? There are two aspects to this. First, there are laws of general application, but they are more likely to apply to older persons than others. Second, some laws affect older persons, but they are not the dominant age group.

An example of the first category is the Deprivation of Liberty Safeguards (DoLS), which the Liberty Protection Safeguards may eventually replace. In 2020–21, the number of DoLS applications in England completed per 100,000 adults was 119 for the eighteen to sixty-four age group, 534 for the sixty-five to seventy-four age group, 2,126 for the seventy-five to eight-four age group, and 7,232 for

51 H. Bows, 'Violence and abuse of older people: A review of current proposals for criminalisation' (2020) *Criminal Law Review* 10, 877.

52 KL Tang, and JJ Lee, 'Global social justice for older people: The case for an international convention on the rights of older people' (2006) British Journal of Social Work 36(7) 1135; I Doron and I Apter, 'The debate around the need for an international convention on the rights of older persons' (2010) *Gerontologist* 50(5) 586-93; JE Ataguba, DE Bloom, and AJ Scott, 'A timely call to establish an international convention on the rights of older people' (2021) *The Lancet Healthy Longevity* 2(9) e540.

53 J Williams, 'An international convention on the rights of older people?' in M Odello and S Cavandoli (eds) *Emerging areas of human rights* (Routledge, 2012) 138.

eighty-five and over.[54] Similarly, for 2021–22 in Wales, 88% of applications to Health Boards and 87% to local authorities were for those over sixty-five.[55] The Court of Protection has a high proportion of people aged eighty and above using its jurisdiction.[56] Given the dominance of older persons affected by such laws, they are particularly relevant for the elder law lawyer, and the older person's perspective is essential in policy development and analytical research, given that they are primary users.

The second category considers how the law of more general application applies to and works for older persons. It differs from the first category in that older persons are one of many groups to whom this law applies and are not primarily affected by it. But it does apply to them. Two examples will illustrate this category. First, the criminal law and the criminal justice system. How are older persons treated within the investigative process and the broader criminal justice system? Is there an awareness of issues that may be more prevalent amongst older persons than other age groups? For example, is there an awareness of mental capacity, mobility, and medication? How are older persons sentenced to imprisonment treated? Are necessary adjustments made to ensure that they do not experience discrimination? Second, human rights law. How visible are older persons in discussions on human rights? Do they enjoy the full benefits of the rights bestowed upon 'everyone' or 'all people,' or are they marginalised?

As noted above, COVID-19 highlighted governments' failure to treat older persons as equals in the enjoyment of their human rights and health and social care entitlements.[57] This was not only about the direct consequences of COVID-19 but also indirect consequences, such as the ability to access general medical care. A report by the Older People's Commissioner for Wales discusses the challenges older persons face when accessing GP practices. The report assesses the impact of COVID-19 on their access to GP services and makes recommendations for improving it. During the pandemic, older persons faced difficulties when seeking medical attention, especially those who were isolated or living with dementia. The shift towards virtual and telephonic medical services benefited some older persons but

54 NHS Digital, 'Mental capacity act 2005, deprivation of liberty safeguards - 2020-21' (*NHS*, 19 August 2021) <https://digital.nhs.uk/data-and-information/publications/statistical/mental-capacity-act-2005-deprivation-of-liberty-safeguards-assessments/2020-21> – accessed 28 September 2024.

55 Care Inspectorate Wales and Healthcare Inspectorate Wales, 'Deprivation of liberty safeguards annual monitoring report for health and social care 2021-22' (*NHS*, 19 August 2021). <https://www.careinspectorate.wales/sites/default/files/2023-02/230207-dols-2021-22-en.pdf> – accessed 28 September 2024.

56 S Gurbai, E Fitton, and W Martin, 'Insight under scrutiny in the Court of Protection: A case law survey' (2020) *Frontiers in Psychiatry* 11, 560329.

57 See A Wyllie, 'The human rights of older people during covid-19: Social wellbeing and access to care and support for older people in the United Kingdom - research repository' in C Ferstman and A Fagan (eds) *Covid-19, law and human rights: Essex dialogues* (1st ed, School of Law and Human Rights Centre, University of Essex, 2020) 197 <http://repository.essex.ac.uk/28042/> - accessed 28 September 2024; Williams, J, 'Taking it on the chin: Older people, human rights and COVID-19' (2021) *The Journal of Adult Protection* 23(2) 86.

caused problems for others, particularly those without internet access. Some older persons reported that they could not participate in online or video call appointments with their GP and could not secure in-person appointments.[58] They felt marginalised and denied equal treatment.

Conclusion

Elder law lawyers, whether they are practitioners, teachers, students or researchers, will encounter ageist assumptions and discrimination. The diversity of older persons must be welcomed and reflected in how the State and society respond to the fact that we live longer. Creating a positive image and celebrating longevity are essential, as is addressing older people's struggles. Intergenerationality must be encouraged. Although younger and older persons may have different priorities, many share the burden of poverty, inadequate housing, poor health, malnutrition, fuel poverty, and unemployment. Those who promote intergenerational antagonism do a disservice to all. Such posturing may set social media alight; however, it does not enable us to work for an inclusive and well-integrated society.[59]

Elder law is an exciting and dynamic area in which to work. It is not a backwater but can confidently stand alongside other legal specialisms as a sub-discipline that helps governments, policymakers and others to address the prospect of people enjoying a longer life, hopefully in good health and robust well-being.

Bibliography

Age UK, 'Number of pensioners living in poverty tops two million, with Black and Asian older people most at risk' (2021) https://www.ageuk.org.uk/latest-press/articles/2021/number-of-pensioners-living-in-poverty-tops-two-million/#:~:text=The%20number%20of%20pensioners%20in%20poverty%20has%20now,hard-pressed%20to%20check%20their%20eligibility%20for%20Pension%20Cre - accessed 28 September 2024.

Aronson L, *Elderhood: Redefining aging, transforming medicine, reimagining life* (Bloomsbury Publishing, 2019).

At what age can I…. (Law Stuff, undated) https://lawstuff.org.uk/at-what-age-can-i/ - accessed 28 September 2024.

Ataguba JE, Bloom DE, and Scott AJ, 'A timely call to establish an international convention on the rights of older people' (2021) *The Lancet Healthy Longevity* 2(9) e540.

Baska M, 'Worker asked if she had Alzheimer's by manager wins age discrimination case' (*People Management*, 27 November 2020) https://www.peoplemanagement.co

58 Older People's Commissioner for Wales, 'Access to GP practices in Wales' (2024) <https://olderpeople.wales/resource/difficulties-accessing-gp-practices-leaving-many-older-people-suffering-in-pain-and-living-with-deteriorating-conditions-warns-commissioner/> – accessed 28 September 2024.

59 See, for example, P Toynbee, 'My generation is sucking Britain's young people dry. Why are politicians too scared to admit it?' *Guardian* (London, 14 February 2023); W Gore, 'After the disaster of the Biden/Trump debate, is it time to consider upper age limits for politics?' *Independent* (London, 30 June 2024) <https://www.independent.co.uk/voices/biden-trump-age-elderly-reform-politics-b2571368.html> – accessed 28 September 2024.

.uk/article/1747131/worker-asked-alzheimers-manager-wins-age-discrimination-case. - accessed 28 September 2024.

BBC Wales News, 'Operation Jasmine inquiry: Justice demanded over homes neglect' (2013) http://www.bbc.co.uk/news/uk-wales-22761073 - accessed 28 September 2024.

Bows H, 'Violence and abuse of older people: A review of current proposals for criminalisation' (2020) *Criminal Law Review* 10, 877.

Bradney A, 'Law as a parasitic discipline' (1998) *Journal of Law and Society* 25(1) 71, 84.

Bushby M, 'Welsh surgery apologises over "do not resuscitate" instruction' (*Guardian*, 31 March 2020).

Butler RN, 'Age-ism: Another form of bigotry' (1969) *The Gerontologist* 9(4, Part 1) 243.

Butler RN, *Why survive? Being old in America* (1975) Harper and Row.

Cahn N, Huntington C, and Scott ES, 'Family law for the one-hundred-year life' (2023) *Yale LJ* 132, 1691.

Canocchi C, 'Almost a third of over 60s still in work - and 40% of those are working full-time' (*This Is Money*, 15 October 2016) https://www.thisismoney.co.uk/money/pensions/article-3838417/Almost-60s-work-40-working-time.html - accessed 28 September 2024.

Care Inspectorate Wales, and Healthcare Inspectorate Wales, 'Deprivation of liberty safeguards annual monitoring report for health and social care 2021-22' (*NHS*, 19 August 2021) https://www.careinspectorate.wales/sites/default/files/2023-02/230207-dols-2021-22-en.pdf - accessed 28 September 2024.

Centre for Ageing Better, 'How the media fuels negative views about older people and ageing' (18 April 2023) https://ageing-better.org.uk/blogs/how-media-fuels-negative-views-about-older-people-and-ageing - accessed 28 September 2024.

Chappel J, Golden Years (1st edn., Basic Books 2024).

Collins D, 'The introduction of old age pensions in Great Britain' (1965) *Historical Journal* 8(2), 246, 247.

Cotter A-M, *Just a number: An international legal analysis on age discrimination* (Routledge, 2016) 25.

Cotterrell R, *Law's community: Legal theory in sociological perspective* (Clarendon Press, 1996) 381.

Doron I and Apter, 'The debate around the need for an international convention on the rights of older persons' (2010) *Gerontologist* 50(5) 586-93.

Employment Equality (Repeal of Retirement Age Provisions) Regulations 2011, SI 2011/1069.

Equality Commission for Northern Ireland, 'Response to OFMdFM consultation on a commissioner for older people in Northern Ireland' (January 2009) https://www.equalityni.org/ECNI/media/ECNI/Consultation%20Responses/2009/OFMDFMCOPConsultationFinal2009.pdf?ext=.pdf - accessed 28 September 2024.

Frolik LA, 'The developing field of elder law redux: Ten years after' (2002) *Elder Law Journal* 10, 1.

Gereontology Research Group, 'World supercentenarian rankings list' (2024) World Supercentenarian Rankings List – https://www.grg-supercentenarians.org/world-supercentenarian-rankings-list/ - accessed 28 September 2024.

Goosey S, 'Ageism as a hate crime: The case for extending aggravated offences to protect age groups' (2021) *Oxford Journal of Legal Studies* 41(3), 612.

Gore W, 'Is it time we talked about an upper age limit for politics?' (*Independent*, 30 June 2024) https://www.independent.co.uk/voices/biden-trump-age-elderly-reform-politics-b2571368.html - accessed 28 September 2024.

Greenwood PR, 'The criminal justice response to elder abuse' in *Elder Abuse* (2020) 241-56.

Grubb A, 'The emergence and rise of medical law and ethics' (1987) *Modern Law Review* 50(2) 241, 267.

Gurbai S, Fitton E, and Martin W, 'Insight under scrutiny in the Court of Protection: A case law survey' (2020) *Frontiers in Psychiatry* 11, 560329.

Harasty C, and Ostermeier M, 'Population ageing: Alternative measures of dependency and implications for the future of work', International Labour Organization Working Paper -- Issue 5 5 POPULATION AGEING (2020) https://www.ilo.org/publications/population-ageing-alternative-measures-dependency-and-implications-future-1 - accessed 28 September 2024.

Hazell K, 'Over 65s prefer "grey panthers" over "old-age pensioner"' (*HuffPost*, 30 July 2012).

HM Inspector of Prisons, 'Social Care in Prisons in England and Wales a Thematic Report' (2018) https://www.justiceinspectorates.gov.uk/hmiprisons/wp-content/uploads/sites/4/2018/10/Social-care-thematic-2018-web.pdf - accessed 28 September 2024.

Ishikawa M, 'Internalization of negative societal views on old age into self-perceptions of aging: Exploring factors associated with self-directed ageism' (2023) *Frontiers in Sociology* 8, 1291325.

Kang H, and Kim H, 'Ageism and psychological well-being among older adults: A systematic review' (2022) *Gerontology and Geriatric Medicine* 8, 23337214221087023.

Kirkwood T, *The end of age* (Profile Books, 2001).

Kohn N, Brown M, and Doron I, 'Building bridges between gerontology and elder law' (2019) *Gerontology* 65(1), 98

Kohn N and Spurgeon E, 'Elder law teaching and scholarship: An empirical analysis of an evolving field' (2010) *Journal of Legal Education* 59, 414, 431.

Lorenc T, Petticrew M, Whitehead M, et al. 'Environmental interventions to reduce fear of crime: Systematic review of effectiveness' (2013) *Systematic Reviews* 2, 1.

Marques S, Mariano, Mendonça J, et al. 'Determinants of ageism against older adults: A systematic review' (2020) *International Journal of Environmental Research and Public Health* 17(7) 2560.

Mullan P, *The imaginary time bomb* (I.B. Tauris, 2002), 215.

Nguyen D, Mika G, and Ninh A, ' Age-based exclusions in clinical trials: A review and new perspectives' (2022) *Contemporary Clinical Trials* 114, 106683.

NHS Digital, 'Mental Capacity Act 2005, deprivation of liberty afeguards - 2020-21' (*NHS*, 19 August 2021) https://digital.nhs.uk/data-and-information/publications/statistical/mental-capacity-act-2005-deprivation-of-liberty-safeguards-assessments/2020-21- accessed 28 September 2024.

Nissani M, 'Fruits, salads, and smoothies: A working definition of interdisciplinarity' (1995) *The Journal of Educational Thought* 121-28.

Office for National Statistics, 'Life expectancy for local areas of the UK: Between 2001 to 2003 and 2018 to 2020' (ONS, 2020) https://www.ons.gov.uk/releases/lifeexpectancyforlocalareasoftheukbetween2001to2003and2018to2020 - accessed 28 September 2024.

Office for National Statistics, 'Living longer and old-age dependency – What does the future hold?' (2019) https://www.ons.gov.uk/peoplepopulationandcommunity/birthsdeathsandmarriages/ageing/articles/livinglongerandoldagedependencywhatdoesthefuturehold/2019-06-24 - accessed 28 September 2024.

Office for National Statistics, 'Population and household estimates, England and Wales: Census 2021' (Census 2021, 2 November 2022) https://www.ons.gov.uk/peoplepopulationandcommunity/populationandmigration/populationestimates/bulletins/populationandhouseholdestimatesenglandandwales/census2021 - accessed 28 September 2024.

Office for National Statistics, 'Unpaid care by age, sex and deprivation, England and Wales: Census 2021' (ONS, 2023) https://www.ons.gov.uk/peoplepopulationandcommunity/healthandsocialcare/socialcare/articles/unpaidcarebyagesexanddeprivationenglandandwales/latest#unpaid-care-by-age-sex-and-geography-2021 - accessed 28 September 2024.

Older People's Commissioner for Wales, 'Access to GP practices in Wales' (2024) https://olderpeople.wales/resource/difficulties-accessing-gp-practices-leaving-many-older-people-suffering-in-pain-and-living-with-deteriorating-conditions-warns-commissioner/ - accessed 28 September 2024.

OrimoIto H, Suzuki T, Araki A, et al. 'Reviewing the definition of "elderly"' (2006) *Geriatrics & Gerontology International* 6(3), 149, 157.

Paine T, *Basic writings of Thomas Paine: Common sense, rights of man, age of reason* (Wiley, 1942).

Powell DH, *The nine myths of aging: Maximizing the quality of later life* (WH Freeman, 1998).

Sanderson W, What is old age? (*World Economic Forum*, 21 April 2015) https://www.weforum.org/agenda/2015/04/what-is-old-age/ - accessed 28 September 2024.

Shaw A, 'Past it at 40? Artists fight "culture of ageism" in the art world' (*The Art Newspaper*, 31 January 2022).

Tang KL, and Lee JJ, 'Global social justice for older people: The case for an international convention on the rights of older people' (2006) *British Journal of Social Work* 36(7) 1135.

Thane P, *Old age in English history: Past experiences, present issues* (OUP, 2000), 236.

Toynbee P, 'My generation is sucking Britain's young people dry. Why are politicians too scared to admit it?' (*Guardian*, 14 February 2023).

Trades Union Congress, Older workers after the pandemic: creating an inclusive labour market (2022) https://www.tuc.org.uk/research-analysis/reports/older-workers-after-pandemic-creating-inclusive-labour-market - accessed 28 September 2024.

Tully BA, 'The growth and business of elder law' (2020) *ACTEC LJ* 46, 113.

UNHCR, 'Emergency handbook: Older persons' (UNHCR, 2020) https://emergency.unhcr.org/protection/persons-risk/older-persons - accessed 28 September 2024.

Vanleerberghe P, Claes C, Campens J, et al. 'The mediating role of self-directed ageism on frailty and quality of life in community-dwelling older people' (2024) *Discover Social Science and Health* 4(1) 1.

Westwood S, Willis P, Fish J, et al. 'Older LGBT+ health inequalities in the UK: Setting a research agenda' (2020) *Journal of Epidemiology and Community Health* 74(5) 408.

Williams J, 'An international convention on the rights of older people?' in Odello M and Cavandoli S (eds) *Emerging areas of human rights* (Routledge, 2012) 138.

Williams J, 'Care home design and human rights' (2011) *Elder Law Journal* 1(4) 395.

Williams J, 'Social care and older prisoners' (2013) *Journal of Social Work* 13(5) 471.

Williams, J, 'Taking it on the chin: Older people, human rights and COVID-19' (2021) *The Journal of Adult Protection* 23(2) 86.

World Health Organisation, 'Life expectancy at birth (years)' (Global Health Observatory, 2020) https://www.who.int/data/gho/data/indicators/indicator-details/GHO/life-expectancy-at-birth-(years)#:~:text=The%20average%20number%20of%20years%20that%20a%20newborn,in%20a%20given%20country%2C%20territory%2C%20or%20geographic%20area.- accessed 28 September 2024.

Wyllie A, 'The human rights of older people during covid-19: Social wellbeing and access to care and support for older people in the United Kingdom – Research repository' in Ferstman C and Fagan A (eds) *Covid-19, law and human rights : Essex dialogues* (School of Law and Human Rights Centre, University of Essex, 1st ed, 2020) http://repository.essex.ac.uk/28042/ 197 - accessed 28 September 2024.

2 Older persons and human rights

Introduction

Eleanor Roosevelt, one of the architects of the Universal Declaration of Human Rights, addressing the United Nations in 1958, posed the 'great question,' namely,

> (W)here, after all, do universal rights begin? In small places, close to home – so close and so small that they cannot be seen on any maps of the world. Yet they are the world of the individual person; the neighbourhoods he lives in; the school or college he attends; the factory, farm or office where he works. Such are the places where every man, woman, and child seek equal justice, equal opportunity, equal dignity without discrimination. Unless these rights have meaning there, they have little meaning anywhere.[1]

Human rights are not a remote and abstract set of political aspirations. For everyone, they are real and touch on all aspects of life; they are pervasive. Dignity, justice, and liberty are fundamental parts of being human. Equality of treatment for all defines us as a society. A quotation attributed to Mahatma Gandhi states that '(T)he true measure of any society can be found in how it treats its most vulnerable members.' Why should people experience discrimination based on gender, race, disability, religion, sexual orientation, or age? The othering of individuals and groups denies them human rights and humanity. Human rights are not new, although it was not until after World War II that the term became widely used. They trace their origins back to ancient Greece and Rome and the belief that human conduct should be judged according to natural law or the immutable law of the gods. However, obligations were emphasised rather than rights and slavery and serfdom were tolerated. There began a long transition from a concept based on natural law and duties to one reflected in post–World War II international, regional, and national human rights instruments.

Human rights belong to everyone by virtue of being human. They are not bestowed upon us or granted by governments; they must be 'protected and

1 Eleanor Roosevelt, 'Where do human rights begin?' (10th Anniversary of the UDHR, 27 March 1958). <https://www.futurelearn.com/info/courses/the-universal-declaration-of-human-rights/0/steps/58216> – accessed 28 September 2024.

DOI: 10.4324/9780203798058-3

guaranteed.'[2] There are three generations of human rights. The first generation embraces civil and political rights, including liberty, freedom of speech, and a fair trial before the law. They also include the right to be treated with dignity and safety and to live without discrimination. First-generation rights are often called negative rights, requiring the State to refrain from actions rather than impose obligations to do something. However, the European Court of Human Rights (ECtHR) has recognised that the European Convention on Human Rights (ECHR) includes positive obligations.[3] Second-generation rights are known as economic, social, and cultural rights. They refer to providing employment, housing, food, clothing, social and healthcare, and social security. Such rights require the State to do something – to provide pensions, healthcare, and social care. They feature strongly in the African Charter on Human and People's Rights, which includes, for example, the rights to work, health, and education. The main focus of the ECHR is on civil and political rights. However, the ECtHR recognises rights can include socioeconomic rights such as obligations under Articles 2,3, and 8 ECHR to address basic human needs such as healthcare and welfare for vulnerable people. Nevertheless, it remains cautious in challenging national resource allocation policies.[4] Third-generation rights involve collective rights such as the right to a clean environment, development, and belonging to a stable, cohesive society. The Welsh Assembly enacted the Well-being of Future Generations (Wales) Act 2015, which imposes a duty on public authorities to safeguard the well-being of future generations.[5] Included are duties relating to sustainable development. Future generations include future generations of older persons, so their well-being must be considered under this legislation.

Human rights must be enjoyed without discrimination. In its many manifestations, the State must not unlawfully interfere with a person's rights, such as unlawfully depriving them of their liberty. It is also incumbent on the State to protect rights rather than only act when rights are violated. This applies with equal force to older persons. At the international level, a 2010 Human Rights Council Working Paper recognised that,

> (T)oday, millions of elderly people across the world face unequal treatment or denial of basic rights, specifically in terms of chronic poverty, violence

2 J Ife, *Human rights and social work: Towards rights-based practice* (Cambridge University Press, 2012).

3 See, for example, in relation to Article 3 ECHR *A v United Kingdom* App no 100/1997/884/1096 (*ECtHR*, 23 September 1998); Akandji-Kombe J-F, 'Positive Obligations under the European Convention on Human Rights' (Directorate General of Human Rights Council of Europe, 2007) <https://rm.coe.int/168007ff4d> accessed 28 September 2024.

4 See, African Union, 'Protocol to the African charter on Human and peoples' Rights on the Rights of older persons In Africa' (2016) <https://au.int/sites/default/files/pages/32900-file-protocol_on_the_rights_of_older_persons_e.pd accessed 28 September 2024; Palmer E, 'Positive Obligations under the European Convention on Human Rights' (2009) 2 Erasmus Law Review, Vol. 2, No. 4, pp. 397-425, 2009 397.

5 See H Davies, 'The Well-being of Future Generations (Wales) Act 2015' (2016) *Environmental Law Review* 18(1) 41.

> and abuse, lack of education, little or no access to the law, and exclusion from social and political participation. Age discrimination can be direct, such as by denying work to a person because of their age, or indirect, such as in the exclusion of elderly people from HIV and AIDS prevention programmes.[6]

The work of the United Nations Open-Ended Working Group on Ageing is discussed in Chapter 8.

In 1949, ten Western European Nations, including the United Kingdom, founded the Council of Europe in response to the atrocities of World War II. Its remit is to uphold human rights. The Council must be distinguished from the European Union; Brexit does not affect the United Kingdom's Council membership. Two significant achievements of the Council were the ECHR and the ECtHR. The United Kingdom was the first State to ratify the ECHR on 8 March 1951, albeit against a background of domestic political concern over the implications of being party to the Convention. Potential troublemakers in the colonies, the individual right to petition the ECtHR, inconsistency with the idea of a planned economy, and the ability of tax inspectors to use powers of search and seizure were some of the misgivings put forward by politicians opposed to the idea.[7] Little was done on a domestic law level in response to the ECHR until the Human Rights Act 1998. This was a radical development for the United Kingdom as it made the ECHR enforceable in courts and tribunals in the four nations and requires public authorities to act in accordance with the ECHR.[8] The human rights of older persons are now a central topic of discussion for elder law lawyers and a lens for measuring how effectively law works for older persons.[9]

Dignity

Dignity underpins human rights. McCrudden says of dignity,

> that each human being possesses an intrinsic worth that should be respected, that some forms of conduct are inconsistent with respect for this intrinsic worth and that the state exists for the individual, not vice versa.[10]

In making health and social care decisions, public authorities must consider their impact on the person's dignity. The ECtHR, in Pretty v United Kingdom,[11] said

6 C Chung, 'The necessity of a human rights approach and effective United Nations mechanism for the human rights of the older person' (2010) (UN Doc. A/HRC/AC/4/CRP) 4.

7 A Lester and D Pannick (eds), *Human Rights Law and Practice* (2nd edn, Lexis Nexis, 2004) 4–8.

8 J Williams, 'Human Rights Act: Social work's new benchmark' (2001) *British Journal of Social Work* 31(6) 831.

9 F Mégret, 'The human rights of older persons: a growing challenge' (2011) *Human Rights Law Review* 11(1) 37.

10 C McCrudden, 'Human dignity and judicial interpretation of human rights' (2008) *The European Journal of International Law* 19(4) 655.

11 App no. 2346/02 (ECtHR 29 April 2002) [65].

the very essence of the Convention was respect for human dignity and freedom. The ECtHR in McDonald v United Kingdom confirmed this.[12] Dignity is not a new concept. It is prominent in the Universal Declaration of Human Rights. Article 1 states, 'All human beings are born free and equal in dignity and rights.' Defining dignity is difficult. Dupré argues that defining it presents 'such a scholarly challenge that the best we can hope for might be a fragmented and partial picture.'[13] Despite such difficulties, indignity is easily recognised. There are many examples of the dignity of older persons not being respected. A few examples are a failure to afford justice to older persons who experience abuse and neglect, the abuse and neglect of older residents in some care homes, and the experience of older persons during the COVID-19 pandemic. Former General Secretary of the United Nations, Ban Ki-moon, put it this way,

> As I see it, justice and dignity are not abstractions. They are not mere aspirations. They are rights of people, – they are the responsibilities of Governments to deliver... They are core American values; they are core trans-Atlantic values, increasingly widely shared around the world. Our challenge is to continue to spread these principles all around the world – and this universal code.[14]

Non-discrimination in the enjoyment of rights under the ECHR

Despite very few references to older persons in international and municipal law, human rights are no less important or relevant to them. Older persons cannot be airbrushed from the human rights discourse. Article 14 ECHR prohibits discrimination in the enjoyment of the Convention rights. The article is parasitic and can only be invoked to support a claim under one of the substantive rights; it is not a freestanding right. It says,

> The enjoyment of the rights and freedoms set forth in this Convention shall be secured without discrimination on any ground such as sex, race, colour, language, religion, political or other opinion, national or social origin, association with a national minority, property, birth or other status.

Health status is not mentioned explicitly in Article 14. However, the ECtHR in JD and A v United Kingdom[15] said that a person's health status, including disability and various health impairments, falls within the term' other status' in Article 14. Similarly, older age is not mentioned but falls within 'or other status.' The

12 App no. 4241/12 (ECtHR 20 May 2014) [47].

13 C Dupré, *Age of Dignity* (1st edn, Hart 2015) 4.

14 Secretary-General's Remarks at the Atlantic Council, 'The Great Transition' (7 May 2012) https://www.un.org/sg/en/content/sg/statement/2012-05-07/secretary-generals-remarks-the-atlantic-council-the-great-transition-delivered - accessed 4 March 2025.

15 App nos 32949/17 and 34614/17 (ECtHR, 24 October 2019).

ECtHR has recognised this.[16] The ECtHR has yet to fully support ending age discrimination, which is interesting given that between 2000 and 2010, on average, 11.9% of its caseload involved older persons. The absence of any reference to age may make it more difficult for older persons to seek justice for violations of their rights. However, the ECtHR's jurisprudence in cases involving children or people with disabilities suggests that States must also prevent human rights abuses against older persons.[17]

The ECtHR considered age discrimination in British Gurkha Welfare Society and Others v the United Kingdom.[18] This well-publicised case involved the pension rights of Gurkha soldiers. The relocation of the Gurkha's home base to the United Kingdom led to the government bringing their pensions into line with other soldiers in the British Army. However, it only allowed the transfer of rights accrued after 1 July 1997. Longer-serving Gurkha soldiers argued that this cut-off point meant they were treated less favourably than non-Gurkha soldiers in the British Army and younger Gurkha soldiers. The Court rejected the applicants' arguments. On age discrimination, the Court concluded that any difference in treatment due to age was objectively and reasonably justified. The 1997 date was, in the opinion of the Court, chosen because they had no ties with the United Kingdom before that date. Whether this is a sufficient justification is contentious. Sangroula is critical, saying that the Court failed to justify its decision.[19]

Discrimination based on age featured in the case of Carvalho Pinto de Sousa Morais v Portugal.[20] It involved a medical negligence case where a woman had non-pecuniary damages awarded because the negligence resulted in her inability to have sexual intercourse. The Portuguese Supreme Administrative Court reduced the damages, basing it on the fact that she was fifty years old and already had two children; at her age, having sex was not as important as in her younger years. In two earlier cases before the Portuguese courts involving men aged fifty-five and fifty-nine, the courts found that their inability to have regular sexual intercourse lowered their self-esteem. Although the ECtHR found a breach of Article 14 in the Morais case, Mantovani et al. argue that the majority of the Court gave too little consideration to her age as opposed to sex discrimination, which they observe was a point picked up by the dissenting judges. Although impressed that the majority went beyond traditional legal literature when addressing sex discrimination, they noted a failure to do the same for older age or ageism. They conclude,

> Are we sure that a continent whose population is increasingly old is creating the right conditions for millions of individuals to spend their last years well?

16 See *Schwizgebel v Switzerland* App no 25762/07 (ECtHR, 10 June 2010).

17 B Mikołajczyk, 'Is the ECHR ready for global ageing?' (2013) *The International Journal of Human Rights* 17(4) 511.

18 App no 44818/11 (ECtHR, 15 September 2016).

19 GP Sangroula, 'Gurkha's quest for justice: Possible remedies for Gurkhas under international Human Rights system' (2019) *Kathmandu School of Law Review* 7, 21.

20 App no 17484/15 (ECtHR, 25 July 2017).

> What do we mean by being old? What do we expect? How do we view and understand the experience of ageing and of being old? What limits do we put? It is high time that human rights law starts contributing, from its own standpoint and according to its own parameters, to the new reality of ageing societies and ageism. To do so, one must first acknowledge it.[21]

Both cases recognise that age is embraced by Article 14; however, it received relatively little attention from the ECtHR, which appeared to pay greater attention to other forms of discrimination. In neither case was age regarded as a suspect ground.[22] A suspect ground will trigger stricter scrutiny and require weightier evidence by the State to justify differential treatment.

The Human Rights Act 1998

Upon winning the 1997 election, Tony Blair embarked on a radical constitutional reform programme, including devolution, freedom of information, and House of Lords reform. Perhaps the most radical change was the Human Rights Act 1998 (HRA 1998). He appointed Derry Irvine as Lord Chancellor, who was central to implementing the constitutional reform legislative programme.[23] Getting the Human Rights Bill through Parliament was difficult. Irvine reassured the House of Lords that the Bill did not cede powers to Europe, nor did it allow the courts to override Acts of Parliament.[24] Irvine was later to be critical of the courts for 'slavishly following' the jurisprudence of the ECtHR; domestic courts are not subordinate to the Strasbourg court.[25] Section 2 imposes a duty on the domestic courts to 'take into account' the Court's judgments, decisions, declarations, or advisory opinions. They do not set a rigid binding precedent.

Article 1 ECHR imposes a duty on contracting parties to 'secure to everyone within their jurisdiction' the rights and freedoms in the Convention. Although the ECHR was traditionally thought of as imposing negative obligations (states must refrain from violating rights), it is now accepted that it also imposes positive obligations in some situations (states must intervene to ensure rights). So, for example, Article 2 ECHR states that '(E)veryone's right to life shall be protected by law.' This not only requires the State to respond to failure to protect life, but it also involves taking preventive operational measures to protect life. The ECtHR has developed positive duties to ensure that the ECHR remains relevant and effective.[26]

21 E Mantovani, B Spanier, B, and I Doron, 'Ageism, human rights, and the European Court of human rights: A critical analysis of the Carvalho v. Portugal case (2017)' (2018) *DePaul Journal for Social Justice* 11(1) 14.

22 Gurkha case (n18) [88].

23 A Seldon, *Blair* (The Free Press 2004) 206–207.

24 HL Deb 3 November 1997, vol 582, col 227–312.

25 M Wolfe-Robinson and O Bowcott, 'Lord Irvine: Human rights law developed on false premise' *Guardian* (London, 15 December 2011).

26 A Mowbray, 'The development of positive obligations under the European Convention on Human Rights by the European Court of Human Rights' in A Mowbray (ed), *The development of positive*

However, the State must have some knowledge of the risk to life, a point made by the ECtHR in Osman v UK, where it said it was sufficient,

> for an applicant to show that the authorities did not do all that could reasonably be expected of them to avoid a real and immediate risk to life of which they ought to have knowledge.[27]

What does the HRA 1998 do, and how well has it protected and promoted the human rights of older persons? Williams notes that in its early life, the HRA 1998 was expected to be reactive in its approach, particularly by addressing the pre-existing human rights deficit; it would respond through complaints or litigation to violations that had taken place. However, he said that 'before too long the [ECHR] will be deeply embedded in social work culture and that rights will be centre stage.'[28] Whether this has been fully achieved is questionable; austerity and political failure to address the crisis in social care risks minimising or excluding, in some cases, human rights considerations. A key provision of the HRA 1998 is the incorporation of the ECHR into the domestic law of the United Kingdom. The ECHR rights can be argued before domestic courts and tribunals; previously, cases had to be taken to the ECtHR. Applications may still be made to the ECtHR, although applicants must show that they have personally and directly been a victim of a violation of their rights. Achieving victim status was discussed by the ECtHR in the 2024 case of Verein Klimaseniorinnen Schweiz and Others v Switzerland.[29] The case involved an application to the ECtHR by four women aged over eighty against Switzerland's failure to mitigate the effects of climate change. In dismissing their claim for direct and potential victim status, the ECtHR said,

> As regards the applicants' status as potential victims of a violation of Articles 2 and 8, the [Intergovernmental Panel on Climate Change] work had demonstrated that a real risk of them seeing their rights under Articles 2 and 8 of the Convention violated in the near future could not be established. Acknowledging potential risks for the future was uncertain and raised the question whether the applicants, who were women already over the age of 80, would themselves be individually affected by the effects invoked when global warming reached 1.5°C in 2040 in line with the relevant predictions. The further away the date damage would occur was, the more uncertain it was that it would occur and what the impact on the persons concerned would be.[30]

---

obligations under the European Convention on Human Rights by the European Court of Human Rights (Hart Publishing, 2004) 1-255; TS Güler, '"Positive obligations" doctrine of the European Court of Human Rights: Is it cogent or obscure?' (2017) *European Journal of Multidisciplinary Studies* 2(6) 358.

27 App no 87/1997/871/1083 (ECtHR, 28 October 1998).

28 Williams (n8) 843.

29 App no 53600/20 (ECtHR, 9 April 2024).

30 Ibid para 344–345.

This is a troubling line of reasoning by the ECtHR as it assumes none of the individual applicants have the potential to live until they are one hundred. The chilling words 'whether the applicants, who were women already over the age of 80' are dismissive of the potential people have to live well into their nineties and beyond. Arguably, it also ignores the incremental harm of climate change as the world approaches the 2040 target and any legitimate concerns they have for the well-being of future generations. However, the ECtHR accepted that the organisation to which the women belonged had the status of a victim as they acted on behalf of those people who could claim to be affected by specific threats or adverse effects resulting from climate change on their lives, health, well-being, and quality of life. On this basis, the ECtHR found that Switzerland had violated the ECHR. The case is celebrated as a landmark environmental ruling and one that was brought about by the determination of older people to challenge governments.[31] However, the ruling does not offer reassurance that the ECtHR is fully aware of the need to avoid making assumptions based on age. Applicants to the ECtHR must also show that they have exhausted all available domestic remedies.

Legislation, 'so far as it is possible to do so,' must be read or interpreted in a way compatible with the ECHR rights. This applies to pre and post-1998 legislation and primary and secondary legislation across all four legislative bodies in the United Kingdom.[32] If a higher court determines that Westminster legislation is incompatible with the ECHR, it can be declared incompatible under Section.4 HRA 1998. An early example of a declaration of incompatibility arose in R (on the application of H) v MHRT.[33] This involved the compatibility of Section.72 and Section.73 Mental Health Act 1983 (MHA 1983), which enabled patients to challenge the legality of their detention. Sections 72 and 73 required the patient to prove that the detention criteria were not satisfied; this placed the burden of proof on the patient rather than those who wished to continue detention. The court issued a declaration of incompatibility. This does not invalidate the legislation. Instead, it invites but does not require the relevant Secretary of State to use a special parliamentary procedure to align it with the ECHR.[34] Unlike the Welsh Senedd, the Westminster Parliament can, if it chooses, pass a law incompatible with the ECHR. Section 3 Wales Act 2017 prevents the Senedd from passing an incompatible law. The HRA 1998 is not entrenched in United Kingdom law as the Westminster Parliament can amend, repeal or disapply it.[35]

The HRA 1998 applies where any public authority has breached one or more of the rights in the ECHR. It can be used in direct proceedings against a public authority for breach of an ECHR right, in judicial review proceedings, before tribunals such as the Mental Health Review Tribunal, and in any action brought against a

31 C Mantovani and G Tétrault-Farber, 'Switzerland underestimated elderly women in climate case, plaintiff says' *Reuters* (12 April 2004).

32 See Human Rights Act 1998, Section 3.

33 [2001] EWCA Civ 415, 61 BMLR 163.

34 Human Rights Act 1993, Section 10; Mental Health Act 1983 (Remedial) Order 2001 No 3712.

35 See, for example, the Safety of Rwanda (Asylum and Immigration) Bill 2023.

victim by a public authority. Under Section 6 HRA 1998, public authorities must act in a way compatible with an ECHR right except where the wording of the legislation in question prevents it from doing so. Given that older persons are regular users of services provided by public authorities, such as health and social care, it is necessary to define public authority. Unhelpfully, Section 6(3) HRA 1998 states that public authority includes 'any person certain of whose functions are functions of a public nature'. There are obvious candidates. Specifically mentioned in the HRA 1998 are courts and tribunals. Local authorities, the police, NHS bodies, government departments, prisons, ombudspersons, and the Crown Prosecution Service are further examples. The duty applies when an older person receives services directly from, for example, a local authority. However, local authorities directly provide very little social care as it is delivered mainly by independent providers – either for profit or not for profit. In 2002, the Court of Appeal held that a local authority–funded resident in a privately operated care home could not bring proceedings under the HRA 1998 because the operator, Leonard Cheshire, was not a public authority. The argument was that as a private provider could provide a care home, it could not be a public function.[36] This defence of the purity of public law ignored the rapid growth in the delivery of public services by the private sector. From the human rights perspective, this was arbitrary, and the reality of the blurring of the lines between public and private was ignored. If human rights are to work effectively in social care, they must overlap both the public and private spheres.[37] The case meant that older persons in private care homes, fully or partially funded by a local authority, were not directly protected by the HRA 1998, while those placed in local authority–owned homes would be protected. Resolving this anomaly was a matter for Parliament. It was not until the Care Act 2014 (CA 2014) that the issue was almost entirely resolved. Section 73 CA 2014 applies across all four nations. For England and for Wales, registered providers of home-based personal care or accommodation with nursing or personal care will be regarded as a public authority where the care has been arranged or funded by a local authority. The only gap in the protection is what may be termed the pure self-funder; this is the person who makes arrangements themselves and pays for the care.

Deciding whether an ECHR right has been violated is more complex than often portrayed in the media and by politicians less friendly to human rights. Many myths suggest human rights are there for the asking without structure or balance.[38] When ascertaining potential human rights violations, a careful calculation must involve balancing individual and community rights. In Soering v United Kingdom, the ECtHR said,

36 *Callin, Heather and Ward v Leonard Cheshire* [2002] EWCA Civ 366, [2002] 2 All E.R. 936. See also *YL v Birmingham City Council* [2007] UKHL 27, [2008] 1 AC 95.

37 See S Palmer, 'Public, private and the Human Rights Act 1998: An ideological divide' (2007) *Cambridge Law Journal* 66(3) 559.

38 Guardian Legal, 'Catgate: Another myth used to trash human rights' *The Guardian* (London, 4 October 2011).

> inherent in the whole of the convention is a search for a fair balance between the demands of the general interest of the community and the requirements of the protection of the individual's fundamental rights.[39]

Lord Steyn, in Brown v Stott, put it this way.

> The fundamental rights of individuals are of supreme importance, but those rights are not unlimited: we live in communities of individuals who also have rights.[40]

This was an issue during the COVID-19 pandemic and government responses in Westminster and Cardiff. What is a fair balance between curtailing the rights of older persons to see their family and the wider community's interests in controlling the spread of COVID-19? This is discussed below.

When considering balance, the nature of the right must be considered. The ECHR classifies rights as absolute, limited, or qualified. The State cannot restrict absolute rights. Article 2 (the right to have life protected) and Article 3 (prohibition of inhuman or degrading treatment) are absolute rights. The State cannot interfere with or derogate these rights in an emergency. Limited rights may be interfered with in specified circumstances and in accordance with the law. For example, Article 5 ECHR guarantees the right to liberty and security of person. People can only be deprived of their liberty under a procedure prescribed by law and for one of a specified number of reasons. These include where a person is, under Article 5(1)(e), of 'unsound mind.' Thus, a deprivation of liberty is allowed if there is a Deprivation of Liberty authorisation under the Mental Capacity Act 2005. A qualified right is one where the article identifies the conditions to be satisfied for a lawful interference with the right. Article 8 is a qualified right; it guarantees respect for private life and family life, home, and correspondence. Article 8(2) lists the criteria for interfering with the substantive right. Similar provisions can be found in articles 9(2), 10(2), and 11(2). Any interference must have a basis in statutory or common law.[41] Non-statutory guidance does not provide an adequate legal basis. Statutory guidance, such as that issued under the CA 2014 or the Social Services and Well-being (Wales) Act 2014 (SSWA 2014), counts as a legal basis. The law should be easily understood, but the need for a lawyer to explain it does not make it inaccessible. Criteria for decision-making that may lead to interference must be publicly available.[42] Any consequence of a restriction, such as eligibility, must be foreseeable. Interference must be for a legitimate aim; these are listed in Article 8(2). For older persons, the legitimate aim of public safety, prevention of disorder or crime, protection of health or morals, and the protection of the rights and freedoms of others are relevant. Finally, the interference must be 'necessary

39 App no 14038/88, (ECtHR, 7 July 1989) [89].
40 [2004] UKHL 43, [2003] 1 AC 681, 707.
41 *Sunday Times v United Kingdom* App no 6538/74 (ECtHR, 26 April 1979).
42 *Silver v United Kingdom* App no 5947/72 (ECtHR, 25 March 1983).

in a democratic society.' The reason for interference must be other than political expediency – there must be a pressing social need that relates to the legitimate aim being claimed.[43] In deciding this, regard must be had to the situation in the country.[44] It is also essential that the State justifies its decision to interfere by assessing the relevant facts.[45] Balance is an integral part of this calculation.[46] Minorities must be protected, and the needs of the majority must not overrule their rights.[47] Thus, it is not permissible to ignore the rights of older persons, a minority group, to protect the rights of the rest of the population. As noted above, human rights belong to everyone.

Where the ECHR allows any of its rights to be restricted in specified circumstances, any interference must be proportional. Proportionality is associated with the need to balance rights. It requires that the intervention is essential for achieving the legitimate goal being pursued and is proportionate to that goal. Lord Clyde in de Freitas v Permanent Secretary of the Ministry of Agriculture, Fisheries, Land and Housing[48] said proportionality involves asking if,

1. The legislative aim is sufficiently important to justify limiting a fundamental right.
2. The measure designed to meet the legislative objective is rationally connected to it.
3. The means used to impair the right or freedom are no more than are necessary to accomplish the aim.

Where the State's proposed interference is substantial, the public interest gain must also be significant, a point relevant to the experience of older persons under the COVID-19 restrictions in England and Wales.[49]

Principal ECHR rights affecting older persons

Article 2 – the right to have life protected

> 2(1). Everyone's right to life shall be protected by law. No one shall be deprived of his life intentionally *save in the execution of a sentence of a court following his conviction of a crime for which this penalty is provided by law.*

43 *Observer and Guardian v United Kingdom*, App no 13585/88 (ECtHR, 26 November 1991) [71].
44 *Lingens v Austria* App no 9815/82 (ECtHR, 8 July 1986).
45 *Oberschlick v Austria* App no 20834/92 (ECtHR, 1 July 1997) [60].
46 See, for example, *Cambridge University Hospitals NHS Foundation Trust v AH* [2021] EWCOP 64, [2021] 12 WLUK 175.
47 *Young, James and Webster v United Kingdom* App no 7601/76; 7806/77 (ECtHR, 13 August 1981) 63.
48 [1999] 1 AC 69
49 J Rivers, 'Proportionality and variable intensity of review' (2006) *The Cambridge Law Journal* 65(1) 174.

Protocol No. 6, passed in 1983, abolished the death penalty in peacetime, so the italicised words no longer apply.[50] This article does not give a right to life but rather a right to have life protected by law. The positive nature of Article 2 has implications for healthcare. The ECtHR has held that the State has a positive obligation to prevent self-harm by persons under the control of the State. For example, where an older person is detained under the MHA 1983, subject to a deprivation of liberty authorisation, or is in hospital voluntarily with a mental disorder, the State must take reasonable measures to protect their life. In Centre for Legal Resources on behalf of Valentin Câmpeanu v Romania, the ECtHR held that where the authorities are aware of appalling conditions that led to the death of older persons placed in care homes or hospitals but did nothing, Article 2 is engaged.[51] In Dodov v Bulgaria,[52] the ECtHR considered the case of the disappearance of an Alzheimer's patient from a nursing home operated by the State. The applicant was one of her children who claimed, amongst other things, that the nursing home had, through negligence, placed his mother's life at risk. The Court found that the nursing home's failure to supervise his mother, despite being told not to leave her alone, was the cause of her disappearance. In this regard, there had been a violation of Article 2. The courts have distinguished between those detained subject to statutory powers and those in the hospital voluntarily. The duty is heightened in the case of detained patients or residents.[53] However, there is no general obligation to protect people from deliberate self-harm, even when the authorities were aware of or should have been aware of a real and immediate risk of death if these were a consequence of a truly autonomous decision. The State would have had no authority to intervene, and those decisions would have deserved respect as an expression of the person's autonomy and protected by Article 8 ECHR.[54]

The Westminster and Cardiff governments' responses to COVID-19 engaged the right. Older age was a factor in triaging and prioritising treatment. The March 2020 guidance issued by the National Institute for Health and Care Excellence (NICE) required that upon hospital admission, whether for COVID-19 or otherwise, the person should be assessed under the Clinical Frailty Scale (CFS). However, this guidance was not to be used for younger persons or those with longer-term disabilities, as disability organisations successfully argued that doing so would be discriminatory. No such recognition was given to older persons. The critical care referral criteria required that discussions with the critical care team should be held when,

50 Council of Europe, *Protocol No. 6 to the Convention for the Protection of Human Rights and Fundamental Freedoms Concerning the Abolition of the Death Penalty*, Strasbourg 28.IV.1983.

51 App no. 47848/08 (ECtHR, 17 July 2014).

52 App no. 59548/00 (ECHR, 17 January 2008).

53 See *Savage v South Essex Partnership NHS Foundation Trust* [2008] UKHL 74, [2009] 1 A.C. 6; *Rabone v Pennine Care NHS Trust* [2012] UKSC 2, [2012] 2 AC 72; *Fernandes de Oliveira v. Portugal* App no 78103/14 ECtHR, 31 January 2019) [124].

54 *R (on the application of Gary Parkin) v His Majesty's Assistant Coroner for Inner London (East)* [2024] EWHC 744 (Admin), [2024] All ER (D) 63 (Apr).

> the assessment suggests the person is more frail (for example, a CFS score of 5 or more), there is uncertainty regarding the likely benefit of critical care organ support, and critical care advice is needed to help the decision about treatment.[55]

A CFS score of 5 refers to a person who is 'mildly frail.' It covers a person with more evident slowing and may need help in high-order instrumental activities of daily living (finance, heavy housework, medications, transportation). Mild frailty 'progressively impairs shopping and walking outside alone, meal preparation and housework.'[56] It does not necessarily mean a lack of capacity or the inability to live an autonomous life, although it may affect recovery time. The criteria risked screening out many older persons. Chong et al. were concerned about the guidance and emphasised,

> that frailty identification should not simply result in a 'label' but rather impact management in a meaningful context-appropriate way that is used to make care rational and not to ration care.[57]

Without compelling clinical evidence that this guidance was reasonable and appropriate, the lives of many older persons were denied the protection of Article 2. In addition, the early practice of discharging persons from hospitals into care homes without COVID-19 testing disproportionally affected older persons.[58]

Another disturbing feature of the COVID-19 pandemic was the reported increase in the number of older persons and persons with disabilities placed under Do Not Attempt Cardiopulmonary Resuscitation Notices (DNACPR). The Care Quality Commission in England found that some older persons in care homes were denied lifesaving treatment in the early stages of the pandemic by the misuse and abuse of DNACPR notices. They reported that providers sometimes conflated decisions about cardiopulmonary resuscitation with decisions about whether to admit a person to a hospital or provide treatment for COVID-19. This led to delays in calling ambulances and doctors. Relatives were not consulted.[59] A study by The Queen's Nursing Institute found that one in ten care homes surveyed was instructed to place blanket DNACPR notices on residents. In addition, decisions regarding resuscitation were made by GPs or hospital staff without consulting the

55 National Institute for Health and Care Excellence, 'COVID-19 rapid guidelines: Critical care in adults' (2020) *Guidelines* <https://www.nice.org.uk/guidance/ng159/chapter/2-Admission-to-critical-care> para 2.2- accessed 4 March 2025.

56 ibid paras 1.1.

57 E Chong, M Chan, H Tan, and W Lim, 'Use of the Clinical Frailty Scale for critical care decisions' (2020) *Journal of the American Geriatrics Society* 68(6) E30–E32.

58 J Williams, (2021) 'Taking it on the chin: older people, human rights and COVID-19' (2021) *The Journal of Adult Protection* 23(2) 86.

59 Care Quality Commission, 'Review of Do Not Attempt Cardiopulmonary Resuscitation Decisions Duringthe COVID-19 Pandemic Interim report' (2020) 26; Dyer C. 'Some care home residents may have died because of blanket DNR orders, says regulator.' BMJ. 2020; 371:m4733 <https://www.bmj.com/content/371/bmj.m4733.full>

residents, their families, or the care home staff, to free up hospital beds.[60] Failure to follow the General Medical Council Guidance on DNACPR[61] notices led to wishes being ignored. The guidance is reinforced by the Court of Appeal's decision in R (Tracey) v Cambridge University Hospitals NHS Foundation Trust.[62] The Court held that there is a strong presumption of involving patients in DNACPR decisions, and doctors must not exclude them because it is likely to cause distress that falls short of physical or psychological harm. Where the doctor's clinical judgement is that resuscitation would be futile, this must be sensitively discussed with the patient unless this would cause them serious harm. Importantly, the futility assessment must not be based on age but on prognosis. Amnesty International's report on the UK government's failure to protect older persons during COVID-19 included a disturbing finding.

> Discussing how the CCG guidance came to be issued, a senior local figure told Amnesty International that it was clear from conversations he had with senior figures in the local health system that they were under 'an enormous amount of pressure from upwards' and that they were given instructions orally which were not sent in writing or would be worded differently when sent in writing. This would explain why so many CCGs and GPs asked care homes to put [DNACPR] instructions on their residents in a blanket approach even though there is no written record of any such government policy.[63]

Suppose an unlawful DNACPR notice leads to the death of an older person. This would engage Article 2 unless a credible clinical judgement considers the intervention futile and not in the patient's best interest. In Hristozov and Others v Bulgaria, the ECtHR held that Article 2 is engaged when a person's life is put at risk by the denial of healthcare that is available to others.[64] Article 2 is an absolute right. The right of a person to have their life protected cannot be qualified in the interests of others, although this does not give an open-ended right to life-sustaining treatment; that remains a clinical judgement.

Poor provision of care in care homes or domestic settings, which puts an older person at risk of death, may also engage Article 2. Failure to report and address abuse and neglect places older persons at risk of death and denies necessary

60 The Queen's Nursing Institute 'The Experience of Care Home Staff During Covid-19 A Survey Report by the QNI's International Community Nursing Observatory International Community Nursing Observatory.' (2020) <https://www.qni.org.uk/wp-content/uploads/2020/08/The-Experience-of-Care-Home-Staff-During-Covid-19-2.pdf> - accessed 12 Feb. 2025.

61 General Medical Council, 'Treatment and care towards the end of life: Good practice in decision making content' (2022) <https://www.gmc-uk.org/professional-standards/professional-standards-for-doctors/treatment-and-care-towards-the-end-of-life/cardiopulmonary-resuscitation-cpr> – accessed 28 September 2024.

62 [2014] EWCA Civ 822, [2015] QB 543.

63 Amnesty International, 'As if expendable: The UK government's failure to protect older people in care homes during the Covid-19 pandemic' (London, 2020).

64 App nos 47039/11 and 358/12 (ECtHR, 15 February 2018).

protection. The absence of a coherent and workable adult safeguarding policy may also engage Article 2. A line of ECtHR cases suggests that the article may be engaged even though the person has not died, but a serious threat to life existed.[65] Other examples that may engage the right are poor control of medication, incorrect medication, and inadequate staffing, leading to gaps in observing residents that may put lives at risk.[66] It does not follow that Article 2 will be engaged in all cases where an older person dies because of the actions of a public authority. In Watts v the United Kingdom, a 106-year-old was moved from a care home where she had lived for several years to another care home. She argued that this move placed her life at risk, reducing her life expectancy by 25%. It is recognised that such transfers may pose a risk to life, particularly when they are poorly managed. However, when deciding whether the application was admissible, the ECtHR recognised the difficulties local authorities face due to lack of funding and that it had carefully planned the move and taken steps to minimise the risk. It held that the positive duty under Article 2 was met.

Article 3 – the right not to be subject to inhuman or degrading treatment

> 3. No one shall be subjected to torture or to inhuman or degrading treatment or punishment.

It is generally accepted that Article 3 is an absolute right.[67] However, the threshold for inhuman or degrading is relative and depends upon the circumstances. Treatment that does not meet the requirements of Article 3 may engage Article 8. The ECtHR has said,

> The assessment of this minimum is relative: it depends on all the circumstances of the case, such as the nature and context of the treatment, its duration, its physical and mental effects, and in some instances, the sex, age and state of health of the victim.[68]

Poor medical or social care may engage Article 3.[69] A physical or mental illness that risks being worsened by treatment for which the State has a responsibility may

65 *Selahattin Demirtaş v. Turkey* App nos 14305/17 (ECtHR, 22 December 2020).

66 For example, see Commissioner for Older People Northern Ireland, 'Home truths: A report on the Commissioner's investigation into Dunmurry Care Home (2018) 196 https://copni.org/assets/general/resources/copni-home-truths-report-web-version.pdf – accessed 28 September 2024; M Flynn, 'In Search of Accountability: A review of the neglect of older people living in care homes investigated as Operation Jasmine' (2015) 328 <https://www.gov.wales/sites/default/files/publications/2019-06/in-search-of-accountability-a-review-of-the-neglect-of-older-people-living-in-care-homes-operation-jasmine_1.pdf> – accessed 28 September 2024.

67 MK Addo and N Grief, 'Does Article 3 of the European Convention on Human Rights enshrine absolute rights?' (1998) *European Journal of International Law* 9(3) 510.

68 *MC and AC v Romania* App no 12060/12107 (ECtHR, 12 April 2016) [107].

69 *Tanko v Finland* App no 23634/94 (ECtHR, 2 December 2008); *Herczegfalvy v Austria* App no 10533/83 (ECtHR, 24 September 1992).

fall within Article 3, for example, the inappropriate use of antipsychotic drugs to keep people living with dementia sedated. There are reports of increased use of 'archaic and dangerous' antipsychotic drugs during the COVID-19 pandemic despite their potential to shorten life and affect its quality. In a recent study, Mok et al. found that using antipsychotics in adults living with dementia is associated with negative outcomes, such as pneumonia, kidney injury, stroke, fracture, heart failure, and more. They recommend that antipsychotics should only be used if other interventions are ineffective or if patients are at high risk. When prescribed, doctors should use the lowest effective dose for the shortest possible time. This study highlights the importance of considering these risks before prescribing antipsychotics to people living with dementia.[70] The Article 3 threshold may be lower when an older person is detained under the law or is de facto detained. For example, a relatively slight injury may still be inhuman and degrading if the older person is detained under the MHA 1983 or the deprivation of liberty provisions of the Mental Capacity Act 2005, as they are more vulnerable by having to remain in a closed community.[71]

The Coronavirus Act 2020 gave the governments in England and in Wales the power to disapply many social care duties in the CA 2014 and the SSWA 2014. These duties include assessment of need, financial assessments, provision of support, review, and the duty to provide NHS continuing care. As older persons are the primary users of social care, they would be most affected if the powers were used. Lack of overnight care, toileting help, and the increased risk of falls were likely outcomes of no engagement with social care. Cognitive ability is expected to decline faster for older persons living with dementia without social care support and support for their carers; in some instances, this would engage Article 3 as inhuman and degrading. In the end, neither government used these powers. However, their presence in the statute book shows a disturbing lack of sensitivity to the human rights of older persons.

The abuse and neglect of older persons may engage Article 3. Based on the evidence received during its inquiry, the Westminster Parliament's Joint Committee on Human Rights, in its report, The Human Rights of Older People in Healthcare, identified some examples of poor treatment that engaged Article 3.

Malnutrition and dehydration
Abuse and rough treatment
Neglect, carelessness and poor hygiene
Inappropriate medication and use of physical restraint
Inadequate assessment of a person's needs
Bullying, patronising, and infantilising attitudes towards older persons

70 R Howard, et al. 'Antipsychotic prescribing to people with dementia during COVID-19' (2020) *The Lancet Neurology* 19(11) 892; P Mok, M Carr, B Guthrie et al. (2024) 'Multiple adverse outcomes associated with antipsychotic use in people with dementia: population based cohort study' (2024) *BMJ* 385, e076268.

71 *Ribbitsch v Austria* App no 18896/91 (ECtHR, 4 December 1995).

Examples of such treatment feature in many reports examining cases of elder abuse.[72] In the report on the abuse of older persons in care homes in South Wales, Margaret Flynn found evidence of residents with grade four sores so deep they possibly reached the bone. Nothing was done by the homes in question.[73] No criminal prosecutions were forthcoming. The State's failure to intervene to protect older persons from such inhuman and degrading treatment compounds the abuse and neglect they have experienced. The State is failing in its positive duty to protect. Looking at Northern Ireland, the findings of the Cherry Tree House Review[74] and the Commissioner's Home Truths Report[75] provide further examples of older residents being exposed to unbearable and unacceptable treatment, with nothing being done about it. In Home Truths, the Commissioner pointed to a case where a resident had only had two showers within six weeks; one former employee reported that washing was taking too long, and they were told to tick the sheet to say it had been done. Residents were never hoisted – 'too much hard work.'[76] Several television documentaries have used undercover reporters to expose ill-treatment and neglect in care and nursing homes and hospitals. They include examples of rough handling, giving morphine to a resident to 'shut her up,' unanswered alarms, slapping, and inadequate nutrition and hydration.[77]

The State is also responsible for ensuring that older persons are safe and free from inhuman or degrading treatment in their homes. The ECtHR in A v United Kingdom[78] considered the case of a nine-year-old boy who was beaten with a cane by his stepfather. The stepfather was charged under Section 47 Offences Against the Person Act 1861 with assault occasioning actual bodily harm. His defence was lawful chastisement, a defence inexplicably accepted by the jury. The ECtHR found that the child's right under Article 3 had been violated as the force exceeded the minimum severity level. The United Kingdom failed to provide adequate protection to which children and vulnerable persons are particularly entitled. Although the State did not inflict the punishment, it still had a duty to protect the child in his home. The same principle applies to those older persons who experience abuse or neglect at the hands of family and others outside of institutional settings.

72 Joint Committee on Human Rights, *The Human Rights of Older People in Healthcare* (HC 2006-07 156-1) 14

73 Flynn (n66).

74 Regulation and Quality Improvement Authority 'Independent review of the actions taken in relation to concerns raised about the care delivered at Cherry Tree house.' (RQIA. 2014) <https://www.rqia.org.uk/RQIA/files/1f/1fc36cdd-154f-47a6-bd5d-366dcea2f3bf.pd> -accessed 28 September 2024.

75 Commissioner for Older People Northern Ireland (66).

76 ibid 37–8.

77 See 'Nursing Homes Undercover' *Panorama* (25 November 2016) <https://www.bbc.co.uk/programmes/b0844wq3>– accessed 28 September 2024.

78 *A v United Kingdom* (n3) 65.

Article 5 – the right to liberty

> 5(1). Everyone has the right to liberty and security of person. No one shall be deprived of his liberty save in the following cases and in accordance with a procedure prescribed by law.
>
> (e). the lawful detention of persons for the prevention of the spreading of infectious diseases, of persons of unsound mind, alcoholics or drug addicts or vagrants…
>
> 4. Everyone who is deprived of his liberty by arrest or detention shall be entitled to take proceedings by which the lawfulness of his detention shall be decided speedily by a court and his release ordered if the detention is not lawful.

Detention of an older person under the MHA 1983 is considered to be compliant with this article. Although the detention rate declines as people age, the MHA 1983 is still used to deprive older persons of their liberty.[79] The MHA 1983 sets out criteria for admission, although arguably, they are too vague and open to subjective interpretation to provide satisfactory safeguards. In Mohammed v Ministry of Defence, the Supreme Court emphasised that the criteria and rules governing detention must not be so broad as to be beyond effective legal control.[80] People should be able to foresee the consequences of the restrictions imposed upon them. Under the MHA 1983, review procedures include the hospital managers and the Mental Health Review Tribunals. Detention time limits are fixed but renewable, subject to the patient still meeting the criteria. Article 5 is also the basis for the Deprivation of Liberty Safeguards. In HL v UK,[81] the ECtHR found that a person who was admitted informally into a hospital for treatment for his mental disorder and who did not appear to resist or run away was still detained by the State. He was under continuous supervision and control and was not, in fact rather than in theory, free to leave. The procedures available to him to challenge his detention must satisfy Article 5(4). Restricting permission to leave a care home without a 'procedure prescribed by law' breaches Article 5.[82] If a deprivation of liberty is imputable to the State, it does not matter that it took place in a State-controlled facility, a private facility, or the older person's home.[83] This is consistent with the State's positive duty to prevent unlawful deprivation of liberty.[84] The MHA 1983 and the Deprivation of Liberty Safeguards are discussed in Chapter 7. The ECtHR has emphasised the importance of liberty. Nobody should be arbitrarily deprived of their liberty. The need for a procedure prescribed by law is an essential safeguard

79 NHS Digital, 'Mental Health Act Statistics, Annual Figures England 2022–23' (2024) <https://digital.nhs.uk/data-and-information/publications/statistical/mental-health-act-statistics-annual-figures/2022-23-annual-figures> – NHS England Digital – accessed 28 September 2024.

80 [2017] UKSC 2, | [2017] AC 821.

81 App no 45508/99 (ECtHR, 5 October 2005).

82 *Stanev v Bulgaria* App no 36760/06 (ECtHR, 17 January 2012).

83 *Cheshire West and Chester Council v P* [2014] UKSC 19, [2014] AC 896.

84 [2016] EWCA Civ 1317, [2017] Fam 278.

against this, particularly where the older person lacks the capacity to consent or is a person with mental ill health.[85] In N v Romania,[86] it was held that the continued detention of the person after a decision had been taken to release him was arbitrary, even though he agreed to remain in detention until social services found appropriate support in the community. The conditions under which the person is detained must be consistent with the purposes of the detention.[87]

Whoever intends to deprive an older person of their liberty has the burden of proving that the criteria are met. In Winterwerp v Netherlands, the ECtHR set out three requirements for detaining a person because of an unsound mind. First, it must be proven by objective medical evidence that the person has a mental disorder, except in cases of emergency. Second, the mental disorder must be serious enough to justify confinement and necessary given the circumstances. Finally, the mental disorder must continue throughout detention.[88] 'Persons of unsound mind' lacks precision but was probably the best term available when the ECHR was drafted. The ECtHR has recognised that it is an imprecise term and one that is constantly developing from medical and social perspectives. The unsoundness of the mind must be so serious that it requires that the person is placed in a setting appropriate for mental health patients,[89] such as a hospital, care home, or similar.[90] Transferring to an unsuitable setting, other than temporarily before transfer to suitable settings, may render the deprivation unlawful and also a breach of Article 3.

Article 6 – the right to a fair and public hearing

> 6(1). In the determination of his civil rights and obligations or of any criminal charge against him, everyone is entitled to a fair and public hearing within a reasonable time by an independent and impartial tribunal established by law. Judgment shall be pronounced publicly but the press and public may be excluded from all or part of the trial in the interest of morals, public order or national security in a democratic society, where the interests of juveniles or the protection of the private life of the parties so require, or the extent strictly necessary in the opinion of the court in special circumstances where publicity would prejudice the interests of justice.
>
> (2). Everyone charged with a criminal offence shall be presumed innocent until proven guilty according to law.
>
> (3). Everyone charged with a criminal offence has the following minimum rights:

85 *Stanev v. Bulgaria*, Application no 36760/06 (ECtHR 17 January 2012).
86 App no 38048/18 (ECtHR, 16 November 2021) paras 165–7.
87 *Brown v Parole Board for Scotland* [2017] UKSC 69, [2018] AC 1.
88 App no 6301/73 (ECtHR, 24 October 1979).`See Chapter 7.
89 *Ilnseher v. Germany* App nos10211/12 and 27505/14 (ECtHR, 2 February 2017).
90 *Ashingdane v United Kingdom* App no 8225/78 (ECtHR, 28 May 1985).

(a). to be informed promptly, in a language which he understands and in detail, of the nature and cause of the accusation against him;

(b). to have adequate time and facilities for the preparation of his defence;

(c). to defend himself in person or through legal assistance of his own choosing or, if he has not sufficient means to pay for legal assistance, to be given it free when the interests of justice so require;

(d). to examine or have examined witnesses against him and to obtain the attendance and examination of witnesses on his behalf under the same conditions as witnesses against him;

(e). to have the free assistance of an interpreter if he cannot understand or speak the language used in court.

The first part of the article guarantees fair and public hearings within a reasonable time for determining civil rights, obligations, or criminal charges. The second part concerns criminal proceedings and the necessary safeguards to ensure fairness and justice. Older persons may have contact with the legal system in different ways. Of particular importance is the role of the Court of Protection in deciding matters under the Mental Capacity Act 2005. Older persons may also be involved in criminal proceedings as victims, witnesses or the accused. Ensuring older persons have access to justice is crucial to uphold their civil and human rights. However, they often face barriers due to ageism, lack of support, invisibility, and fear of victimisation.[91]

When is the article engaged? Its application to decisions by public authorities is less clear-cut than may appear. In Begum v Tower Hamlets LBC,[92] the House of Lords considered the local authority's duty towards homeless persons under the Housing Act 1996. The applicant had refused accommodation offered by the authority because the area was 'drug addicted' and racist. The housing officer rejected the refusal and argued that the authority had discharged its duty under the Act. There was a right under the Act to appeal to the county court, but only on a point of law; the court had to accept the factual finding of the officer. On appeal to the House of Lords, it was accepted that the council official was not an 'independent and impartial tribunal' under Article 6. However, it was noted that there were procedural safeguards designed to ensure the fairness of the housing officer's review. Because of this, even though the county court could not review the factual evidence, only points of law, this did not violate Article 6. The Supreme Court in Ali v Birmingham City Council[93] considered a similar case under the Housing Act 1996. One of the issues in the case was the definition of 'civil rights' in Article 6. Lord Hope distinguished two categories of social security and welfare benefit cases. First, where the legislation clearly defines those benefits, thus amounting to an individual civil right and, therefore, within article 6. Second, those benefits

91 AS Gutterman, 'Older persons' right to access justice' (2022) ,<<https://papers.ssrn.com/sol3/papers.cfm?abstract_id=4050576>accessed 28 September 2024.

92 [2003] UKHL 5, [2003] 2 AC 430.

93 [2010] UKSC 8, [2010] 2 AC 39.

which require a judgement by the public authority. The latter does not confer individual rights. In the absence of a personal right, the applicant in the case could not consider themself as the holder of a civil right and therefore fell outside of Article 6. The Secretary of State for Communities intervened in this case. His interest was primarily in the working of the homelessness legislation; however, the intervention was also driven by a concern that the outcome could indirectly affect how decisions are made in other areas, such as social care. This limiting approach is driven by a desire to conserve judicial resources and fear of 'judicial creep' into administrative decision-making.[94] It has implications for older persons who may wish to challenge administrative decisions concerning social care and similar matters.

The requirement that the hearing must take place within a reasonable time is an essential component of the right. If there is an unreasonable delay, article 6 is engaged. In Bock v Germany,[95] the ECtHR concluded that there was excessive judicial activity focussing on the mental capacity of the person to undertake legal proceedings. The German courts continued to have doubts even though five reports and two guardianship applications all pointed to the person having the necessary capacity. Consequently, the case lasted over nine years.

When an older person is a victim or witness in a criminal trial, their interests must be balanced against those of the accused. The right to a fair hearing applies to the accused, witnesses, and victim. In Doorson v the Netherlands, the ECtHR said,' (P)rinciples of fair trial also require that in appropriate cases the interests of the defence are balanced against those of witnesses or victims called upon to testify.'[96] Special measures designed to assist a victim or witness when giving evidence at a criminal trial are available under Part II Youth Justice and Criminal Evidence Act 1999. Older persons considered 'vulnerable witnesses' may benefit from these. Using these measures may be the difference between prosecution or no action being taken and help address a justice deficit for older persons.[97]

Article 8 – right to respect for private and family life.

> 1. Everyone has the right to respect for his private and family life, his home and his correspondence.
>
> 2. There shall be no interference by a public authority with the exercise of this right except such as is in accordance with the law and is necessary in a democratic society in the interests of national security, public safety or the economic well-being of the country, for the prevention of disorder or crime,

94 E Laurie 'Homelessness and the 'over-judicialisation' of welfare' (2021) Legal Studies 41(39) 52–53

95 App no 41604/98 (ECtHR, 28 July 2005).

96 *Doorson v The Netherlands* 54/1994/501/503 para 70. See also P Bates 'Youth Justice and Criminal Evidence Act -the evidence of children and vulnerable adults' (1999) 11 *Child and Fam LQ* 289.

97 See, for example, KJ Brown and F Gordon, 'Improving access to justice for older victims of crime by reimagining conceptions of vulnerability' (2022) Ageing and Society, *42*(3) 614; K Brown, and F Gordon, 'Exploring and overcoming barriers to justice for older victims of crime' (2020) *Criminal Law Review* 12 1127.

> for the protection of health or morals, or for the protection of the rights and freedoms of others.

Article 8 is a qualified right, and interference with it must be lawful and necessary to achieve one of the purposes listed in Article 8(2) and be proportionate. For older persons, this right is of particular importance. Rights to private life, family, and home become at greater risk as people age, partly because of ageism but also, in some cases, because of increasing vulnerability and greater dependence on others. A precise definition of private life is elusive, although Mustill LJ's attempt is worthy of note. He said,

> [T]he privacy of a human being denotes at the same time the personal 'space' in which the individual is free to be itself, and also the carapace, or shell, or umbrella, or whatever other metaphor is preferred, which protects that space from intrusion. An infringement of privacy is an affront to the personality, which is damaged both by the violation and by the demonstration that the personal space is not inviolate.[98]

Unjustified intervention into the personal space of an older person violates their right to that personal space or private sphere. Dignity is at the core of this right.[99]

An older person is entitled to have their private life respected in such diverse areas as physical and psychological integrity, personal development, identity, the way they choose to live, sexuality, sexual orientation, and making decisions. The right to self-determination is part of private life. It covers decisions on whether to accept or refuse medical treatment, including life and death decisions. The Court of Appeal underlined the significance of private life in end-of-life decisions in the Tracey case.

> A decision as to how to pass the closing days and moments of one's life and how one manages one's death touches in the most immediate and obvious way a patient's personal autonomy, integrity, dignity and quality of life.[100]

Private life is as important when life ebbs away as it is at other stages of life.

Although an older person may choose to live their life to the exclusion of others, private life embraces existing relationships as well as establishing and developing new ones. An older person has the right to interact with others and build friendships and intimate relations; they have the right to a private social life.[101] Environmental factors may deny older persons the right to maintain relationships and develop new ones. The poor state of public transport and age-unfriendly towns and cities may

98 *R v Broadcasting Standards Commission ex p BBC* [2000] EWCA Civ 116, [2000] 3 All ER 989.
99 J Miller, 'Dignity: A relevant normative value in "access to health and social care" litigation in the United Kingdom?' in A Diver and J Miller (eds), *Justiciability of human rights law in domestic jurisdictions* (Springer, 2016) 71.
100 Tracey (n62) [29].
101 *Bărbulescu V. Romania* App no 61496/08 (ECtHR, 5 September 2017) [71].

make them prisoners in their own homes.[102] Also of concern is the placement of older persons in care homes far from their communities. Out-of-area placements can isolate older persons from friends, families, community organisations, and familiar environments. Distance may make it difficult for family and friends to visit, thus depriving the older person of essential stimuli. It may restrict access to community resources and delay or prevent rehabilitation.[103]

Article 8's right to private life does not include an absolute right to health or social care, as the ECHR does not include second-generation rights. With limited exceptions the ECtHR has recognised that signatory States are best placed to decide how scarce resources are allocated in their health and social care arrangements, and they have what is referred to as a wide margin of appreciation. Allocation of resources arose in the case of McDonald v United Kingdom,[104] a case before the ECtHR. Ms McDonald required support to continue living at home after a stroke. As she needed to use the toilet at night, the local authority initially assessed her as needing overnight support to use a commode, although she was not incontinent. This was deemed an eligible need. Initially, a care worker provided sleep-in care for seven nights a week. However, as part of a cost-cutting exercise, the local authority wrote to tell her that sleep-in care would be cut to four days a week and they would supply her with incontinence pads for the other three days. In doing so, the authority failed to follow the legal rules for re-assessing a person's needs when changing their care package. It was not until twelve months later that the authority re-assessed, confirming their decision to reduce night care. She challenged the decision. The United Kingdom courts rejected her claim, arguing that allocating resources was a matter for the local authority.[105] An application was made to the ECtHR. The Court agreed that the case engaged Article 8 ECHR. In doing so, it emphasised that the very essence of the ECHR was respect for human dignity and freedom. As Article 8 was engaged, local authorities must conduct a proportionality assessment.[106] The next question was whether the local authority had lawfully reduced her care package. It found that the authority acted unlawfully for the twelve months between the original communication and the reassessment. Therefore, reducing the care package for that period was incompatible with her

102 J Williams, 'Care homes and communities: A human rights approach to age-friendliness' in C Gardiner and E O'Brien Webb (eds) *The Age-friendly Lens* (Routledge, 2023) 107.

103 Care Quality Commission 'Brief guide: Out of area placements in rehabilitation units' (*CQC*, 2019) <https://www.cqc.org.uk/sites/default/files/Brief_Guide_Out_of_Area_Placements_in_Rehabilitation_Units_0.pdf> – accessed 28 September 2024; |National Development Team for Inclusion, 'Close to Home: Review and recommendations for reducing out of area placements for adults with mental health conditions' (NDT, 2020)<tps://www.ndti.org.uk/news/introduction-to-close-to-home-ndtis-review-into-out-of-area-placements> – accessed 28 September 2024.

104 McDonald case (n12).

105 *R (on the application of McDonald) v Royal Borough of Kensington and Chelsea* [2011] UKSC 33, [2011] 4 All ER 881.

106 M Amos, 'The Influence of British courts on the Jurisprudence of the European Court of Human Rights' in R McCorquodales and J Gauce (eds) *British influences on international law, 1915–2015* (Brill Nijhoff, 2016) 213.

right to private life. She was awarded a thousand Euros for this violation of her rights. Once the reassessment had taken place, the unlawfulness was removed, thus satisfying the requirement of lawfulness in Article 8(2). The Court was, therefore, content that the decision was, at this point, lawful and proportionate given the authority's duty to consider the needs of other service users towards whom it had responsibilities. On the positive side, the Court's decision establishes that withdrawing care engages Article 8 and could amount to a breach which impacts dignity and independence. Furthermore, if the State is acting unlawfully, it cannot justify interfering with the enjoyment of the right. McDonald is also interesting in that the ECtHR had little regard for the principles in the Convention on the Rights of Persons with Disabilities; the case was a missed opportunity to explore the relationship between the Disabilities Convention and the ECHR.[107]

Elder abuse also engages the right to private life. This is particularly the case where the State (for example, the police or adult safeguarding in local authorities or the NHS) is aware of the risks of physical or psychological violence against an older person. In Volodina v Russia (no 2), a failure to conduct an effective investigation into the many instances of cyberviolence led to no prosecution being undertaken. The State had failed to protect the person who was experiencing serious abuse. The introduction of the HRA 1998 placed pressure on governments in the United Kingdom to introduce specific laws to address the rising number of cases of abuse of vulnerable adults.[108] England, Scotland, and Wales have responded, albeit in different ways.[109] Northern Ireland is currently debating the introduction of adult safeguarding legislation .

The right to family life is another component of Article 8 ECHR affecting older persons. Families may provide care and support for an older person. Older persons often value relationships with their grandchildren; divorce or separation can sever those relationships, negatively impacting the grandparent's well-being.[110] The ECtHR recognises that the grandparent/grandchild relationship is included in the article. However, given that it differs from the parent/child relationship, the degree of protection is less and involves the right to maintain a 'normal' grandparent/grandchild relationship. Contact between them will be subject to parental agreement and the child's welfare.[111] It is argued that there should be a presumption regarding grandparent involvement with grandchildren post-breakdown. A con-

107 L Pritchard-Jones, 'Night-time care, Article 8 and the European Court of Human Rights: A missed opportunity?' (2015) *Journal of Social Welfare and Family Law* 37(1) 108.

108 J Williams, 'Public law protection of vulnerable adults'(2002) *Journal of Social Work* 2(3) 293.

109 J Williams, 'Safeguarding adults at risk: An asymmetrical approach to reform across the four nations' (2015) *Elder Law Journal* 5(4) 343; see Chapter 6.

110 LM Drew and M Silverstein, 'Grandparents' psychological well-being after loss of contact with their grandchildren' (2007) *Journal of Family Psychology* 21(3) 372; M Jappens and J Van Bavel, 'Parental divorce, residence arrangements, and contact between grandchildren and grandparents' (2016) *Journal of Marriage and Family* 78(2) 451.

111 *Mitovi v. the Former Yugoslav Republic of Macedonia* App no. 53565/13 (ECtHR, 16 July 2015); Children Act 1989, Section 1.

trary argument is that this may prejudice the interests of mothers and children.[112] Grandparents are often involved in raising their grandchildren, which may include assisting parents who, for example, work, or it may involve complete responsibility for their upbringing and care. When grandparents have assumed responsibility for bringing up their grandchild, the right to family life is much stronger.[113] When parents are unable or unwilling to care for a child, grandparents often act as kinship carers. Assumptions are made about their ability or willingness to take on this role. Australian research highlights the importance of not regarding kinship care by grandparents as a cost-saving measure; grandparents need support to enable them to be involved in their grandchildren's upbringing.[114] Hunt reviews the United Kingdom's position of grandparents as kinship carers. She concludes,

> (I)rrespective of children's need for external services, it is their grandparents who are likely to be their primary source of support, and the essential instrument in their recovery and healthy functioning. Hence, it is vital that grandparents also receive the support they need.[115]

Necessary support includes information, financial support, peer group contact, day and respite care, education and guidance, therapeutic, counselling, mental health services, practical assistance, legal help, transport, and help with the involvement of the child's parents and parental contact. Despite some progress, Hunt points out that such support is not always available.

Acknowledging grandparents' role in providing childcare support to working families is essential, as is the need to ensure that their rights are protected. Research shows that one in four working families and one in three working mothers rely on grandparents for this assistance. A significant 63% of grandparents with grandchildren under sixteen offer childcare support, and one in five grandmothers provide at least ten hours per week. In 2013, Age UK estimated that the collective value of this help amounted to £7.3 billion. As people retire later in life, many grandparents find themselves juggling childcare responsibilities with their work commitments and sometimes feel compelled to give up employment. Sweden has partially addressed this by introducing a law allowing grandparents to take paid parental leave while caring for their grandchildren, which is one of its family-friendly policies. Under this law, parents can transfer up to 45 days of their 480-day joint parental leave entitlement to the grandparents during the child's first year. For single parents, the

112 F Kaganas and C Piper, 'Grandparent contact: Another presumption?' (2020) *Journal of Social Welfare and Family Law* 42(2) 176.

113 *Terna v. Italy* App no 21052/18 (ECtHR, 14 April 2021).

114 I Zuchowski, S Gair, D Henderson and R Thorpe, 'Convenient yet neglected: The role of grandparent kinship carers' (2019) *The British Journal of Social Work* 49(3) 615.

115 J Hunt, 'Grandparents as substitute parents in the UK' (2018) *Contemporary Social Science* 13(2) 175, 182.

transfer can be up to 90 days. The importance of protecting the rights of grandparents and their role in their families is acknowledged by this policy.[116]

The ECtHR adopts a broad definition of what constitutes family life. It is not confined to the traditional husband, wife, and children. Marriage is not a legal or social prerequisite. The Court looks at the facts in individual cases. The parties may cohabit, and their relationship may be longstanding and robust, or they may be married or have gone through a formal ceremony. Their relationship may or may not include physical intimacy. LGBTQ+ older adults face difficulties when ensuring that their partners are recognised and accepted by service providers as family. Skeldon and Jenkins found that for older LGBTQ+ persons, care homes and nursing homes are not always welcoming environments, and they identify a need for more training. Among the issues identified is the assumption by staff in some cases that the older person is heterosexual, which can force the person to deny their sexuality. They may experience discrimination by other residents and fear isolation from their social networks.[117] Older LGBT+ persons may be afraid to access care services due to negative experiences, causing them to delay or avoid planning for future care transitions.[118] This can lead to disorganised and stressful moves into formal care settings. Inclusive and supportive healthcare services that are stigma-free are needed for the LGBT+ community to address inequalities in healthcare.[119] There is also the risk of their loved one being ignored in favour of so-called 'more traditional' family members. Such attitudes and behaviour interfere with the right to family life.

Continued contact with family can contribute towards maintaining and promoting an older person's well-being, particularly for those in residential care. Concern was expressed about the restrictions on visiting care homes during the COVID-19 pandemic. Was this a proportionate restriction when measured against the risk of infection?[120] Imposing restrictions on contact by family members and an older person engages the right. In SR v A Local Authority,[121] a couple had been married for fifty-eight years; the wife developed dementia and was in a care home subject to

116 Department for Work and Pensions, *Looking after the grandchildren? Make sure it counts towards your State Pension* (26 July 2013) <https://www.gov.uk/government/news/looking-after-the-grandchildren-make-sure-it-counts-towards-your-state-pension> – accessed 28 September 2024; Katie Rosseinsky, '"Grandpaternity" leave may be a childcare breakthrough' *Independent* (London, 9 July 2024).

117 L Skeldon and S Jenkins, Experiences and Attitudes of the LGBTQ+ Community on Care/Nursing Homes. Journal of Homosexuality, (2022(70(13), 1–33. doi:https://doi.org/10.1080/00918369.2022.2086751.

118 D Kneale, J Henley, J Thomas, et al., 'Inequalities in older LGBT people's health and care needs in the United Kingdom: A systematic scoping review' (2021) *Ageing & Society* 41(3) 493.

119 ibid.

120 J Andrews, 'Irrational restrictions' *New Scientist* (London, 14 November 2020) 23; J Williams, 'Taking it on the chin: Older people, human rights and COVID-19' (2021) *The Journal of Adult Protection* 23(2) 86.

121 [2018] EWCOP 36, [2018] 6 WLUK 685.

a Deprivation of Liberty authorisation.[122] Her husband had strong pro-euthanasia views. The local authority restricted his ability to take her out unaccompanied due to concern about his pro-euthanasia stance and the risk it allegedly posed. This restriction was successfully challenged as the authority could only make the order with the court's approval. The court accepted that the restriction interfered with the Article 8 right to private and family life and was not justifiable, proportionate or necessary. Such extreme limitations on the right to family life required strict scrutiny by the court and not a local authority decision.

Home can be very precious for older persons. It contains many memories, happy and sad. It can be a focal point for family reunions, with adult children still referring to it as 'home' despite leaving many years ago. A home is a place for personal possessions, photographs, and pets. It helps define us and reflects our character. As with private and family life, home is difficult to define. The ECtHR in Buckley v UK described it as follows.

> 'Home' is an autonomous concept which does not depend on classification under domestic law. Whether or not a particular habitation constitutes a 'home' which attracts the protection of Article 8(1) will depend on the factual circumstances, namely, the existence of sufficient and continuous links.[123]

Lord Bingham in Qazi adopted a 'down-to-earth and pragmatic' approach to the meaning of 'home.'[124] Lord Millett in Collins referred to the home as the place where a person lives to which they return and which forms the centre of their existence.[125] It is the personal nexus between the person and their home that matters. In her compelling diary of her time in care homes in Australia, Ellen Newton refers to 'home' as being 'your peculiar treasure.'[126] An essential part of the right to respect for home is that the State may only enter for a lawful reason as there is no blanket power of entry.[127] Powers exist under Section 135 MHA 1983 and in Wales under Section 127 SSWA 2014. The police also have powers of entry, as does public health.

When an older person moves to residential care, the care home becomes their home. The care home must ensure that residents' dignity is protected and privacy respected. Staff and others should knock on a resident's door before entering. The home's design must be human rights compliant, particularly protecting the right to liberty.[128] The choice and personalisation of private space must be protected within the requirements of the health, safety, and well-being of other residents. Such matters are equally important for people living with dementia in care homes. The home

122 See Chapter 7.
123 App no 20348/92 (ECtHR, 29 September 1996).
124 *Harrow LBC v Qazi* [2003] UKHL 43, [2004] 1 A.C. 983.
125 *Uratemp Ventures Ltd v Collins* [2001] UKHL 43, [2002] 1 AC 301.
126 E Newton, *This Bed My Centre* (Virago 1980).
127 *Jarrand v France* App no 56138/16 (ECtHR 9 March 2022) [75]
128 J Williams, 'Care home design and human rights' (2011) *Elder Law Journal* 1(4) 395.

should be designed, furnished, and decorated to support a range of activities which maximise personal enjoyment and provide a stimulating environment.[129]

The final component of Article 8 is the right to respect for correspondence. The right covers the range of correspondence such as letters, texts, emails, social media messages, and telephone calls. Any interception of an older person's correspondence engages the right. Only if it is lawful, necessary and proportionate is it justifiable. Subject to strict controls, Sections 134 and 134A MHA 1984 provide a lawful basis for withholding correspondence sent or received by a person detained under the Act. Care homes and hospitals must respect the right to correspondence. Interference includes opening mail, showing mail to a third party without permission or legal justification, and listening to private phone conversations.

Article 9 – freedom of thought, conscience and religion

> 1. Everyone has the right to freedom of thought, conscience and religion; this right includes freedom to change his religion or belief and freedom, either alone or in community with others and in public or private, to manifest his religion or belief, in worship, teaching, practice and observance.
>
> 2. Freedom to manifest one's religion or beliefs shall be subject only to such limitations as are prescribed by law and are necessary in a democratic society in the interests of public safety, for the protection of public order, health or morals, or for the protection of the rights and freedoms of others.

Older persons have the right to practice a religion or not to do so. The right to hold or not hold religious beliefs is absolute; only the manifestation of those beliefs is qualified by Article 9(2), similar to Article 8(2). Dietary laws required by a religion fall within the article. So, for example, meat-free meals, halal food, and no beef or pork may be part of an older person's religious beliefs and should be respected. A Muslim should be able to celebrate Ramadan and fast between dawn and sunset. Healthy older Muslims continue fasting during Ramadam, although those with health conditions such as diabetes or kidney or heart conditions are excused. Religious symbols and clothing may also come within Article 9. Social care and healthcare providers must be alert to the diversity of older persons and recognise and respond to different religious beliefs and practices. In London Borough of X v MR and Ors, the court was asked to decide whether MR, who lacked the capacity to determine where he should live, should be placed in a Jewish care home. The court was required to balance the opposing views of family members with what MR's wishes regarding his faith would have been if he had the capacity. After reviewing the evidence, including his involvement in the Jewish community, it was decided

129 S Davis, S Byers, R Nay and S Koch, 'Guiding design of dementia friendly environments in residential care settings' (2009) *Dementia* 8(2) 185.

that given that he only had months to live, he would benefit from familiar religious and communal activities at the Jewish care home.[130]

Article 10 Freedom of expression

> 1. Everyone has the right to freedom of expression. This right shall include freedom to hold opinions and to receive and impart information and ideas without interference by public authority and regardless of frontiers. This Article shall not prevent States from requiring the licensing of broadcasting, television or cinema enterprises.
>
> 2. The exercise of these freedoms, since it carries with it duties and responsibilities, may be subject to such formalities, conditions, restrictions or penalties as are prescribed by law and are necessary in a democratic society, in the interests of national security, territorial integrity or public safety, for the prevention of disorder or crime, for the protection of health or morals, for the protection of the reputation or rights of others, for preventing the disclosure of information received in confidence, or for maintaining the authority and impartiality of the judiciary.

Older persons must be able to express their opinions and beliefs, popular or otherwise. This may involve campaigning against authority or being critical of how a service is provided for them. They must not be discriminated against when accessing services based on their views. However, this right may be limited under Article 10(2). Restrictions imposed by law include breaching confidentiality, harassment, defamation, or using threatening, abusive or insulting words or behaviour with intent to provoke a breach of the peace, or racist language.

Article 13 – right to marry

> Men and women of marriageable age have the right to marry and to found a family, according to the national laws governing the exercise of this right.

To enter a valid marriage, both parties must possess the necessary capacity. The capacity to marry involves more than just participating in a wedding ceremony or understanding the words. It requires understanding the nature and quality of marriage, including the responsibilities and duties that come with it. These include maintaining a mutual and reciprocal relationship, living together, and sharing a common home and domestic life. The MCA 2005 does not allow anybody else to consent to marriage or a civil partnership on behalf of another person. The courts do not have jurisdiction to consider whether a particular marriage was in a patient's

130 [2022] EWCOP 1, [2022] 1 WLUK 248.

best interests.[131] DMM (Alzheimer's: power of attorney)[132] concerned the proposed marriage of a man with Alzheimer's to his long-term partner. Did he have the necessary capacity? If he had the capacity, his marriage would adversely affect the financial expectations of his daughters as it would revoke his will under which they were beneficiaries. Once he was married, he could potentially lack the capacity to make a new will, and the intestacy rules would apply. This would disinherit the daughters. The Court confirmed the need for capacity to enter a marriage. It referred to the Mental Capacity Act 2005, saying he must be able to understand, retain, use, and weigh the information as to the reasonably foreseeable financial consequences of his marriage, including that the marriage would automatically revoke his earlier will. The Court said the threshold for capacity was low; there was no requirement for detailed knowledge of the rules relating to will and intestacy, and he had capacity. Reliance was placed on expert evidence that he understood the consequences of his marriage, namely that the children would be disinherited as he may lack the capacity to reinstate them as beneficiaries.

The Older People's Commissioner for Wales

The Older People's Commissioner for Wales was established by the Commissioner for Older People (Wales) Act 2006.[133] According to Section 5, the Commissioner must 'seek to promote' the well-being of older persons who require care and support and their carers who require support. The Commissioner has a variety of general functions, including raising awareness about the interests of older persons in Wales and the need to protect those interests. The Commissioner must ensure that older persons in Wales have equal opportunities and are not subject to discrimination. Furthermore, the Commissioner encourages best practices in the treatment of older persons and reviews the adequacy and effectiveness of laws that impact the interests of older persons in Wales. These powers can only be used in areas within the Welsh devolution settlement, which means that non-devolved matters are not included. For example, the powers cannot be used concerning the administration of justice. The Commissioner can examine any topic related to the welfare of older persons in Wales and make representations to the Welsh Ministers, the

131 See MCA 2005 Section.27(1)(a); Sheffield City Council v E [2005] 1 FLR 965, [2005] Fam 326;

132 [2017] EWCOP 32, [2017] 7 WLUK 588; Southwark London Borough v KA and others (Capacity to Marry) [2016] EWCOP 20, [2016] 3 WLUK 657: Department for Constitutional Affairs, *Mental Capacity Act 2005 Code of Practice* (The Stationery Office, 2007) <https://assets.publishing.service.gov.uk/government/uploads/system/uploads/attachment_data/file/921428/Mental-capacity-act-code-of-practice.pdf> para 2.1 – accessed 28 September 2024.

133 See generally A Sherlock, J Williams, and E Royles, 'A Welsh Model of Commissioners' (2015) *Cambrian Law Review* 45, 74-95; A Sherlock, and J Williams, (2017). 'The Children's Commissioner for Wales and the Older People's Commissioner for Wales and the Administrative Justice System' in S Nason (ed) *Administrative Justice in Wales and Comparative Perspectives* (Gwasg Prifysgol Cymru, 2017) 125.

First Minister for Wales, or the Counsel General to the Welsh Government regarding these matters.

When exercising the office's functions, the Commissioner must 'have regard to the United Nations Principles for Older Persons.' This is in addition to the Section 6 HRA 1998 duty not to act in a way incompatible with the ECHR. Much of the Commissioner's work has focused on human rights. In 2014, the Commissioner led an advisory group to inform the Welsh Government on the potential, scope, and impact of a declaration of the rights of older persons in Wales. Although not legally binding, the Declaration outlines the rights of older persons in an accessible form. A similar approach was adopted in an easy guide to rights published by the Commissioner.[134] Human Rights are at the forefront of the Commissioner's work, a point reflected in her commitment to the work of the United Nations Open-Ended Working Group on Ageing.

Northern Ireland also has a Commissioner for Older People. An interesting use of the Commissioner's powers was investigating the treatment and experience of older persons living in Dunmurry Care Home. This was conducted using the Commissioner's powers to investigate under Section 4(3) and (4) and Schedule 2 Commissioner for Older People Act (Northern Ireland) 2011. The resulting report, Home Truths,[135] has reinvigorated a discussion in Northern Ireland on the need for an adult safeguarding law.

Conclusion

Does the HRA 1998 work for older persons? Theoretically, it should, particularly if an older person is at an enhanced risk because of disability, poverty, or abuse. Unfortunately, the COVID-19 experience shows that governments can downgrade older persons' human rights in times of crisis. Times of crisis are when human rights are fundamental to ensuring that older persons are not discriminated against and are fully recognised as human beings. In his report, Home Truths, the Commissioner for Older People Northern Ireland uncovered failings by public authorities to respect the human rights of residents and to respond appropriately to concerns that these rights were being violated. He refers to 'a slow and inadequate response from the authorities involved in ensuring that minimum standards of care were being met.'[136] The report usefully maps the many failures in the home and by the authorities onto the rights in the ECHR. Flynn's report on abuses in care homes in Gwent paints a similar picture of professional cruelty and indifference, being exacerbated by systemic failure in the State apparatus designed to protect the older residents.[137] Were these findings treated with the same anger and repulsion

134 Older People's Commissioner for Wales, 'Know your rights: An easy guide' (2018) <https://older-people.wales/wp-content/uploads/2024/04/Rights-Booklet-e-2024.pdf> – accessed 28 September 2024.

135 Commissioner for Older People Northern Ireland (n66).

136 ibid 4.

137 Flynn (n66).

as they would, rightly, if they involved children? Harold Shipman was Britain's most prolific serial killer. He is thought to have killed 250 plus older persons. Were we as shocked and appalled about Shipman as we rightly were about the Soham murderer Ian Huntley, who killed two young girls at the time Shipman was on trial? Miles Kington, writing in the Independent in 2003, contrasted the public response to Huntley and his demonisation with that of the reaction to Shipman's crimes.

> despite having killed scores of people, [Shipman] never seems quite to have caught the fancy of the British people. But then, he was most unBritish in that he only killed people older than himself, not teenagers. And we still haven't worked out how we really feel about older people yet.[138]

Although written over twenty years ago, Kington's point about understanding how we feel about older persons still resonates. This presents obstacles to older persons enjoying human rights as equal citizens. Changing societal ageist attitudes cannot be achieved by law alone. Clough and Brazier conclude,

> (H)uman rights law can help us set standards of civilised behaviour. Securing implementation of those standards for those less able to defend their own rights is a task that cannot be done by laws or lawyers alone.[139]

The existence of human rights law and the opportunity to challenge past violations do not guarantee that the rights of older persons and others will be respected. What is needed is to ensure that human rights are embedded in our public services and that older persons are valued.[140]

When discussing the American experience, Cox and Pardasani argue for a rights-based approach to social work with older adults. They distinguish between 'needs' and 'human rights'.

> Human rights are frequently confused with needs although the two are clearly distinguishable. Tangible needs exist as phenomena that can be objectively identified and measured such as needs for food, housing, support, or income... However, needs can also be subjective, wherein society decides whether they actually exist. In contrast to human rights, which are constant, social values and perspectives are influential in determining needs.[141]

Elder law lawyers, social workers, and other practitioners must use their knowledge and understanding of older persons to influence and educate policymakers to ensure policies uphold rather than undermine human rights. Chapter 8 discusses

138 M Kington, 'Kenneth Williams knew what his fans wanted' *Independent* (London, 1 December 2003).

139 B Clough and M Brazier, 'Never too old for health and human rights?' (2014) *Medical Law International* 14(3) 133, 154.

140 Williams (n8).

141 C Cox, and M Pardasani, 'Aging and human rights: A rights-based approach to social work with older adults' (2017) *Journal of Human Rights and Social Work* 2, 98, 99.

whether a bespoke international convention on the rights of older persons will enhance their human rights.

Bibliography

Addo MK and Grief N, 'Does Article 3 of the European Convention on Human Rights enshrine absolute rights?' (1998) *European Journal of International Law* 9(3) 510.

African Union, 'Protocol to the African Charter on Human and Peoples' Rights on the Rights of Older Persons in Africa' (2016) https://au.int/en/treaties/protocol-african-charter-human-and-peoples-rights-rights-older-persons - accessed 28 September 2024.

Akandji-Kombe J-F, 'Positive Obligations under the European Convention on Human Rights' (Directorate General of Human Rights Council of Europe, 2007) <https://rm.coe.int/168007ff4d> accessed 28 September 2024.

Amnesty International, *As if expendable: The UK government's failure to protect older people in care homes during the Covid-19 pandemic* (Amnesty International, 2020).

Amos M, 'The influence of British Courts on the Jurisprudence of the European Court of Human Rights' in McCorquodales R and Gauce J (eds) *British influences on international Law, 1915-2015* (Brill Nijhoff, 2016) 213.

Andrews J, 'Irrational restrictions' (*New Scientist*, 14 November 2020) 23.

Bates P, 'Youth Justice and Criminal Evidence Act - The evidence of children and vulnerable adults' (1999) *Child and Fam LQ* 11, 289.

BBC, 'Nursing Homes Undercover' Panorama (*BBC One,* 25 November 2016) https://archive.org/details/BBCNEWS_20161125_033000_Nursing_Homes_Undercover_-_Panorama- accessed 28 September 2024.

Brown K and Gordon G, 'Exploring and overcoming barriers to justice for older victims of crime' (2020) *Criminal Law Review* 12, 1127.

Brown KJ and Gordon F, 'Improving access to justice for older victims of crime by reimagining conceptions of vulnerability' (2022) *Ageing and Society* 42(3) 614.

Care Quality Commission, 'Brief guide: Out of area placements in rehabilitation units' (CQC, 2019) Brief_Guide_Out_of_Area_Placements_in_Rehabilitation_Units_0.pdf (cqc.org.uk) - accessed 28 September 2024.

Care Quality Commission, 'Review of do not attempt cardiopulmonary resuscitation decisions during the COVID-19 pandemic. Interim report' (Care Quality Commission, 2020) 26.

Chong E, Chan M, Tan H, and Lim W, 'Use of the clinical frailty scale for critical care decisions' (2020) *Journal of the American Geriatrics Society* 68(6) E30–E32.

Chung C, 'The necessity of a human rights approach and effective United Nations mechanism for the human rights of the older person' (2010) (UN Doc. A/HRC/AC/4/CRP) 4.

Clough B and Brazier M, 'Never too old for health and human rights?' (2014) *Medical Law International* 14(3) 133.

Commissioner for Older People Northern Ireland, 'Home truths: A report on the commissioner's investigation into Dunmurry Manor Care Home' (2018) 196-196 copni-home-truths-report-web-version.pdf - accessed 28 September 2024.

Council of Europe, Protocol No. 6 to the Convention for the Protection of Human Rights and Fundamental Freedoms concerning the abolition of the death penalty, Strasbourg 28.IV.1983.

Cox C and Pardasani M, 'Aging and human rights: A rights-based approach to social work with older adults' (2017) *Journal of Human Rights and Social Work* 2, 98.

Davies H, 'The Well-being of Future Generations (Wales) Act 2015' (2016) *Environmental Law Review* 18(1) 41.

Davis S, Byers S, Nay R, et al. 'Guiding design of dementia friendly environments in residential care settings' (2009) *Dementia* 8(2) 185.

Department for Work and Pensions, Looking after the grandchildren? Make sure it counts towards your state pension (26 July 2013) https://www.gov.uk/government/news/looking-after-the-grandchildren-make-sure-it-counts-towards-your-state-pension - accessed 28 September 2024.

Drew LM and Silverstein M, 'Grandparents' psychological well-being after loss of contact with their grandchildren' (2007) *Journal of Family Psychology* 21(3) 372.

Dupré C, *The age of dignity* (1st ed, Hart, 2015), 4.

Dyer C, *Some care home residents may have died because of blanket DNR orders, says regulator* (British Medical Journal Publishing Group, 2020).

Flynn M, 'In search of accountability: A review of the neglect of older people living in care homes investigated as Operation Jasmine' (2015) 328-328 https://www.gov.wales/sites/default/files/publications/2019-06/in-search-of-accountability-a-review-of-the-neglect-of-older-people-living-in-care-homes-operation-jasmine_1.pdf- accessed 28 September 2024.

General Medical Council, 'Treatment and care towards the end of life: Good practice in decision making content' (2022) https://www.gmc-uk.org/professional-standards/the-professional-standards/treatment-and-care-towards-the-end-of-life#:~:text=This%20guidance%20provides%20you%20with%20a%20framework%20to,useful%20section%20on%20neonates%2C%20children%20and%20young%20people.- accessed 28 September 2024.

Gerards J, 'The discrimination grounds of article 14 of the European Convention on Human Rights' (2013) *Human Rights Law Review* 13(1) 99.

Guardian Legal, 'Catgate: Another myth used to trash human rights' (*The Guardian*, 4 October 2011).

Güler TS '"Positive obligations" doctrine of the European Court of Human Rights: Is it cogent or obscure?' (2017) *European Journal of Multidisciplinary Studies* 2(6) 358.

Gutterman AS, 'Older persons' right to access justice' (2022) https://papers.ssrn.com/sol3/papers.cfm?abstract_id=4050576- accessed 28 September 2024.

Howard R, Burns A, and Schneider L, 'Antipsychotic prescribing to people with dementia during COVID-19' (2020) *The Lancet Neurology* 19(11) 892.

Hunt J, 'Grandparents as substitute parents in the UK' (2018) *Contemporary Social Science* 13(2) 175.

Ife J, *Human rights and social work: Towards rights-based practice* (Cambridge University Press, 2012).

Jappens M and Van Bavel J, 'Parental divorce, residence arrangements, and contact between grandchildren and grandparents' (2016) *Journal of Marriage and Family* 78(2) 451.

Joint Committee on Human Rights, The human rights of older people (HC 2006-07 156-1) 14.

Kaganas F and Piper C, 'Grandparent contact: Another presumption?' (2020) *Journal of Social Welfare and Family Law* 42(2) 176.

Kington M, 'Kenneth Williams knew what his fans wanted' (*Independent*, 1 December 2003).

Kneale D, Henley J, Thomas J, et al. 'Inequalities in older LGBT people's health and care needs in the United Kingdom: A systematic scoping review' (2021) *Ageing & Society* 41(3) 493.

Laurie E, 'Homelessness and the 'over-judicialisation'of welfare' (2021) *Legal Studies* 41, 39.

Lester A and Pannick D (eds), *Human Rights Law and Practice* (2 ed, Lexis Nexis, 2004).

Mantovani C and Tétrault-Farber G, 'Switzerland underestimated elderly women in climate case, plaintiff says' (*Reuters*, 12 April 2004).

Mantovani E, Spanier B, and Doron I, 'Ageism, human rights, and the European Court of Human Rights: A critical analysis of the Carvalho v. Portugal Case (2017)' (2018) *DePaul Journal for Social Justice* 11.1, 14.

Mays H, 'Care homes "ordered not resuscitate" as coronavirus pandemic took hold' (*The Times*, 24 August 2020).
McCrudden C, 'Human dignity and judicial interpretation of human rights' (2008) *The European Journal of International Law* 19(4) 655.
Mégret F, 'The human rights of older persons: A growing challenge' (2011) *Human Rights Law Review* 11(1) 37.
Mikołajczyk B, 'Is the ECHR ready for global ageing?' (2013) *The International Journal of Human Rights* 17(4) 511.
Miller J, 'Dignity: A relevant normative value in "access to health and social care" litigation in the United Kingdom?' in Diver A and Miller J (eds) *Justiciability of human rights law in domestic jurisdictions* (Springer, 2016) 71-90.
Mok P, Carr M, Guthrie B, et al. 'Multiple adverse outcomes associated with antipsychotic use in people with dementia: Population based cohort study' (2024) *BMJ* 385, e076268.
Mowbray A, 'The development of positive obligations under the European Convention on Human Rights by the European Court of Human Rights' in Mowbray A (ed.) *The Development of Positive Obligations under the European Convention on Human Rightsby the European Court of Human Rights* (Hart Publishing, 2004).
National Development Team for Inclusion, 'Close to Home: Review and recommendations for reducing out of area placements for adults with mental health conditions' (NDT, 2020) https://www.ndti.org.uk/assets/files/Close_to_Home-NDTi2C_February_2020.pdf - accessed 28 September 2024.
National Institute for Health and Care Excellence, 'COVID-19 rapid guidelines: Critical care in adults. Guidelines' (2020) https://www.nice.org.uk/guidance/ng159/chapter/2-Admission-to-critical-care - accessed 28 September 2024.
Newton E, *This bed my centre* (Virago, 1980).
NHS Digital, 'Mental Health Act statistics, annual figures England 2022-23' (2024) https://www.gov.uk/government/statistics/mental-health-act-statistics-annual-figures-2022-23 accessed 28 September 2024.
Older People's Commissioner for Wales, 'Know your rights: An easy guide' (2018) https://olderpeople.wales/resource/know-your-rights-an-easy-guide/ - accessed 28 September 2024.
Palmer S, 'Public, private and the Human Rights Act 1998: An ideological divide' (2007) *Cambridge Law Journal* 66(3) 559.
Pritchard-Jones L, 'Night-time care, article 8 and the European Court of human rights: A missed opportunity?' (2015) *Journal of Social Welfare and Family Law* 37(1) 108.
The Queen's Nursing Institute 'The Experience of Care Home Staff During Covid-19 A Survey Report by the QNI's International Community Nursing Observatory International Community Nursing Observatory' (2020) <https://www.qni.org.uk/wp-content/uploads/2020/08/The-Experience-of-Care-Home-Staff-During-Covid-19-2.pdf> - accessed 12 Feb. 2025].
Regulation and Quality Improvement Authority 'Independent review of the actions taken in relation to concerns raised about the care delivered at cherry tree house The Regulation and Quality Improvement Authority.' ' (Belfast, 2014) <https://www.rqia.org.uk/RQIA/files/1f/1fc36cdd-154f-47a6-bd5d-366dcea2f3bf.pdf> - accesssed 28 September 2024..
Rivers J, 'Proportionality and variable intensity of review' (2006) *The Cambridge Law Journal* 65(1) 174.
Roosevelt E, 'Where do human rights begin?' (10th Anniversary of the UDHR, 27 March 1958) https://www .futurelearn .com /info /courses /the -universal -declaration -of -human -rights /0 /steps /58216 - accessed 28 September 2024.
Rosseinsky K, '"Grandpaternity" leave may be a childcare breakthrough' (*Independent*, 9 July 2024).
Sangroula GP, 'Gurkha's quest for justice: Possible remedies for Gurkhas under international human rights system' (2019) *Kathmandu School of Law Review* 7, 21.

Secretary-General's Remarks at the Atlantic Council, 'The great transition' (7th May 2012) https://press.un.org/en/2012/sgsm14274.doc.htm - accessed 28 September 2024.
Seldon A, *Blair* (The Free Press, 2004).
Sherlock A and Williams J, 'The children's commissioner for Wales and the older people's commissioner for Wales and the administrative justice system' in Nason S (ed.) *Administrative Justice in Wales and Comparative Perspectives* (Gwasg Prifysgol Cymru, 2017) 125.
Sherlock A, Williams J, and Royles E, 'A Welsh Model of Commissioners' (2015) *Cambrian Law Review* 45, 74-95.
.Skeldon, L. and Jenkins, S. 'Experiences and Attitudes of the LGBTQ+ Community on Care/Nursing Homes.' Journal of Homosexuality, (2020) 70(13), 1–33. doi:https://doi.org/10.1080/00918369.2022.2086751.
Williams J, 'Care home design and human rights' (2011) *Elder Law Journal* 1(4) 395.
Williams J, 'Care homes and communities: A human rights approach to age-friendliness' in Gardiner C and O'Brien Webb E (eds) *The age-friendly lens* (Routledge, 2023) 107.
Williams J, 'Human Rights Act: Social work's new benchmark' (2001) *British Journal of Social Work* 31(6) 831.
Williams J, 'Public law protection of vulnerable adults' (2002) *Journal of Social Work* 2(3) 293.
Williams J, 'Safeguarding adults at risk: An asymmetrical approach to reform across the four nations' (2015) *Elder Law Journal* 5(4) 343; see Chapter 6.
Williams J, 'Taking it on the chin: Older people, human rights and COVID-19' (2021) *The Journal of Adult Protection* 23(2) 86.
Wolfe-Robinson M and Bowcott O, 'Lord Irvine: Human rights law developed on false premise' (*Guardian*, 15 December 2011).
Zuchowski I, Gair S, Henderson D, et al. 'Convenient yet neglected: The role of grandparent kinship carers' (2019) *The British Journal of Social Work* 49(3) 615.

3 Older persons and mental capacity

Introduction

The World Health Organisation estimates that fifty-five million people worldwide are living with dementia. It is projected to increase to eighty-two million in 2030 and one hundred and fifty-two million in 2050.[1] Alzheimer's research estimates that 982,000 people across the United Kingdom are living with dementia 65% of whom are women. About 52% of the public knows someone who has been diagnosed with a form of dementia. There are many different types of dementia, the most common ones being Alzheimer's disease, vascular dementia, Lewy body dementia, frontotemporal dementia, and mixed dementia; each type interferes with the proper functioning of neurons in specific brain areas, affecting memory, thinking, and speech. Alzheimer's is the most common form of dementia, followed by vascular dementia. Dementia does not only affect older persons, as over 70,800 people in the UK under sixty-five are living with the condition. However, one in fourteen people over sixty-five is living with dementia.[2] A diagnosis of dementia does not necessarily mean a lack of capacity. In the early stages, the older person may be able to make many decisions, but this ability declines as it progresses. Those working with, supporting or advising older persons with a diagnosis must be aware of this and not assume that a diagnosis always means a lack of capacity. As will be discussed, assessments are time and subject-sensitive.

Dementia is not the only condition that can affect an older person's mental capacity. Loss of capacity may be associated with mental illness, significant learning disability, long-term effects of brain damage, a stroke, physical or mental conditions that cause confusion or drowsiness, delirium, concussion following injury, and the symptoms of alcohol or drugs. Some of these may cause temporary incapacity; they are often treatable. For example, a urinary tract infection can cause delirium. As always, early diagnosis and treatment of such conditions can be effective. This is particularly important as the infection may speed up the progression of dementia and also run the risk of misdiagnosis.

1 World Health Organisation, 'Mental Health of Older Adults' (2017) <https://www.who.int/news-room/fact-sheets/detail/mental-health-of-older-adults> – accessed 28 September 2024.

2 Alzheimer's Research UK, 'Dementia Statistics Hub' (2022) <https://dementiastatistics.org/statistics/numbers-of-people-in-the-uk-2/> – accessed 28 September 2024.

DOI: 10.4324/9780203798058-4

The European Court of Human Rights (ECtHR) has consistently held that assessing somebody as lacking mental capacity interferes with their right to respect for private life under Article 8 European Convention on Human Rights (ECHR). A balance must be struck between the interests of the person lacking capacity and other legitimate interests.[3] Therefore, the decision to do so must be considered carefully, and procedural and substantive safeguards must be in place to ensure the power is not misused or abused. However, understanding what mental capacity means is complex. One approach is to determine mental capacity by reference to age. As discussed in Chapter 1, this approach is used for children and young persons. However, as the Gillick case showed, fixed age limits are not always workable or desirable.[4] To set an age at which people lose mental capacity would be contrary to human rights law, unreliable, and nonsensical. 'All people over seventy-five lack capacity' would not and should not work. Another approach is to decide mental capacity on the grounds of health status. For example, a person detained under the Mental Health Act 1983 could be considered automatically lacking capacity. Again, this is not sensible; many people under the Act have full mental capacity, and the Act assumes this is the case for some purposes. A third possibility is assessing mental capacity based on the rationality of decisions. But how do we decide what is rational and what is irrational? It is a highly subjective judgement. More important, does it matter if the older person makes a decision that others may consider irrational? As Lord Donaldson in the case of Re T said,

> (T)his right of choice is not limited to decisions which others might regard as sensible. It exists notwithstanding that the reasons for making the choice are rational, irrational, unknown or even non-existent.[5]

Older persons may still be victims of the rationality of the decision approach, often through benevolent ageism. The desire to do what is 'best' for an older person may wrongly deprive them of decision-making ability and be disempowering.

Prior to the Mental Capacity Act 2005 (MCA 2005), the courts rejected these tests. They developed a functional approach instead[6] which involves the person being able to receive information and retain it long enough to make a decision. The MCA 2005 adopted this approach, However, the approach is not without its critics. Bartlett argues that the passage of time since the 1995 Law Commission report and the MCA 2005 has changed the understanding of mental capacity. He questions why the criteria for decision-making should be limited to a narrow subset of factors that do not align with the decision-making processes used by most people.[7] It

3 *AN v Lithuania* App no 37553/05 (ECtHR, 15 October 2015).

4 See p 10.

5 *Re T (Adult: Refusal of Treatment)* [1993] Fam 95, 102.

6 See, for example, See *Re C (Adult: Refusal of Medical Treatment)* [1994] 1 W.L.R. 290; *Re MB (Caesarean section)* [1997] 2 FLR 426 CA; *St George's Healthcare NHS Trust v S (No.1)* [1998] 3 All E.R. 673.

7 P Bartlett, 'Rethinking the Mental Capacity Act 2005: Towards the next generation of law' (2023) *Modern Law Review* 86(3) 659; Law Commission, *Mental Incapacity* (Law Com 231, 1995).

is also argued that the functional approach violates Article 12 of the Convention on the Rights of Persons with Disabilities (Disabilities Convention). In General Comment No. 1,[8] the Committee on the Rights of Persons with Disabilities said it was flawed in two respects. First, it is discriminatory as it only applies to persons with disabilities. Second, the functional approach presumes an ability to assess the mind's inner workings accurately. If the person does not pass the test, they are denied equal treatment. It concludes,

> (I)n all of those approaches, a person's disability and/or decision-making skills are taken as legitimate grounds for denying his or her legal mental capacity and lowering his or her status as a person before the law. Article 12 does not permit such discriminatory denial of legal capacity, but, rather, requires that support be provided in the exercise of legal capacity.[9]

The relationship between the Disabilities Convention and the MCA 2005 is discussed below.

Before the MCA 2005, the courts decided cases of mental capacity using the doctrine of necessity. They incorporated the functional approach with a best interests test for decision-making where a person lacked capacity.[10] Of the four nations in the United Kingdom, Scotland was the first to introduce mental capacity legislation, the Adults with Incapacity (Scotland) Act 2000. England and Wales followed with the MCA 2005, amended by the Mental Health Act 2007 and the Mental Capacity Amendment Act 2019. These amendments involved safeguards for people deprived of their liberty. Paragraph 169 Schedule 7A Government of Wales Act 2006 (as amended) lists the MCA 2005 as one of the matters reserved to the Westminster Parliament. Northern Ireland passed the Mental Capacity Act (Northern Ireland) in 2016.

The statutory Principles

For England and Wales, the MCA 2005 includes statutory Principles that must be applied 'for the purposes of this Act.'[11] This follows the Adult with Incapacity (Scotland) Act 2000 pattern. In arguing for including principles in the MCA 2005, which were absent from the original draft Bill, the Joint Parliamentary Committee examining the Bill said that they would be helpful for non-lawyers who would

8 Committee on the Rights of Persons with Disabilities Eleventh Session 31 March–11 April 2014 'General Comment No. 1' (2014) https://www.ohchr.org/en/documents/general-comments-and-recommendations/general-comment-no-1-article-12-equal-recognition-1_– accessed 28 September 2024.

9 Ibid para 15.

10 See *F v West Berkshire HA* [1990] 2 AC 1, discussed below.

11 MCA 2005, Section.1; See P Letts, 'Mental Capacity Act 2005: The statutory principles and best interests test' (2005) *Journal of Mental Health Law* 150; R Griffith and C Tengnah, 'Mental Capacity Act 2005: Statutory principles and key concepts' (2008) *British Journal of Community Nursing* 13, 233.

have primary responsibility for working under the legislation.[12] Including the Principles in the body of the legislation rather than in a code or guidance emphasises their importance. They are *statutory* Principles. In proceedings in the Court of Protection, for example, practitioners should be able to provide evidence of how they have been applied. The Code of Practice issued under the MCA 2005 identifies their role. The Principles aim to,

- protect people who lack capacity and
- help them take part, as much as possible, in decisions that affect them. They aim to assist and support people who may lack capacity to make particular decisions, not to restrict or control their lives.[13]

Section 42(4) MCA 2005 imposes a duty on those having functions under the Act to have regard to the Code. These include people acting as Lasting Power of Attorneys, Court of Protection Deputies, researchers, Independent Mental Capacity Advocates, and anyone involved in the Deprivation of Liberty procedures. The Principles apply to any decision taken under the MCA 2005. There are five Principle

Principle 1: 'A person must be assumed to have capacity unless it is established that they lack capacity.' An older person does not have to prove that they have mental capacity to make a decision. The burden of proving incapacity lies with whoever is claiming the older person lacks capacity. They must prove incapacity to the standard of a balance of probabilities – it is more likely than not.[14] The presumption applies to everyone and does not become less important as people age. Hayden J emphasised this point in QJ v A Local Authority.[15] QJ, who was eighty-seven and lived in a care home, was assessed as lacking capacity to decide where to live and what care he should receive. He was diagnosed as having vascular dementia. Did he have the mental capacity to decide about hydration and medical treatment? Doctors asked QJ whether he wanted a nasogastric tube inserted; he shook his head. Based on the facts of the case, it may be easy to conclude that the presumption was rebutted. He was eighty-seven, lacked capacity in essential aspects of his life, and was living with dementia. Hayden J disagreed. He referred to the presumption as a fundamental safeguard of human autonomy requiring cogent, clear and carefully analysed information before it can be rebutted. On this basis, he concluded that the presumption was not rebutted. The case is noteworthy for several reasons. First, it shows that mental capacity is divisible; a

12 House of Lords and House of Commons Joint Committee on the Draft Mental Incapacity Bill, *Draft Mental Incapacity Bill* (2003 HL 189-I, HC 1083-I) 40.

13 Department for Constitutional Affairs, *Mental Capacity Act 2005 Code of Practice* (The Stationery Office, 2007) <https://assets.publishing.service.gov.uk/government/uploads/system/uploads/attachment_data/file/921428/Mental-capacity-act-code-of-practice.pdf> para 2.1 – accessed 28 September 2024.

14 MCA 2005, Section.2(4).

15 [2020] EWCOP 7, [2020] 1 WLUK 374.

person can lack mental capacity for one purpose and have it for another. Second, a diagnosis of dementia does not end all mental capacity.[16] Third, the presumption applies with equal weight to an eighty-seven-year-old as it does to somebody who is twenty-seven. Finally, the consequences of QJ's decision were severe, but this did not influence the decision.

A balanced and proportionate approach to the presumption is required. In PH v A Local Authority, Baker J noted,

> in cases of vulnerable adults, there is a risk that all professionals involved with treating and helping that person – including, of course, a judge in the Court of Protection – may feel drawn towards an outcome that is more protective of the adult and thus, in certain circumstances, fail to carry out an assessment of capacity that is detached and objective.[17]

In the absence of significant legal powers of intervention, for example, in elder abuse or neglect cases, rebutting the presumption may be the only way to provide protection. However, this must follow from an assessment of mental capacity based on the MCA 2005 and not be driven by a well-intentioned desire to protect the older person.

In what circumstances should the presumption be questioned? In Bank of Scotland PLC v AB, the Employment Appeal Tribunal recognised the importance of the presumption but said it had 'logical limits.' Although this was a case of litigation capacity, it has broader implications. The Tribunal noted that when there is 'good reason for cause for concern' or 'legitimate doubt as to capacity to litigate,' the presumption should not be used to avoid taking responsibility for assessing and deciding on mental capacity. However, it added that 'good cause' requires careful consideration, and a decision should not be taken lightly.[18] Important though the presumption is, failure to challenge it in appropriate circumstances may deny older persons who lack mental capacity the safeguards of the MCA 2005. If there is evidence that gives good cause for concern that the person may lack mental capacity, then professional curiosity requires further enquiries.

Principle 2: 'A person is not to be treated as unable to make a decision unless all practicable steps to help him to do so have been taken without success.' In various ways, people need support when making complex decisions. It may be from a lawyer, financial adviser, doctor, nurse, social care practitioner, or others. Friends and family may also provide support. Some older persons require particular forms of support that need practitioners to adapt how they provide information and interact with the older person. For example, the Royal National Institute for the Deaf

16 *Re Deceasedumbrella.com Ltd (Formerly Trading as Racs Collective Ltd)*, Chancery Division [2021] 11 WLUK 389.

17 [2011] EWHC 1704 (Fam), [2011] 6 WLUK 749. See also *A Local Authority v H (by her litigation friend* the Official Solicitor), [2023] EWCOP 4, 192 BMLR 1.

18 *Bank Of Scotland Plc v AB* Employment Appeal Tribunal, 2020 WL 00999593. Subsequent Court of Appeal treatment [2021] EWCA Civ 345, [2021] 3 WLUK 205.

reported that more than 70% of people over seventy have hearing loss ranging from mild (26.7%) to profound (1.3%).[19] An older person's inability to hear during a capacity assessment may result in a wrong decision. If there is doubt, assessors should undertake a hearing test rather than let the older person struggle. An older person's eyesight may be affected by age-related eye problems such as presbyopia, glaucoma, dry eyes, age-related macular degeneration, cataracts, and temporal arteritis. What support can be provided to mitigate the effects of these conditions when assessing capacity? Assistance will maximise the ability of the older person to participate fully despite impairments in hearing or eyesight. The Code includes examples of how practitioners can support decision-making,

- Using a different form of communication, such as non-verbal.
- Providing information in more accessible form – photos, drawings.
- Treating a medical condition that may be affecting the person's capacity.
- Having a structured programme to improve a person's capacity to make particular decisions, such as helping a person with learning disabilities to learn new skills.[20]

An Independent Mental Capacity Advocate (IMCA) is a specialist advocate who supports people who lack capacity under the MCA 2005. The role of IMCAs is outlined in Sections 35–39 MCA 2005. Special provisions apply to IMCAs acting in Deprivation of Liberty Safeguards (DoLS) cases and are discussed in Chapter 7. The role of the IMCA is to provide independent protection for people unable to make important decisions due to a lack of capacity. When an older person lacks capacity and has no one else to support them other than someone providing professional care or treatment for payment, an IMCA must be appointed and consulted if an NHS body is considering giving serious medical treatment, or when an NHS body or local authority is arranging accommodation in a hospital for more than twenty-eight days or a care home for more than eight weeks. Additionally, an IMCA may be appointed to support the older person during a care review when no other support is available. In adult safeguarding cases, an IMCA may be appointed, regardless of whether the person has family, friends or others to support them.[21]

Practitioners often have to spend time with the older person to build rapport and understand the most effective communication methods. A critical consideration is the timing and location of the assessments. For example, an older person living with early stage dementia may function better in their home in the afternoon rather than a doctor's surgery first thing in the morning. The amount of time set aside for the assessment needs careful consideration. If the older person feels rushed, it may compromise their ability to participate. Interpreters should be used when

19 Action on Hearing Loss (2020) *Hearing Matters* https://rnid.org.uk/wp-content/uploads/2020/05/Hearing-Matters-Report.pdf – accessed 28 September 2024.

20 MCA Code (n13) para 2.7.

21 See MCA 2005, ss. 35–41.

necessary; care must be taken when using family or close friends as interpreters, as there may be conflicts of interest and confidentiality issues. For those few cases that go to the Court of Protection, capacity assessors will probably be required to provide evidence of what they did to support the person in making their own decision.

Article 12(3) Disabilities Convention requires signatory states to,

> take appropriate measures to provide access by persons with disabilities to support they may require in exercising their legal capacity.[22]

General Comment No 1, issued by the United Nations Committee on the Rights of Persons with Disabilities,[23] identifies two elements of legal capacity. The first is legal standing, which means the person is a person before the law. For example, older persons who lack mental capacity or have other forms of disability have a right to recognition as persons before the law; disability does not justify any lesser status. The second is legal agency, or active legal capacity, which entails acting within the legal system's framework and deciding for self rather than others imposing decisions.[24] How far can this right to determine for oneself be applied to older persons who lack the capacity to decide? Donnelly points out that Article 12 gives people with dementia some degree of control for as long as possible and is an essential reminder that cognitive decline does not mean an end to moral personhood.[25] But are there limits to its applicability to mental capacity under the MCA 2005, a piece of legislation based on substitute decision-making? While welcoming the Disabilities Convention, Pritchard-Jones raises concerns about the implications of Article 12 for people living with dementia. She points out that despite approximately fifty million people in the world living with dementia, there was a relative lack of dementia organisations involved in drafting the Convention.[26] Nor does the Convention feature prominently in the profiles of organisations representing older people and Alzheimers. Lush argues that Article 12 does not require eliminating all forms of substitute decision-making. It requires states to take appropriate measures to provide access to 'the support they may require in exercising their legal capacity.' The MCA 2005, he argues, meets this requirement, particularly the second Principle. Lush concludes,

22 UN General Assembly, *Convention on the Rights of Persons with Disabilities: Resolution / adopted by the General Assembly* 24 January 2007, A/RES/61/106, <https://www.refworld.org/docid/45f973632.html> – accessed 28 September 2024.

23 General comment (n8).

24 B McSherry, 'Legal capacity under the Convention on the Rights of Persons with Disabilities' (2012) 20 *Journal of Law and Medicine* 22, 23–24.

25 M Donnelly, 'Deciding in dementia: the possibilities and limits of supported decision-making' (2019) 66 *International Journal of Law and Psychiatry* 101466.

26 L Pritchard-Jones, 'Exploring the potential and the pitfalls of the United Nations Convention on the Rights of Persons with Disabilities and General Comment no. 1 for people with dementia' (2019) 66 *International Journal of Law and Psychiatry* 101467.

> (T)here are many cases where supported decision-making is no longer feasible, and some form of substituted decision-making is essential. This is particularly so in cases involving people with advanced dementia, who numerically represent by far the largest client group within the jurisdiction of the Court of Protection, or, to give a more extreme example, where P is in a permanent vegetative state.[27]

Law reform bodies in several countries have considered incorporating Article 12 into domestic laws.[28] No clear model emerges.[29] Implementing the right into law has proved challenging for those countries that have done so.[30] The Law Commission for England and Wales discussed it as part of the deprivation of liberty law review. It proposed the appointment of a 'supporter' to help the person in decision-making, although this recommendation was not included in the Mental Capacity (Amendment) Act 2019. The Commission was committed to supporting a person in exercising their legal capacity. However, it recognised 'that there are some situations in which it may nonetheless be necessary and proper to overrule the ascertainable wishes and feelings of a person lacking the mental capacity to make a particular decision or decisions.'[31]

Ruck Keene et al., in their detailed analysis of the implications of the Disabilities Convention, argue against it being a paradigm shift and instead bestow that title on the functional approach adopted by the MCA 2005, despite its limitations. The UN Committee on the Rights of Persons with Disabilities has prompted a change in England and Wales by emphasising the importance of wishes and feelings in decision-making and raising awareness of the need to provide support. They point to the greater awareness that a person cannot be found functionally to lack capacity unless appropriate support is given without success. [32] Their conclusion, however, is unambiguous and, it is submitted, correct.

> Some might feel that it is so vital to challenge both the concept and the conditions for considering capacity that it is necessary, in effect, to pull down the house around them in the hopes that a new one can be constructed. Others

27 D Lush, 'Article 12 of the United Nations Convention on the Right of Persons with Disabilities' (2011) *Elder Law Journal* 61.

28 See, for example, the Assisted Decision-Making (Capacity) Act 2015 (Ireland); Law Commission of Ontario, *Legal Capacity, Decision-making and Guardianship* (Law Commission of Ontario 2017); Adult Guardianship and Co-decision-making Act 2000 (Saskatchewan); and Australian Law Reform Commission, *Equality, Capacity and Disability in Commonwealth Laws* (ALRC Report 124, 2014).

29 S Then, T Camey, C Bigby et al. 'Supporting decision-making of adults with cognitive disabilities: The role of law reform agencies – recommendations, rationales and influence' (2018) 61 International *Journal of Law and Psychiatry* 64, 74.

30 See Pritchard-Jones (n26); M Hall, 'Situating dementia in the experience of old age: Reconstructing legal response' (2019) *International Journal of Law and Psychiatry* 66, 101468.

31 Law Commission, 'Mental Capacity and Deprivation of Liberty' (Law'Com No 372, 2017) paras 14.51–56.

32 A Ruck Keene, N Kane, S Kim et al., 'Mental capacity—why look for a paradigm shift?' (2023) 31 *Medical Law Review*, 340.

> (and we belong here) may feel that the intellectual, emotional, and other resources of those concerned with securing the rights of those with impairments are better directed to testing, probing, and refining the processes necessary for a legitimate concept of mental capacity.[33]

Supported decision-making maximises the chance of an older person being assessed as having capacity and, therefore, able to make their own decisions. As a result, by raising awareness of it, the Disabilities Convention has contributed to better mental capacity and general disability decision-making. More can be done. However, there are limits to what supported decision-making can achieve. In those cases, substitute decision-making is needed. Lush's example of a person in a persistent vegetative state effectively illustrates this point.

Principle 3: 'A person is not to be treated as unable to make a decision merely because he makes an unwise decision.' It is a feature of life that we make decisions others consider daft, dangerous, deluded, or simply wrong. Others may helpfully or otherwise point out what they see as the error of our ways, but we have the right to decide, providing our decision is lawful. There may be adverse consequences, but that does not affect the validity of the decision. As noted above, Lord Donaldson recognised that the reasons for such a choice might be rational, irrational, unknown or non-existent.[34] The courts recognised this right before the MCA 2005.[35] For practitioners, this presents ethical dilemmas. For example, a social care assessment of an older person might conclude that they will likely benefit from a move to residential care because of the dangers of remaining in their home. They would be safer, and the residential care environment would promote their well-being; nevertheless, the older person refuses to move. The deciding factors may be their attachment to their home, possessions, pets, and community; some wish to die at home. Other examples include an older person refusing necessary medical treatment, a social care assessment, or the offer of support in self-neglect cases. Decision-makers must avoid the dangers of benevolent paternalism, which ignores the person's personal autonomy. Principle 3 reminds us of our right to make decisions with which others disagree. This was reflected in PH v Betsi Cadwaladar UHB, where the court recognised that PH's refusal to eat was distressing, but he had the capacity to refuse.[36]

Despite the need to protect the right to make 'unwise decisions,' the Principle uses the word 'merely,' thus recognising that such a decision, or a series of them, may raise doubts about capacity. While an older person cannot be found to lack capacity solely because their proposed decision is thought by others to be unconventional,

33 ibid 357.

34 Re T (n5).

35 See, for example, *Re C (Adult: Refusal of Medical Treatment)* [1994] 1 All ER 819; *Re MB (Caesarean section)* [1997] 2 F.L.R 426; *St George's Healthcare NHS Trust v S* [1998] 3 WLR 936; and J Herring, 'Caesarean sections and the right of autonomy' (1998) *The Cambridge Law Journal* 57(3) 429.

36 [2022] EWCOP 16, (2022) 186 BMLR 148.

irrational or unwise, it may, in some instances, trigger an assessment of their capacity. However, this does not inevitably lead to a finding of incapacity.[37]

Principle 4: 'An act done, or decision made, under this Act for or on behalf of a person who lacks capacity must be done, or made, in his best interests.' When a person lacks the mental capacity to consent to medical treatment, that is not a valid reason to deny them treatment. Before the MCA 2005, the courts developed the best interests approach as the basis for decision-making if a person lacks capacity. Lord Goff said,

> the doctor must act in the best interests of the patient, just as if he had received the patient's consent to do so. Were this not so, much useful treatment and care could, in theory at least, be denied. [38]

Arguably, best interest is not the most suitable term because of its potentially patronising nature. Would reference to 'promoting and protecting the person's human rights' be better? The Joint Committee on the Mental Incapacity Bill thought not as it would impose too onerous a burden on carers and other informal decision-makers.[39] However, Donelly argues it is time to revisit best interests and move towards a rights-based approach.[40]

General Comment No 1 is critical of the best interest tests for different reasons. As a safeguard, it argues that it is incompatible with Article 12 of the Disabilities Convention as it denies people the right to legal capacity on an equal basis with others. It argues that where it is not practicable to identify a person's wishes and preferences, the 'best interpretation of will and preferences' must replace best interests.'[41] The will and preference paradigm is open to criticism. Appelbaum says it would deny the ability to protect loved ones with dementia by managing their assets or placing them in residential care.[42] Steinert contends that it violates human rights such as the right to life and health, both of which feature in the Disabilities Convention. By implication, the European Court of Human Rights disagreed with the General Comment's interpretation of Article 12 when finding that the appointment of a mentor and substituted decision-making were compatible with Article 12 of the Disabilities Convention and article 8 of the ECHR.[43] This interpretation is supported by some signatories to the Disabilities Convention who

37 See *A County Council v MS*, 2014 WL 1219394, 60; An *NHS Trust and another v WA and another [*2020] EWCOP 37; *PC (by her litigation friend the Official Solicitor) v A Local Authority* [2013] EWCA Civ 478; Joint Committee (n12) 2.,.11.

38 Re F (n10) 50.

39 Joint Committee (n12).

40 M Donnelly, 'Best interests in the Mental Capacity Act: Time to say goodbye?' (2016) 24 *Medical Law Review* 318.

41 General Comment (n8) 21.

42 PS Appelbaum, 'Protecting the rights of persons with disabilities: An international convention and its problems' (2016) 67 *Psychiatric Services* 366, 367.

43 *A-MV v Finland*, App no 53251/13 (ECtHR, 23 March 2017).

have made declarations and reservations supporting substituted decision-making.[44] Some older people, particularly those living with advanced dementia, would be at a disadvantage if the states followed the General Comment. Article 12(3) of the Disabilities Convention obliges signatories to support people with disabilities in making decisions but does not proscribe substitute decision-making using best interests. Principle 4 reflects this. Comment No 1's reading of Article 12 would discriminate against older people living with advanced dementia.

Principle 5: 'Before the act is done, or the decision is made, regard must be had to whether the purpose for which it is needed can be as effectively achieved in a way that is less restrictive of the person's rights and freedom of action.' This Principle is based on the requirement that any decision must be proportionate. So, for example, decision-makers may have several options when deciding on the living arrangements for an older person who lacks capacity. They should consider arrangements that best promote the person's autonomy while addressing their identified need. However, the Principle states that 'regard must be had' to the least restrictive option; on occasions, the older person's best interests will take priority, which may result in an intervention that is not the least restrictive.[45] As always, each case depends upon its facts. In Reading BC v PSS, HS, and KS,[46] the court had to decide whether P should remain in a care home placement or have a trial period of care with her daughter. There was family disagreement, with the daughter objecting to the care home placement and showing some hostility towards the care home. Almost counter-intuitively, the court found the least restrictive option was to remain in the care home placement; even though she was deprived of her liberty, the placement enabled her to have contact with all her family members.

Consideration must be given to the statutory Principles. They are integral to the working of the MCA 2005 alongside the definition of capacity.[47] Actions or decisions that conflict with them are likely to be found to be unlawful. Principles 1–3 assist in assessing whether the person has mental capacity; Principles 4 and 5 support decision-making. Within the Principles, there are tensions. Principle 5 may conflict with Principle 4. A balancing exercise is needed, but Principle 4 requires that any act or decision *must* be done or made in the older person's best interests. When deciding on best interests, both autonomy and protection must be considered.

What is incapacity?

Section 2(1) MCA 2005 states,

44 See, for example, Canada, Australia, and Estonia. United Nations, *United nations treaty collection, convention on the rights of persons with disabilities* (United Nations, 2008)

45 *R (on the application of C) v A Local Authority* [2011] EWHC 1539 (Admin), [2011] All ER (D) 171 (Jun); *Havering London Borough Council v LD* [2010] 6 WLUK 641.

46 [2022] EWCOP 27.

47 *A Local Authority v JB* [2012] UKSC 52, [2013] 1 AC 484.

> a person lacks capacity in relation to a matter if at the material time he is unable to make a decision for himself in relation to the matter because of an impairment of, or a disturbance in the functioning of, the mind or brain.

A mental capacity assessment is decision-specific and time-specific; it involves deciding on a particular matter at a particular time. The required capacity levels vary depending on the decision. For example, there is a difference between choosing to travel abroad for a short holiday and emigrating; similarly, there is a difference between deciding on a dental check-up and undergoing heart surgery.[48]

There must be an impairment of or disturbance in the functioning of the mind or brain. As a result, the person must be unable to decide on the matter in question – the functional component of the assessment.[49] When assessing capacity, the assessor should first address the functional ability to make a decision – are they unable to decide on that matter at that time? An assessment should occur at a time that maximises the opportunity for the older person to decide. If they cannot decide, the next question is whether there is an impairment or disturbance of the mind or brain, such as dementia, learning disability, brain damage, delirium, concussion, or the effects of alcohol or drug use. The causal connection is essential. The co-existence of the two does not inevitably lead to incapacity unless the inability to decide is a consequence of the impairment or disturbance.[50] In Re SB (A Patient: Capacity to Consent to Termination), the fact that a patient detained under the Mental Health Act 1983 was paranoid and had delusional thoughts did not mean that she lacked mental capacity.[51] Similarly, a diagnosis of advanced dementia does not indicate a complete lack of capacity, as noted in QJ v A Local Authority discussed above.[52]

Some older people may frequently or occasionally lapse into and out of mental capacity. There may be times and situations when they can clearly state their wishes; at other times, that may be impossible. Therefore, the timing and physical environment are important considerations; when and where is the older person most likely to be able to decide? This is consistent with Principle 3 as it is one practical step that may help the older person to decide. In addition, the incapacitating effects of any medication may wear off and capacity restored. Section 2(2) MCA 2005 says it does not matter whether the impairment or disturbance is permanent or temporary. Temporary incapacity can refer to situations where the older person may have lost capacity because of, for example, a UTI capable of being successfully treated with antibiotics, at which point capacity returns. Decisions should be delayed whenever possible until the older person can decide. Alternatively, temporary incapacity may arise where the older person fluctuates in and out of mental

48 *PC v City of York Council* [2013] EWCA Civ 478, [2014] Fam 10.

49 Mental Capacity Code (n13) paras 4.11–13.

50 *PC (by her litigation friend the Official Solicitor) v NC and City of York Council* [2013] EWCA Civ 478, [2014] Fam 10.

51 [2013] EWHC 1417 (COP),[2013] 3 F.C.R. 384; see also the pre-MCA 2005 case of *Re C (Adult: Refusal of Treatment)* [1994] 1 WLR 290.

52 *QJ v A* case (n15).

capacity. For example, those living with dementia may have moments when they are able to make decisions, whereas, at other times, they cannot.

Responding to fluctuating capacity is complex, particularly if decisions relate to ongoing matters such as care, medical treatment, and financial affairs. For example, is it necessary to reassess capacity every time a decision is needed about an item of expenditure? The specific time and decision requirements in the MCA 2005 suggest it is required. However, in its report on the Deprivation of Liberty Safeguards, the Law Commission concluded that the complex nature of fluctuating capacity is not addressed fully in the MCA 2005 nor in the Code of Practice. It identified a disconnect between the MCA 2005 and practice.[53] The Code of Practice highlights the importance of assessing mental capacity concerning a particular issue. It points out it may be possible to put off the decision until the person regains mental capacity.[54] A more nuanced approach is found in the Deprivation of Liberty Safeguards Code. If an older person experiences short-term fluctuations in their mental capacity, it is important to strike a balance between terminating a DoLS authorisation if their capacity is regained, albeit fleetingly, and using resources to constantly review, remove, and renew it as their mental capacity changes. Cases must be treated on their facts, and the authorisation must end if there is consistent evidence of regaining capacity on a longer-term basis. If the regaining of capacity is temporary, the authorisation remains but must be kept under review.[55] The recent draft code of practice considers fluctuating capacity in greater depth than the current Code. It distinguishes isolated decisions and repeated decisions. Isolated decisions should be delayed until the person regains capacity with only minimal intervention in the meantime. This would apply to, for example, making a will or elective surgery. Where ongoing decisions are required, for example, administering finance or managing diabetes, a longer-term view should be taken. This is particularly the case where decisions have serious consequences, and capacity is transient.[56]

Hedley J in Cheshire West and Chester Council v PWK considered what is referred to as longitudinal capacity. PWK's capacity fluctuated; during periods of anxiety, he lacked capacity, although that was not always the case. Hedley J referred, with obvious approval, to an earlier decision of his in A, B & C v X, Y & Z where he held,

> (I)n the light of [the medical] evidence, I am satisfied on balance that he lacks capacity to manage his own affairs. In so finding I acknowledge, as I have done in relation to the other matters, that there would be times when a snapshot of his condition would reveal an ability to manage his affairs. But the general concept of managing affairs is an ongoing act and, therefore,

53 Law Com No 372 (n31) paras 9.38–58.

54 Mental Capacity Code (n13) paras 4.26–27.

55 Ministry of Justice, *Mental Capacity Act 2005, Deprivation of Liberty Safeguards* (The Stationery Office, 2008) paras 8.22–24.

56 HM Government, *Mental Capacity Act 2005 Code of Practice Including the Liberty Protection Safeguards* (2022) paras 4.51–56.

quite unlike the specific act of making a will or making an enduring power of attorney. [57]

Applying this principle to PWK, he concluded that the relevant decision-making involved repeat rather than isolated decisions, such as residence, social media, care and support needs, and consequently, he lacked capacity even though a snapshot of his condition might show an ability to manage his affairs. Newton J in RB Greenwich v CDM adopted a similar approach in a case involving a sixty-four-year-old's capacity to manage diabetes medication.[58] Although she could sometimes make individual decisions about her diabetes management, viewed on a 'global basis,' she lacked capacity. Each case turns on the facts, and caution in drawing too many conclusions is necessary. However, they are a pragmatic response to the, at times, perverse consequences of the decision and time approach of the MCA 2005.[59]

Under Section 2(3) MCA 2005, a person cannot be found to lack mental capacity merely by reference to their age or appearance. Perceiving older people as inherently frail and lacking in capacity is stigmatising. Such perceptions are a product of cultural ageism, which hinders healthcare professionals from providing older people with the best health, mental health, and pastoral services.[60] The presumption of capacity applies with equal force, whatever the person's age. Similarly, the subsection says that lack of mental capacity cannot be established merely by reference to any condition the person has or an aspect of their behaviour 'which might lead others to make unjustified assumptions' about their capacity. It must be noted that Section 2(3) MCA 2005 uses the word 'merely': age, condition, and behaviour may be relevant if other factors point to incapacity.

'Unable to decide'

The term 'unable to make a decision' is defined in Section 3 MCA 2005.

3(1) A person is unable to make a decision if unable–

(a) to understand the information relevant to the decision,
(b) to retain that information,
(c) to use or weigh that information as part of the process of making the decision,
(d) to communicate the decision (whether by talking, using sign language or any other means).

57 Cheshire West and Chester Council v PWK [2029] EWCOP 57; A B and C v X Y and Z [2012] EWHC 2400 (COP); [2012] 7 WLUK 953, 41.

58 *RB Greenwich v CDM* [2019] EWCOP 32; [2019] 4 W.L.R. 130.

59 M Curtice, 'Fluctuating capacity: The concept of micro-and macro-decisions' (2020) *BJPsych Advances* 26(4) 238; R Griffith, 'Assessing capacity in cases of fluctuating decision-making ability' (2020) *British Journal of Nursing* 29(15) 908; A Mogg and A Bartlett, 'Refusal of treatment in a patient with fluctuating capacity-theory and practice' (2005) *Journal of Forensic Psychiatry & Psychology* 16(1) 60.

60 M Kane and R Jacobs, 'Assumptions about frailty and the tenacity of ageism among care professionals' (2018) *Journal of Pastoral Care & Counseling* 72(3) 190, 193.

The inability to meet any of these requirements shows the person is unable to decide.

Chapter 4 discusses the importance of information as an important component of decision-making and Section 3(1) MCA 2005 recognises this. Therefore, when assessing an older person's mental capacity, particular regard must be given to the second Principle, namely taking all practicable steps to help the person maximise their chances of deciding for themselves. This involves providing information in an accessible and appropriate form.[61] Section 3(4) MCA 2005 requires that relevant information includes the reasonably foreseeable consequences of deciding one way or the other or failing to make a decision. An older person asked to decide whether to move into residential care should, for example, have information on the financial implications of moving to a care home, the benefits of moving, the location of the care home, visiting arrangements, and any information on the proposed home. They must also get information on what alternatives are available and any inherent risks they may entail; any questions must be answered.

When assessing capacity, information overload must be avoided. Assessors must not expect a greater insight from the older person being assessed than they would of themselves or others.[62] Too much information can be an obstacle to decision-making. Baker J in CC v KK and STCC emphasised that,

> it is not necessary for a person to demonstrate a capacity to understand and weigh up every detail of the respective options, but merely the salient factors.[63]

In this case, the Court of Protection had to decide whether an eighty-two-year-old woman with Parkinson's possessed the capacity to decide about residence and care. Baker J held that she understood she needed carers four times daily and depended on them for support in her daily living. Furthermore, she understood the need to eat and drink, even though she occasionally needed prompting; she had views on the food she disliked. She knew she would be lonely at home and could not routinely rely on the lifeline for company. There was an understanding that the risks of living at home were more significant than living in residential care. Even though she could not evaluate every nuance or detail, Baker J held she could decide for herself as she understood the salient factors, which is no different from how most people make complex decisions. They grasp the broad principles of, for example, a mortgage or complicated surgery but no more. Detailed knowledge is not required.

Section 3(1)(b) MCA 2005 requires that the person retains the information, which raises the question, 'for how long?' The fact that information can only be retained for a short time does not prevent the person from being able to make a

61 MCA 2005 Section.3(2).

62 A Local Authority v GP (Capacity: Care, Support and Education) [2020] EWCOP 56, [2021] COPLR 1.

63 [2012] EWHC 2136 (COP); [2012] 7 WLUK 861, 69.

decision.[64] However, retention must be long enough to process the information and to communicate a decision. A Local Authority v AK and Ors discussed retention. It involved the capacity to marry a man who suffered catastrophic head injuries following two falls. As a result, he had significantly impaired cognitive capacity and executive function. The court held that he lacked the capacity to marry partly because of his inability to know or remember his marital status and that of his spouse, other than for very short periods. Body J said,

> (T)he reference to the retention of information for 'a short period' in s.3(3) of the Act cannot seriously be interpreted to mean, in the context of the lifetime commitment of marriage, for so short a period as AK is able to recall whether he is married at all, or reliably (when he does remember) to whom.[65]

Rapid fluctuations may result in an inability to retain information long enough to process it or to communicate a decision, in which case the older person will be unable to decide.

Moore et al. identify the risk of a 'cloak of competence' resulting in the older person appearing more capable in an assessment environment than in a functional one.[66] This is a more general point: assessments should go beyond the question 'Can you make a cup of tea?' to include 'Let's go and make a cup of tea?' The older person must be able to use or weigh the information provided and retained as part of the decision-making process.[67] One judge described this process as having enough jigsaw pieces to see the whole picture. Assessors must apply the older person's values to the decision in question.[68] The older person must believe the information provided when using or weighing it as part of the process. For example, in Re TS (Pacemaker), TS[69] had delusional beliefs that the police, medical authorities, and local authorities were persecuting him. He did not believe he had mental health problems. A pacemaker would enable him to receive antipsychotic medication to help him regain capacity. His delusions prevented him from using or weighing the information to decide whether to have a pacemaker fitted.[70]

The final component of the assessment of the inability to decide is that the older person must be able to communicate the decision using sign language or similar when required. This is a residual category but must not be used to avoid providing communication support to maximise decision-making capacity. Examples include patients in a coma or unconsciousness. Another example is locked-in syndrome, which results in paralysis of voluntary muscles other than those controlling the eyes. As the person can think and reason, they will probably satisfy the first three

64 MCA 2005 Section.3(1)(b).
65 [2012] EWHC B29 (COP); [2012] 11 WLUK 947, 51.
66 S Moore, R Wotus, A Norman et al. 'Behind the cloak of competence: Brain injury and mental capacity legislation' (2019) *The Journal of Adult Protection* 21(4) 201.
67 Section.3(1)(c) MCA 2005.
68 *S v Birmingham Women's And Children's NHS Trust* [2022] EWCOP 10; [2023] 1 F.L.R. 458, 58.
69 *Chesterfield Royal Hospital NHS Foundation Trust v TS* [2021] EWCOP 41; [2021] 6 WLUK 284.
70 See also *Liverpool City Council v CMW* [2021] EWCOP 50; [2021] 7 WLUK 644.

requirements of Section 3(1) MCA 2005. They may be able to communicate through eye movements. Whether this is acceptable was discussed in AK (Medical Treatment: Consent), where the patient's only means of communication was moving one eyelid; this enabled him to answer 'yes' or 'no.' The healthcare practitioners asked the court to decide whether to take him off his ventilator; the patient knew this would lead to his death. In deciding that AK had the mental capacity, the court recognised the difficulty of communication and ensuring he indicated his wishes. On the evidence, it held that he did.[71] Eye movement, hand squeezing or other methods of communication should be explored, although it is necessary to show that they are genuine and reliable.[72] Recent developments in methods of communication include brain–computer interface technology, which is currently being trialled in cases of locked-in syndrome.[73]

The 'best interests' test

Principle 4 MCA 2005 requires that any act or decision made for a person lacking mental capacity must be in their best interests. Section 4 MCA 2005 contains a checklist for decision-makers to observewhen using the best interests test. The factors referred to in the checklist must be followed, although the relative weight given to each will vary.[74] The correct approach to deciding best interests is to use the checklist and then ask whether the conclusion is necessary and proportionate.[75] Thorpe LJ suggests that courts create a balance sheet listing benefits and counterbalancing disbenefits. As well as courts, this is a helpful approach for all decision-makers as it helps to clarify both sides of the argument. However, the length of one column does not dictate the decision. Although the checklist identifies specific factors, decision-makers must consider all the relevant circumstances in addition to those listed. [76] 'Relevant circumstances' is defined in Section 4(11) MCA 2005 as those of which the decision maker is aware and which it would be reasonable to regard as relevant. The Code recognises that these vary with each case. For example, it highlights clinical needs, potential benefits and burdens of treatment, and life expectancy in medical treatment cases. However, it says it would not be reasonable to consider life expectancy when working out if it would be in somebody's best interests to be given medication for a minor problem.[77] Medical evidence is only part of the best interests calculation. Professionals from different disciplines

71 [2000] 8 WLUK 112, [2001] 1 F.L.R. 129.
72 Mental Capacity Code (n13) paras 4.23–25.
73 M Branco, E Pels, F Nijboer et al. 'Brain–computer interfaces for communication: Preferences of individuals with locked-in syndrome, caregivers and researchers' (2023) *Disability and Rehabilitation: Assistive Technology* 18(6) 963.
74 *Re M, ITW v Z* [2009] EWHC 2525 (Fam); [2011] 1 WLR 344, 32.
75 *K v A Local Authority* [2012] EWCA Civ 79, [2012] 1 FCR 441.
76 MCA 2005 Section. 4(2).
77 Mental Capacity Code (n13) para 5.19.

may be involved, as well as relatives, unpaid carers, and friends.[78] What is particularly important is to hear from those who know the older person well. Relatives are important, but there must be evidence that they have an ongoing and positive relationship with the older person. The autonomy, beneficence, non-maleficence, and justice principles should guide decision-making. These help ensure that older persons receive the best possible care while respecting their rights, promoting their well-being, avoiding harm, and treating them fairly and equitably.[79] For example, the Court of Appeal in A Local Authority and another v B and another upheld the lower court's rejection of a submission that AB should not be told about covert HRT medication. The judge regarded frankness as offering the best chance of persuading her to take it voluntarily, which was a judgement he was entitled to make.[80]

Decisions on a person's best interests should not be made 'merely' based on their age, appearance, or a condition of their behaviour, which might lead to others making unjustified assumptions about their best interests.[81] The word 'merely' recognises that, in some cases, they may be relevant; however, decision-makers must avoid general assumptions, which are often ageist. So, for example, they should avoid the idea that it is always in an older person's best interests to be in residential care because that is where they are safest. Similarly, when an older person makes lifestyle choices that others find odd, this is not grounds for assuming it is in their best interests to intervene and radically change how they live. Given that it is always better that a person decides for themself, the checklist reminds decision-makers to consider whether the person may regain capacity. If they are likely to regain mental capacity, when will that be, and can the decision be delayed until then? So far as is 'reasonably practicable,' the person must be encouraged to participate in the process and assisted to improve their ability to contribute.[82] Although older persons may lack capacity, dignity requires that if they can express a point of view, it should be considered.

The best interests checklist seeks to minimise the effect of the decision-makers subjective opinions and maximise the information available to them about the person to reflect them as an individual. An essential part of this involves getting an insight into the person's personality and what drives them. Therefore, decision-makers must consider past and present wishes and feelings 'so far as is reasonably ascertainable.' Where it is impossible to ascertain past or present wishes and feelings, the Court of Protection proceeds based on how a reasonable citizen would approach the matter.[83] A written statement made during capacity should be considered if relevant. Where the Court of Protection is using its power to execute

78 *Aintree University Hospitals NHS Foundation Trust v James* [2013] UKSC 67; [2014] AC 591.

79 G Mead, 'Shared decision making in older people after severe stroke' (2024) *Age and Ageing* 53(2), afae017.

80 *A Local Authority and another v B and another* [2024] EWCA Civ 572 [2024] All ER (D) 21 (Jun).

81 MCA 2005 Sections. 4(1)(a) and (b).

82 MCA 2005 Sections. 4(3) and 4.

83 *Secretary of State for the Home Department v Skripal (by her Litigation Friend the Official Solicitor) and another* [2018] EWCOP 6, [2018] Med LR 276.

a will under its property and affairs jurisdiction, it may refer to, for example, a previous will or a draft will prepared by the person.[84] How much weight is given to the ascertainable wishes and feelings will vary. Re M emphasised that wishes and feelings will always be significant, but their weight will be fact-specific.[85] No *a priori* weight can be given to them. For example, when an older person cannot understand the seriousness of their illness and the risks of living at home, minimal weight may be attached to wishes and feelings. However, the strength and consistency of the views will be important, as will the degree of incapacity. AC and GC (Capacity: Hoarding: Best Interests)[86] involved a best interest decision to allow the return of a ninety-two-year-old woman (AC) to her home where her son (GC) was her primary carer. AC and GC had been diagnosed with hoarding disorder. The judge decided that a trial period at home was in her best interests. Important factors were the consistency of her wish to return home and her strong sense of belonging to her home with its memories. Her relationship with GC and her attachment to her pets were important to her. Hoarding presented a risk, but the judge concluded it was manageable.

Beliefs and values are also to be considered insofar as they would have been likely to influence their decision if they had the capacity. Religious beliefs, especially long-held ones, are relevant in assessing best interests but must be balanced against any risks to health and well-being that customs and practices may pose. The Islamic observance of fasting during Ramadan and removing body hair were considered in Re IH (Observance of Muslim Practice).[87] The Court of Appeal held that it was not in IH's best interests to fast during Ramadan or to have his body hair removed. Interestingly, the Court heard that under Islamic law, a person lacking capacity was under no obligation to observe either practice, even though it was apparent that IH would have followed them if he had mental capacity.[88] In addition to beliefs and values, the decision-maker must consider any other factors the older person would have considered if able to do so.

Section 4(7) MCA 2005 requires the decision-maker, if practicable and appropriate, to obtain the views of anybody named by the older person, anyone engaged in caring for them or interested in their welfare, a donee of a Lasting Power of Attorney, or a deputy appointed by the Court of Protection. The above are not consulted on their personal preferences but on what is in the older person's best interest, having particular regard to any known wishes, feelings, or beliefs and values. A failure to meet the requirements of Section 4(7) MCA 2005 violates the

84 See MCA 2005 Sections.16(1)(h)(i) and *Re D (statutory will)* [2010] EWHC 2159 (Ch), [2012] Ch 57

85 Re M; ITW v Z [2009] EWHC 2525 (Fam) 35.

86 [2022] EWCOP 39; [2022] 8 WLUK 222.

87 [2017] EWCOP 9; [2017] All ER (D) 61 (Jun).

88 J Two, and M Curtice, 'The Islamic faith and best interests' (2019) *BJPsych Bulletin* 43(4) 177.

older person's rights under Article 8 ECHR in the absence of a convincing reason not to consult.[89]

Decisions taken by practitioners and others regarding mental capacity and best interests significantly affect the life of the older person being assessed. They often involve medical treatment, place of residence, financial matters, life and death, and deprivations of liberty. Professional judgments, knowledge, and skills are needed to transform the words of the MCA 2005 into an actual decision affecting an individual. The difficulties of mental capacity and best interests decisions lead to the possibility of disagreement over assessments. These may come from other practitioners, the older person, family, friends or advocates. Courts recognise that different people may reach different conclusions based on the same information, but be wholly professional and careful in how they do it.

Acts done in connection with care and treatment

Decision-makers and others working under the MCA 2005 are protected from civil and criminal liability if something goes wrong, provided they have acted in good faith. Section 5 MCA 2005 provides protection. It applies to acts done by a person (D) in connection with the care or treatment of another person (P) where D, before doing the act, takes 'reasonable steps' to establish whether P lacks capacity. When doing the act, D must reasonably believe that P lacks the necessary capacity and that it will be in P's best interest that the act is done. D does not incur any liability in respect of the act that they would not have incurred if P had capacity to consent and did consent. However, this does not exclude any liability in civil or criminal law resulting from negligence in doing the act. Section 5 MCA 2005 does not authorise doing any act which falls within the scope of the authority of a lasting power of attorney or a deputy of the Court of Protection. However, this does not apply if D is providing life-sustaining treatment or doing something D reasonably believes is necessary to prevent a deterioration in P's condition, pending a decision from the Court. Section 5 is modified by Section.6 MCA 2005, which applies to the use of restraint. The Code gives guidance on the use of restraint. If restrictions are necessary while in care, they should be kept to a minimum and for the shortest time possible.[90] Restraint involves using or threatening the use of force to ensure that P does something they are resisting or where it restricts P's liberty, regardless of whether P resists.[91] Two further conditions must be met before the defence is available. First, D must reasonably believe it is necessary to restrain to prevent harm to P. Second, the restraint must be proportionate to the likelihood of harm and its seriousness.

89 *Winspear v City Hospitals Sunderland NHS Foundation Trust* [2015] EWHC 3250 (QB); [2016] Q.B. 691.
90 Mental Capacity Code (n13) paras 6.40-6.44.
91 MCA 2005 Section. 6(4).

Conclusion

Sadly, losing mental capacity can be a consequence of ageing for some people. The MCA 2005 attempts to capture the progress made by the judges and place it within a statutory context. In many respects, it is a good piece of legislation as it provides a structured framework for assessments and best-interest decisions. However, as discussed above, some argue it violates Article 12 of the Disabilities Convention; others have countered this argument by pointing to the need to protect those incapable of deciding for themselves. The MCA 2005 is a necessary safeguard for many older people but can work against them. Graham refers to the 'unintended consequences' for older service users' emotional well-being. He highlights evidence of,

> risk averse practice where it is suggested that where potential for significant risk is present then professionals may err on the side of caution resulting in, at best, people whose capacity is questioned being over-assessed and, at worst, determining a 'lack of capacity attitude' actually prevailing within practice.[92]

He points to Court of Protection judgments that have openly criticised how the wishes and feelings of older people are being ignored in MCA 2005 decision-making. This is unacceptable; the MCA 2005 should be a source of protection and not a threat to maximising autonomy. The MCA 2005 is about the older person and not about legitimising a preconceived idea of what is 'good' for the older person regardless of their capacity.

Szelepet questions whether the MCA 2005 can achieve the aims of Parliament, namely empowerment, protection and support. She argues that,

> (T)he aims of the law for the elderly should run deeper than those originally expressed by Parliament; they should encompass the significance and value of old age and respect for the knowledge and experience acquired by a person of advanced years.[93]

COVID-19 restrictions created unease among mental capacity professionals. Kuylen et al. were particularly concerned about residents in care homes during the pandemic. In such crises, legal safeguards have a heightened role to play. Human rights were not suspended during the pandemic, although the tension between the rights of individuals and the broader interests of society became more evident. Participants in their study identified confusion about the remit of the MCA 2005 during a public health crisis, expressing concern about the pandemic restrictions'

92 M Graham, 'Understanding of the Mental Capacity Act in work with older adults exploring the "unintended consequences" for service users' emotional wellbeing' (2016) *Working with Older People* 20(3) 151.

93 E Szelepet, 'The Mental Capacity Act 2005 best interests test as applied to the elderly–is it fit for purpose?' (2018) *Medico-Legal Journal* 86(3) 142, 145.

impact on older people with impaired capacity. Disturbingly, they found uncertainty about the remit of the MCA 2005.

> Participants in our study reported that some care homes considered obligations under the MCA to be secondary to, or even superseded by, public health and infection control guidance. We also found renewed uncertainty among professionals as to when a restrictive measure engages the DoLS system.[94]

A systematic literature review of the MCA 2005 by Hinsliff-Smith et al.[95] identified three overarching themes with specific reference to older people. These were,

1) The inherent tensions between the requirements of the Act and its implementation in the everyday realities of clinical practice.
2) The limited effectiveness of current approaches to education and training about the Act and its application.
3) The lack of knowledge and awareness about the Act on the part of lay and informal carers.

The third theme is significant as non-professionals will make many capacity decisions, such as what to eat or wear. Decision-makers who are practitioners identified inconsistencies in applying the MCA 2005 across various care settings. In conclusion, the authors highlight the importance of training and the need to apply learning to practice.[96] Limited understanding of the MCA 2005 can lead to negative experiences and poor outcomes, particularly for people with intellectual disabilities, dementia, and mental health disorders. MCA 2005 training is not always mandatory, leading to assumptions being made that the person cannot make their own decisions. Although training is valued, research points to lingering anxieties and a lack of confidence in applying the legislation effectively among some practitioners.[97] The House of Lords report, the Mental Capacity Act 2005: Post-legislative Scrutiny,[98] recognised the visionary nature of the Act and how it continues to be held in high regard. However, it points to patchy understanding and awareness, and

94 M Kuylen, A Wyllie, V Bhatt et al. 'COVID-19 and the Mental Capacity Act in Care Homes: Perspectives from Capacity Professionals' (2022) 30(5) *Health & Social Care in the Community* e3018–e3028.

95 K Hinsliff-Smith, R Feakes, G Whitworth et al., 'What do we know about the application of the Mental Capacity Act (2005) in healthcare practice regarding decision-making for frail and older people?' (2017) *Health & Social Care in the Community* 25(2) 295.

96 See also J Manthorpe, K Samsi, and J Rapaport, '"More of a leg to stand on": Views of and usage of the Mental Capacity Act 2005 among staff of local Alzheimer's society and carer organisation' (2012) *Ageing & Mental Health* 16 (1) 102, 109.

97 C Jenkins, N Webster, A Smythe et al. 'What is the nature of mental capacity act training and how do health and social care practitioners change their practice post-training? A narrative review' (2020) *Journal of Clinical Nursing* 29(13–14) 2093.

98 Select Committee on the Mental Capacity Act 2005 *Mental Capacity Act 2005: Post-legislative scrutiny* (2013–14, HL 139).

some practitioners believe it is an optional add-on. In addition, paternalism and risk aversion have resulted in the empowering ethos not being delivered, thus violating the rights of older people to dignity and autonomy.

Chapters 4 and 7 discuss the provisions of the MCA 2005 regarding decision-making and deprivation of liberty for older people lacking capacity.

Bibliography

Action on Hearing Loss, Hearing matters (2020) <https://rnid.org.uk/wp-content/uploads/2020/05/Hearing-Matters-Report.pdf> - accessed 28 September 2024.

Aintree University Hospitals NHS Foundation Trust v James [2013] UKSC 67; [2014] AC 591.

Alzheimer's Research UK, 'Dementia statistics hub' (2022) <https://dementiastatistics.org/statistics/numbers-of-people-in-the-uk-2/> - accessed 28 September 2024.

Appelbaum PS, 'Protecting the Rights of Persons with Disabilities: An international Convention and its Problems' (2016) *Psychiatric Services* 67, 66, 367.

Australian Law Reform Commission, 'Equality, Capacity and Disability in Commonwealth Laws', Final report (ALRC report 124, 2014).

Bartlett P, 'Rethinking the Mental Capacity Act 2005: Towards the next generation of law' (2023) *Modern Law Review* 86(3) 659; Law Commission, *Mental Incapacity* (Law Com 231, 1995).

Branco M, Pels E, Nijboer F, et al. 'Brain-computer interfaces for communication: Preferences of individuals with locked-in syndrome, caregivers and researchers' (2023) *Disability and Rehabilitation: Assistive Technology* 18(6) 963.

Committee on the Rights of Persons with Disabilities Eleventh Session 31 March–11 April 2014 'General comment no. 1' (2014) <https://www.ohchr.org/en/documents/general-comments-and-recommendations/general-comment-no-1-article-12-equal-recognition-1> - accessed 28 September 2024.

Curtice M, 'Fluctuating capacity: The concept of micro-and macro-decisions' (2020) *BJPsych Advances* 26(4) 238

Department for Constitutional Affairs, 'Mental Capacity Act 2005 Code of Practice' (The Stationery Office, 2007) <https://assets.publishing.service.gov.uk/government/uploads/system/uploads/attachment_data/file/921428/Mental-capacity-act-code-of-practice.pdf> para 2.1 - accessed 28 September 2024.

Donnelly M, 'Best interests in the Mental Capacity Act: Time to say goodbye?' (2016) *Medical Law Review* 24, 318.

Donnelly M, 'Deciding in dementia: The possibilities and limits of supported decision-making' (2019) *International Journal of Law and Psychiatry* 66, 101466.

Graham M, 'Understanding of the Mental Capacity Act in work with older adults exploring the "unintended consequences" for service users' emotional wellbeing' (2016) *Working with Older People* 20(3) 151.

Griffith R, 'Assessing capacity in cases of fluctuating decision-making ability' (2020) *British Journal of Nursing* 29(15) 908.

Griffith R and Tengnah C, 'Mental Capacity Act 2005: Statutory principles and key concepts' (2008) *British Journal of Community Nursing* 13, 233.

Hall M, 'Situating dementia in the experience of old age: Reconstructing legal response' (2019) *International Journal of Law and Psychiatry* 66, 101468.

Herring J, 'Caesarean sections and the right of autonomy' (1998) *The Cambridge Law Journal* 57(3) 429.

Hinsliff-Smith K, Feakes R, Whitworth G, et al. 'What do we know about the application of the Mental Capacity Act (2005) in healthcare practice regarding decision-making for frail and older people?' (2017) *Health & Social Care in the Community* 25(2) 295.

HM Government, 'Mental Capacity Act 2005 Draft Code of Practice: Including the Liberty Protection Safeguards' (2022).
House of Lords and House of Commons Joint Committee on the Draft Mental Incapacity Bill (2003 HL 189-I, HC 1083-I) 40.
Jenkins C, Webster N, Smythe A, et al. 'What is the nature of Mental Capacity Act training and how do health and social care practitioners change their practice post-training? A narrative review' (2020) *Journal of Clinical Nursing* 29(13–14) 2093.
Kane M and Jacobs R, 'Assumptions about frailty and the tenacity of ageism among care professionals' (2018) *Journal of Pastoral Care & Counseling* 72(3) 190, 193.
Kuylen M, Wyllie A, Bhatt V, et al. 'COVID-19 and the Mental Capacity Act in care homes: Perspectives from capacity professionals' (2022) *Health & Social Care in the Community* 30(5) e3018–e3028.
Law Commission, 'Mental Capacity and Deprivation of Liberty' (Law'Com No 372, 2017) paras 14.51-56.
Law Commission of Ontario, 'Legal capacity, decision-making and guardianship' (Toronto, 2017).
Letts P, 'Mental Capacity Act 2005: The statutory principles and best interests test' (2005) *Journal of Mental Health Law* 1, 150.
Lush D, 'Article 12 of the United Nations Convention on the Right of Persons with Disabilities' (2011) *The Elder Law Journal* 61.
Manthorpe J, Samsi K, and Rapaport J, '"More of a leg to stand on": Views of and usage of the Mental Capacity Act 2005 among staff of local Alzheimer's Society and carer organisation' (2012) *Ageing & Mental Health* 16(1) 102, 109.
McSherry B, 'Legal capacity under the cConvention on the Rights of Persons with Disabilities' (2012) 20 *Journal of Law and Medicine* 22, 23–24.
Mead G, 'Shared decision making in older people after severe stroke' (2024) *Age and Ageing* 53(2) afae017.
Ministry of Justice, *Mental Capacity Act 2005: Deprivation of Liberty Safeguards* (The Stationery Office, 2008) paras 8.22–24.
Mogg A and Bartlett A, 'Refusal of treatment in a patient with fluctuating capacity-theory and practice' (2005) *Journal of Forensic Psychiatry & Psychology* 16(1) 60.
Moore S, Wotus R, Norman A, et al. 'Behind the cloak of competence: Brain injury and mental capacity legislation' (2019) *The Journal of Adult Protection* 21(4) 201.
Pritchard-Jones L, 'Exploring the potential and the pitfalls of the United Nations Convention on the Rights of Persons with Disabilities and General Comment no. 1 for people with dementia' (2019) *International Journal of Law and Psychiatry* 66, 101467.
Ruck Keene A, Kane N, Kim S, et al. 'Mental capacity – Why look for a paradigm shift?' (2023) *Medical Law Review* 31, 340.
Secretary of State for the Home Department v Skripal (by her Litigation Friend the Official Solicitor) and another [2018] EWCOP 6, [2018] Med LR 276.
Select Committee on the Mental Capacity Act 2005, 'Mental Capacity Act 2005: Post-legislative Scrutiny' (2013–2014, HL 139).
Szelepet E, 'The Mental Capacity Act 2005 best interests test as applied to the elderly – Is it fit for purpose?' (2018) *Medico-Legal Journal* 86(3) 142, 145.
Then S, Camey T, Bigby C, et al. 'Supporting decision-making of adults with cognitive disabilities: The role of law reform agencies – Recommendations, rationales and influence' (2018) 61 *International Journal of Law and Psychiatry* 64, 74.
Two J and Curtice M, 'The Islamic faith and best interests' (2019) *BJPsych Bulletin* 43(4) 177.
UN General Assembly, 'Convention on the Rights of Persons with Disabilities: Resolution / adopted by the General Assembly, 24 January 2007', A/RES/61/106 https://www.refworld.org/docid/45f973632.html - accessed 28 September 2024.
World Health Organisation, 'Mental health of Older Adults' (2017) <https://www.who.int/news-room/fact-sheets/detail/mental-health-of-older-adults> - accessed 28 September 2024.

4 Older persons and decision-making

Introduction

Decision-making is a feature of life. People decide on many seemingly trivial matters, such as what clothes to wear, what to eat, what to watch on television, and whether to take sugar in tea. Though these decisions may appear minor, they can hold significant value for some. For instance, an older person living with dementia may still retain the ability to decide on these issues and should be encouraged to do so. Making such decisions allows the older person to exercise a degree of control over their life which must be respected. Older persons have the right to make their own decisions, which is vital in preserving their dignity and control. Other decisions involve more complex matters. Making a will, transferring property, or making a Lasting Power of Attorney are activities with legal consequences. Medical treatment or social care decisions also impact the lives of some older persons. The ability to decide is a part of the right to dignity and autonomy. The European Court of Human Rights emphasises that respect for human dignity and freedom is the essence of the European Convention on Human Rights (ECHR). Article 8 ECHR contains the right to respect for private life, including dignity and the right to independence and to exercise choice. For many, such rights and freedoms are taken for granted. Practitioners rarely question mental capacity, even in the most complex of decisions. For some older persons, the experience is different. There is a sense that things are done to them rather than with them. This ignores the basic rules of consent and refusal. People have considerable freedom to decide for themselves. The law may restrict the extent of our decision-making, and social conventions may limit what we can do. However, people are usually free to decide how they live their lives and, importantly, have the right to make what others consider unwise decisions. How people live is up to them. Unfortunately, ageist attitudes deny some older persons the right to choose. Such ageism may be misguided benevolence whereby it is thought that the kindest thing to do is to relieve the older person of the responsibility of deciding. Although well-intentioned, this takes away a fundamental right. The other form of ageism is ill-intentioned and, through coercion or otherwise, takes away the right to decide, often leading to personal gain for the perpetrator. The process of making decisions has many aspects. It can involve agreeing to something or, just as importantly, refusing something. Essential though mental capacity is, it is necessary to consider the other requirements for valid

DOI: 10.4324/9780203798058-5

consent or refusal. Three elements are needed. In addition to mental capacity discussed in Chapter 3, the older person must be given information and be able to decide using their free will.

Information

Information is essential when making decisions. For an older person choosing whether to have medical treatment or social care, entering into a legal agreement, or deciding where to live, awareness of the implications of saying yes or saying no is necessary. Information is empowering and a valuable way of supporting decision-making. This begs the question of how much information is needed to enable the person to make an informed decision. There is no easy answer, as people want different amounts of information. Indeed, an older person may refuse to receive any information or only a bare minimum. This is their right, although they should be made aware of the implications of their decision. Where the decision involves complex medical, financial, or legal matters, how much technical detail is necessary to satisfy the duty? To expect a layperson to understand a technical explanation of a heart bypass operation or a property transfer is possibly asking too much. Technical language and jargon must be avoided by those seeking a decision. Also, the format in which information is provided must have regard to any special communication needs, such as those arising from visual or hearing impairments. Special aids to communication may improve the older person's ability to receive and understand information.

Solicitors advising clients must inform them about the services they need, how they will be delivered, and the cost. This is part of the duty of client care. The client care letter also reinforces information given during an interview to help them make an informed decision; it should use an easily readable font and have a clear layout.[1] Solicitors should have available leaflets on topics relevant to older clients. These include information leaflets from public bodies and charities, including the Office of Public Guardian, the Department for Work and Pensions, and charities working for older persons and their carers. They may also prepare in-house publications aimed at older clients.[2] Solicitors have a duty beyond simply drawing up the necessary documentation, particularly for a gift. They must ensure the older client understands the benefits and risks (particularly concerning home transfer), the foreseeable consequences of their action, and the nature of what they are doing. This ensures that the decision is well-informed and that the client makes it of their own free will.

1 Solicitors Regulatory Authority (2019) 'Guidance: Client Care Letters' (2019) <https://www.sra.org.uk/solicitors/guidance/client-care-letters/> – accessed 28 September 2024.

2 J Pierce, 'The older client practice' in C Bielanska (ed) *Elderly Client Handbook* (Legal Handbooks, 6th edn, The Law Society 2019) 98.

For doctors, the law was changed by the Supreme Court in Montgomery v Lanarkshire Health Board.[3] Previously, the doctor's duty to give information was based on two cases, Bolam v Friern Hospital Management Committee[4] and Sidaway v Board of Governors of the Bethlem Royal Hospital.[5] Bolam considered a negligence claim arising from injuries sustained during electroconvulsive therapy, ECT. The court found that doctors would not be negligent if they had acted under a practice accepted at the time as proper by a responsible body of medical opinion. Other doctors may do things differently, but that does not matter. The relevance of Bolam to giving patients information was discussed in Sidaway by Lord Diplock, who argued that doctors must exercise their professional skill and judgement to decide which risks to inform their patients about and how to convey such information. This decision should be based on expert medical evidence, and the Bolam test should be applied. Lord Scarman warned against information that could confuse or alarm patients. He believed doctors should act in their patient's best interests to protect them from this. This was a highly paternalistic approach. Montgomery rejected this approach and adopted a patient-centred test. The Supreme Court said it would be a mistake to view patients as uninformed and incapable of understanding medical matters. Patients should not be regarded as dependent on information from doctors; they have the right to self-determination. Doctors were obliged to take reasonable care to ensure the patient was aware of any material risks involved in the treatment and any reasonable alternatives. What is a material risk? A risk is material if a reasonable person in the patient's position would likely attach significance to it. Alternatively, a risk will be material where the doctor *was or should reasonably be aware* the patient would likely attach significance to it. Assessing the risk cannot be reduced to percentages. A gloss was put on the Montgomery case by the Supreme Court in McCulloch v Forth Valley Health Board.[6] It involved assessing what information on alternative treatments should be given to the patient. Should the doctor adopt the Montgomery approach, or should Bolam apply? The Supreme Court ruled in favour of using clinical judgment, the Bolam test, in determining what reasonable alternative treatment options should be shared with the patient, accepting the arguments of the British Medical Association and the General Medical Council.

Doctors must engage in a dialogue with the patient rather than make assumptions based, for example, on the patient's age. In some circumstances, the doctor can withhold information using therapeutic privilege if it is reasonably considered that disclosure would harm the patient's health. However, doctors should respond

3 [2015] UKSC 11, [2015] AC 1430. See also C Milo, 'The law and ethics of informed consent after Montgomery and the safeguard of patients' safety' in J Tingle, C Milo, G Msikska, R Millar (eds) *Research Handbook on Patient Safety and the Law* (Edward Elgar Publishing, 2023) 22.

4 [1957] 1 WLR 583.

5 [1985] AC 871.

6 [2023] UKSC 26, [2023] 3 WLR 321. See also the Court of Appeal in *Bilal and another v St George's University Hospital NHS Foundation Trust* [2023] EWCA Civ 605, [2023] All ER (D) 37: J MacLeod, 'Double duty: McCulloch v Forth Valley Health Board' (2024) *Edinburgh Law Review* 28(1) 130.

openly to a direct question, notwithstanding the possibility that it may upset the patient. Despite reaffirming the principle of therapeutic privilege, the Supreme Court in Montgomery did not discuss the parameters in detail. These still need to be clarified.[7] However, being overprotective of an older person by not being open and honest may amount to benevolent ageism. In its guidance, the General Medical Council lists seven principles of decision-making and consent.

1. All patients have the right to be involved in their treatment and care decisions and to be supported in making informed decisions.
2. Decision-making is an ongoing process focused on meaningful dialogue: the exchange of relevant information specific to the individual patient.
3. All patients have the right to be listened to, given the information they need to decide, and given the time and support they need to understand it.
4. Doctors must try to find out what matters to patients so they can share relevant information about the benefits and harms of proposed options and reasonable alternatives, including the option to take no action.
5. Doctors must start from the presumption that all adult patients have the mental capacity to decide about their treatment and care. A patient can only be judged to lack the mental capacity to make a specific decision at a specific time and only after assessment in line with legal requirements.
6. The choice of treatment or care for patients who lack mental capacity must benefit them overall, and decisions should be made in consultation with those close to them or advocating for them.
7. Patients whose right to consent is affected by law should be supported in decision-making and, if possible, in exercising choice.[8]

The General Medical Council issued guidance on treating older persons, requiring doctors to ensure that information is received and understood. The guidance points out that older persons may have hidden physical or other conditions, which means they need help understanding the information given during a consultation. These conditions may include visual or hearing impairments. It advises using accessible formats such as large print leaflets, electronic amplifiers, and speech and language therapists. It is also essential to be satisfied that there are no other barriers to communication; failure to do so may lead to incorrect assessments of, for example, the older person's mental capacity. Older persons must be treated as individuals

7 R Mulheron, 'The defence of therapeutic privilege in Australia' (2003) *Journal of Law and Medicine* 11 201; AM Finnerty, 'The privilege of information—an examination of the defence of therapeutic privilege and its implications for pregnant women' (2021) *Medical Law Review* 29 639.

8 General Medical Council, 'Decision Making and Consent' (2020) <https://www.gmc-uk.org/-/media/documents/gmc-guidance-for-doctors---decision-making-and-consent-english_pdf-84191055.pdf>, 7 – accessed 28 September 2024.

and should not be treated differently based on age. Doctors have duties under the Equality Act 2010 to avoid discrimination and to make reasonable adjustments.[9]

Social care practitioners must also obtain informed consent from an older person when deciding on assessments, social care packages, place of residence, and safeguarding.[10] They must provide relevant information to enable the older person to decide. If the older person has mental capacity, subject to the decision being made freely, they retain the right to refuse care even though care is assessed as being in their best interest. Under the British Association of Social Workers' Code of Ethics, social workers should ensure that people have the information they need to make informed choices and decisions.[11]Older persons lacking mental capacity may have a point of view and should be allowed to share it with their social worker. All information should be provided in a form consistent with the older person's ability to understand. As with medical practitioners, information should not be withheld because it may lead the older person to make decisions not thought to be in their best interest. The person's vulnerability may suggest that keeping some information from them is safer, but they have a right to receive material information. The approach taken by the Supreme Court in the Montgomery case provides valuable guidance for social care practitioners.

Decisions must be freely made

The right to decide free of undue influence has long been a principle of our law. Historically, it has applied to legal contracts or agreements such as wills or property transfers. Some older persons experience undue influence when making their wills. For example, in Schrader v Schrader.[12] the mother's original will divided her estate equally between her two sons. However, a later will, the final one, left it to one son only. The other son contested the will, arguing that his brother coerced his mother into changing her will in his favour. The evidence showed that the mother, who was ninety-six, was vulnerable and relied heavily on the son named as the beneficiary. He was described as a forceful man with a violent history who was instrumental in preparing the new will. He did not involve the mother's usual solicitor and tried to cover up his involvement in drafting the new will. The court concluded that on the evidence there was no other rational reason for her changing her will other than undue influence and found the will to be invalid.

Undue influence comes in two forms: first, is a rebuttable presumption of undue influence and second, is actual undue influence. Royal Bank of Scotland PLC v

9 General Medical Council, 'Ethical Guidance for Doctors: Practical steps to include older adults in their care' (2024)<https://www.gmc-uk.org/professional-standards/ethical-hub/older-adults?msclkid=52115fc8a5ff11ec82b5c435ceb20d02> – accessed 28 September 2024.

10 F Reamer, 'Informed consent in social work' (1987) *Social Work* 32(5) 425.

11 British Association of Social Workers, 'The BASW Code of Ethics for Social Work' (July 2021), <https://new.basw.co.uk/sites/default/files/resources/basw_code_of_ethics_-_2021.pdf>, 10 – accessed 28 September 2024.

12 [2013] EWHC 466 (Ch), [2013] 3 WLUK 258.

Etridge[13] held that a presumption of undue influence arises if there is a relationship of trust and confidence between the parties, giving one of them a measure of power they then abuse. In addition, there must be a transaction between them that the relationship cannot readily explain. The presumption applies to lifetime gifts and transfers only and not to wills. For wills, actual undue influence must be proven.[14] Certain types of relationships are automatically considered ones of trust and confidence. These include parent and child (both ways), trustee and beneficiary, solicitor and client, and doctor and patient. The relationship between husband and wife does not, by itself, raise the presumption.[15] However, it does apply to a fiancée. Other relationships may raise the presumption that the donor had trust and confidence in the recipient. This can include an unpaid carer. In Hammond v Osborn,[16] P gave a significant gift to O, his neighbour, who provided him with care and friendship. The gift represented over 90% of P's liquid assets and exposed him to a substantial tax liability. O argued that her conduct was blameless and that there were no hidden motives behind the gift. H, one of P's cousins, claimed that the presumption of undue influence had arisen and was not successfully rebutted by O. The Court of Appeal agreed that the presumption arose as a substantial gift was given when the donor and donee had a relationship of trust and confidence. O failed to rebut this presumption; she could not prove that the gift was made after the donor had given it full, free, and informed thought. Simply showing that there was no wrongdoing on her part was insufficient. The burden of rebutting the presumption falls on the donee, who must prove that the donor, in making the gift, did so freely.

Actual undue influence is where there is no relationship of trust and confidence, but there has been coercion or pressure put on the older person to act. Actual undue influence must be proved rather than presumed. As the testator will likely be dead when a will's validity becomes an issue, it may be difficult to gather sufficient evidence to show coercion or pressure. However, a witness to a will may be called upon to establish whether the person was coerced into signing. In actual undue influence, the burden of proof is on the person claiming it was present during the transaction. The alleged influencer does not have to prove that it was entered freely. The person alleged to have exercised undue influence must be shown by the person challenging the decision to have exercised coercion over the older person.[17] The influence must be undue; persuasion does not necessarily amount to undue influence. Attempts to persuade the older person to pursue a particular course of action are acceptable without pressure and coercion. Disagreement is permitted.

Solicitors and others advising an older person should be clear about who the client is. A family member or close friend may make an appointment; however, they are not the client. The older person should be seen alone on at least one occasion.

13 [2001] UKHL 44, [2002] 2 AC 773.

14 *Re Edwards (Deceased)* [2007] EWHC 1119 (Ch), [2007] 5 WLUK 72; *Re Williams (Deceased)* [2022] EWHC 1334 (Ch), [2022] 5 WLUK 527.

15 *Midland Bank v Shepherd* [1988] 3 All ER 17.

16 [2002] EWCA Civ 885, 2002 WL 1310756.

17 *Wingrove v Wingrove* (1885) 11 PD 81; *R v Edwards* (n14).

Advisors must be alert to attempts to exert undue influence by others having a vested interest or an over-benevolent approach. Gifts, wills, property transfers, and establishing trusts are prime targets for undue influence. It features in other areas. A vulnerable older person may be pressured into making an advance decision under the Mental Capacity Act 2005 (MCA 2005) or signing a DNACRP notice. A certificate provider for Lasting Powers of Attorney must ensure that the donor understands what they are doing and that they are not being pressured.

In the Re T (Adult: Refusal of Treatment) case, the Court of Appeal discussed the effects of outside influence on a patient's decisions on medical treatment. The Court considered, amongst other things, whether pressure applied by a mother on her pregnant daughter to refuse a blood transfusion invalidated the daughter's refusal. It emphasised that a patient is entitled to receive advice and assistance from others. However, doctors must be satisfied that the decision is that of the patient. Two aspects are relevant for older patients who may be vulnerable.

> First, the strength of the will of the patient. One who is very tired, in pain or depressed will be much less able to resist having his will overborne than one who is rested, free from pain and cheerful. Second, the relationship of the 'persuader' to the patient may be of crucial importance. The influence of parents on their children or of one spouse on the other can be, but is by no means necessarily, much stronger than would be the case in other relationships.[18]

The Court held that persuasion based on religious belief can be more compelling, particularly if deployed by somebody close to the patient. The fundamental question is, does the patient mean what they say?

Undue influence is closely related to coercive and controlling behaviour, although the former looks primarily at an individual transaction (gift, will, property transfer, etc.). Where coercive and controlling behaviour is present in a relationship, financial and other decisions made by an older person are likely to be open to challenge because of the lack of free will. Such behaviour may create barriers for an older person seeking help and support.[19] Section 42(3) Care Act 2014 includes being pressured about money or property as financial abuse. Section 1 Domestic Abuse Act 2021 defines domestic abuse as including controlling or coercive behaviour. Engaging in controlling or coercive behaviour towards another person that has a serious effect on them is an offence under Section 76 Serious Crime Act 2015 (as amended by the Domestic Abuse Act 2021), where the perpetrator and victim are personally connected, and the perpetrator either knows or should know the impact of their behaviour on the victim. In broad terms, 'personally connected' includes people who are married or in civil partnerships, engaged, in a civil partnership

18 *Re T (Adult: Refusal of Treatment)* [1993] Fam 95, 114.

19 S Wydall, and R Zerk, 'Domestic abuse and older people: Factors influencing help-seeking' (2017) The *Journal of Adult Protection* 19(5) 247; S Wydall, A Clarke, J Williams et al., 'Domestic abuse and elder abuse in Wales: A tale of two initiatives' (2018) *British Journal of Social Work* 48(4) 962.

agreement, in an intimate personal relationship, or in a parental relationship. This is discussed further in Chapter 6.

Mental capacity: decision-making

Making decisions for an older person assessed as lacking mental capacity is based on the best interests test under Sections 1 and 4 MCA 2005, as discussed in Chapter 3. However, as part of the MCA 2005's underlying philosophy, people are encouraged to plan for possible future incapacity in the same way they make wills and ensure that their expressed views are respected if they lose capacity. At a time when they have the capacity, they can put in place provisions whereby their preferences, for example, about medical treatment or social care, have legal effect. This can be done under the MCA 2005. However, formal processes do not negate the importance of informal methods of recording preference through, for example, conversations with family, trusted friends, or professionals. People may record their wishes in writing. Chapter 3 shows that these discussions may help when making best interests decisions. Everybody should be encouraged to discuss their wishes with trustworthy family and friends. The MCA 2005 provides formal ways in which people can ensure that their wishes and feelings are still respected in the event of a loss of capacity.

Lasting Power of Attorney

Lasting Powers of Attorney (LPAs) replaced Enduring Powers of Attorney (EPAs), made under the now-repealed Enduring Power of Attorney Act 1985. The EPA was designed to solve the problem of ordinary powers of attorney being automatically revoked if the donor lost mental capacity. It was thought helpful if a power of attorney continued even after the loss of capacity; this would allow an attorney to decide on behalf of the donor according to their wishes. The EPA was restricted to property and financial matters. Since 1 October 2007, it has not been possible to create an EPA, although, under the MCA 2005, transitional provisions protect EPAs completed before that date.[20] The MCA 2005 introduced LPAs.[21] An LPA allows a person ('the donor') to grant decision-making authority to an attorney(s) to be exercised if the donor becomes mentally incapacitated; the attorney is also referred to as the donee. In deciding if a person has the capacity to make an LPA, Sections 2 and 3 of the MCA 2005 and Chapters 2–4 of the Code of Practice apply. In addition, Poole J in The Public Guardian v RI, D, RS, RO[22] gives guidance on what information a donor needs to understand to have the capacity to make their LPA. This includes understanding the effect of the LPA, who the attorneys are, the scope of the attorney's powers, how the MCA 2005 restricts an attorney's use of

20 MCA 2005 Schedule 4.
21 ibid Sections 9–14.
22 [2022] EWCOP 22, [2022] 6 WLUK 23.

the power, when the attorneys can exercise their powers, the assets the attorneys can deal with, the power of the donor to revoke the LPA when they have the capacity to do so, and the pros and cons of executing the LPA or not. It is also necessary for the donor to understand that the LPA needs to be registered before it can be used.[23] It is incumbent on solicitors to ensure that their client has the necessary capacity to make an LPA.[24] In The Public Guardian v RI and Others case, the court found that when the LPA was executed in 2009, the donor lacked capacity because of his learning disability and diagnosis of chronic schizophrenia. He was incapable of managing his property and financial affairs and lacked the capacity to revoke or execute an LPA. The presumption of capacity was rebutted.[25]

To create a valid LPA, a certificate provider must certify that the donor was not coerced into signing it and fully understands the agreement. They should discuss the LPA with the donor and be prepared to raise any concerns about the donor's capacity to make the LPA. Certificate providers must be independent of the donor, so family members, proposed attorneys, and anyone connected to a care home where the donor lives cannot provide the certificate. Certificate providers are often solicitors or doctors. There is also a provision for the donor to choose people they want to notify when the LPA is about to be registered. These are usually friends, neighbours, or relatives the donor knows well and would be willing to raise concerns about the LPA, such as suspected coercion or fraud. An LPA can be registered by either the donor or one of the attorneys. Whichever it is, that person must tell those people that the LPA is being registered using the form provided. Upon notification, persons notified can raise any concerns within three weeks. This is an added safeguard. Under the the Powers of Attorney Act 2023, when it enters into force, only the donor can initiate the registration process and the duty to notify named persons will fall to the Office of Public Guardian. Additional safeguards in the 2023 Act are the need for ID verification for donors, certificate providers, attorneys, and replacement attorneys.

The donor can appoint one or more attorneys aged eighteen years or older who have the capacity to undertake the role. They may be trusted friends, relatives, professionals, or a combination of these. For an older person making an LPA, it is helpful to consider appointing a younger person to act alongside a spouse, partner, or friend of the same age. Appointing replacement attorneys is possible if an original attorney cannot act. The donor can choose whether the attorneys act jointly or severally, or jointly for some decisions and severally for others; the choice may depend on the gravity or complexity of the decision, for example, serious medical treatment or a property transaction such as the sale of a home. The LPA must be completed in the prescribed form and registered with the Public Guardian, which

23 *Re Collis* (unreported) 27 October 2010.

24 The Law Society, *Practice Note: Lasting Powers of Attorney* (The Law Society, 2023) 3.1 <https://www.mentalhealthlaw.co.uk/media/2022-08-17_Law_Society_LPA_practice_note.pdf> - accessed 28 January 2024.

25 *RI* case (n22).

has a supervisory role over LPAs. A fee is payable. Registering an LPA as soon as possible is advisable to avoid potential complications. For example, if the donor delays too long, they may be unable to make amendments or re-process the application through loss of capacity.

LPA forms are available from the Office of Public Guardian and can be completed online, although a physical signature is still needed rather than a digital one. However, the Powers of Attorney Act 2023 will allow the Office of the Public Guardian to implement a new digital process alongside an improved paper application system. Professional legal advice is not formally required, although it is often advisable to use a solicitor or a third-sector organisation providing an LPA writing service. Attorneys should comply with the statutory principles and act in the best interests of the donor. Their powers are also subject to any conditions or restrictions in the LPA. They must assess whether the donor has the capacity to make decisions. If they lack capacity, the attorney should consider the possibility of them regaining it in the future. This may allow for the decision to be postponed until they are able to decide.[26]

Unlike EPAs, two types of LPA may be made – personal welfare and property and affairs.[27] A person may make one or both of these. The introduction of the personal welfare LPA was first recommended in the Law Commission's 1995 Mental Incapacity report[28] and was eventually included in the MCA 2005. Personal welfare decisions can only be made under the LPA if the donor lacks capacity or the attorney reasonably believes this is the case.[29] It does not apply if the donor becomes physically incapable but has mental capacity.[30] The MCA 2005 Code states that 'welfare' covers various social care and accommodation issues. These include where the donor should live and with whom, day-to-day decisions on food and dress, consenting to and refusing medical treatment, assessments for social care, personal correspondence and papers, and the right to complain about the donor's care or treatment.[31] For some older persons, the attorney might have to decide whether they should enter a care home. In making the LPA, the donor may impose instructions or preferences on what the attorney can do and the areas of personal welfare to which the LPA will apply. Examples of preferences include having pets for as long as possible, spending time outdoors, living near a relative or friend, and engaging in social activities. Alternatively, they may allow the attorney to make all such decisions. The attorney can only make decisions within the terms of the LPA. If the decision falls outside of the LPA's remit, it may be necessary to apply to the Court of Protection.[32] A welfare LPA cannot include powers over the

26 MCA 2005 Section 9(4).
27 ibid Section 9(1)(a) and (b).
28 Law Commission, *Mental Incapacity* (Law Com No 231, 1995) para 7.7.
29 MCA 2005 Section 11(7).
30 *Re Azancot* (2009) COP 27/5/09.
31 Department for Constitutional Affairs, *Mental Capacity Act 2005 Code of Practice* (The Stationery Office, 2007) para 7.21.
32 ibid 7.56.

donor's property and affairs as these can only be made under a finance LPA, even though welfare and finance are often linked. The MCA Code requires decision-makers to consult with attorneys about whether a decision comes within the LPA.[33]

During the parliamentary debates on the Mental Capacity Bill, there was unease that personal welfare LPAs and other measures would indirectly legalise euthanasia. The Joint Committee of the Lords and Commons recognised the intensity of these concerns but believed, correctly, they were unfounded. Nevertheless, in response, they proposed that the bill should include clarification that nothing in the legislation legalises euthanasia.[34] Section 62 MCA 2005 states that to avoid doubt, nothing in the Act is to be read as affecting the law of murder, manslaughter, or suicide. In addition, it does not authorise an attorney to decide on initiating or continuing life-sustaining treatment unless the LPA explicitly provides for this. Life-sustaining treatment means treatment which, in the view of the person providing health care for the donor, is necessary to sustain life.[35] In The Public Guardian v DA and others,[36] the LPAs included instructions or preferences which required that, in certain circumstances, the attorney should take or encourage steps to be taken that would bring about the donor's death. Baker LJ held that such instructions or preferences encouraged the attorney to commit an unlawful act, were ineffective, and should be severed. They were impossible directions. So, for example, a term in a welfare LPA instructing or encouraging the attorney to take the donor to Dignitas would be severed as doing so could be an offence under Section 2 Suicide Act 1961, namely encouraging or assisting suicide. If a decision to withdraw or withhold life-sustaining treatment is challenged, Section.6(7) MCA 2005 permits its continuation, or the taking of any action reasonably believed to be necessary to prevent a significant decline in a person's condition, pending a decision by the Court of Protection regarding any relevant issues.. If the donor retains the capacity to decide a specific health or welfare matter, they have a right to decide. The capacity assessment may restrict incapacity to more serious treatment, such as major surgery. The donor may retain the capacity to consent to less intrusive procedures such as an X-ray or minor dental treatment. For a donor who is a patient under Part IV or 4A of the Mental Health Act 1983, the treatment provisions of that Act apply.

Unlike a welfare LPA, a property and finance LPA may be used with the donor's consent before they lose capacity; donors must choose on the forms whether the attorney can act immediately upon registration. Property and finance are similar to the previous EPAs. They can give the attorney powers over managing bank accounts, buying and selling property, investments, paying bills, and managing savings. The attorney has the authority to make gifts on 'customary occasions' to people who are related to or connected with the donor, including the attorneys

33 ibid 7.57.

34 House of Lords and House of Commons Joint Committee on the Draft Mental Incapacity Bill, *Draft Mental Incapacity Bill* (2003 HL 189-I, HC 1083-I) 204.

35 MCA 2005 ss.11(8a) and 4(10).

36 *The Public Guardian v DA and others* [2018] EWCOP 26, [2018] EWCOP 26.

themselves.[37] Customary occasions include birthdays, weddings, civil partnerships, and seasonal celebrations. Additionally, the attorney can make gifts to charities the donor supported or would have likely supported. This could be a charity the donor cares about, like an animal welfare charity. However, the value of all gifts must be reasonable considering the donor's overall estate.[38] Making gifts on the donor's behalf is subject to there being no contrary conditions or restrictions in the LPA.

LPAs ensure that people can plan for older age and the possible loss of capacity, although younger people will also benefit from them. Thinking ahead is essential, and delaying making an LPA risks leaving it too late. However, LPAs are not immune from criticism. Former Senior Judge Denzil Lush has some concerns regarding the weak supervision of attorneys by the Office of Public Guardian and identifies the need for more robust procedures to be implemented. He argues that when choosing an attorney, people may have less autonomy than claimed, and attorneys often benefit from this. It is important to consider how creating an LPA may affect family relationships. Those who are not chosen may feel hurt and lose trust in the attorney.[39] Australian research identifies risk factors that may result in powers of attorney being used as an instrument of abuse. These include inadequate knowledge of powers of attorney, family conflicts, feelings of entitlement by family members and others, and a lack of planning for financial decision-making.[40]

Advisors should be aware of two issues when advising someone on making an LPA. First, they must ensure the donor has the necessary capacity to make an LPA. Second, they must ensure that the donor is not being coerced or influenced and that there is no collusion by those involved to register an LPA concerning a person who lacks capacity. Regrettably, LPAs can be used to abuse older persons, and it is often hard to identify when this happens. If there is evidence of abuse of the LPA, the Public Guardian may apply to the Court of Protection to remove attorneys. In Re SB,[41] the donor had Alzheimer's and was in a nursing home. She appointed her sons as attorneys. They acted in a way that contravened their authority and in a way that was not in SB's best interest. The Court revoked the LPA and appointed a deputy to act with a panel deputy from a solicitors firm.

The Ministry of Justice and the Office of Public Guardian report that in 2023-24 1.37million LPAs were registered. The number is growing on an annual basis. The OPG has nearly seven million LPAs and EPAs on their register. Some applications are rejected. The main reasons for rejection relate to instructions and preferences, signing in the wrong order, illegible information, missing information, and misspelling of names. Care is neeeded when completing the paperwork. If an LPA

37 *Re Various Lasting Powers of Attorney* [2019] EWCOP 40, [2020] 3 All E.R. 879.

38 MCA 2005 Section 12.

39 M Walters, 'I would never sign a power of attorney – retired judge' (*Law Society Gazette* 2017) <https://www.lawgazette.co.uk/law/i-would-never-sign-a-power-of-attorney-retired-judge/5062465.article> – accessed 28 September 2024.

40 NM Ries, 'Enduring Powers of Attorney and financial exploitation of older people: A conceptual analysis and strategies for prevention' (2022) *Journal of Aging & Social Policy* 34(3) 357.

41 [2015] EWCOP 7, [2015] 2 WLUK 399.

made by an older person with declining mental capacity is rejected, any delay in correcting mistakes could lead to a revised application being denied due to an intervening loss of capacity.

How well do LPAs work for older persons? They allow younger and older persons to prepare for future capacity loss. It has all the benefits of making a will with the bonus of the donor being alive when it is used and having their wishes respected. Some older persons may delay making an LPA. It may be that a dementia diagnosis at an early stage persuades the person to act. However, this can be a sensitive matter as it involves formally recognising a distressing prognosis. Existing safeguards are inadequate to protect older persons.[42] Issues still need to be addressed, particularly around the supervision of attorneys and the lack of auditing of annual accounts in finance and property LPAs involving transactions above a certain amount. The Powers of Attorney Act 2023 is intended to simplify LPA procedures. Its primary objective is to digitise the LPA process, allowing donors to sign and execute LPAs electronically. It will allow for electronic signatures and registration. However, lawyers are concerned about the safety and robustness of verifying signatories' identities.[43] Donors may lack digital access, and there is no requirement to notify the registration of an LPA. The role of certifiers in the new digital system needs to be clarified. Will they be required to assess capacity and look for potential coercion? Scotland has a more robust requirement for donors to obtain a certificate of capacity before the power can be registered and used.[44] Stanyer suggests that random sampling checks would provide some reassurance.[45]

Health and welfare LPAs are complex due to the vast array of decisions that need to be made regarding an older person who lacks capacity. Although considered a way of respecting their wishes and feelings, there is a concern that complex and personal decisions are rarely discussed during capacity. This makes it difficult for the attorney, who may be a family member, to decide what the donor would have wanted.[46] At best, LPAs are a structured way of maximising the voice of an older person in the event of losing capacity. The ability to plan is empowering but requires much discussion with attorneys before registration. At worst, LPAs can be a way of regularising abuse and neglect with minimal chances of detection. Independent advice is, as always, an important safeguard. Regrettably, along with

42 O P O'Sullivan, 'Financial abuse, statutory provisions and the courts: Adequacy and analysis of enduring and Lasting Powers of Attorney' (2021) *The Journal of Adult Protection* 23(4) 253.

43 M Duddles 'The Powers of Attorney Act 2023 – how far does it go to protect the vulnerable?' (2023) <https://www.bondsolon.com/the-powers-of-attorney-act-2023-%E2%80%93-how-far-does-it-go-to-protect-the-vulnerable/> – accessed 28 September 2024.

44 C Stephens, A Stanyer, R Anderson, et al., 'Changing policy landscape around elder abuse in England and Wales' (2024) *British Medical Journal* 384.

45 A Stanyer, 'Lasting Powers of Attorney-are they good enough protection against financial abuse' (2017) *Elder Law Journal* 225.

46 M Curtice, I Katuwawela, and R McCollum, 'Lasting Powers of Attorney: Implications for clinicians' (2012), *Advances in Psychiatric Treatment* 18(3) 205.

many aspects of adult protection safeguarding law, LPAs must be considered as work in progress.

Advance decisions to refuse treatment

An advance decision (AD), also called a living will or advanced directive, allows a person to decide in advance what medical treatment they want to refuse if they lose capacity. It is impossible to use an AD to insist on a specific type of medical treatment as that is a clinical decision based on various factors, including the likely value of the treatment and the prognosis. ADs are made while the person can decide and help ensure their wishes are respected if they cannot decide in the future. Sections 24–26 MCA 2005 give ADs legal standing, although the concept is not new. A 2001 case, Re AK (Medical Treatment: Consent),[47] is a case in point. The patient had indicated that if he lost the ability to communicate, he would want to stop being ventilated. Could the doctor withdraw the ventilation and allow the patient to die? Hughes J reiterated that doctors cannot proceed with treatment if they know that a patient with capacity has clearly expressed their refusal. These wishes may also be expressed in anticipation of losing capacity. Verifying that the anticipatory statements accurately represent the patient's desires is necessary. This necessitates an examination of the timing and context in which the wishes were expressed, as well as the information available at the time. All of these aspects must be carefully considered.

Usually, an AD does not need to be in writing. However, given the concern that the MCA 2005 risked allowing euthanasia, additional safeguards apply to advance decisions involving life-sustaining treatment. They are only valid if they are in writing and signed by the maker or another person in their presence and with their direction. The signature must be made in the presence of a witness and signed by the witness in the maker's presence. As a matter of good practice, GPs, hospitals, families, social care professionals, and carers should be aware of the written AD and how they can access it if needed. Otherwise, the maker's wishes may be bypassed. Healthcare professionals and others are not liable if they undertake treatment if they are unaware of the AD. Similarly, there is no liability for withholding or withdrawing treatment if they reasonably believe a valid and applicable AD exists. Taking action to save a life or prevent serious deterioration is permitted while waiting for a Court of Protection decision on an AD's validity, existence, or applicability.[48]

An older person may decide they do not want doctors to strive to keep them alive if the prognosis is poor. They may wish their lives to end at a time of their choosing with as much dignity as possible and without intrusive and, in some cases, futile interventions. Relatives may wish to prolong the life of their loved one for as long as possible, but the older person does not. In addition to life-sustaining

47 [2001] 1 FLR 129.
48 MCA 2005 Section 26(2), (3), (4), and (5).

treatment, an older person may not wish to have particular types of treatment for personal or other reasons. They may distrust doctors or have an aversion to hospitals. They may have concerns about the side effects of the treatment. Their religious or other beliefs may not allow them to accept certain types of treatment. In such circumstances, an advance decision clarifies the older person's wishes and, ideally, is the outcome of conversations between them and the healthcare professionals, their families, and trusted friends. They allow for the older person's wishes to be respected. Section 24 MCA 2005 outlines the basics of an AD. When making the AD, a person must be eighteen or over and have capacity. An AD will stipulate that if a healthcare provider proposes a specific treatment at a later time and in the circumstances specified by the maker and they lack the capacity to decide at that time, the treatment should not be carried out or continued. According to Section 64(1) MCA 2005, 'treatment' includes 'a diagnostic or other procedure.' One area of concern for older persons is hydration and nutrition. In different circumstances, the House of Lords in Airedale NHS Trust v Bland[49] established that artificial hydration and nutrition are treatments if the patient cannot ingest food or fluids. Does this definition apply to ADs? Although an older person may have refused 'treatment,' in the strict clinical sense, does it include basic care and maintaining hydration and nutrition? What happens if they specifically refuse hydration, nutrition, and basic care in an AD? Clinically assisted nutrition and hydration (CANH) is a medical treatment because it involves intrusive procedures. An older person may validly refuse it when they have the capacity or in an AD. What about basic care such as warmth, hygiene, and encouraging the patient to eat or drink by mouth? Not providing such basic and essential care would be distressing for family, carers, and healthcare staff and would lead to suffering by the patient. For this reason, the MCA Code clarifies that an AD cannot refuse actions that make the person comfortable.[50] An AD can be revoked at any time.[51] Munby J in HE v A Hospital NHS Trust emphasised that it was fundamental that an anticipatory decision was revocable and that a clause making it irrevocable was contrary to public policy and void.[52] It may be amended during capacity; usually, it need not be in writing unless it applies to life-sustaining treatment. In expressing their wishes in advance, the older person is not expected to use complex medical terms; layperson language will suffice. If the context is clear, phrases like 'don't plug me into a machine' or 'don't cut off any parts' maysuffice.

An AD does not apply if the person has capacity concerning the proposed treatment, even though they lack the capacity to consent or refuse other forms of treatment. Nor is it applicable if the treatment is not specified in the AD or the specific circumstances are absent.[53] There are circumstances when an AD is not valid. One

49 [1993] AC 789 HL.
50 Mental Capacity Code (n31) 9.28
51 MCA 2005 Section 25(2)(a).
52 [2003] EWHC 1017 (Fam), [2003] 2 FLR 408.
53 MCA 2005 Section 25(3).

is where the maker has subsequently made an LPA, which gives the attorney the power to make decisions anticipated in the AD.[54] There is also a proviso that the AD ceases to be valid if the maker 'has done anything else clearly inconsistent with the advance decision remaining his fixed decision.'[55] In Re PW (Jehovah's Witness: Validity of Advance Decision), an advanced decision was made in 2001 to refuse consent for blood transfusions. At the time of the hearing, the maker was eighty years old and living with dementia. Poole J concluded,

> I recognise that the evidence before me does not all go one way. However, weighing all the matters discussed, I am satisfied, on the balance of probabilities, that Mrs W has done things clearly inconsistent with the advance decision remaining her fixed decision.[56]

He relied on her actions in making an LPA, which, although it did not include life-sustaining treatment, was inconsistent with the AD remaining her fixed intention. She had also requested the removal of a DNR notice without telling her family and possibly her clinicians about the AD. He held that the word 'done' in Section 25(2)(c) MCA 2005 includes words and actions. 'Fixed' does not involve just doing something inconsistent with the AD, but with that being a fixed decision; thus, fluctuating adherence to the AD may be incompatible with it being a fixed intention but this will depend on the facts of each case.

Before the MCA 2005, an anticipatory decision to refuse treatment was generally considered binding, even though the maker was unaware of what the circumstances would be when it became relevant.[57] However, in the 2003 case of HE v A Hospital Trust,[58] a woman born and brought up a Muslim became a Jehovah's Witness and signed an advanced directive refusing blood and blood products. She became seriously ill and required a transfusion. However, her circumstances had changed, as she was betrothed to marry a Muslim on the condition that she converted back to Islam. She had distanced herself from the Jehovah's Witnesses and had failed to mention the advanced directive when admitted to the hospital at a time when she had the capacity to do so. Was the advanced directive still valid? Munby J reiterated that ADs were revocable. He argued that an advance directive's continuing validity and applicability is a question of fact. The essential and compelling aspect was her rejection of the faith upon which the advance directive had been founded. He granted a declaration that treatment, including a blood transfusion, was lawful. Interestingly, he said that if there was doubt about its continued validity, this should be decided in favour of the preservation of life.

54 ibid Section 25(2)(b).
55 ibid Section 25(2)(c).
56 [2021] EWCOP 52, [2021] 9 WLUK 212, para 57.
57 A Grubb, J Laing, J McHale, et al., *Principles of Medical Law* (OUP 2010) para 4.114 citing the Ontario Court of Appeal decision in *Malette v. Shulman* (Ont. C.A.), 1990 CanLII 6868 (ON CA).
58 [2003] 2 FLR 408, [2003] 2 F.L.R. 408.

The issue for Parliament was whether Munby J's approach should be incorporated into the MCA 2005 or whether ADs should be binding, whatever the circumstances. This presents ethical dilemmas for doctors, some of which were raised during the scrutiny of the Mental Incapacity Bill by the Joint Committee of the House of Lords and House of Commons. When making an AD, it is difficult for the maker to predict how they would want to be treated if they lost the ability to decide for themselves at some unknown time. Personal circumstances may change, as well as improvements in treatment. For example, the birth of grandchildren or entering into a relationship might have caused a person to rethink their AD to refuse treatment when they had the capacity to do so.[59] To address these concerns, Section 25(4)(c) MCA 2005 provides that an AD does not apply to the treatment in question if 'there are reasonable grounds believing that circumstances exist which [the maker] did not anticipate at the time of the AD and which would have affected [their] decision had [they] anticipated them.' Consideration should be given to the following factors when reviewing the applicability of an AD: how long ago it was made, any changes in the patient's personal life that may affect its validity, and any unforeseen progress in medical treatments such as new medication, therapies, or treatments. The first point raises the question of whether ADs should be time-limited, say for five years. This would require the person to revisit them and revise them if necessary. Most of them are unwritten, so it isn't easy to see how that could be achieved in practice.

Advanced decisions are not immune from abusive practices. The use of blanket so-called advance decisions, particularly DNACPR, during COVID-19 demonstrated a woeful lack of understanding of what they are and of the importance of the person's right to choose and to be involved. Examples of the blanket imposition of DNACPR on some older persons were unlawful, contrary to General Medical Council guidance, and a human rights violation.[60] Care must also be taken to ensure that the maker has not been coerced into making an AD, although this may be difficult when it was made many years ago. Some older persons may make an AD at a crisis point. Admission to hospital following a crisis may involve a discussion with healthcare professionals and social care workers on whether, for example, to resuscitate in the event of cardiac arrest. There must be a discussion, and the older person must be the one to decide. In such cases, an AD made during a crisis must not routinely follow the older person if they return to their home or a care home. Circumstances have changed, and the older person is entitled to reconsider their decision.

59 Joint Committee (n34).

60 M Lyne and J Parker, 'From Ovid to COVID: The metamorphosis of advanced decisions to refuse treatment into a safeguarding issue' (2020) *Journal of Adult Protection* 22 (6) 361; J Williams, 'Taking it on the chin: Older people, human rights and COVID-19' (2021) *The Journal of Adult Protection* 23(2) 86.

The Court of Protection

LPAs and ADs allow an older person's wishes and preferences to be captured and used when decisions are required if they lose capacity. If an older person does not have an LPA or AD, alternative decision-making methods are necessary in the event of no capacity. The best interests test, discussed in Chapter 3, is used primarily concerning care and treatment decisions. The Section 5 MCA 2005 defence applies to care and treatment decisions and absolves decision-makers from liability if they reasonably believe the person lacks capacity and the decision is in their best interests. Reasonable steps should be taken to establish whether there is a lack of capacity.[61] However, this may not be an appropriate process, particularly if the decision is serious and has significant implications for the older person. At this stage, involving the Court of Protection may be necessary. The Court, which has the same powers, rights, privileges, and authority as the High Court, was created under Section 45 MCA 2005.[62] It operates through designated judges within the court structure, with district and circuit judges hearing less complex cases and High Court judges presiding over complex ones. This gives it a more extensive geographical footprint, making it less London-centric than its predecessor. In addition, unlike the old Court, the Court now has jurisdiction over welfare matters, finance, and property. As well as having declaratory and decision-making powers and the ability to appoint deputies, the Court exercises the inherent jurisdiction for people lacking capacity and disputes arising from LPAs. In urgent cases, Section 48 MCA 2005 enables the Court to make interim orders and directions if there is 'reason to believe' the person lacks the necessary capacity on a matter within its jurisdiction where a delay is not in the person's best interests. Section 48 involves balancing the state's duty to promote independent decision-making by adults with its obligation to protect vulnerable persons and prevent harm. The use of Section 48 MCA requires careful consideration and cannot be regarded as a perfunctory gateway to a protective regime. [63]

Under Section 15 MCA 2005, the Court can make declarations regarding a person's capacity to make a single decision or a series of decisions and the legality of any actions taken or 'yet to be done' concerning that person. Unlike Section 48 MCA 2005 interim orders, Section 15 requires incapacity to be established rather than there being 'a reason to believe.' An example of a declaration is E v Hammersmith and Fulham LBC.[64] An eighty-year-old woman, E, was diagnosed with dementia, schizophrenia and type II diabetes; she lacked capacity. E lived in a care home throughout the COVID-19 pandemic. Her son objected to her having a COVID-19 vaccination. Her legal representative applied to the Court for a Section 15(1)(c) MCA 2005 declaration that vaccination would be lawful. In accordance

61 See Chapter 3.

62 See J Weston, 'Managing mental incapacity in the 20th century: A history of the Court of Protection of England & Wales' (2020) *International Journal of Law and Psychiatry* 68, 101524.

63 *DP v Hillingdon LBC* [2020] EWCOP 45, (2021) 180 BMLR 179.

64 [2021] EWCOP 7, [2021] EWCOP 7.

with the best interests test in the MCA 2005, the Court considered the son's opinions on what would be most beneficial for her. However, it concluded that his views 'were a facet of his own temperament' rather than reflecting E's character. E had willingly accepted the flu vaccination and appeared to trust the healthcare professionals caring for her. Hayden J concluded that vaccination was in E's best interest and, therefore, lawful.

> By virtue of her vulnerabilities, the prospects for her if she contracts the virus are not propitious; it is a risk of death, and it is required to be confronted as such. The vaccination reduces that risk dramatically and I have no hesitation in concluding that it is in her best interests to receive it. Accordingly, I make the declaration, sought by Mrs E's representatives, pursuant to section 15 MCA 2005.[65]

There is some uncertainty about the meaning of an act 'yet to be done' in Section 15 MCA 2005. Does this permit the court to make a pre-incapacity declaration whose coming into effect would be contingent on future loss of capacity? In Guys and St Thomas' NHS Foundation Trust v R,[66] the Court held that declarations could be made to anticipate future incapacity; they would take effect if capacity were lost. Under this approach, it would be possible in some cases to have contingency plans in place, such as a healthcare decision, where an older person has capacity, but it is declining. This would enable a proactive approach, possibly avoiding a reactive crisis response at the point of incapacity. In a later case, Mostyn J disagreed. He argues,

> In my judgment, the court cannot make a proleptic finding of incapacity, saying, pursuant to s2(4) [MCA 2005], that it is satisfied that it is more likely than not that at some point in the future that the person will lose capacity. This is because Part 1 of the [MCA 2005] only applies to persons who are presently incapacitated, not to persons who are not incapacitated but who might become at some point in the future incapacitated.[67]

Thus, Section 15 declarations are restricted to those who have already lost capacity, and anticipatory declarations are inconsistent with the MCA 2005. Mostyn J's approach is more compatible with the wording and intentions of the MCA 2005, although maybe at the expense of anticipatory planning.

Under section 16 MCA 2005, the Court may issue orders making decisions on behalf of the person, or appoint a deputy, in relation to personal welfare, or property and affairs. The role of the deputy is to help somebody make a decision or, if that is not possible, decide on their behalf. Section 20(1) MCA 2005 makes it clear that the deputy does not have the power to decide if they know or have

65 ibid [19].
66 [2020] EWCOP 4, [2020] 4 W.L.R. 96.
67 *An NHS Foundation Trust v Amira (by her litigation friend, the Official Solicitor)* [2023] EWCOP 25, [2023] 6 WLUK 145, [35].

reasonable grounds for believing that the person has capacity. This reflects the underpinning principle that capacity is subject and time-sensitive. They must act in the person's best interests and adhere to the terms imposed by the Court. An annual report should be made to the Office of Public Guardian explaining their decisions. Deputies must be at least eighteen and can be relatives or friends. A professional, such as an accountant or lawyer, may also be appointed in cases involving significant sums of money or assets. The Court can grant powers and impose duties on a deputy. Any powers given to a deputy should be limited in scope and time as is reasonably practicable, which aligns with the Principles in Section 1(6) MCA 2005, namely the least restrictive intervention. Deputies can be removed if they behave in a way that contradicts the authority given under the deputyship or propose to do so. According to Section 16(4) MCA 2005, a court decision is preferred over the appointment of a deputy, although deputies are more appropriate if a series of decisions or ongoing supervision is required. They are more likely for property and financial affairs than personal welfare as Section 5 MCA 2005 protects ongoing personal welfare decision-makers. When the Court makes a decision or appoints a deputy under Section 16 MCA 2005, the Section 1 MCA 2005 Principles apply as do the provisions of Section 4, the best interests.

Regarding Section.16 MCA 2005 personal welfare decisions for older persons, the Court may, under Section 17 decide on living arrangements, social interactions, restricting contact with specific persons, providing or withholding consent for healthcare, and designating a different person to provide healthcare. There are many examples of such decisions. In UR v Derby City Council,[68] the issue before the Court was whether it was in the best interest of a sixty-eight-year-old nursing home patient lacking capacity to return home to Poland and be cared for by her family. It was held that it had power under Section 15 to make a declaration on her lack of capacity. A decision could then be made under Section 16 to specify where she should live based on what was in her best interests. The evidence supported the move back to Poland. A similar issue arose in AC (Capacity: Hoarding: Best Interests).[69] A ninety-two-year-old woman lacked the capacity to consent to return home to live with her son, who suffered from a hoarding disorder. A trial of living at home would involve a manageable risk and would be in her best interests. In this case, the Court appointed a property and affairs deputy. The advantage of a deputy was that, as part of the attempts to address the hoarding, the deputy could give precise directions and perform inspections. These cases illustrate the difference between the Court making a one-off decision, as in the UR case, and cases where a degree of ongoing supervision and decisions are required, as in AC. The appointment of a deputy prevents constant referrals back to the Court.

Restrictions are imposed on a welfare deputy by Section 20 MCA 2005. Unlike under a Court direction, the deputy cannot restrict contact with a named person or require somebody different to take over healthcare. They cannot do anything

68 [2021] EWCOP 10, [2021] 1 WLUK 399.
69 [2022] EWCOP 3, [2022] 2 WLUK 59.

inconsistent with a valid LPA. Also excluded from their powers is the refusal to consent to life-sustaining treatment. Restraint by a deputy of an older person to protect them from harm is only allowed if the Court has granted authority, the person lacks or the deputy reasonably believes they lack capacity, and restraint is necessary to prevent harm. Any restraint must be proportionate to the likelihood of suffering harm and its seriousness.[70]

The Court's power under Section 16 MCA 2005 concerning property and finance are extensive and include,

1. Managing and controlling property.
2. Selling, exchanging, charging, gifting, or disposing of property.
3. Acquiring property in the person's name or on their behalf.
4. Conducting any profession, trade or business on behalf of the person.
5. Making decisions dissolving a partnership in which the person is a member.
6. Fulfilling any contracts entered into by the person.
7. Settling debts and obligations, whether legally enforceable or not.
8. Settling any property belonging to the person, whether for their benefit or others.
9. Executing a will for a person eighteen years or older.
10. Exercising any power vested in the person, whether beneficially or as a trustee or otherwise.
11. Conducting legal proceedings in the person's name or on their behalf.[71]

As with a welfare deputy, Section 20 MCA 2005 limits the authority a deputy can be given. Deputies cannot be authorised to settle property, carry out powers granted to the person as a beneficiary or trustee, or make a will; only the Court can do these through a decision under Section 16 MCA 2005.[72] Deputies must act according to the terms of the appointment.

Problems arise when an older person with little or no capacity inherits money or property intestate or via a will that does not consider the possibility of exploitation. How can they be protected? A reference to the Court will often be necessary. In Watt v ABC,[73] the decision involved whether a substantial personal injury settlement should be administered by a deputy or through a trust executed under the powers of the Court. There was a fear that the person lacked the capacity to make significant decisions and was vulnerable to abuse. The Court held that appointing a deputy had advantages over a trust. A trust is governed by trust law and the trust deed; compared to a deputyship, it is rigid. Section 20(1) provided flexibility and promoted autonomy. It provided a structure for the deputy to allow the person to

70 MCA 2005 Section 20(7)–(12).
71 ibid Section 18(1).
72 ibid Section 20(3).
73 [2016] EWCOP 2532, [2017] 4 W.L.R. 24.

make decisions when they could and decide for them when they could not. The Court emphasised that each case involves a detailed weighing of the evidence.

In addition to the Court of Protection, the Office of Public Guardian safeguards against abuse. It has an overall supervisory role over attorneys and deputies and maintains a register of people acting as such. Any concerns should be reported to the OPG, who will take action. It will investigate reports of abuse or neglect. The OPG also registers LPAs.[74] In addition, the Lord Chancellor may appoint Court of Protection Visitors to assist the OPG in supervising deputies. They can visit clients, deputies, attorneys, and agencies such as social services and care home managers and provide written reports to the OPG or Court.[75]

When hearing cases, the Court needs to involve older persons with impaired capacity as much as possible. Though they may be unable to decide, their opinions should still be considered. According to Section 1(3) MCA 2005, a person should not be treated as unable to decide unless all possible steps have been taken to assist them. While much preparation may take place before the Court hearing, the proceedings must acknowledge and uphold this Principle. More research is needed to ensure that participation is achieved. Watkins et al. note that there can be confusion around the definition of participation and the lack of training, resources, and time to implement it fully.

> To date there has been a notable lack of special measures legislation for the [Court of Protection] and of financial backing from the Ministry of Justice for the introduction of participation-enabling technology as standard in [Court of Protection] courtrooms. The absence of a special measures scheme together with the risks and ambiguity of purpose associated with judges meeting with P, creates the same barriers to participation that have troubled the Family Court in its attempt to support the participation of vulnerable adults and children.[76]

Ruck Keene et al. report on the cases brought before the Court. In 32.5% of cases, dementia and related disorders were cited as the reason for lack of capacity, although multiple capacity issues were often mentioned. The main issues where capacity was contested were residence (42.5%) and care (37.5%). Property and affairs accounted for 20% of cases. The authors underline the necessity of the Court and all decision-makers being able to clearly explain the basis of their decisions in a way that addresses statutory criteria transparently and robustly, ensuring a clear and accountable process.[77]

74 MCA 2005 Sections 57–60.

75 ibid Section 61.

76 M Watkins, P Cooper, and R Stickler, 'Participation in the Court of Protection: A search for purpose' (2022) *International Journal of Mental Health and Capacity Law* 29(3) 21.

77 A Ruck Keene, N B Kane, S Y Kim, et al. 'Taking capacity seriously? Ten years of mental capacity disputes before England's Court of Protection' (2019) *International Journal of Law and Psychiatry* 56-76, 62.

The inherent jurisdiction

The MCA 2005 introduced a comprehensive and codified law on mental capacity. It defines incapacity and provides a set of principles and a framework within which decisions can be made affecting the well-being of older persons who lack capacity. Before the MCA 2005, decisions were made using the inherent jurisdiction of the High Court. The House of Lords in the 1990 case of Re F (Mental Patient: Sterilisation)[78] decided that in the absence of any legislation, the High Court could, under the inherent jurisdiction, declare that a proposed operation was in the patient's best interests. Today, the case would fall within the MCA 2005. Does that mean the inherent jurisdiction no longer has a role? Traditionally, the jurisdiction exists to protect those who cannot protect themselves and fall outside existing legislative frameworks such as the MCA 2005 or the Mental Health Act 1983. It recognises that the ability to decide may be compromised by reasons other than mental capacity, highlighting its crucial role in protecting vulnerable persons.

There is a case for the inherent jurisdiction, although the vagueness of its boundaries is concerning. The MCA 2005 only applies to people assessed as lacking mental capacity under Part 1. In the absence of legislation, the inherent jurisdiction provides a residual means of safeguarding 'vulnerable' persons who may be coerced into making decisions against their free will and may need protection. An example of the use of the inherent jurisdiction is A Local Authority v DL.[79] This involved an application by a local authority to use the inherent jurisdiction to protect D's parents, who were eighty-nine and ninety years old. Both parents had mental capacity. The local authority alleged that D physically assaulted his parents, threatened them, prevented them from leaving the house, and controlled who could visit them, including health and social care professionals. It was further alleged that D was trying to coerce his parents into transferring their house to him and to have his mother removed into a care home against her wishes. There was evidence from a social worker that the ability of his parents to make decisions was compromised by his behaviour or prevented altogether. D argued that as his parents fell outside of the MCA 2005, the court had no jurisdiction to intervene.

In a comprehensive review of existing case law, McFarlane LJ recognised the importance of individual autonomy. He said there is a strong argument for the inherent jurisdiction to be available in such cases. In this case, the jurisdiction was used to' enhance or liberate the autonomy of a vulnerable adult' where it has been compromised by a reason other than mental incapacity. He described the jurisdiction as follows.

78 [1990] 2 AC 1.

79 *A Local Authority v DL* [2012] EWCA Civ 253, [2013] Fam 1. See Munby J in Re SA (Vulnerable adult with capacity: Marriage) [2005] EWHC 2942 (Fam), [2006] 1 FLR 867; Theis J in DL Local Authority [2011] EWHC 1022 (Fam), [2012] 1 FLR 1119; and A Local Authority v EBY and others [2023] EWHC 2494 (Fam), [2024] 2 WLR 579.

> The question for consideration is whether, despite the extensive territory now occupied by the MCA 2005, a jurisdictional hinterland exists outside its borders to deal with cases of 'vulnerable adults' who fall outside that Act and which are determined under the inherent jurisdiction.[80]

The judge approved the reasoning of Munby J and Theis J. He held that the safety net jurisdiction should be available in cases where a person is at risk, including where they are:

1. Under constraint.
2. Subject to coercion or undue influence.
3. For some other reason, they are deprived of the capacity to make the relevant decision, or disabled from making a free choice, or incapacitated or disabled from giving or expressing real and genuine consent.[81]

This approach aligns with Article 8 ECHR, as it seeks to protect the parents' rights to private and family life while ensuring their safety and well-being. As Davies LJ put it,

> It would be most unfortunate if, by reference to their personal autonomy, they were to be beyond the reach of judicial protection. For the reasons given by my Lords, they are not.[82]

The Court of Appeal approved Macur J's reasoning in LBL v RYJ and VJ that the objective was to facilitate the process of unencumbered decision-making free of external pressure or physical restraint.[83]

The need for a facilitative rather than a dictatorial approach featured in Islington LBC v EF,[84] where the Court was asked to prevent a vulnerable young woman who had capacity, from travelling abroad to continue what the local authority regarded as an inappropriate relationship with a man. Its decision emphasised that the power was to be used sparingly. The jurisdiction should only be used to enhance Article 8 rights; in this case, it would have the opposite effect. A worldwide travel ban would be highly intrusive. The instinctive desire to protect vulnerable people against 'bad decisions' should not overpower their right to choose if they have the capacity. There was a similar reluctance to intervene in Southend-on-Sea BC v Meyers.[85] It involved a ninety-eight-year-old man who was blind and diabetic but otherwise in good health. He lived with his son, with whom, in the court's words, he had a dysfunctional relationship that was felt to be the essence of his vulnerability. His

80 ibid *A v Local Authority* [1].
81 ibid [54].
82 ibid [79].
83 [2010] EWHC 2665 (Fam), [2010] 9 WLUK 378.
84 [2022] EWHC 803 (Fam), [2022] 3 WLUK 548.
85 [2019] EWHC 399 (Fam), (2019) 168 B.M.L.R. 91.

decision-making was compromised, but not due to his son's coercive influence. Instead, the intensity of their relationship damaged his ability to make rational and informed decisions. The court refused to intervene in his decision-making power to protect him from his unwise choices as he had capacity; a well-intentioned desire to protect him from his unwise decisions was a dangerous course that threatened personal autonomy.

The DL decision is not without its critics or those who have reservations about its implications.[86] The understandable fear is that it could lead to over-interference in autonomy. This is a genuine concern. However, given the current law, what else could be done to protect the parents in the DL case? The parents could not exercise their autonomy; their son deprived them of that. It must not be forgotten that the use of the inherent jurisdiction helped shape the MCA 2005. But in using the jurisdiction to address the legislative lacunae, there was judicial unease that it operated on a case-by-case basis. In the pre-MCA 2005 case of Re F (2000), Sedley LJ stated the problem faced by the court where the person was unable to judge what was in her best interests and concluded that 'no humane society could leave her adrift and at risk simply because she has reached the age of 18.'[87] However, Butler-Sloss emphasised that using the inherent jurisdiction does not lessen the need for a well-structured and clear statutory framework for protecting adults lacking mental capacity. The inherent jurisdiction is meant to address individual problems and not to provide general guidance; it is there in the absence of other practicable options. The lack of a statutory framework for incapacity was addressed by the MCA 2005. Should a similar legal framework be created to protect people unable to make decisions due to coercion or other vulnerabilities? It would need to include robust safeguards but could reduce the need to resort to the inherent jurisdiction.

The case for such legislation encounters three issues. To whom would such a jurisdiction apply? What would the reach of the legislation be? What safeguards would there be against unjustified intrusions into personal autonomy? Existing case law discusses these issues, particularly the dangers of overreach in an attempt to protect people from themselves. The Meyers and the LBC case give some insight into how restrictions may be imposed. Importantly, in the case of an older person, such as the man in the Meyers case, care must be taken not to be overprotective to the point of violating Article 8 rights. Getting the balance right is challenging but best achieved within a statutory framework rather than a case-by-case approach of the inherent jurisdiction. Careful consideration should be given to the safeguards needed. It would be impossible to anticipate all circumstances. The Joint Committee of the House of Lords and House of Commons considered extending the Mental Capacity Bill to include the inability to decide caused by undue

86 See, for example, E Cave, 'Protecting patients from their bad decisions: Rebalancing rights, relationships, and risk' (2017) *Medical Law Review* 25(4) 527; L Pritchard-Jones, '"Palm tree justice": The Inherent Jurisdiction in Adult Welfare Cases' (2023) *The Modern Law Review 86(6)* 1358-1389; B Hewson, 'Neither Midwives Nor Rainmakers: Why "DL" is wrong' (2013) *Public Law* 3 451.

87 *Re F (Adult: Court's Jurisdiction)* [2001] Fam 38, 54.

influence or coercion. However, the Committee did not feel confident in recommending this.[88] Nevertheless, there is an argument for a statutory framework that addresses vulnerabilities other than lack of capacity and provides statutory safeguards and definitions. These safeguards should balance protection and autonomy and minimise reliance on a case-by-case approach.

End-of-life decisions

Withdrawing treatment

End-of-life decisions can be among the most challenging for older persons, whether deciding for themselves or their loved ones. In such cases, an older person with the capacity to act freely can refuse life-sustaining treatment or request its withdrawal. This is an absolute right, regardless of what doctors or family members may think of the decision. In Re B (Consent to Treatment: Capacity),[89] a patient with tetraplegia asked to be taken off the ventilator, but the hospital refused. Butler-Sloss P highlighted the dangers of benevolent paternalism, which fails to recognise the personal autonomy of severely disabled patients. Despite her disabilities, the patient had the necessary capacity. She was entitled to exercise her right to end life-sustaining treatment, which must be respected despite the well-intentioned reservations of the doctors. When involved in these decisions, the General Medical Council's guidance requires doctors to identify clinically appropriate options, which may include taking no action. These must be discussed with the patient; whereas doctors may recommend, they must not pressurise the patient. For the older patient, a discussion is necessary to ensure that their wishes and feelings are fully considered and that ageist assumptions do not influence the decision-making process.[90] Research has found that older LGBT+ people face inequalities in end-of-life care and bereavement support. Non-disclosure of their relationships adds to the worry, making the grieving process more difficult. Specialised care and support services are needed to ensure they receive compassionate and appropriate care.[91] After weighing the pros and cons, a patient can accept or refuse an option without the need to justify their decision. A patient may request a particular form of treatment which the doctor considers clinically inappropriate. Although this enables the doctor to explore the reasons behind the request, the treatment should not be provided if the doctor believes it would not help the patient. The doctor's clinical judgement prevails; however, the reason for refusing the request must be explained to the patient.

88 Joint Committee (n34) 270.

89 [2002] EWHC 429 (Fam), [2002] 2 All E.R. 449.

90 General Medical Council 'Treatment and care towards the end of life: Good practice in decision making' (2022) <https://www.gmc-uk.org/professional-standards/professional-standards-for-doctors/treatment-and-care-towards-the-end-of-life> – accessed 28 September 2024.

91 D Kneale, J Henley, J Thomas, et al., 'Inequalities in older LGBT people's health and care needs in the United Kingdom: A systematic scoping review' (2021) *Ageing & Society* 41(3) 493.

Where a patient lacks mental capacity and has no relevant LPA or AD, the decision is made using the best interests test. Section 4(5) MCA 2005 says that in deciding whether commencing or continuing life-sustaining treatment is in the patient's best interests, the decision-maker must not be motivated by a desire to bring about their death. This is consistent with Section 62 MCA 2005, which clarifies that nothing in the Act affects the law of murder, manslaughter, or suicide. In NHS Trust v L,[92] it was decided that it was not in the best interests of a patient with extremely severe anorexia nervosa, who was in the closing stages of her life, to be subjected to forcible feeding. In making the best interests assessment, the Court of Protection recognised the futility of the proposed treatment and the likelihood that it would cause her death. The declaration sought to alleviate distress and allow her to die with dignity with her family around her. Airedale NHS Trust v Bland, a pre-MCA 2005 case, was followed.[93] Bland held there was a strong presumption that preserving life is in a patient's best interest, but that is not sacrosanct and can be rebutted. In making a decision, all the factors in Section 4 MCA 2005 must be considered, particularly the views of those involved in the patient's care and any ascertainable past and present wishes. The patient's wishes and feelings will be significant but must be considered along with 'all the relevant circumstances.'[94]

Suicide

Under Section 1 Suicide Act 1961, suicide ceased to be a crime, but Section 2 makes it an offence to intentionally encourage or assist another person to attempt or commit suicide. This follows the general rule that taking another person's life is a crime. The compatibility of Section 2 with the ECHR has been challenged, particularly where the person has the capacity but is physically unable to end their life. In R (on the application of Conway) v Secretary of State for Justice,[95] the appellant was a sixty-eight-year-old man diagnosed with motor neurone disease; he had less than six months to live. He requested,

> I would like to be able to seek assistance from a medical professional so that I may be prescribed medication which I can self-ingest to end my life successfully, if I wish to do so. If I am unable to take the medication by drinking a prescribed medication, I would also be prepared to receive medication in a different format, by activating a switch for example. I do not believe that unsupervised alternative methods of suicide are humane or acceptable and would be additionally distressing for my loved ones.

92 [2012] EWHC 2741 (COP), [2012] 8 WLUK 345.
93 *Bland* (n49).
94 *Local Authority X v MM (by the Official Solicitor) and KM* [2007] EWHC 2003 (Fam), [2009] 1 FLR 443, [121]-[124] and MCA 2005 Section 4(2).
95 [2018] EWCA Civ 1431, [2020] QB 1.

In his submission, he proposed an alternative scheme for assisted suicide containing safeguards and criteria. He did not wish his life to continue beyond the point where he could not enjoy it. Section 2 amounted, he argued, to a blanket ban and denied him the assistance of a medical professional who would enable him to die humanely. Was it a valid interference with his Article 8 ECHR right? Was it 'necessary in a democratic society for the purposes of the protection of health and morals and the protection of the rights of others'? The Court of Appeal dismissed his appeal on the grounds that the legitimate aims of the section were to protect the weak and vulnerable, preserve the sanctity of life and promote trust between patient and doctor.

The General Medical Council has published guidance for doctors where patients seek advice or information on assistance to die. Suppose a patient raises the issue or asks for information that might encourage or assist in taking their own life. In that case, the guidance clarifies that respecting patient autonomy cannot justify illegal action. The doctor should explain that assisted suicide is a criminal offence, be objective about any lawful clinical options such as sedation or palliative care, and explore whether there are any unmet needs for palliative care, such as pain management. At all times, they should be respectful and compassionate. Nothing in the Guidance prevents doctors from prescribing medicine or treatments to alleviate pain or other symptoms.[96] Following recent activity in the courts and Parliament, the British Medical Association in 2021 reviewed its stance on physician-assisted suicide, or more appropriately, physician-assisted dying, and moved to a position of neutrality. A 2020 survey of members showed that 50% personally supported changing the law on prescribing drugs for eligible patients to self-administer to end their own lives, 39% were neutral, and 11% were undecided. When asked what the BMA's position should be on changing the law on doctors administering drugs to end an eligible patient's life, 30% were supportive, 23% neutral, 40% opposed, and 7% undecided.[97]

Mercy killings

There has been much media coverage of mercy killings involving the ending of another person's life who is very ill, which reflects the settled decision of that person and is a way of relieving suffering and avoiding a long, drawn-out, undignified death. The compassionate motive behind a mercy killing is irrelevant in deciding

96 General Medical Council, 'Patients seeking advice or information about assistance to die' (2022) <https://www.gmc-uk.org/professional-standards/professional-standards-for-doctors/when-a-patient-seeks-advice-or-information-about-assistance-to-die/when-a-patient-seeks-advice-or-information-about-assistance-to-die> accessed 28 September 2024.

97 British Medical Association, 'Physician-assisted dying' (2023) <<https://www.bma.org.uk/advice-and-support/ethics/end-of-life/physician-assisted-dying> – accessed 28 September 2024; British Medical Association, 'Physician-assisted dying survey' (2023) <https://www.bma.org.uk/advice-and-support/ethics/end-of-life/physician-assisted-dying/physician-assisted-dying-survey> – accessed 28 September 2024.

whether it is murder, although it may be a mitigating factor in sentencing. The question arises whether prosecutions are in the public interest, which is one of the factors that must be considered by the Crown Prosecution Service (CPS) when deciding on prosecution. Recently, the CPS revised its guidance on when it will prosecute mercy killing cases.[98] After strongly emphasising that acting to end the life of another with the intention to kill is murder, it sets out factors in favour of and against a prosecution. Among the thirteen factors in favour of prosecution are the victim's lack of capacity under the MCA 2005, no evidence of a clear and settled informed decision, the victim was physically able to take their own life, the suspect was not wholly motivated by compassion, and the suspect was acting in their capacity as a healthcare provider. Prosecution is less likely, although the guidance states that it will probably happen, if, among other things, there is a voluntary, clear and settled intention on the part of the victim and they have mental capacity, the suspect is motivated by compassion, and the suspect's actions may be characterised as reluctant. However, the Director of Public Prosecutions has stressed that the starting point is that prosecution is almost always required in the public interest because the suspect has 'culpably taken the life of another.' He did not envisage that the new guidelines would lead to fewer prosecutions.[99]

Suicide pacts

A related issue is suicide packs. These are defined by Section 4(3) Homicide Act 1957 as a common agreement between two or more people which has as its objective the death of them all. The intention is that they end their lives together. For example, an eighty-year-old woman gave her terminally ill husband a fatal dose of medicine. She and her husband had formed a pact to end their lives. However, despite taking the medication, she survived. The issue was whether she should be prosecuted for her husband's death. Under the 1957 Act, the surviving pact member can be charged with manslaughter and not murder. The revised CPS guidance also applies to decisions to prosecute the survivor of a suicide pact. One factor against a prosecution is that the survivor simultaneously attempted to end their own life. However, the essential caveat, which must not be minimised, is that prosecution is highly likely.

98 Crown Prosecution Service, 'Homicide: Murder, manslaughter, infanticide and causing or allowing the death or serious injury of a child or vulnerable adult' (2023) <https://www.cps.gov.uk/legal-guidance/homicide-murder-manslaughter-infanticide-and-causing-or-allowing-death-or-serious> – accessed 28 September 2024.

99 J Rosenberg, 'New guidance for mercy killings' (*A Lawyer Writes*, 5 October 2023). <https://open.substack.com/pub/rozenberg/p/new-guidance-for-mercy-killings-333?r=1qy0s9&utm_medium=ios&utm_campaign=post> – accessed 28 September 2024.

Assisted dying

In many ways, the ultimate decision in life is whether to continue living. It involves complex issues such as dignity, family, prognosis, enjoyment of life, and what can be done to mitigate suffering. Many attempts have been made in Parliament and the courts to change the absolute position of the law, and they have not been successful. The court's message is that this is an issue for Parliament, which is correct. Such a law cannot be developed on a case-by-case basis. Safeguards are needed against abuse. It is also essential that palliative care must be readily available to those facing such decisions. If the law is changed, a right to good palliative care must be included to ensure that the choice is not between ending life now and enduring avoidable suffering. Backbench MP Kim Leadbeater introduced the Terminally Ill Adults (End of Life) Bill in the Westminster Parliament in October 2024. If passed, it will allow terminally ill adults to seek assistance in ending their lives. The Bill incorporates safeguards to protect vulnerable persons, but some question whether these are sufficiently robust. The eligibility criteria stipulate that applicants must be at least 16 years old, diagnosed with a terminal illness, and possess the mental capacity to make such a request. A terminal illness is defined as an advanced, progressive, and incurable condition expected to lead to death within six months. The applicant must make the decision free of coercion. The Bill requires that two medical practitioners (the coordinating doctor and the independent doctor) must confirm the diagnosis of a terminal illness. A 14-day reflection period is included, during which the applicant can reconsider the decision. To qualify for assisted dying, a person must have resided in the United Kingdom for at least one year. Although the Bill was approved at the second reading in the House of Commons, many issues remain to be resolved during the committee stage, particularly concerning the involvement of the courts. After an initial declaration and evaluation by the two doctors, the original drafting of the bill required approval from the High Court as one of the principal safeguards. The High Court would approve if satisfied that the applicant meets the criteria, including being terminally ill, having decision-making capacity, and making the declaration voluntarily and without coercion. The applicant and the doctors may be required to appear before the Court. Concerns were raised regarding whether the court system has the capacity to hear applications quickly enough. Additionally, there are questions about their ability to properly investigate potential coercion as such behaviour is often difficult to prove and may involve evidence going back many years. The inclusion of an advocate for the applicant is a necessary safeguard and must be included. An amendment proposed at the committee stage would replace the High Court with a panel of experts. This has proved controversial. Some older people may feel pressured into agreeing to assisted dying as they do not wish to be a burden. Such internal and societal coercion may be even more difficult to prove. Accurately diagnosing how long a person has to live can be difficult, and a case has been made to extend the period to twelve months. Once the Court or expert panel approves, the applicant must then make a second declaration, after a fourteen-day reflection period, consenting to assistance in ending their life. The coordinating doctor provides and prepares the approved substance for self-administration but does not administer it. The person must take the final act of self-administration. The doctor stays with the person until the procedure is completed or cancelled. Finally, after assistance has been provided and the person has passed away, the coordinating doctor is responsible for completing a final statement for the person's medical records. Despite the safeguards in the Bill, it may face legal challenges regarding human rights, particularly concerning Article 8 ECHR. However, case law from the European Court of Human Rights suggests that states have a significant margin of appreciation regarding assisted dying. Similar bills are being considered in Scotland, Jersey, and the Isle of Man.

Conclusion

The freedom to make decisions and have them respected is part of autonomy. Some older persons experience others making decisions on their behalf, even though they can decide for themselves. To take away an older person's right to choose, whether for benevolent or malevolent reasons, is wrong. For some, there may be a need for support in making decisions. This involves ensuring that they make the decision freely and have accessible information. Better access to advocacy is required to ensure older persons are not disadvantaged. An independent advocate can assist older persons and carers in understanding information, expressing needs, defending rights, and obtaining care. Under Section 67 CA 2014, older persons with significant difficulties understanding or retaining relevant information, using or weighing information as part of the process, or communicating their views, wishes, or feelings have the right to an independent advocate. This applies to assessments, creating or modifying care and support plans or support plans, a child's needs assessment, and a child or young carer's assessment. However, if the local authority is satisfied that there is somebody appropriate to represent and support the person involved who is not providing support in a professional capacity or being paid, the duty does not apply. When a local authority provides an independent advocate, it must consider the advocate's representations and provide assistance to them in supporting the person.[100] The SSWA 2014 allows for regulations to be made to provide advocacy services. However, the Welsh Government chose not to use this power and instead make provision for advocacy services through a Code of Practice. Under the Code local authorities in Wales must provide an independent professional advocate when a person needs help to participate fully but lacks somebody appropriate to assist them. The Code identifies circumstances where the need for an advocate is heightened. These include significant issues such as assessments, care planning, changes in care arrangements, safeguarding inquiries, and hospital discharges. Advocates are also necessary when external factors, such as provider failures or care home closures. If there is disagreement regarding the need for an independent advocate, the person must be informed of their right to access

100 Care and Support (Independent Advocacy Support) (No 2) Regulations 2014, SI 2014/2889.

the complaints procedure and be provided with the necessary support.[101] A 2024 study reveals a concerning decline in both the number of services and people supported in Wales, indicating systemic issues within the advocacy framework. The study highlights the increasing complexity of cases handled by advocates, leading to greater demands on their time and resources[102]. Other specialised advocacy and support services are available in both nations. An Independent Mental Health Advocate may be appointed under the Mental Health Act 1983 and an Independent Mental Capacity Advocate under the MCA 2005. Independent Sexual Violence Advisors (ISVA) and Independent Domestic Violence Advisors (IDVA) provide practical, emotional or moral support for victims of violence and assist and support them in engaging with the court process and out-of-court discussions. Third-sector organisations also provide advocacy services, including advocacy for persons living with dementia and their carers.

Many older persons are perfectly adept at making decisions, sometimes with significant consequences for how they live and where they live. Others may need help with decision-making even though they have capacity. Supporting these older persons in making decisions, rather than assuming a benevolent approach, is necessary out of respect for their autonomy. Advice, guidance, and other forms of support are often helpful. However, a careful balance must be struck to ensure the decision is freely made. The provision of information in an appropriate and accessible form is essential. Wherever possible, decision-making must be at the older person's pace, although speed may be needed in an emergency. Delaying a decision, when possible, may be beneficial, allowing the older person to mull something over to arrive at a thoughtful decision truly reflecting their wishes.

Bibliography

Age Cymru, 'A Review of Advocacy Services for Adults in Wales with a Particular Focus on Older People ' (2024) <https://www.agecymru.wales/siteassets/documents/gtap/advocacy-counts/age-cymru-advocacy-counts-9-english.pdf> accessed> 5 February 2025

British Association of Social Workers, 'The BASW Code of Ethics for Social Work' (July 2021) <https://new.basw.co.uk/sites/default/files/resources/basw_code_of_ethics_-_2021.pdf, 10> - accessed 28 September 2024.

British Medical Association, 'Physician-assisted dying' (2023) <https://www.bma.org.uk/advice-and-support/ethics/end-of-life/physician-assisted-dying>
accessed 28 September 2024.

British Medical Association, 'Physician-assisted dying survey' (2023) <https://www.bma.org.uk/advice-and-support/ethics/end-of-life/physician-assisted-dying/physician-assisted-dying-survey> - accesssed 28 September 2024.

101 Welsh Government 'Social services and well-being (wales) act 2014 part 10 code of practice (advocacy)' (2015) https://gov.wales/sites/default/files/publications/2019-05/part-10-code-of-practice-advocacy.pdf – accessed 28 September 2024.

102 Age Cymru, 'A Review of Advocacy Services for Adults in Wales with a Particular Focuson Older People ' (2024) accessed 5 February2025

Cave E, 'Protecting patients from their bad decisions: Rebalancing rights, relationships, and risk' (2017) *Medical Law Review* 25(4) 527.

Crown Prosecution Service, 'Homicide: Murder, Manslaughter, Infanticide and Causing or Allowing the Death or Serious Injury of a Child or Vulnerable Adult' (2023) https://www.cps.gov.uk/legal-guidance/homicide-murder-manslaughter-infanticide-and-causing-or-allowing-death-or-serious - accessed 28 September 2024.

Curtice M, Katuwawela I, and McCollum R, 'Lasting Powers of Attorney: Implications for clinicians' (2012) *Advances in Psychiatric Treatment* 18(3) 205.

Department for Constitutional Affairs, *Mental Capacity Act 2005 Code of Practice* (The Stationery Office, 2007).

Duddles M, 'The Powers of Attorney Act 2023 - How far does it go to protect the vulnerable?' (2023) - <https://www.bondsolon.com/news-and-insights/the-powers-of-attorney-act-2023-how-far-does-it-go-to-protect-the-vulnerable/> - accessed 28 September 2024.

Finnerty AM, 'The privilege of information - An examination of the defence of therapeutic privilege and its implications for pregnant women' (2021) *Medical Law Review* 29, 639.

General Medical Council, 'Decision making and consent' (2020) <https://www.gmc-uk.org/professional-standards/the-professional-standards/decision-making-and-consent> - accessed 28 September 2024.

General Medical Council, 'Ethical guidance for doctors: Practical steps to include older adults in their care' (2024) <https://www.gmc-uk.org/professional-standards/ethical-hub/older-adults#Age-discrimination> - accessed 28 September 2024.

General Medical Council, 'Patients seeking advice or information about assistance to die' (2022) https://www .gmc -uk .org /professional -standards /professional -standards -for -doctors /when -a-patient -seeks -advice -or -information -about -assistance -to -die / when -a -patient -seeks -advice -or-information -about -assistance -to -die - accessed 28 September 2024.

General Medical Council, 'Treatment and care towards the end of life: Good practice in decision making' (2022) https://www.gmc-uk.org/professional-standards/professional-standards-for-doctors/treatment-and-care-towards-the-end-of-life - accessed 28 September 2024.

Grubb A, Laing J, McHale J, et al. Principles of Medical Law (OUP 2010) para 4.114 citing the Ontario Court of Appeal decision in Malette v. Shulman (Ont. C.A.), 1990 CanLII 6868 (ON CA).

Hewson B, 'Neither midwives nor rainmakers: Why "DL" is wrong' (2013) *Public Law* 3, 451.

House of Lords and House of Commons Joint Committee on the draft mental incapacity bill (2003 HL 189-I, HC 1083-I).

Kneale D, Henley J, Thomas J, et al. 'Inequalities in older LGBT people's health and care needs in the United Kingdom: A systematic scoping review' (2021) *Ageing & Society* 41(3) 493.

Lyne M and Parker J, 'From Ovid to Covid: The metamorphosis of advanced decisions to refuse treatment into a safeguarding issue' (2020) *Journal of Adult Protection* 22(6) 361.

MacLeod J, 'Double duty: McCulloch v Forth Valley Health Board' (2024) *Edinburgh Law Review* 28(1) 130.

Milo C, 'The law and ethics of informed consent after Montgomery and the safeguard of patients' safety' in Tingle J, Milo C, Msikska G and Millar R (eds) *Research handbook on patient safety and the law* (Edward Elgar Publishing, 2023) 22.

Mulheron R, 'The defence of therapeutic privilege in Australia' (2003) *Journal of Law and Medicine* 11, 201.

O'Sullivan OP, 'Financial abuse, statutory provisions and the courts: Adequacy and analysis of enduring and lasting powers of attorney' (2021) *The Journal of Adult Protection* 23(4) 253.

Pierce J, 'The older client practice' in Bielanska C (ed.) *Elderly Client Handbook* (Legal Handbooks, 6 edn The Law Society, 2019) 98.

Pritchard-Jones L, '"Palm tree justice": The inherent jurisdiction in adult welfare cases' (2023) *The Modern Law Review 86(6) 1358-1389.*

Reamer F, 'Informed consent in social work' (1987) *Social Work* 32(5) 425.

Ries NM, 'Enduring powers of attorney and financial exploitation of older people: A conceptual analysis and strategies for prevention' (2022) *Journal of Aging & Social Policy* 34(3) 357.

Rosenberg J, 'New guidance for mercy killings' (*A Lawyer Writes*, 5 October 2023) https://open.substack.com/pub/rozenberg/p/new-guidance-for-mercy-killings-333?r=1qy0s9&utm_medium=ios&utm_campaign=post - accessed 28 September 2024.

Ruck Keene A, Kane NB, Kim SY, et al. 'Taking capacity seriously? Ten years of mental capacity disputes before England's Court of Protection' (2019) *International Journal of Law and Psychiatry* 56-76.

Solicitors Regulatory Authority, 'Guidance: Client care letters' (2019) https://www.sra.org.uk/solicitors/guidance/client-care-letters/ - accessed 28 September 2024.

Stanyer A, 'Lasting powers of attorney - Are they good enough protection against financial abuse' (2017) *The Elder Law Journal* 23, 225.

Stephens C, Stanyer A, Anderson R, et al. 'Changing policy landscape around elder abuse in England and Wales' (2024) *British Medical Journal* 384.

The Law Society, *Practice note: Lasting Powers of Attorney* (Law Society ,London, 2023) <https://www.mentalhealthlaw.co.uk/media/2022-08-17_Law_Society_LPA_practice_note.pdf> - accessed 28 September 2024.

Walters M, 'I would never sign a power of attorney - Retired judge' (*Law Society Gazette*, 2017) https://www.lawgazette.co.uk/law/i-would-never-sign-a-power-of-attorney-retired-judge/5062465.article - accessed 28 September 2024.

Watkins M, Cooper P, and Sticklerm R, 'Participation in the court of protection: A search for purpose' (2022) 29 *International Journal of Mental Health and Capacity Law* 3, 21.

Welsh Government, 'Social Services and Well-being (Wales) Act 2014 part 10 Code of Practice (Advocacy)' (2015) https://gov.wales/sites/default/files/publications/2019-05/part-10-code-of-practice-advocacy.pdf - accessed 28 September 2024.

Weston J, 'Managing mental incapacity in the 20th century: A history of the Court of Protection of England & Wales' (2020) *International Journal of Law and Psychiatry* 68, 101524.

Williams J, 'Taking it on the chin: Older people, human rights and COVID-19' (2021) *The Journal of Adult Protection* 23(2) 86.

Wydall S, Clarke A, Williams J, et al. 'Domestic abuse and elder abuse in Wales: A tale of two initiatives' (2018) *British Journal of Social Work* 48(4) 962.

Wydall S and Zerk R, 'Domestic abuse and older people: Factors influencing help-seeking' (2017) *The Journal of Adult Protection* 19(5) 247.

5 Older persons and social care

Introduction

Fixing social care has been an elusive goal for governments over the years, with little progress towards a solution. The term 'kicking the can down the road' aptly encapsulates the politics of social care; action is delayed rather than addressing and resolving the underlying issues. Social care faces a confluence of challenges. Lack of resources is a perennial problem as inflation has eroded any cash increases in funding. There are problems with recruiting and retaining staff to meet growing demand. Longer-term planning is frustrated by short-termism. Underpinning this is the ongoing and central debate on whether social care should be means-tested or free, a decision that could significantly impact the lives of older persons. The crisis in social care affects the provision of NHS services as a lack of social care services in care homes or the community may delay the hospital discharge of older persons; regrettably, this is often referred to as bed blocking. However, this is not the only reason for the delays in discharging patients. The Chair of the Local Government Association's Community Wellbeing Board emphasised the importance of the link between social care, hospital admissions and discharge, and the role of preventative work.

> We agree that the answer to tackling hospital pressures is a considerable bolstering of primary and community-based support – both to support discharge from hospital and to prevent people attending hospital in the first place. Councils and providers always strive to reflect, learn and improve, but it is becoming increasingly hard to fully fund statutory services.[1]

Originally, Section 74 Care Act (CA 2014) allowed the NHS in England to charge local authorities for discharge delays. If a local authority received the required

1 Local Government Association, 'Further urgent investment needed in social care – LGA on King's Fund report' (*LGA*, 14 February 2024) <https://www.local.gov.uk/about/news/further-urgent-investment-needed-social-care-lga-kings-fund-report> – accessed 28 September 2024; F Cavallaro, F Grimm, L Allen et al., *Why are delayed discharges from hospital increasing? Seeing the bigger picture* (The Health Foundation, 2003) <https://www.health.org.uk/publications/long-reads/why-are-delayed-discharges-from-hospital-increasing-seeing-the-bigger#:~:text=Social%20care%20is%20often%20seen,without%20the%20care%20they%20need> – accessed 28 September 2024.

DOI: 10.4324/9780203798058-6

notices from an NHS body but failed to perform a needs or carer's assessment, preventing safe patient discharge, the NHS body could require the authority to contribute to the cost of any delays.[2] Wales did not introduce such a scheme. Discharge delay payments were a clumsy attempt to promote integrated working. The provision was repealed by the Health and Care Act 2022. The new section now requires that an NHS Trust involves the patient and, if applicable, their carer in discharge planning.

The Law Commission's 2011 review of adult social care in England and Wales noted that the law was found in a 'disparate range of legislative provision...[which] reflects the differing policy imperatives and understandings current at various times since 1948.'[3] The Commission's report formed the basis of the CA 2014 in England and the Social Services and Well-being (Wales) Act 2014 in Wales (SSWA 2014). It initially recommended a single statute covering both nations unless policy in Wales diverged enough to require separate legislation.[4] Following the 2011 Welsh referendum approving primary law-making powers for Wales, the Commission concluded it would be 'infelicitous' to propose either a single bill or for Westminster to impose a separate bill on Wales, particularly as social care is a devolved matter.[5] The Commission suggested that, wherever possible, legislation should be consistent, not least because of the cross-border portability of social care packages. Although portability across Offa's Dyke is a practical issue, political realities must be considered. The politics of Westminster and Cardiff are not always harmonious, and a more generous devolution settlement now provides greater scope for Wales to do things differently. Whether this has been used to its full potential is debatable.[6] However, one area of difference is that the SSWA 2014 combined social care for children and adults as part of the Welsh Government's integrated social care policy. However, child protection in Wales is still covered by the Children Act 1989, whereas adult safeguarding comes within the SSWA 2014.

Older persons and social care

In 2022–23 in England, the number of new requests for publicly funded long-term social care received from older persons increased to 1.39 million in 2022–23 from 1.37 million in the previous year, reversing a decline during the COVID-19 pandemic. During this period, the number of older persons receiving long-term care rose from 529,000 to 542,545; this represents a 7.7% fall since 2015–16. Although local authorities allocated similar amounts of funding for long-term support for working-age adults (£9.1 billion) and older persons (£9.3 billion), the distribution of spending differed. Over two-thirds of the funding for eighteen to sixty-four-year-olds

2 CA 2014 Section 74 and Schedule 3 (as originally enacted).

3 Law Commission, *Adult Social Care* (Law Com No 326, 2011) para 1.2.

4 Law Commission, *Adult Social Care: A Consultation Paper* (Law Com No 192, 2011) paras 2.9–2.12

5 Law Com 326 (n3) para 3.9.

6 I Ferguson, 'Increasing user choice or privatizing risk? The antinomies of personalization' (2007) *The British Journal of Social Work* 37(3) 387.

went on community-based support, whereas for older persons, nearly two-thirds was spent on care homes.[7] The Welsh Local Government Association in its survey of the twenty-two Welsh local authorities found that over 70% reported that meeting the complex physical and mental health needs of the ageing population was a ''very high priority.' Managing this pressure is challenging due to the increased demand for social care, capacity issues causing delays in assessments, difficulties in providing adequate home-based care, rising waiting lists, and resulting delays that impact the well-being of people, particularly unpaid carers.[8]

Glasby et al. explored the growing gap between social care needs and available funding in England, referring to a 'lost decade' where warnings in 2010 were not heeded. They identified severe cutbacks in social care services and argued that these may appear more acceptable when applied to older persons. This is partly attributable to ageist attitudes and assumptions about the role and needs of older persons; they conclude,

> (W)hen social care for older people is cut to the bone, lives are blighted, distress and pressure increase, and the resilience of individuals and their families is ground down. Yet this happens slowly day by day, week by week and month by month. It is not sudden, dramatic or hi-tech in the way a crisis in an Accident and Emergency department may be, and tends to attract less media, political and popular attention.[9]

Advances have been made in services for younger persons with disabilities, which are long overdue and a cause for celebration and must be continued. However, the needs of an ageing population must be recognised even when they do not always present in an acute form but gradually, often masked by unpaid care by families and others and reluctance by some older persons to use services.

A particular problem for older persons is accessing the social care system. AgeUK reported a 28% increase in people in England awaiting assessments, care, or direct payments between November 2021 and February 2022; in 2020–21, it was estimated that 37,370 older persons died without receiving the care they were waiting for. Lack of support adds to carer stress; 4.87 million unpaid carers worry about the impact of caring on their physical and mental health. Many feel overwhelmed

7 The King's Fund, 'Social Care 360' (2024) <https://assets.kingsfund.org.uk/f/256914/x/10453129ad/social_care_360_2024.pdf> – accessed 28 September 2024.

8 Welsh Local Government Association, 'A question of priorities: social care in the context of the impact of austerity, rising demand, and the pandemic' (2023) <https://www.wlga.wales/SharedFiles/Download.aspx?pageid=62&mid=665&fileid=3740> – accessed 28 September 2024; Care Inspectorate Wales, 'Chief Inspector's Annual Report 2022–23' (2023) <https://www.careinspectorate.wales/sites/default/files/2023-10/261020-CI-Report-22-23-en.pdf#:~:text=Chief%20Inspector%E2%80%99s%20Annual%20Report%202022-23.%20Overview%20of%20our> – accessed 28 September 2028.

9 JON Glasby et al, 'A lost decade? A renewed case for adult social care reform in England' (2021) *Journal of Social Policy* 50(2) 406, 428.

and lonely. The COVID-19 pandemic made matters worse.[10] A similar picture emerges in Wales. In two recent reports, Age Cymru highlighted older people's experience of the social care system. It reported delays in older persons accessing social care assessments and having them completed. There are several reasons for delays in access for people fifty-five and over, including increased demand due to the pandemic, long waiting times for care assessments, delays in implementing care packages, workforce shortages, poor communication, hospital discharge issues, complex charging arrangements, and reliance on short-term funding. These delays encompass systemic issues from demand management to communication and financial structure challenges within the social care framework. In its 2024 survey of older persons' experience of social care, Age Cymru found that those accessing it were over three times as likely to report very poor physical health and more than twice as likely to experience very poor mental or emotional health. Additionally, those in need of social care were more likely to report abuse, with 5% reporting it compared to 2.5% of those not requiring care.[11] Delays in older persons accessing assessments for social care and health services worsen prognoses and lead to needs becoming critical and expose older persons to unacceptable risks, such as falls, for longer. Oliver argues that delay is equivalent to rationing care. Delaying decisions about the care of,

> vulnerable older people flies in the face of platitudinous organisational values on person-centred care. Procedure, bureaucracy, and money come first—not people. And this forces caring health and social care professionals to make decisions that they know full well aren't always driven by the best course of action for the patient or family.[12]

It also impacts the lives of carers who provide ever more complex and demanding care as the health and well-being of the person cared for decline. Of particular concern are delays in diagnosing dementia. Early diagnosis helps preserve functioning for longer, allowing the person to adjust whilst still being able to engage. It also helps family and carers to adjust emotionally and practically.[13]

10 Age UK, 'Why can't I get care? Older people's experiences of care and support' (2022) https://www.ageuk.org.uk/globalassets/age-uk/documents/campaigns/care-in-crisis/why-cant-i-get-care-report.pdf – accessed 28 September 2024.

11 Age Cymru, 'Why are we still waiting? Delays in social care in Wales' (2024) <https://www.agecymru.wales/siteassets/documents/why-are-we-still-waiting/why-are-we-still-waiting.pdf> – accessed 10 February 2025; Age Cymru, 'What matters to you? Current experiences of people aged 50 or over in Wales' (August 2024) <https://www.ageuk.org.uk/cymru/our-work/policy/annual-survey/>– accessed September 2024.

12 D Oliver, 'Rationing care by delaying decisions' (2019) *British Medical Journal* (Online) 367.

13 See, for example, J Rasmussen and H Langerman, 'Alzheimer's disease–why we need early diagnosis' (2019) *Degenerative Neurological and Neuromuscular Disease* 123-130.

Social care law

The CA 2014 and the SSWA 2014 represent the first comprehensive reform of social care law in over sixty years. Although many practitioners bring skills and knowledge from their experience of the earlier law, the 2014 legislation necessitated adjusting to a new legal framework. Social care decision-making relating to older persons is often complex and challenging. There may be disagreement on the outcome of assessments and care plans, but that is inevitable given the range of factors identified and the need to weigh them against each other. Professional disagreement can be productive. The courts recognise legitimate debate and differing opinions, but their role is confined to determining whether the decision was made lawfully and not second-guessing which professional opinion should prevail. In Bolam v Friern Hospital Management Committee,[14] a 1957 medical negligence case, the court was reluctant to state the weight given to each factor in any assessment; judges are not qualified to undertake that task. Instead, courts must be reassured that doctors have followed a practice accepted by a responsible body of medical professionals skilled in that particular art. This does not give doctors complete freedom to decide what is negligent amongst themselves; the decision must be sensible and logical.[15] Although Bolam was about medical negligence, the test of reasonable skill and care applies to social care practitioners who must act in accordance with a practice accepted by a responsible body of social work opinion, even though another body of practitioners supports a different course.[16] The Court of Appeal, in an early appeal on the CA 2014, recognised that the claimant and her family strongly disagreed with the authority's decision to reduce his personal budget, but this did not make the decision unlawful as it had carefully considered the effect of its decision and that its decision was reasonable.[17] Courts are primarily concerned with how decisions are made rather than the merits of individual cases. The actions of public authorities must be reasonable, done for a proper purpose, proportionate, procedurally fair, and, at all times, impartial. All relevant factors must be considered, and irrelevant ones must be disregarded. Failure to meet these requirements may result in a judicial review; for example, where material evidence was not considered when assessing a person's social care needs, the assessment was held unlawful.[18]

Before discussing the 2014 legislation, it is helpful to understand the broader legal context in which social care is located. Public authorities, such as local authorities, NHS bodies, and some third-sector or for-profit providers, must act

14 [1957] 1 WLR 583 (QBD) (584); see Chapter 4.
15 *Bolitho v City and Hackney Health Authority* – [1997] 4 All ER 771.
16 *ABB vilton Keynes Council* [2011] EWHC 2745 (QB); [2012] 1 F.L.R. 1157.
17 *R (Davey) v Oxfordshire CC* [2017] EWCA Civ 1308; [2017] 9 WLUK 7.
18 *R (on the application of JG) v Southwark LBC* [2020] EWHC 1989 (Admin; [2020] 7 WLUK 355; *R (JF) v The London Borough of Merton* [2017] EWHC 1519 (Admin); [2017] 6 WLUK 674;. *R (on the application of Raja and another (by their mother and litigation friend)) v Redbridge London Borough Council* [2020] EWHC 1456 (Admin), [2020] All ER (D) 48 (Jun).

compatibly with the European Convention on Human Rights.[19] A knowledge of the Mental Capacity Act 2005 (MCA 2005) is necessary when working under the 2014 legislation. Additionally, some older persons come within the Mental Health Act 1983 (MHA 1983) and need social care support to live safely in the community rather than being detained under the Act. Practitioners may also encounter other areas of law, such as criminal law, negligence, domestic abuse, health and safety, data protection, and employment law. The Equality Act 2010 protects people from discrimination in the provision of public services. There are nine protected characteristics: age, disability, gender reassignment, marriage and civil partnerships, pregnancy and maternity, race, religion or belief, sex, and sexual orientation.[20] Discrimination may be direct, indirect, harassment, or victimisation. Section 14 of the Act addresses combined discrimination, which occurs when one person discriminates against another based on a combination of two relevant protected characteristics. However, this section is not yet in force. Section 149 Equality Act 2010 includes a public sector equality duty (PSED). When exercising their functions, the PSED duty requires public authorities in England, Scotland, and Wales to have 'due regard' to the need to eliminate discrimination, harassment, victimisation, and any other conduct prohibited by the Act. A failure to properly apply the PSED may lead to the decision being successfully judicially reviewed. For example, in the Norfolk case, the Court recognised that an authority's revised policy resulted in a higher proportion of the claimant's income being taken in charges compared to less severely disabled persons who could work and had their income disregarded. This differential treatment was deemed unnecessary, irrational, and disproportionate.[21]

Public authorities must actively promote equality of opportunity between people with a protected characteristic and those without. They should also foster good relations between those who share a protected characteristic and those who do not. This proactive role is further highlighted in Wales, where regulations require specified Welsh public authorities to consider the equality impacts of their decisions and take steps to promote equality. These bodies must publish equality objectives outlining strategies for addressing inequalities and promoting equality of opportunity. They must conduct equality impact assessments to see how their policies and practices affect people with protected characteristics. Engaging with stakeholders is required to ensure they listen to those affected by their decisions. Additionally, they must report on their progress in meeting their equality objectives and evaluate the impact of any initiatives. Finally, they must collect and use data to monitor and review the effects of their policies on people with protected characteristics. The regulation aims to ensure equality and human rights are integrated into the operations and decision-making processes of public bodies in Wales. A socioeconomic

19 See Chapter 2, and Section 6 Human Rights Act 1998.

20 Equality Act 2010 Sections 4–12.

21 See *R (on the application of SH) v Norfolk County Council and another* [2020] EWHC 3436 (Admin), [2021] PTSR 969; *R (on the application of YVR (a protected party by his litigation friend YUL)) v Birmingham City Council* [2024] EWHC 701 (Admin); *R (on the application of Sepulchre) v Royal Borough of Kensington and Chelsea* [20023] EWHC 2913 (Admin).

duty under the Equality Act 2010, was introduced in Wales in 2021; it requires public bodies to have due regard to how their decisions can reduce inequalities linked to socioeconomic disadvantage. This duty aims to improve outcomes for those affected by such disadvantages. It complements the PSED by encouraging public bodies to promote a more inclusive and equitable society in Wales. These duties apply only to public authorities specified in the regulations, including the Welsh Ministers, local authorities, local health boards, and NHS Trusts. Scotland has also introduced the socioeconmic duty, but England has not. The Future Generations (Wales) Act 2015 complements the socioeconomic duty by focusing on long-term well-being and sustainability, while the socioeconomic duty aims to reduce socioeconomic inequalities.[22]

Section 78 CA 2014 requires local authorities in England to act under general guidance issued by the Secretary of State, including when they exercise discretion. The Secretary of State must consult appropriate persons or bodies when preparing general guidance and have regard to local authorities' general duty to promote well-being. This is similar to the repealed Section 7 Local Authority Social Services Act 1970, other than 'shall' has been replaced by 'must.' In R v Islington LBC ex p Rixon,[23] a case under the 1970 Act, Sedley J emphasised that local authorities were not free to take it or leave it; they must follow the path charted by the guidance but may deviate when, on admissible grounds, there is a good reason to do so. They cannot take a substantially different course. The Law Commission recommended, in line with the MCA 2005 and the MHA 1983, that guidance should be subject to parliamentary scrutiny and included in a code of practice. The recommendation was not adopted in England, so the guidance does not require parliamentary scrutiny. The Secretary of State published the Care and Support Statutory Guidance, updated in September 2024.[24] A different approach is taken in Wales. Section 145 SSWA 2014 provides that Welsh Ministers may issue codes which can impose requirements, issue guidance, and set out aims, objectives, and other matters. Unlike England, and following the Commission's recommendation, draft codes, including revisions, must, following consultation, be laid before the Senedd. If, within forty days, the Senedd decides not to approve the draft, it cannot be issued in that form.[25] Democratic scrutiny of codes is a safeguard against weakening the Act. Welsh local authorities must comply with any requirement in a code and have regard to any guidance. However, this is subject to Section 147

22 Equality Act 2010 Sections.149-157; Equality Act 2010 (Statutory Duties) (Wales) Regulations 2011/1064; Equality Act 2010 (Authorities subject to a duty regarding Socioeconomic Inequalities) (No. 2) (Wales) Regulations 2021/1351.

23 [1997] ELR 66.

24 Department of Health and Social Care, 'Care and Support Statutory Guidance' (*Gov.UK*, 2023) https://www.gov.uk/government/publications/care-act-statutory-guidance/care-and-support-statutory-guidance_– accessed 28 September 2024. The list of changes made in September 2024 can be found at <https://www.gov.uk/government/publications/care-act-statutory-guidance/list-of-changes-made-to-the-care-act-guidance> - accessed 28 September 2024.

25 SSWA 2014 Section 146.

SSWA 2014, which permits a departure from requirements in a code where a local authority considers there is 'good reason' for so doing. It must agree on an alternative policy and issue a policy statement under Section 148 SSWA 2014, identifying how the function will be exercised differently from the requirement in the Code and the reason for the departure. The statement must be published, and a copy sent to the Welsh Ministers. A code may specify that Section 147 is not to apply to a requirement contained in it. There is a general exemption from complying with a requirement in a code or following a policy statement where 'it would be unreasonable for the authority' to do so; this applies to individual cases and to categories of cases.[26] Several codes have been issued, including general functions, assessments, meeting needs, charging and financial assessment, safeguarding, and advocacy.[27]

The 2014 legislation imposes duties on local authorities and grants powers; they must do some things and may do others. For example, Section 9(1) CA 2014 says local authorities 'must' assess a person if it appears they need care and support; this is a duty. In contrast, Section 19(3) says that they 'may' meet a need for care and support in urgent cases; this is a discretionary power. Similar provisions are found in Section 19(1) and Section 36(1) SSWA 2014. The local authority cannot adopt an overly rigid policy that would effectively fetter the exercise of a discretionary power.[28] Bankes LJ distinguished two situations. The first is when a public authority has a policy which includes reassurance that cases will be heard but that the policy will be followed unless the case is exceptional. The second is where an authority says it will not hear any request to depart from the policy.[29] The former is lawful; the latter is not. If the evidence shows an urgent need for care and support under Section 19(3) CA 2014 or Section 36 SSWA 2014, such as night care for an older person, and the local authority applies a blanket policy of non-provision, that is unlawful.[30]

General duties and general functions

In addition to assessment, eligibility, and service delivery reforms, the CA 2014 and the SSWA 2014 include general responsibilities or functions applicable to local authorities when delivering social care in their areas. The most significant of these is the adoption of the Law Commission's recommendation that there should be a single overarching principle that social care must promote or contribute to the well-being of people. The report emphasised the person-centred nature of social care and the need for the legislation to be read alongside the Human Rights Act 1998 and the Equality Act 2010.[31] Both Acts have a similar idea of

26 ibid Section 147(3).

27 See Welsh Government, 'Social Services Codes of Practice' (2024) <https://www.gov.wales/social-services-codes-practice#Codesofpractice>_– accessed 28 September 2024.

28 *Attorney General ex rel Tilley v London Borough of Wandsworth* [1981] 1 All ER 1162.

29 *R v Port of London Authority, ex parte Kynoch Ltd* [1919] 1 KB 176, CA, Bankes LJ.

30 *R (on the application of Raja and another (by their mother and litigation friend)) v Redbridge London Borough Council* [2020] EWHC 1456 (Admin), [2020] PTSR 2129.

31 Law Commission 326 (n3) para 24.

Table 5.1 Well-being indicators – CA 2014 and SSWA 2014

Section 1(2) Care Act 2014	*Section 2(2) Social Services and Well-being (Wales) Act 2014*
a. Personal dignity (including treatment of the individual with respect).	a. Physical and mental health and emotional well-being.
b. Physical and mental health and emotional well-being.	b. Protection from abuse and neglect.
c. Protection from abuse and neglect.	c. Education, training, and recreation.
d. Control by the individual over day-to-day life (including over care and support, or support, provided to the individual and the way in which it is provided).	d. Domestic, family, and personal relationships.
e. Participation in work, education, training, or recreation.	e. Contribution made to society.
f. Social and economic well-being.	f. Securing rights and entitlements.
g. Domestic, family, and personal relationships.	g. Social and economic well-being.
h. Suitability of living accommodation.	h. Suitability of living accommodation.
i. The individual's contribution to society.	i. Control over day-to-day life. j. Participation in work.

what well-being entails, although there are some differences – see Table 5.1. The recommendation is partially acknowledged in both pieces of legislation. Section 1 CA 2014 imposes a 'general duty' on local authorities in England to promote the well-being of persons who may need care and support or support if they are carers. The Explanatory Memorandum to the CA 2014 states that the general duty 'is not intended to be directly enforceable as an individual right, but to carry indirect legal weight' where a local authority fails to follow the principle.[32] In Wales, Section 5 SSWA 2014 imposes a 'duty' to 'seek to promote' the well-being of people in need of care and support and carers. The words 'seek to promote' can be read as limiting the provision's potential. These are not the strongest legal duties, although in the Merton case, the court held that an assessment was unlawful if it failed to assess the impact of the claimant's needs based on the well-being outcomes.[33] Whether the two pieces of legislation contain principles in the same way as the MCA 2005 is debatable. Nevertheless, well-being is an essential touchstone for practitioners and users alike.

Including personal dignity in the CA 2014 resulted from a House of Lords amendment to the Bill. Although the SSWA 2014 does not refer to dignity as a well-being indicator, it is included in Section 6(2)(b), which states that anybody exercising functions under the Act must have regard to the importance of 'promoting and respecting' personal dignity. Both Acts refer to 'control' over day-to-day life despite the Law Commission recommending that 'choice' was more appropriate when making decisions such as direct payment and choice of accommodation;

32 Explanatory Notes to the Care Act 2014, para 57.
33 Merton case (n18).

neither nation accepted the suggestion.[34] Well-being is a broad concept. For example, in a case involving a child placement under the SSWA 2014, Judge Gareth Jones considered well-being alongside the welfare principle in Section 1 Children Act 2014. He held that,

> (O)ne might, therefore, reasonably infer that 'well-being' is wider than 'welfare' since 'welfare' is included [in the SSWA 2014] within 'well-being' as an element thereof.[35]

In addition to well-being, local authorities in England and in Wales must adhere to the factors in table 5.2 below.

Although not included in the CA 2014, the Guidance clarifies that the well-being principle is intended to cover components of the Convention on the Rights of

Table 5.2 Factors to which local authorities must have regard

Section 1(3) CA 2014 – a local authority must have regard to	*Section 6(2) (3) SSWA 2014 – a person exercising functions under the Act must comply with the following duties*
a) Beginning with the assumption that people are best placed to judge their own well-being. b) The person's views, wishes, feelings, and beliefs. c) The importance of preventing or delaying the development of needs and reducing existing needs. d) The need to have regard to all the person's individual circumstances – decisions must not be based on an individual's age or appearance or any condition of the individual's or aspect of their behaviour which might lead others to make unjustified assumptions about their well-being. e) The importance of the person participating as fully as possible in decision-making and being provided with information and support to enable participation. f) The importance of achieving a balance between the person's well-being and that of any friends or relatives involved in their care. h) The need to protect from abuse or neglect. i) The need to ensure that restrictions on a person's rights or freedoms are kept to the minimum necessary to achieve its purpose.	a) So far as is reasonably practicable, ascertain and have regard to the individual's views, wishes and feelings. b) Have regard to the importance of promoting and respecting the dignity of the individual. c) Have regard to the individual's characteristics, culture, and beliefs (including, for example, language). d) Have regard to the importance of providing appropriate support to enable the individual to participate in decisions that affect them to the extent appropriate in the circumstances, particularly where the individual's ability to communicate is limited for any reason. e) Have regard to the importance of beginning with the presumption that people are best placed to judge their own well-being. g) Have regard to the importance of promoting the person's independence where possible.

34 Law Commission 326, (n3) para 4.25.

35 *In re E (A Child) (Care Proceedings: Placement Outside Jurisdiction)* [2017] 4 W.L.R. 99, [2017] 2 WLUK 622, [57].

Persons with Disabilities, particularly article 19, the right to live independently and be included in the community.[36] The Welsh Code also regards well-being as including aspects of independent living, as found in Article 19 of the Convention.[37] Well-being recognises the value of maximising personal independence and maintaining autonomy. Both nations emphasise the importance of community engagement, employment, education, training, and contributing to society. For older persons, these remain essential for well-being. An older person's ability to access educational opportunities may be as important to them as to younger persons. Identifying an older person's well-being must not be predicated on paternalism, risk aversion, and assumptions about what older persons need or want. A formulaic approach to meeting an older person's needs, whether through domiciliary or residential provision, may ignore individual preferences and aspirations. In their review of forty studies focussing on older persons living at home with chronic conditions in the United Kingdom, Abdi et al. found that many services and care delivery models are not based on the needs of older adults. There is a need to tailor services to meet the needs of older persons and respect their right to maximum independence. Generic adult social care services are not always appropriate. They conclude,

> (I)t was clear from the evidence reviewed that older adults living with chronic conditions are faced with some challenges in their social lives, psychological health, and activities related to self-care, domestic lives and mobility. It was also clear that despite these challenges older adults valued independence and demonstrated a desire to cope with their illness.[38]

Well-being in both nations must be seen through the lens of older persons and their specific needs, abilities, and aspirations. In planning services, local authorities must engage with older persons. The Welsh Strategy for Older People prioritises involving them in decision-making through older people forums, which empower older persons to have a voice in policies that affect them. Fifty-plus forums allow older people to express their needs, identify solutions, and form a collective voice locally.[39] One provision unique to Wales is the Section 7(1) SSWA 2014 duty to have 'due regard' to the United Nations Principles for Older Persons. This duty applies to any person carrying out functions under the Act concerning adults with

36 Care Act Guidance (n24) para 1.18–19.

37 Welsh Government, *Social Services and Well-being (Wales) Act 2014: Part 2 Code of :Practice (General Functions)* (Welsh Government, 2024) para 54.

38 S Abdi, A Spann, J Borilovic et al., 'Understanding the care and support needs of older people: A scoping review and categorisation using the WHO International Classification of Functioning, disability and Health Framework (ICF)' (2019) *BMC Geriatrics* 19(1) 1, 3.

39 SG Milsom, 'The benefits of independent older people's representation and why its development should be supported' (2023) *Working with Older People* 27(4) 304; Welsh Government, 'Age friendly wales: Our strategy for an ageing society' (2021) <https://publichealthnetwork.cymru/age-friendly-wales-our-strategy-for-an-ageing-society/#:~:text=The%20Welsh%20Government%20has%20launched%20Age%20Friendly%20Wales%3A,the%20way%20we%20think%20and%20feel%20about%20ageing>. - accessed 28 September 2024.

needs for care and support and carers in need of support. The due regard duty is not the strongest, but it must be exercised in substance, with rigour, and with an open mind.[40] The UN Principles are discussed in Chapter 8.

Section 2 CA 2014 requires local authorities to provide or arrange services, resources, facilities, or other things to prevent or delay the need for care and support arising in their areas. A similar duty applies to prevent or delay a carer's need for support. Authorities must identify existing resources and how they may meet the unmet needs of those needing care and support and carers who require support. Section 15(1)–(9) SSWA 2014 contains a similar duty. Welsh local authorities must provide a range of services that contribute towards preventing or delaying and reducing people's need for care and support, minimising the effect of a person's disability, contributing towards preventing abuse or neglect, and enabling people to live as independently as possible. Services include those provided under Sections 34 and 35 SSWA 2014, as discussed below. They include care and support and support for carers. Available services should be identified, including those provided by the third sector, when deciding what to provide or arrange. Assessing the cost-effectiveness of prevention is difficult, especially defining what prevention means. Evidence of its effectiveness is patchy.[41] Additionally, it can be challenging to identify causality between preventative services and their outcomes. However, according to Tew et al., prevention initiatives can avoid the progression of needs and reduce costly long-term care requirements, such as nursing homes.[42] They point out that austerity strengthened the need for more prevention but perversely made it difficult for authorities to invest in it. Loneliness experienced by older persons is associated with an increased possibility of having to leave their homes.[43] Befriending face-to-face or virtually can be an effective way to address loneliness. The third sector often provides preventative services, including physical activities to promote well-being, such as yoga, tai chi, dance, and Nordic walking, which help reduce falls and lessen anxiety. However, the public sector's financial problems also restrict the third sector's contribution as they rely heavily on public funding, and cuts limit their preventative work. Many rely on short-term funding that may not be renewed. Cuts in funding and reduced community support increase the likelihood of avoidable care home admissions.[44]

40 Social Care Wales, 'Making rights work for older people: Guidelines for health and social care' (undated) <https://www.gov.wales/sites/default/files/publications/2022-05/making-rights-work-for-older-people-guidelines-for-health-and-social-care.pdf> – accessed 28 September 2024.

41 K Allen, and J Glasby, '"The billion dollar question": Embedding Prevention In Older People's Services – ten "High-impact" Changes' (2013) *The British Journal of Social Work* 43(5) 904.

42 J Tew, S Duggal, S Carret al., *Implementing the Care Act 2014: Building social resources to prevent, reduce or delay needs for care and support in adult social care in England* (University of Birmingham, 2019).

43 B Hanratty, D Stow, D Collingridge Moore et al., 'Loneliness as a risk factor for care home admission in the English longitudinal study of ageing' (2028) *Age and Ageing* 47(6) 896.

44 M Knapp, KC Chua, M Broadbent et al., 'Predictors of care home and hospital admissions and their costs for older people with Alzheimer's disease: findings from a large London case register' (2016) *BMJ Open* 6(11) e013591.

Given the importance of information in enabling older persons to make informed choices about their social care, Section 4 CA 2014 and Section 17 SSWA 2014 require local authorities to provide information and advice on how the legislation operates in their areas, the available choices of providers, how to access care and support, raising safeguarding concerns, and financial information. The Equality Act 2010 requires reasonable adjustments to ensure equal access to information, advice, and assistance services. In England, local authorities must ensure accessibility in providing information and advice services by considering the languages used within the community and making necessary adjustments to accommodate non-English speakers. They must be aware of the ethnic makeup and language diversity within their local area to ensure that information and advice services are easily accessible to all. Regardless of language, everyone has the right to equal access to the information and advice provided. Different languages and methods should be used, such as face-to-face interaction, peer-to-peer communication, telephone, mass media, and digital platforms, including websites and email. Certain groups may have special needs for information and advice services. Local authorities must recognise and consider these needs to ensure their services are inclusive and accessible. In Wales, local authorities must ensure that they provide information, advice, and assistance in a way that is easily accessible and meets the population's needs. Furthermore, local authorities must ensure that people receive the necessary support to access the service and provide a service to assist people with accessing social care. The information must be aimed at those needing care and support and their carers and must be accessible and sufficient to enable the person to make plans for meeting their needs.

Both nations recognise the importance of cooperation between public authorities. Section 6(1) CA 2014 and Section 162(1) SSWA 2014 impose duties on local authorities to cooperate with 'relevant partners' in exercising their social care functions. Relevant partners include other local authorities, NHS bodies, police, ministers or the Welsh Ministers, and probation. The duty is reciprocal, although the relevant partner can only cooperate within the terms of its statutory remit. In addition to relevant partners, the local authority must cooperate with any other person or body it considers appropriate if they have adult social care functions.[45] This duty is not reciprocal. Such persons or bodies include providers of care and support, carer's support services, pharmacists, NHS primary health providers, independent hospitals, and registered social housing providers. Cooperation is important between public authorities and also within local authorities who must ensure that their officers responsible for adult social care, housing, public health, and children's services cooperate to provide integrated services.[46] Working with Children's Services is essential for older persons who are cared for by children or young persons and those with care responsibilities for grandchildren. In addition to requiring general cooperation, Section 7 CA 2014 allows a local authority to request a rel-

45 CA 2014 Section 6(2); SSWA 2014 Section 162(2).
46 CA 2014 Section 6(4); SSWA Section 162(2).

evant partner's cooperation in individual cases. The relevant partner must comply with the request unless it considers it outside its duties and functions. Reasons for a refusal must be given, which could lead to legal challenges if unreasonable. A similar duty is found in Section 164 SSWA 2014.

Linked to cooperation is integration. Greater health and social care integration has generated much debate but minimal progress. Integration aims to prevent need and enhance the quality of care provided. Health and social care are inextricably linked; it is sometimes difficult to identify a need as a health or a social care one. Cooperation between health and social care helps promote the well-being of older persons needing care and their carers. It can improve the quality of care by avoiding duplication and providing seamless care. It is also crucial in preventing, identifying, and responding to abuse and neglect. Again, both nations seek to promote greater integration through their legislation. Section 3 CA 2014 requires local authorities to integrate health and health-related services with their care and support functions if it promotes the well-being of adults needing care and support and their carers needing support. Care and support functions refer to services meeting the needs of those requiring care and support and carers; health provision refers to services provided by the healthcare system. 'Health-related provision' does not fall under either health or social care but may impact an older person's health. Housing is included in health-related provision. Similar duties for Wales are found in Section 165 SSWA 2014. The Welsh Government's guidance on hospital discharge highlights the need for integrated working, sets minimum standards, and outlines how providers can better integrate to provide seamless and timely services.[47] Some progress has been made. The Health and Care Act 2022 established integrated care partnerships in England to bring together the NHS, integrated care boards, local authorities and health and care providers. Their role is to develop and set an integrated care strategy for joined-up care for their area. The Health and Social Care Regional Integration Fund plans to deliver preventative, integrated health and social care in Wales.[48]

Achieving integration is challenging due to structural and intangible barriers. Health services fall within the NHS remit, while social care is primarily the responsibility of local government; each has different politics, financing, terminology, and legal frameworks. This separation has been deeply embedded in the welfare state's structure since its creation. As Aronson puts it, '(T)he line between medical and social care is created by politics, not biology.'[49] The study by Naqvi et al. on integration between primary healthcare and social care points out that lack of funding underpins many obstacles to effective interdisciplinary working. More generally, their findings,

47 CA 2014 Section 3(5); Welsh Government, 'Hospital Discharge Guidance' (December 2023) https://www.gov.wales/hospital-discharge-arrangements-december-2023 – accessed 28 September 2024.

48 Welsh Government, 'Health and Social Care Regional Integration Fund' (2022) <https://www.gov.wales/sites/default/files/publications/2022-02/health-and-social-care-regional-integration-fund-revenue-guidance-2022-2027.pdf> – accessed 28 September 2024.

49 L Aronson, *Elderhood* (Bloomsbury Publishing, 2021) 111.

> indicate that effective communication, trusted relationships between staff and an educated workforce are required prior to making organisational changes, as structural changes have thus far been hindered from being successful by silo mentalities within staff.[50]

This is an interesting perspective, as practitioners argue, with some merit, that structures and finance get in the way of achieving greater integration despite their goodwill. Integrating health and social care systems alone will not yield significant benefits. To develop new seamless care models, it is necessary to overcome professional and cultural barriers, improve information sharing, maintain organisational stability, and provide financial support and flexibility.[51]

One of the most significant changes in social care since the 1980s is the growth of the independent sector as providers of social care, which has largely replaced direct provision by local authorities. The independent sector now provides 83% of residential care. While it offers a diversity of provisions and choices, the We Own It group argues for reversing the policy.[52] The domination of market principles has, it is argued, resulted in a drift from a market economy to being a market society with markets and market values penetrating spheres where they do not belong.[53] Local authorities in England must provide diverse and high-quality care options, collaborate with others, ensure sustainability and quality, and prioritise well-being when procuring services. Access to a range of providers is important for those using social care services.[54] Wales encourages the growth of social enterprises and cooperatives offering care, support, and preventative services. Social enterprises are organisations whose activities might reasonably be considered to be carried on for the benefit of society. They reinvest most of their profits into their social objectives. The involvement of service users in the planning and operation of social enterprises is vital, as is promoting third-sector care, support, and prevention services.[55] A significant change is underway in Wales regarding children being placed in commercially operated care services. The Health and Social Care (Wales) Act 2025 will eliminate profit from the care of restricted children's services which include children's homes, fostering, and secure accommodation services. The Act forbids payment of dividends to shareholders or members and requires that trading surpluses be reinvested into the service, including building appropriate reserves and capital expenditure. Children and young people feel strongly about being cared

50 D Naqvi, A Malik, M Al-Zubaidy et al., 'The general practice perspective on barriers to integration between primary and social care: A London, United Kingdom-based qualitative interview study' (2019) *BMJ Open* 9(8) e029702, 7.

51 See C Ham, D Heenan, Mlongley et al., *Integrated care in Northern Ireland, Scotland and Wales: Lessons for England* (The King's Fund, 2013)

52 We own it, 'Care belongs in public ownership' (2021) <https://weownit.org.uk/public-ownership/care-work> – accessed 28 September 2024; B Hudson, 'Commissioning for change: A new model for commissioning adult social care in England' (2019) *Critical Social Policy* 39(3) 413.

53 MJ Sandel, *What money can't buy: The moral limits of markets* (Macmillan, 2012).

54 CA 2014 Section 5.

55 SSWA 2014 Section 16.

for by privately owned organisations that profit from their experience of being in care. It is unlikely that this initiative will be extended to adults.

The 1998 Griffiths Report, Community Care: Agenda for Action, and the subsequent government White Paper, Caring for People, proposed that local authorities should be responsible for planning and managing social care but not always providing the care directly. This idea was included in the National Health Service and Community Care Act of 1990, superseded by the 2014 legislation adopting the same delivery model. The outsourcing social care model would, it was claimed, create a thriving independent provider sector offering real choice.[56] However, it has created a system where social care provision for older persons relies on market forces. Smaller local providers struggle despite being attractive as more homely and community-based facilities. The collapse of Southern Cross in 2011, placing 31,000 care home residents at risk, exposed the vulnerability of this social care market. The company's business model relied on selling its homes and leasing them back, but the financial crisis of 2007–08 and public sector budget cuts impacted its income.[57] When the company went into liquidation, local authorities struggled to find new homes for the residents. The Southern Cross saga highlights problems with the market approach, as it facilitates competitive risk-taking and removes choice and control from commissioners and users. Scourfield highlights three problems with this approach. First, markets encourage competitive risk-taking. Second, allowing corporate providers to dominate the market removes choice and control from commissioners and users. Third, relying on private markets to provide services to vulnerable groups is fundamentally flawed. Prioritising cost-cutting and profit maximisation is not conducive to providing high-quality and secure care for older and vulnerable persons.[58] The CA 2014 and the SSWA 2014 provide market oversight and temporary powers to intervene in provider failure.[59] Sections 53–57 CA 2014 identify criteria to be applied for market oversight in England. How this can be achieved is unclear, and attempts to find the most appropriate model may risk unsettling the market. More research is needed.[60] In Wales, Section 144B SSWA 2014 requires local authorities to publish local market stability reports. In addition, Section 61 Regulation and Inspection of Social Care (Wales) Act 2016 requires Welsh Ministers to assess a provider's financial stability where the business is at risk. Care home profits in March 2022 were at their lowest level since market oversight was introduced in 2015. Home care profits have also fallen. In 2022–23, workforce capacity and capability, and financial pressures are

56 R Griffiths, *Community care; Agenda for Action* (HMSO, 1988); Department of Health, 'Caring for People: Community care in the next decade and beyond' (1989) *Cm* 849.

57 R Wachman, 'Southern Cross's incurably flawed business model let down the vulnerable' *Guardian* (London, 16 July 2011).

58 P Scourfield, 'Caretelization revisited and the lessons of Southern Cross' (2012) *Critical Social Policy* 32(1), 137, 145.

59 CA 2014, Sections 44–52 and SSWA 2014 Sections189–91.

60 C Needham, K Allen, E Burn et al., 'How do you shape a market? Explaining local state practices in adult social care' (2023) *Journal of Social Policy* 52(3) 640.

forcing some care providers out of the market or increasing reliance on self-funders who pay around 41% more for care in care homes and around £3 more per hour for home care than publicly funded users. It is uncertain whether the 2014 legislation reforms can ensure sustainability and the ability to provide a range of high-quality services.[61]

Ordinary residence

An important feature of social care provision is the idea of ordinary residence. Identifying ordinary residence has been an ongoing matter of contention and confusion across local authorities, but it is an important link between an older person and social care provision. In R v Barnet LBC ex parte Shah,[62] the House of Lords decided that the words should be interpreted according to their natural meaning. 'Ordinary residence' describes a person's chosen place of living in a particular country or area. This choice is made voluntarily and for settled purposes as part of the person's regular order of their life. It does not matter whether it is for a short or long period. Temporary or occasional absences do not disrupt ordinary residence. Factors such as intention, length, and continuity of residence are relevant considerations. Particular problems were encountered regarding serving prisoners. Pre-2014, social care services in prisons were patchy; guidance more or less clarified responsibility on discharge but not during detention.[63] As of 31 March 2024, prisoners aged 60 and over comprised 8.1% of the total prison population, which is approximately 7,110 prisoners. This number is expected to grow.[64] The 2014 legislation clarifies that the local authority in the area where the prison is located is responsible for assessing and meeting these prisoners' care and support needs. A prisoner's previous ordinary residence is irrelevant during detention, and no reference can be made to the ordinary residence criteria.[65] Any dispute regarding ordinary residence must be resolved by the Secretary of State in England or the Welsh Ministers in Wales rather than the courts.[66]

61 Kings Fund (n7) 17; M De Benito Gellner, 'The Declining Profitability of UK Care Homes - Healthcare Business International' (Healthcare Business International17 November 2023) <https://www.healthcarebusinessinternational.com/the-declining-profitability-of-uk-care-homes/ accessed> - accessed 5 February 202.5

62 [1983] 2 AC 309.

63 Prison Reform Trust, 'Doing time: The experiences and needs of older people in prison' (2010) <https://prisonreformtrust.org.uk/wp-content/uploads/old_files/Documents/Doing%20Time%20the%20experiences%20and%20needs%20of%20older%20people%20in%20prison.pdf> – accessed 28 September 2024; J Williams, 'Social care and older prisoners' (2013) *Journal of Social Work* 13(5) 471; J Williams, 'Fifty-the new sixty? The health and social care of older prisoners' (2010) *Quality in Ageing and Older Adults* 11(3) 16.

64 Ministry of Justice 'Her Majesty's Prison and Probation Service Offender Equalities Annual Report 2023 to 2024 (2024) <https://www.gov.uk/government/statistics/hmpps-offender-equalities-annual-report-2023-to-2024/hmpps-offender-equalities-report-202324>– accessed 10 February

65 CA 2014 Section 76; SSWA 2014 Section 185.

66 CA 2014 Section 40; SSWA 2014 Section 195.

In some cases, placing an older person in accommodation outside the local authority area where they are ordinarily resident may be desirable or necessary. Does this change the older person's ordinary residence, and who pays for the care? Out-of-county accommodation may better promote well-being, particularly if local provision is unavailable. The older person may also exercise their right to preferred accommodation in another area. When moving into a 'specified type' of accommodation outside their ordinary residence authority, they will not acquire an ordinary residence in the new authority despite living there. The original local authority continues to be responsible for the care package. The specified accommodation types in England are care homes or shared or supported living accommodation. In Wales, care home accommodation is the specified type.[67] Again, any disputes must be referred to the Secretary of State or the Welsh Ministers rather than the courts.[68]

Schedule 1 CA 2014 contains the United Kingdom rules regarding providing care and support for adults by local authorities in England through arranging accommodation in Wales, Scotland, or Northern Ireland. In such cases, the person is to be treated as still ordinarily resident in the local authority area in England rather than the one in Wales, Scotland, or Northern Ireland where the accommodation is located. Similar rules apply to cross-border placements by local authorities in Wales and Scotland and Health and Social Care Boards in Northern Ireland.[69]

Assessments of an adult's needs for care and support

England and Wales adopt similar approaches when identifying needs. Section 9 CA 2014 and Section 19 SSWA 2014 impose a duty on local authorities to assess people who may need care and support; this is referred to as a needs assessment. Table 5.3 outlines the process for the two Acts and highlights their shared features.Table 5.3

Needs assessments in England and in Wales determine if a person requires care and support based on their identity and characteristics and are the crucial interaction between an older person seeking social care and the local authority. The authority may become aware of a person who requires care and support through another agency, or the person or their carer may request it.[70] An assessment must be carried out regardless of the authority's opinion on the person's need for care

67 Care and Support (Ordinary Residence) (Specified Accommodation) Regulations 2014/2828; Care and Support (Ordinary Residence) (Specified Accommodation) (Wales) Regulations 2015/1499.

68 CA 2014 Section 40; SSWA 2014 Section 195.

69 CA 2014 Schedule 1; Care Act Guidance. Department of Health and Social Care, *Guidance: Principles for maintaining continuity of care when moving across borders within the United Kingdom* (2015) <https://www.gov.uk/government/publications/continuity-of-care-when-moving-across-borders-within-uk/principles-for-maintaining-continuity-of-care-when-moving-across-borders-within-the-united-kingdom#:~:text=The%20aims%20of%20the%20principles,day%20of%20the%20move%20and> – accessed 28 September 2024.

70 *R (on the application of P) v London Borough of Newham* [2001] EWHC Admin 589; (2001) 4 CCL Rep 48.

Table 5.3 Needs assessments under the CA 2014 and the SSWA 2014

	s.9 CA 2014; s.19 SSWA 2014	
Duty to assess	Where it appears to a local authority that an adult may have needs for care and support, the authority must assess—(a) whether the adult does have needs for care and support, and (b) if the adult does, what those needs are.	
	s.9(3) CA 2014; s.19(2) SSWA 2014.	
Matters to be disregarded	The duty to carry out a needs assessment applies regardless of the authority's view of— (a) the level of the adult's needs for care and support, or (b) the level of the adult's financial resources.	
	s.9(2) CA 2014	**s.19(4) SSWA 2014**
Matters to be included in an assessment .	A needs assessment must include an assessment of— (a) the impact of the adult's needs for care and support on the matters specified in section 1(2) CA 2014, (b) the outcomes that the adult wishes to achieve in day-to-day life, and (c) whether, and if so, to what extent, the provision of care and support could contribute to achieving those outcomes.	In carrying out a needs assessment, the local authority must— (a) seek to identify the outcomes that the adult wishes to achieve in day-to-day life, (b) assess whether, and if so, to what extent, the provision of— (i) care and support, (ii) preventative services, or (iii) information, advice or assistance, could contribute to the achievement of those outcomes or otherwise meet needs identified by the assessment, and (c) assess whether, and if so, to what extent, other matters could contribute to achieving those outcomes or otherwise meet those needs.
	S.9(5) CA 2014	***s.19(5) SSWA 2014.***
Who should be involved in the assessment?	A local authority, in carrying out a needs assessment, must involve— (a) the adult, (b) any carer that the adult has, and (c) any person the adult asks the authority to involve or, where the adult lacks capacity to ask the authority to do that, any person who appears to the authority to be interested in the adult's welfare.	A local authority, in carrying out a needs assessment under this section, must involve— (a) the adult, and (b) where feasible, any carer that the adult may have.

and support or their financial situation. The threshold for initiating a needs assessment is low; it only needs to 'appear' to the authority that a person may have needs. Refusing to assess because there is no likelihood of meeting a need is against the law.[71]

71 See *R v Bristol City Council, ex parte Penfold* (1998) 1CCL Rep 315.

In England, an assessment involves considering how the person's needs for care and support impact the well-being outcomes in Section 1(2) CA 2014 and what outcomes they wish to achieve in their daily life. Assessments must consider whether care and support will contribute to the desired outcomes. The word contribute is important as the local authority support is not required to achieve all the outcomes. However, neglecting to consider them is unlawful.[72] In addition to persons listed in Section 9(5) CA 2014, an independent advocate may be used if the person cannot fully participate.[73] When conducting a needs assessment, the authority should consider factors beyond care and support. For example, the Guidance cites a person with physical and mobility-related needs.[74] Consideration should be given to whether the person would benefit from preventative services under Section 2 CA 2014 or information and advice under Section 4.[75] In Wales, a local authority must identify the well-being outcomes a person wishes to achieve on a day-to-day basis. As in England, any services are required to contribute to achieving the outcomes and meeting needs. Under the Code, it is open to the person to invite any other person to support them in participating and fully expressing their view; this could be family, friends, or support networks. Their support can help the person feel as though they are equal partners.[76]

In Wales, it is essential to ensure that the preference of some older persons to be assessed in Welsh is respected. For some older persons, Welsh is their preferred language, particularly when discussing personal matters. Around 224,000 people fifty-five and over in Wales speak some Welsh. Of these, 88,000 are fluent, and 34,000 can speak a 'fair amount' of Welsh. Approximately 15% of older persons speak Welsh beyond a basic level, with 9.4% using the language daily. For fluent Welsh speakers sixty-five and over, approximately 21,000 feel more comfortable communicating in Welsh than in English. The figures differ across local authorities. In Blaenau Gwent, 1.5% aged sixty-five to seventy-four and 1.1% aged seventy-five and over speak Welsh; in Gwynedd, the figures are 55.6% and 60.7%, respectively.[77] Older persons living with dementia may experience a decline in their ability to communicate in English if Welsh has been their primary language throughout their lives. The Code requires,

> assessments should be conducted through the medium of English or Welsh as appropriate to the individual or family concerned. The requirement for an assessment to be in the medium of Welsh should not delay the process.[78]

72 Davey case (n17).

73 Care Act Guidance (n24) para 1.21.

74 ibid para 6.14.

75 CA 2014 Section 9(6).

76 Welsh Government, *Social Services and Well-being (Wales) Act 2014 Part 3 Code of Practice (assessing the needs of individuals)* (Welsh Government, 2015) para 23.

77 Age Cymru, *Older people in Wales: Fact and figures* (Swansea University, 2021) 8–9 <https://www.agecymru.wales/siteassets/documents/policy/age-cymru---older-people-in-wales---facts-and-statistics-2021.pdf?e=MDB X0q> - accessed 28 September 2024.

78 Welsh Assessment Code (n76) para 52.

There is no prescribed format for needs assessments, but they must be conducted proportionately under both Acts.[79] Everybody is different, and that must be reflected in an assessment. James and Clements highlight a practice of conflating 'what matters to you conversations' with needs assessments. An assessment involves more than a conversation, important though that may be. They conclude it would be deeply concerning if people were 'fobbed off by a conversation masquerading as an assessment.'[80] In England, local authorities are required to provide supported self-assessments to older persons who want this type of assessment and have the capacity to participate. The local authority and the older person undertake a supported self-assessment. The authority must take into account the person's preferences, desired assessment outcomes, and the extent of their needs; it should also consider the impact of the person's needs on other family members. Although giving the older person some control over the process, the ultimate assessment of need is that of the practitioner who, with consent, may seek the views of others who have regular contact with the person, such as a GP or other professionals providing care.[81] Wales does not make provision for self-assessment.

Previously, it was unclear if a person could refuse an assessment and, if they did, whether the local authority was still required to assess them. Section 11 CA 2014 and Section 20 SSWA 2014 clarify that an older person has the right to refuse a needs assessment, except when they lack mental capacity or are experiencing or at risk of abuse or neglect.[82] In cases of refusal, the assessment duty is re-engaged if the person changes their mind and requests an assessment. Similarly, it is re-engaged if a local authority considers that the person's needs or circumstances have changed, subject to a further refusal.[83]

Assessments of a carer's need for support

Former First Lady Rosalyn Carter said, '(T)here are only four kinds of people in the world. Those who have been carergivers, those who are currently caregivers, those who will be caregivers, and those who will need a caregiver.' In England and in Wales, unpaid carers, often family or friends, provide significant essential care and support for older persons. According to the 2021 Census, there are approximately 4.7 million unpaid carers in England and around 310,000 in Wales.

79 Care Act Guidance (n24) para 6.35–43; ibid para 81.

80 A James and L Clements, *What matters to carers? 'Is a "what matters" conversation an assessment?'* (Rhydian: Wales Social Welfare Law online, 2017) 1–4 <https://view.officeapps.live.com/op/view.aspx?src=https%3A%2F%2Fwww.lukeclements.co.uk%2Fwp-content%2Fuploads%2F2018%2F07%2F2017-01-What-Matters-briefing.docx&wdOrigin=BROWSELINK> - accessed 28 September 2024..

81 Care Act Guidance (n24) para 6.46–7. See Regulation 2 Care and Support (Assessment) Regulations 2014 SI 2014/2827.

82 CA 2014 Section 11(2)(b); SSWA 2014 Section 20(2). See, for example, *A Local Authority v GP (Capacity: Care, Support and Education)* [2020] EWCOP 56 | [2020] 9 WLUK 449|.

83 CA 2014 Seection 11(3)–(4); SSWA 2014 Section 20(3).

This represents 8.9% and 10.5% of the usual resident population aged five years and over, respectively. In England, the age group with the highest percentage of unpaid carers was women between fifty-five and fifty-nine and men between sixty and sixty-four. Similarly, the highest percentage of unpaid carers in Wales was found in women between fifty-five and fifty-nine and men between fifty-five and sixty-four. In England and Wales, the percentage of women providing unpaid care was higher than that of men; in England, 10.3% of women provided unpaid care compared with 7.6% of men, and in Wales, 12.0% of women compared with 9.0% of men.[84] During the COVID-19 pandemic, the number of carers sixty-five and over doubled to nearly four million, with almost 800,000 in their eighties.[85] Young carers between five and seventeen, who number 120,000 in England and 8,200 in Wales, may perform many tasks and meet the needs of a grandparent, for example. Providing such support may adversely affect the young person's education and development, although some research indicates that there may be positives for them in providing care. However, whatever positives young carers may get from caring, they need support, and any care provided must protect and promote their welfare.

Being a carer can be rewarding and often builds on relationships that have existed over many years. However, it is a demanding and sensitive role and caring for another can significantly impact the carer's well-being. Carers UK highlights the impact of being an unpaid carer. The poverty rate among unpaid carers is 27%, considerably higher than the 18% rate for non-carers. Carers providing over thirty-five hours of care each week face an exceptionally high poverty rate of 43%. Women and ethnic minority unpaid carers experience higher poverty rates compared to their male and white counterparts. Many of those who receive benefits such as Universal Credit or Carer's Allowance still live in poverty; this shows that the current support systems are not enough. Unpaid carers often struggle to maintain paid employment due to their caregiving responsibilities, resulting in lower employment rates than non-carers. Many resort to part-time or lower-paying jobs and frequently feel compelled to leave employment. Financially, unpaid carers face a substantial burden, struggling to meet housing costs and at risk of homelessness. Different support strategies are needed for those with long-term care responsibilities. Former carers need better preparation and support to navigate the challenges after the end of their caring responsibilities.[86] Petrillo and Bennett estimate that the

84 Office for National Statistics, 'Unpaid Care by Age, Sex and Deprivation, England and Wales: Census 2021' (13 February 2023) <https://www.ons.gov.uk/peoplepopulationandcommunity/healthandsocialcare/socialcare/articles/unpaidcarebyagesexanddeprivationenglandandwales/census2021#unpaiCAmded-care-by-age-sex-and-geography-2021>_– accessed 28 September 2024.

85 Age UK, 'New Age UK research finds the numbers of UK over age 65s caring unpaid nearly double during the pandemic to more than 4 million' (2021) <https://www.ageuk.org.uk/latest-press/articles/2021/new-age-uk-research-finds-the-numbers-of-uk-over-65s-caring-unpaid-nearly-double-during-the-pandemic-to-more-than-4-million/> – accessed 28 September 2024.

86 CarersUK, 'Poverty and financial hardship of unpaid carers in the UK: A WPI Economics Report for Carers UK' (2024) <https://www.carersuk.org/media/dnxerxqv/poverty_financial_hardship_uk_web.pdf> – accessed 28 September 2024.

value of the contributions of unpaid carers is roughly the equivalent of the NHS annual budget in England and Wales – approximately £164 billion. Among the many interesting recommendations they make is to amend the Equality Act 2010 to include caring as an additional protected characteristic.[87]

Many people will not readily identify as carers, even though they devote many hours to caring. They see themselves as a spouse, partner, relative, or friend and support the person to maintain their dignity and maximise inclusion.[88] Equally, an older person cared for by a family member or a friend may not recognise them as a carer due to their relationship; instead, they are fulfilling a familial or similar role. This issue arose in a case about whether a child was a young carer, although it has broader implications. The court held that in deciding whether a child was a young carer within Section 17ZA Children Act 1989, the views of the child and the recipient of the care were not definitive.[89] An objective and informed assessment is required rather than how the carer or cared-for person defines their role. Pre-2014 carer assessments were contained in a 'fragmented and multi-layered' web of legislation, whose rationale was opaque and probably non-existent. The Law Commission recommended that there should be a single duty on local authorities to undertake a carer assessment when the person they are caring for requires services.[90] The recommendation was included in the CA 2014 and the SSWA 2014, where carers are featured alongside those needing care and support. The definition of 'carer' in the two Acts is broad. In both, a carer refers to someone providing or intending to care for an adult (and a disabled child in Wales); this departs from the previous law, which restricted carers to those who provided 'a substantial amount of care on a regular basis.' The Law Commission was persuaded to abandon the previous definition mainly because of the inefficiency of requiring local authorities to decide if the care falls within each category.[91] Carer assessments are similar to needs assessments in both Acts.[92]

The broad definition gives practitioners scope to assess whether somebody is a carer. For example, is a neighbour who regularly takes an older person's dog for a walk a carer? Without that help, the dog would have to be adopted. There is persuasive research on the therapeutic value of animals for older persons in tackling loneliness, improving mental and physical health, and helping prevent depression.[93] A

87 M Petrillo and MR Bennett, 'Valuing carers 2021: England and Wales' (2023) <https://centreforcare.ac.uk/updates/2023/05/valuing-carers/> - accessed 28 September 2024.

88 I Hellström, '"I'm his wife not his carer!" – dignity and couplehood in dementia' in LC Hydén, H Lindemann, and J Brockmeier (eds), *Beyond loss: Dementia, identity, personhood* (online edn, Oxford Academic, 18 December 2014) <https://academic.oup.com/book/9216/chapter-abstract/155870161?redirectedFrom=fulltext> – accessed 28 September 2024.

89 *Regina (E) v Islington London Borough Council* [2017] EWHC 1440 (Admin), [2018] P.T.S.R. 349.

90 Law Commission 362 (n3) Recommendation 19.

91 ibid paras 7.15–7.17.

92 CA 2014 Section 10(4); SSWA 2014 Section 24(4).

93 See, for example, CA Krause-Parello, EE Gulick, and B Basin, 'Loneliness, depression, and physical activity in older adults: The therapeutic role of human-animal interactions' (2019) *Anthrozoös* 32(2) 239; MJ Hughes and others, 'Companion animals and health in older populations: A system-

dog walker can significantly contribute to promoting the older person's well-being. Similar arguments can be made for the person who cuts the lawn and tends the garden for a proud gardener who can no longer attend to these matters. A carer may include somebody who takes an older person to see the local football team play – a team they supported all their lives but can now not access the stadium without help. Having a carer's assessment does not guarantee support, but in some cases, it may, and if not, it may signpost to local services such as community transport. An assessment also recognises the unpaid carer's role and contribution to social care.

As discussed, carers now have a single right to an assessment. Well-being outcomes, human rights, and equality duties equally apply to carers. The requirements of a carer assessment are outlined in Table 5.4.

Carer assessments must be proportionate.[94] A carer may refuse an assessment following provisions similar to refusing a needs assessment.[95] The continued ability of a carer to care and the sustainability of the caring relations are critical to a carer's assessment. Although the caring relationship is working reasonably well at the time of the assessment, how sustainable is it likely to be, given, for example, the carer's health and well-being? This may be particularly important when an older person is caring for another older person, and the health and mobility of both are deteriorating. At the same time an older person may be a carer and a person in need of care and support. As seen above, an important part of the assessment is the impact that caring has or may have on well-being in the future. However, the 2014 legislation does not require support to achieve the desired well-being outcomes. It need only contribute toward achieving them.

Supplementary provisions relating to assessments

Sitting underneath the CA 2014 and the SSWA 2014 provisions on assessment are regulations. The English regulations require consideration of support for those involved in caring for the person or anyone else the local authority considers relevant, including support to access information and advice. Specific references are also made to children who care for adults; how does this impact their development, and are they performing inappropriate tasks in the circumstances?[96] The Care and Support (Assessment) Regulations cover supported self-assessment, the impact of assessments on the person's family, and the need for a specially trained person when assessing deafblind persons. Regulation 3(3) addresses fluctuating needs and the importance of the local authority taking account of the person's circumstances over a period of time when assessing the level of need. Information must be provided about the assessment process. Assessors must have the required skills, knowledge,

atic review' (2020) *Clinical Gerontologist* 43(4) 365; and NR Gee, KE Rodriguez, AH Fine et al., 'Dogs supporting human health and well-being: A biopsychosocial approach' (2021) *Frontiers in Veterinary Science* 8, 630465.

94 Care Act Guidance (n24) para 6.28; SSWA 2014 Section 24(7).

95 CA 2014 Section 10(12); SSWA 2014 Section 25.

96 See also Care and Support (Children's Carers) Regulations 2015, SI 2015/305.

Table 5.4 Carers' assessments under the CA 2014 and the SSWA 2014 and the SSWA 2014 ibid s.10(3)(9) and (10) and s.3(4)(7) and (8).

	s.10(1) CA 2014; s.24(1) SSWA 2014	
Duty to assess a carer's need for support	Where it appears to a local authority that a carer may have needs for support (whether currently or in the future), the authority must assess— (a) whether the carer does have needs for support (or is likely to do so in the future), and (b) if the carer does, what those needs are (or are likely to be in the future).	
s.10(2) (9) & (10) CA 2014	**s.3(7), s.24(2) SSWA 2014**	
To whom does the duty apply?	An adult who provides or intends to provide care for an adult needing care. This does not apply to care provided through a contract or voluntary work unless the local authority considers treating them as a carer appropriate.[i]	A carer providing or intending to provide care for— (a) an adult or disabled child who is ordinarily resident in the authority's area, or (b) any other adult or disabled child within the authority's area. This does not apply to care provided through a contract or voluntary work unless the local authority considers treating them as a carer appropriate.
	s.10(4) CA 2014; s.24(3) SSWA 2014	
Matters to be disregarded	The duty applies regardless of the authority's view of— a) the level of the carer's needs for support, or (b) the level of the financial resources of the carer or the person for whom the carer provides or intends to provide care.	
	s.10(5) & (6) CA 2014	**s.24(4) SSWA 2014**
The matters that must be considered during an assessment. . .	An assessment must include assessing the carer's current and future ability and willingness to provide care and the impact of their own support needs on the well-being outcomes. Additionally, the assessment must include the carer's desired outcomes in their day-to-day life and whether providing support could contribute towards achieving these outcomes. Regard must be had to whether the carer works or participates in education, training, or recreation or wishes to do so. Regard must also be had to whether any additional resources available in the community could benefit the carer.	An assessment must include assessing the carer's current and future ability and willingness to provide care. For adult carers, it should identify the outcomes they wish to achieve. For child carers, the assessment should consider the outcomes the carer wishes to achieve, and those the person(s) with parental responsibility wish to achieve in relation to the child. Additionally, the assessment should determine whether support, preventative services, information, advice, or assistance could contribute to achieving those outcomes or meeting identified needs. Finally, other factors that could contribute to achieving outcomes or addressing needs should also be evaluated.
	10(6) CA2014; 24(5) SSWA 2014.	
Other considerations	An assessment must take into account whether the carer is employed or wants to be employed, as well as whether the carer is participating in or wishes to participate in education, training, or leisure activities.	

ibid s.10(3)(9) and (10) and s.3(4)(7) and (8).

and competence and be appropriately trained to work with older persons. When necessary, specialist expertise should be used.[97] A written record of a needs assessment must be provided to the assessed person, and a copy must be given to a carer with the permission of the person receiving care and to anyone else authorised by the assessed person. Similarly, a copy of a carer's assessment must be given to the carer and, if agreed to by the carer, shared with the person cared for or anybody else.[98]

The Welsh regulations require that there is a named person whose role it is to coordinate the assessment.[99] Assessors must have the necessary skills, knowledge, competence, and training, and a person with specialist knowledge must be considered if the person's needs call for their involvement. Any barriers to achieving personal outcomes must be regarded as part of the assessment, as must any risks to the person or others if the outcomes are not fulfilled. Strengths and capabilities must be assessed. Upon completion of an assessment, a written record of the conclusions and the matters the local authority considered in arriving at them must be prepared. The older person assessed has the right to have a copy of the record; it should also be given to anybody acting on their behalf. If the person assessed lacks mental capacity, the record must be given to anybody authorised to act for them. In the absence of such a person, it should be given to someone the local authority considers to be acting in the older person's best interests.

A common criticism by those undergoing assessment is that they have to provide the same information to several health and social care practitioners. Section 12 CA 2014 allows a local authority to combine a needs or carer's assessment with an assessment involving another person, as long as the person being assessed agrees. If the combination involves an assessment of another adult, their consent must also be obtained. If it involves a child, the child must have the capacity or competence to consent to and agree to the combined assessments. If the child lacks capacity or competence, the authority must be satisfied that combining the assessments is in the child's best interests. This enables an assessment of a young carer to be combined with the assessment of the adult they care for.[100] Other public authorities may be involved when assessing an older person's needs. The section also ensures that a local authority, when carrying out a needs or carer's assessment, is able to work together with or act on behalf of another organisation conducting a different assessment for the person or their caregiver. For example, if a local authority is undertaking a carer's assessment and an NHS body is conducting a continuing healthcare assessment for the person being cared for, the authority may collaborate with the NHS body to ensure great integration.[101]

Section 28 SSWA 2014 allows a Welsh local authority to combine a needs assessment and carer's assessment if both parties consent, or in cases of lack of capacity or understanding where doing so is in the person's best interests. An adult

97 SI 2014/2827.
98 CA 2014 Section 12(3) and (4).
99 See Care and Support (Assessment) (Wales) Regulations 2015, SI 2015/1305.
100 CA Section 12(5) and Care Act Guidance (n24) para 6.64.
101 CA 2014 Section 12(7) and Care Act Guidance (n24) para 6.75–77.

and a young person aged sixteen or seventeen are considered to have the capacity to consent to combine. A child under sixteen can agree to combine the assessments if they have sufficient understanding. A person with parental responsibility for a child can consent on behalf of a child under sixteen, but this can be disregarded if the child has sufficient understanding. If a child under sixteen lacks sufficient understanding, the consent of a person with parental responsibility is necessary, but a refusal can be overridden if the authority is satisfied that combining the assessments is in the best interest of the child. When an adult or a sixteen or seventeen-year-old lacks capacity, a person authorised under the MCA 2005 can consent. If there is no authorised person for an adult, the authority can combine if satisfied it is in their best interests. If a sixteen or seventeen-year-old lacks capacity and there is no authorised person, the consent of somebody with parental responsibility is required, but this can be overridden if the authority is satisfied that combining is in the young person's best interests. Section 29 SSWA 2014 provides that when a person appears to be in need of support as a carer and also has needs for care and support in their own right, a local authority can combine the two assessments. As is the case in England, a Welsh local authority can conduct a needs assessment at the same time as another statutory assessment for the same person, either by itself or with another body. This is to make the process more efficient and avoid multiple assessments.

The assessment process identifies if an older person has needs for care and support and whether their carers have needs for support. The next stage is to determine whether the identified needs are eligible needs.

The eligibility criteria – CA 2014

Both Acts place eligibility criteria on a statutory basis rather than in guidance. Once a person has been assessed as having needs, the next stage is to decide whether the need is an eligible need. The introduction of national statutory eligibility criteria sets minimum thresholds and aims to provide uniformity and transparency in service access for carers and persons cared for. The CA 2014 criteria are in the Care and Support (Eligibility Criteria) Regulations.[102] Different criteria apply for persons needing care and support and carers needing support. The criteria for those in need of care and support are outlined in Table 5.5.

The word 'significant' has its everyday meaning; the Oxford Dictionary defines it as beings 'sufficiently great or important to be worthy of attention; noteworthy.' The failure to meet two or more outcomes must have more than a mere impact. Paragraph 6.109–110 of the Care Act Guidance states it must have 'an important, consequential effect on daily living, independence and well-being,' and what may have a significant impact for one person may not have the same effect on another. A person cannot achieve an outcome if they cannot achieve it without assistance or where it would cause significant pain, distress, or anxiety; similarly, when it is likely to endanger their health or safety or that of other people, or it would take significantly longer than would normally be expected. The Guidance provides

102 SI 2015/313.

Table 5.5 Eligibility criteria – need for care and support – CA 2014

An adult's needs meet the eligibility criteria if:	*The outcomes:*
(a) The adult's needs arise from or are related to a physical or mental impairment or illness. (b) As a result of the adult's needs, the adult is unable to achieve two or more of the outcomes. (c) As a consequence, there is, or is likely to be, a significant impact on the adult's well-being.	(a) Managing and maintaining nutrition. (b) Maintaining personal hygiene. (c) Managing toilet needs. (d) Being appropriately clothed. (e) Being able to make use of the adult's home safely. (f) Maintaining a habitable home environment. (g) Developing and maintaining family or other personal relationships. (h) Accessing and engaging in work, training, education or volunteering. (i) Making use of necessary facilities or services in the local community, including public transport and recreational facilities or services. (j) Carrying out any caring responsibilities the adult has for a child.

Section 13 CA 2014 and Regulation 2 Care and Support (Eligibility Criteria) Regulations 2015 SI 2015/313.

illustrations of how local authorities consider each outcome. It gives the example of an older person with arthritis being able to prepare a meal without assistance but being left in great pain and unable to eat it. Similarly, an older person may be able to dress themselves, but it takes a long time and leaves them exhausted and unable to achieve other outcomes.[103]

The CA 2014 eligibility criteria for support of a carer are described in Table 5.6.

A need must arise as a consequence of providing 'necessary' care for an adult, which presupposes that the cared-for adult cannot meet their needs without support from the carer. Whether there is or is likely to be a 'significant impact' on the carer's well-being depends upon whether it has 'an important, consequential effect on daily living, independence and well-being.' The effect of the carer's needs is that any of the circumstances in table 5.6 are met.[104] The guidance provides examples of how the criteria should be interpreted. An older person and their carer may have a caring role for more than one adult; for example, they care for their spouse or partner, their parents, and an adult child with a disability. To what extent does the time spent caring compromise their home environment, nutrition, and ability to maintain personal relationships with family and friends? Finally, how does the caring role impact their ability to engage in broader activities such as education, recreational facilities, and the local community?[105] It is also important to remember

103 Care Act Guidance (n24) para 6.105.
104 ibid Regulation 3.
105 Care Act Guidance (n24) para 6.123 as aemended.

Table 5.6 Eligibility criteria – carer's need for support – CA 2104

A carer's needs meet the eligibility criteria if:	*The circumstances:*
(a) The needs arise as a consequence of providing necessary care for an adult. (b) The effect of the carer's needs is that any of the circumstances specified in column 2 apply to the carer. (c) As a consequence, there is, or is likely to be, a significant impact on the carer's well-being.	(a) The carer's physical or mental health is, or is at risk of, deteriorating. (b) The carer is unable to achieve any of the following outcomes: (i) Carrying out any caring responsibilities the carer has for a child. (ii) Providing care to other persons for whom the carer provides care. (iii) Maintaining a habitable home environment in the carer's home (whether or not this is also the home of the adult needing care). (iv) Managing and maintaining nutrition. (v) Developing and maintaining family or other personal relationships. (vi) Engaging in work, training, education or volunteering. (vii) Making use of necessary facilities or services in the local community, including recreational facilities or services. (viii) Engaging in recreational activities.

Section 13 CA 2014 and Regulation 3 Care and Support (Eligibility Criteria) Regulations 2015, SI 2015/313.

that some older persons have caring responsibility for a grandchild for specific periods (such as when the parents are at work) or permanently through the parent's absence. Kinship caring, where typically children live with grandparents, can be rewarding for some and traumatic for others. In both cases, they need support, in particular respite care.[106]

Eligibility criteria – SSWA 2014

There are differences between the English and Welsh eligibility criteria. The Welsh eligibility criteria for adults in need of care and support and carers in need of support involves four stages.[107] These stages comprise identifying an eligible reason for the need, assessing key tasks, evaluating the inability to meet the need, and

106 A Holt and J Birchall, '"Their mum messed up and gran can't afford to": Violence towards grandparent kinship carers and the implications for social work' (2022) *The British Journal of Social Work* 52(3) 1231.

107 SSWA 2014 Sections 32–33.

determining requirements for local authority support. This sequential approach provides a comprehensive framework for dealing with complex issues that require intervention, as shown in Table 5.7.

In Wales, if the needs do not meet the eligibility criteria, the local authority must decide whether it is still necessary to meet them to protect an older person from abuse or neglect or the risk of it or to protect a child from harm or the risk of it.[108]

The relevant Welsh Code addresses several issues. In identifying barriers to achieving personal outcomes, a local authority must consider any information provided by the person, family, carers, and others. The practitioner's professional judgement is an important consideration, particularly their local knowledge of what is available that would be most beneficial to the person. Assessing risk includes considering the consequences of making people too dependent upon services, which may undermine meeting personal outcomes. The risk assessment should include the time scale, predictability, and complexity of the person's circumstances; in isolation, a risk may be minor, but the cumulative effect of several minor risks must be considered. Risk is part of everyday life and can enhance

Table 5.7 Social Services and Well-being (Wales) Act Eligibility criteria – need for care and support

Stage	*The need of an adult for care and support meets the eligibility criteria if:*	
1	The need arises from the adult's physical or mental ill-health, age, disability, dependence on alcohol or drugs, or other similar circumstances.	
2	The need relates to one or more of these seven factors.	1 Ability to carry out self-care or domestic routines. 2 Ability to communicate. 3 Protection from abuse or neglect. 4 Involvement in work, education, learning, or in leisure activities. 5 Maintenance or development of family or other significant personal relationships. 6 Development and maintenance of social relationships and involvement in the community. 7 Fulfilment of caring responsibilities for a child.
3	The need is such that the adult is not able to meet that need, either-	i. Alone. ii. With the care and support of others who are willing to provide that care and support. iii. With the assistance of services in the community to which the adult has access.
4	The adult is unlikely to achieve one or more of their personal outcomes unless the local authority provides or arranges care and support to meet the need, or the local authority enables the need to be met by making direct payments.	

Regulation 3 Care and Support (Eligibility) (Wales) Regulations 2015, SI 2015/1578.

108 SSWA 2014 Section 32(1)(b).

well-being and independence if properly assessed and managed, but an important question is whether the person is competent to assess the risk and able and willing to accept it. When using the eligibility criteria, there is a balance to be struck between the protection of the person and others against the right to autonomy and independence. It is essential that the older person is involved in this process or that their views are represented.

Table 5.8 below describes the Welsh eligibility criteria for carer support.

Table 5.8 Social Services and Well-being (Wales) Act Eligibility criteria – carers need for support

Stage	*The need of a carer for support meets the eligibility criteria if:*	
1	The need arises as a result of providing care for either an adult who has needs for care and support that are within the eligibility criteria or a disabled child.	
2	The need relates to one or more of these eight factors.	(i) Ability to carry out self-care or domestic routines. (ii) Ability to communicate. (iii) Protection from abuse or neglect. (iv) Involvement in work, education, learning or in leisure activities. (v) Maintenance or development of family or other significant personal relationships. (vi) Development and maintenance of social relationships and involvement in the community. (vii) In the case of an adult carer, fulfilment of caring responsibilities for a child. (viii) In the case of a child carer, achieving developmental goals.
3	The need is such that the adult is not able to meet that need, either	(i) alone. (ii) With the support of others who are willing to provide that support. (iii) with the assistance of services in the community to which the carer has access.
4	The carer is unlikely to achieve one or more of their personal outcomes unless	(i) the local authority provides or arranges support to the carer to meet the carer's need. (ii) the local authority provides or arranges care and support to the person for whom the carer provides care, in order to meet the carer's need. (iii) the local authority enables the need to be met by making direct payments.

Regulation 5 Care and Support (Eligibility) (Wales) Regulations 2015, SI 2015/1578

Clements raises an issue with the Welsh eligibility criteria by pointing out that it may make a person ineligible if their carer indicates a willingness to provide support. This differs from the English guidance, which states that eligibility should be determined based on the person's needs and how they impact their well-being. Any support a carer provides may be relevant to preparing the care and support plan but not eligibility. However, in Wales, this can become a problem if a person is deemed ineligible due to the presence of a 'willing carer.' What happens if the carer suddenly becomes unable or unwilling to continue in their role? In such cases, the assessment process must start again, causing delays and inconvenience. Paragraph 83 of Part 3 of the Code of Practice addresses this concern by stating that a sudden inability of the carer to provide care must not prevent or delay a local authority from taking immediate action to meet the person's needs for care and support. The most recent assessment should inform this. Clements provides another example of the problematic nature of this approach. A person with a disability who requires intimate care may not want a family member to provide it, even if willing to do so. This would make them ineligible, interfere with their ability to control their care arrangements, and be a violation of their dignity. He advises the following,

> To correct this perverse element within the criteria, carers could be advised to state clearly, that they are not able (and therefore not willing) to provide care unless the local authority has first determined that the individual in need is eligible. Then, and only then, will they be able (and therefore willing) to discuss with the individual in need and the authority the nature and extent of the care (if any) they might be willing to provide.[109]

Once the local authority has identified needs and determined that they meet the eligibility criteria, it must decide whether it has a duty or a power to meet those needs.

Meeting needs

The duty to provide services to meet eligible needs for care and support is similar in both Acts and is found in Section 18 CA 2014 and Section 35 SSWA 2014. In both nations, to trigger the duty the person in need of care and support must be ordinarily resident in the local authority's area or of no settled residence but present in the area. A distinction is made between cases where a local authority is prevented from charging and cases where a charge can be made. A local authority must provide where there is no charge for meeting the needs. Both nations have regulations prohibiting local authorities from imposing charges for certain services. The English regulations prohibit charging for aids and minor adaptations, intermediate care, and reablement support services during the first six weeks of a specified period or for the duration if it is less than six weeks. Intermediate care

109 L Clements, 'The Social Services and Well-being (Wales) Act 2014: An overview' (*Rhydian*, 29 November 2023) 17 https://www.lukeclements.co.uk/rhydian-social-welfare-law-in-wales/an-overview-briefing-social-care-law-in-wales/ – accessed 28 September 2024.

helps people to maintain or regain the ability to live independently in their homes. In addition, a local authority cannot charge for meeting needs where care and support are provided to a person with variant Creutzfeldt–Jakob disease. In Wales, local authorities cannot charge for transport to attend a day service if necessary to meet the person's assessed needs. Intermediate care and reablement services are also free of charge, under the same conditions as in England. No charge can be made for advocacy services concerning meeting the needs provisions of the Act nor for a person who has been clinically diagnosed with Creutzfeldt–Jakob disease. Charges may not be made for services provided under Section 117 MHA 1983.[110]

If a charge can be made, the duty to provide arises if one of three conditions in Section 18 CA 2014 in England or in Wales Section 35 SSWA 2014 is met. First, the local authority is satisfied that the person's resources are at or below the financial limit. Second, if the person's financial resources exceed the financial limit that has been set, they may ask the local authority to meet their needs. The local authority may charge them for the services provided and a charge to cover making the arrangements. Third, it has a duty if satisfied the person lacks the capacity to agree to the provision of care and support, and there is nobody authorised to do so under the MCA 2005 or otherwise. However, Section 18(7) CA 2014 clarifies that the Section 18 duty does not apply to any of the person's needs being met by a carer. Similarly, Section 35(6) SSWA 2014 disapplies the duty to meet needs to the extent that the local authority is satisfied that a carer is meeting them.

In addition to the duty, powers to meet needs for care and support are found in Section 19 CA 2014. Following a needs assessment and, if required, a financial assessment, a local authority has the power to meet a person's need for care and support if they are ordinarily resident in its area or present there but of no settled residence and the authority is satisfied that it does not have a Section 18 CA 2014 duty to provide. In addition, a local authority may meet a person's needs for care and support, which meet the Section 13 CA 2014 eligibility criteria if they are ordinarily resident in the area of another local authority. There must be no Section 14 CA 2014 charge for meeting the needs or, if there is a charge, one of the conditions in Section 18 must be met. The authority must notify the other local authority of its intention to meet the needs. Finally, a local authority may meet an adult's needs for care and support, which appear urgent (regardless of whether the adult is ordinarily resident in its area) without having carried out a needs or financial assessment or decided on eligibility. An example given is when the person is terminally ill. In Wales, Section 36 SSWA 2014 provides that a local authority may meet needs for care and support if the person is within the local authority's area or ordinarily resident in its area but outside of it. If the person is ordinarily resident in another local authority's area, it must notify that authority. A local authority may meet needs regardless of whether it has completed a needs or financial assessment. As with England, the power is typically used when urgent needs must be met.

110 Regulation 3 Care and Support (Charging and Assessment of Resources) Regulations 2014, SI 2014/2672; Regulation 4 Care and Support (Charging) (Wales) Regulations 2015, SI 2015/1843.

Section 20 CA 2014 outlines the duties and powers of English local authorities to meet the support needs of carers. It must meet a carer's need for support where it is satisfied that the eligibility criteria and the conditions in the section are fulfilled. The number of carers receiving direct support decreased from 314,000 in 2021–22 to 295,000 in 2022–23. Meanwhile, the number of people provided with respite care increased to 36,000 from 33,000 in 2021–22.[111] The cared for person must be ordinarily resident in the authority's area or present in its area but of no settled residence. If meeting the carer's needs involves providing them with direct support, a duty arises if there is no charge for the service. If there is a charge, one of two conditions must be fulfilled. Either the authority must be satisfied based on the financial assessment that the carer's financial resources are at or below the financial limit, or they are above the financial limit, and the carer asks the authority to meet the needs. Where meeting the carer's needs involves providing care and support to the person cared for, and that person agrees, the duty arises if there is no charge. If a person being cared for has financial resources at or below the limit and agrees to receive care and support, or if they have resources above the limit and ask the authority to meet their needs, there is also a duty. If there is a charge for the services and the person lacks the capacity to arrange for the care and support, a duty to meet the needs arises if no person is authorised to act under the MCA 2005 or otherwise to act on their behalf. This will be subject to the best interests test and follow the MCA 2005. A local authority in England has the power to meet a carer's needs for support even if satisfied it is not required to do so by Section 20 CA 2014. It may also meet a carer's need for support by providing care and support to the cared-for person, even if there is no duty to meet those care and support needs under Section 18 CA 2014. Sections 40 and 41 SSWA 2014 impose similar duties to meet needs in Wales. In both Acts, if a local authority needs to meet some or all of a carer's support needs but cannot do so by providing care and support to the adult in need, it must, if possible, find another way to meet those needs. Section 45 SSWA 2014 provides for the power to support a carer if the person cared for is within its area or is ordinarily resident in the area but outside of it. This power may be exercised irrespective of whether a needs or financial assessment has been undertaken.

A local authority may meet needs directly, but they will most likely be outsourced to an independent provider such as a for-profit or third-sector organisation. Direct payments may also be made. If resources permit, there is room for imaginative and innovative support. Services include accommodation in a care home or similar, care and support at home and in the community, goods and facilities, counselling, information and advice, and occupational therapy. It may also include providing financial support for recreational activities and holidays, but not accommodation needs which should be addressed in the first instance under the Housing Act 1996.[112] These are examples and not a definitive statement of how needs can

111 Kings Fund (n7) 27.

112 CA 2014 Section 8; SSWA 2014 Section 34; *Regina (BG and another) v Suffolk County Council* [2022] EWCA Civ 1047, [2022] 4 WLR 107; *R (on the application of Campbell) v Ealing London*

be met. In England, the CA 2014 requires the preparation of care and support plans for the person being cared for and support plans for carers to record their needs; they may be combined. Plans must identify the needs meeting the eligibility criteria, those the local authority will meet, and how they will be addressed. The care plan outlines how the well-being outcomes the person wishes to achieve will be met and how providing services will contribute to achieving those outcomes. It advises on reducing needs and offers guidance on preventing or delaying their development; any needs to be met by direct payment must be identified, including the payment amounts and frequencies. When preparing a care and support plan, the local authority must involve the person cared for, their carer, and anyone else they want to be included. If they lack capacity, anybody who appears to be interested in their welfare should be involved. A copy of the care and support plan must be given to the person for whom it was prepared and, with their consent, to their carer and anyone they want to receive a copy. When preparing a support plan for a carer, the local authority must involve the carer, the person cared for if the carer agrees, and any other person the carer wants to be included; these people must be given a copy of the plan if the carer agrees along with any other person the carer wishes to receive a copy. The authority must take all reasonable steps to reach an agreement with the person being cared for or the carer on the plan. Plans must include a personal budget detailing the cost to the local authority to meet the needs and, based on the person's financial assessment, identify the amount, if any, the person must contribute. Using this information, the budget determines the amount the local authority is required to contribute towards the cost. The CA 2014 requires local authorities to periodically review the care and support plans and care plans to ensure the needs are being addressed. As part of the review process, the assessed person's involvement is required, and the local authority will consider any changes in their circumstances. The goal is to ensure that the services provided are effective in helping the person maintain their well-being and independence.[113]

In Wales, if a local authority is required to meet a person's needs, it must prepare and maintain a plan for care and support or a support plan, as in England. Copies of the plans must be given to the same people as under the CA 2014. The content of the plans is broadly comparable with the English plans. The local authority must review a plan if it appears to the authority that it is not meeting the eligible needs of the person to whom it relates.[114] A person with a needs assessment or carers assessment may request a review, as may any person authorised to act on their behalf; the local authority must grant the request if satisfied there has been a significant change of circumstances or personal outcomes. If the person's circumstances have changed in a way that affects the plan, the local authority must revise the plan accordingly.

Borough Council [2023] EWHC 10 (Admin), [2023] PTSR 810; *R (on the application of Idolo) v Bromley London Borough Council* [2020] EWHC 860 (Admin), [2020] All ER (D) 175.

113 Care Act Guidance (n24) paras 13.10–13.34.

114 Care and Support (Care Planning) (Wales) Regulations 2015, SI 2015/1335.

Local authorities in England and Wales can charge for services provided to those in need of care and support and carers in need of support.[115] Before deciding if a charge can be made, a financial assessment must be undertaken to ascertain whether the person must pay the total or partial cost or whether the local authority will provide full financial support.[116] Charges can only cover expenses incurred by the local authority. If a person's financial resources exceed the financial limit, they may be charged for services. Carers cannot be charged when their needs are met by providing care and support for the person being cared for. Regulations on charging are made under Section 14 CA 2014 and Sections 61–62 SSWA 2014. Although many older persons requiring care contribute towards its cost, those with ongoing significant health needs can have their care paid for through NHS Continuing Healthcare (CHC). To qualify, an older person must have ongoing and significant physical or mental health issues or both. Once their needs have been assessed, the majority component of their care needs must be focused on addressing and preventing health needs. In England, there is a National Framework for NHS CHC.[117] Wales has a separate framework.[118] These outline the processes for determining CHC eligibility, including whether the care need is a 'primary health need,' a term which lacks a precise legal definition. If an older person has a primary health need, the NHS will provide care beyond what social services can provide. However, there is potential for subjectivity leading to inconsistency in determining primary health needs.[119] Difficulties are encountered by persons living with dementia as they may be unable to perform routine tasks such as personal care, dressing, and feeding themselves; they may need continence care and help with medication. Unfortunately, such needs are not always considered primary health needs but rather social or personal care needs, and consequently, they may be ineligible for CHC. CHC may be provided and funded in an older person's home, care home, or hospice. In the case of a care home, CHC will pay all the fees, whereas, in their own home, it does not cover food, accommodation, and general household support. In England, personal health budgets allocate NHS money to support the person's health and well-being. These can be managed in one of three ways. The first involves direct payments to purchase a care package and reporting on the use of the funds. The second is a notional budget managed by a case manager. The third entails funding an independent care organisation, which becomes the legal employer responsible for managing the care package. Direct payments are currently not available in Wales. However, the Health and Social Care (Wales) Act 2025 includes a provision enabling CHC patients to receive direct payments to

115 CA 2014 Section 14 and SSWA 2014 Section 59.

116 ibid Section 17 and Section 63.

117 Department of Health and Social Care, *National framework for NHC Continuing Health Care and NHS-funded Nursing Care* (Department of Health and Social Care, July 2022).

118 NHS Wales, Welsh Government, *Continuing NHS Healthcare: The National Framework of Implementation in Wales* (NHS Wales, Welsh Government, 2021).

119 L Dalingwater, 'Inequity in supply of health care?: The case of continuing health care in England' (2018) *The International Journal of Health, Wellness and Society* 8(4) 43.

secure services that meet their assessed healthcare needs instead of NHS-provided services. If an older person is ineligible for CHC but requires nursing care in a nursing home, NHS-funded nursing care will cover fees relating to the nursing or medical care provided by a registered nurse. As with the CHC, it is not means-tested. Funded nursing care does not cover accommodation costs, only the nursing care costs.

Choice and personalisation

An English local authority should offer a choice of care homes to those assessed as needing residential care. An older person is not required to choose from the care homes offered by the authority and can make their own choice provided the accommodation satisfies the criteria in the care home regulations. The preferred accommodation must meet the assessed needs, and the cost should be within the personal budget. It must be available, and the provider must agree to the contract on the local authority's terms and within the rate set in the personal budget. The local authority cannot restrict the choice of care home to those with which it has contractual arrangements or homes within its area.[120] The Welsh provisions are similar, although the SSWA 2014 does not require a personal budget to be prepared and included in the care and support plan. The regulations require the local authority to arrange for the person to be accommodated in their preferred care home if it meets their needs and is available. Again, the preferred accommodation provider must agree to the local authority's terms.[121] A third party can cover the difference if the preferred accommodation's cost exceeds the personal budget in England or the typical amount the local authority would pay in Wales. Given that the local authority will enter a contract with the provider, it must be satisfied that the financial offer is genuine and that adequate resources exist to support it. If the top-up fee is not paid, the local authority may move the person to less expensive accommodation unless their assessed needs can only be met at their current placement. Previously, there was a debate about whether residents could use their money to cover top-up accommodation costs. In R v East Sussex County Council, ex parte Ward,[122] Moses J held that these own top-ups were unlawful. However, own top-ups are now available where a twelve-week disregard is in place.[123] This is where the local authority must disregard the value of a person's property for the first twelve weeks of their permanent care home placement. They are also available where there is a deferred payment agreement in place. This is a legal agreement where the local authority provides financial support for care costs on the understanding that it will

120 Care and Support and After-care (Choice of Accommodation) Regulations 2014, SI 2014 No. 2670.

121 Care and Support (Choice of Accommodation) (Wales) Regulations 2015, SI 2015/1840.

122 See *R v East Sussex County Council ex parte Ward* (2000) 3 CCL Rep 132.

123 Care and Support and Aftercare (Choice of Accommodation) Regulations 2014, SI 2014/2670; Care and Support (Choice of Accommodation) (Wales) Regulations 2015, SI 2014/1840 (W 268).

be reimbursed from the proceeds of the future sale of the property.[124] The local authority will register a legal charge on the property to protect its interest. Own top-ups for preferred accommodations are also allowed by Sections 117 and 117A MHA 1983.

Personalisation of care for persons cared for and carers is also promoted through direct payments designed to empower service users and give greater autonomy and choice over the management and organisation of their care. In England, Section 30 CA 2014 allows for an adult with capacity to request that direct payments be used to meet some or all their needs, and the local authority must agree where it considers they are appropriate to meet the needs and that the person, or a nominated person, can manage them. Direct payments can also be used to meet the needs of a person lacking capacity if an authorised person requests it and the authority is satisfied it is an appropriate way to meet the needs. The person must be authorised under the MCA 2005 or nominated by the direct payment recipient. If nobody is authorised, the local authority may appoint somebody they consider appropriate if satisfied they will act in the person's best interest and can manage the payments. Conditions can be included in direct payments, in particular, the stipulation that they can only be used for the specific purpose for which they were given. If the conditions are breached, the local authority can stop the direct payments and ask for the return of payment made. Regulations prohibit using direct payments to pay close relatives unless deemed necessary by the local authority. Direct payment to pay for residential care is limited to four weeks in any twelve months, although the government has undertaken to abolish this restriction.[125]

In Wales, Section 50 SSWA 2014 permits direct payments to be made to carers and those being cared for. The local authority must agree that they are appropriate and can be managed by the recipient. Regulations impose a duty to provide direct payment where these conditions are met.[126] The authority must provide the necessary information to help the person and any authorised persons make informed decisions about whether to request direct payments. Conditions may be included, and if unmet, the local authority can terminate the payments and require repayment of any funds paid out. As is the case in England, direct payments are available for a person lacking capacity where there is somebody suitable to act in their best interests and manage the direct payments on their behalf; this is subject to that person having an enhanced criminal records check. If a person loses capacity after agreeing to direct payments, there are provisions in the regulations that allow for those payments to continue, subject to conditions. Direct payments can only be made to close relatives if the local authority believes it is necessary for the person's well-being.

124 CA 2014 Section 34 and Care and Support (Deferred Payment) Regulations 2014, SI 2014/2671; SSWA 2014 Section 68 and Care and Support (Deferred Payment) Regulations 2014, SI 2014/2671.

125 See CA 2014 Sections 30–33 and Care and Support (Direct Payments) Regulations 2014, SI 2014/2871.

126 Care and Support (Direct Payments) (Wales) Regulations 2015, SI 2015/1815

Woolham et al. question the effectiveness of direct payments to older persons due to limited budgets and a lack of recognition of the different needs of older persons. They suggest radical changes, such as specialised gerontological social work, to provide tailored care and support.[127] Locke and West identify a gap between local authorities and older persons' understanding of the needs and effectiveness of direct payments and suggest that this may reflect the state of social care during a time of austerity.[128] Donoghue and Taylor's Australian-based study found that direct payments can help reduce social isolation, although more service options are needed for older persons. Increasing access to direct payments can help fill service gaps, reduce waiting lists, and provide services such as handypersons, companions, transportation, and cleaning. However, they require more involvement and responsibility than receiving a service directly and managing them requires support. Limited local service options may discourage older persons from using them.[129] The number of people using direct payments in England increased from 117,000 in 2021–22 to 117,737 in 2023-24, while the proportion of users decreased from 27% to under 26%%. According to the King's Fund, 38% of working-age adults and only 15% of older persons in England receiving social care use direct payments. This may be due to the higher level of responsibility and limited choice of local services.[130] In Wales, 36.1% of those receiving direct payments were sixty-five or older, despite older persons making up over 75% of adults receiving social services.[131] As with all aspects of social care, the ravages of austerity adversely affect the implementation of what may be a preferred way of receiving social care support for some older persons. Older persons were initially excluded when introduced by the Community Care (Direct Payments) Act 1996. It is interesting to speculate whether a model initially intended to address the needs of younger persons with disabilities is appropriate for older persons.

Continuity and portability of care

An older person receiving a care package from a local authority may relocate to another area, maybe to be closer to their family or return to the place of their childhood. Previously, this was complex, often involving restarting the assessment process in the new authority. Continuity of care in England and portability in Wales

127 J Woolham, G Daly, T sparks et al., 'Do direct payments improve outcomes for older people who receive social care? Differences in outcome between people aged 75+ who have a managed personal budget or a direct payment' (2017) *Ageing & Society* 37(5) 961.

128 P Locke and K West, 'Direct payments for older adults in an age of austerity' (2018) *Ethics and Social Welfare* 12(3) 216.

129 J Donoghue and C Taylor, 'Over the rainbow: Direct payments and social inclusion' (2010) *Australian Health Review* 34(1) 127.

130 People Places Lives, 'Direct Payments Analysis' 2023/24' (2025) https://www.peopleplaceslives.co.uk/news/direct-payments-analysis-2023-24/ accessed 10 February 2025; The King's Fund (n7).

131 Audit Wales, 'Direct Payments for Adult Social Care' (2022) https://www.audit.wales/blog/audit-wales/2022/6/15/direct-payments-wales_– accessed 28 September 2024.

aim to address this issue. In England, if an older person has an existing care plan and intends to move to a different local authority, they must inform the new authority. If the receiving authority is satisfied that the intention is genuine, they must provide appropriate information, assess the person's and any carers' needs, and create and implement a care and support plan. They must also notify the original authority and obtain a copy of the care plan. If the new authority intends to change the plan, they must give written reasons. Services must be available on the day of arrival in the new authority. If they are not in place, the new local authority must meet the needs identified by the sending authority as far as is reasonably practicable. This is until it conducts an assessment, devises a care plan, and makes necessary provisions. If a person receives care in a care home, shared lives, or supported living placement, the responsibility of meeting their care needs falls within the provisions in Section 39 CA 2014. This means that the local authority responsible for placing them in the accommodation remains responsible for their care needs. However, this rule does not apply if the person receives care outside of these types of accommodation.[132]

In Wales, if an older person receiving care and support from a local authority (the 'sending authority') intends to move to another area in Wales, the sending authority must inform the local authority in the new area (the 'receiving authority') of the person's intention. The sending authority must provide the receiving authority with a copy of the person's care and support plan and any other relevant information about the person and, if there is one, their carer. Once satisfied the person is moving to its area, the receiving authority must notify the sending authority of this and provide the person and any carer with the necessary information. The receiving authority must assess the person, taking account of any changes in their care and support needs resulting from the move, and consider the care and support plan of the sending authority. If the receiving authority has not assessed by the day of the person's move, it must provide the care and support contained in the sending authority's plan until it completes its assessment and decides on the support to be provided.[133]

Registration and inspection

Each nation has a regulatory and inspection framework designed to promote high standards in social care provision. The Care Quality Commission (CQC) regulates, inspects, and sets standards for England's health and adult social care services. Its authority is derived from the Health and Social Care Act 2008, which details the CQC's enforcement powers. The CQC's role involves promoting improvements

132 CA 2014 Section 37.

133 SSWA 2014 Section 56; Welsh Government, 'Social Services and Well-being (Wales) Act 2014 Part 11 Code of Practice (Miscellaneous and General') (Cardiff, 2015) https://www.gov.wales/sites/default/files/publications/2019-05/part-11-code-of-practice-miscellaneous-and-general.pdf – accessed 28 September 2024.

in health and social care services while ensuring that providers meet the needs of their users and use resources effectively. It is also responsible for safeguarding and advancing the rights of service users, particularly those detained under the MHA 1983, subject to a Deprivation of Liberty, or considered vulnerable in other ways. The CQC must consider public views of health and social care services and users' experiences and act proportionately while considering new regulatory approaches and best practices.[134] The Care Inspectorate Wales (CIW) is responsible for registering, inspecting, and taking action to enhance the quality and safety of care services throughout Wales. It performs functions on behalf of Welsh Ministers to ensure service quality and safety. CIW decides who is registered to provide services, inspects and drives improvement of regulated services and local authority social services, and conducts national reviews of social care provision. The primary objectives of CIW are to safeguard, promote, and maintain the safety and well-being of people who use regulated services and to promote and sustain high standards.[135] Healthcare providers in Wales are regulated and inspected by the Healthcare Inspectorate Wales. Healthcare Inspectorate Wales inspects NHS services, regulates independent healthcare providers, and identifies areas for improvement.

Conclusion

An ongoing concern about the sustainability of England and Wales's social care model is how it is funded. In England, in 2023-24, the total expenditure on adult social care was £27.1 billion. In Wales, in 2019–20, the baseline cost of social care for those over sixty-five was £586m and was projected to rise to over £700m for 2022–23.[136] The older person receiving the service often pays in full or contributes to the cost. Charging for social care is contentious, and current arrangements have significant consequences for many older persons and their families. Wittenberg et al.'s survey of public attitudes to funding adult social care identified that the State should meet all healthcare costs regardless of the user's resources. However, for 'old age care,' respondents felt that care costs should be shared between the State and the service user. There was, however, a majority in favour of service users meeting less than half the costs of their care.[137] The arguments for and against paying for social care are balanced. As with healthcare, free social care can be seen

134 Health and Social Care Act 2008, Sections1–4.

135 Regulation and Inspection of Social Care (Wales) Act 2016, Section 2.

136 See NHS Digital, 'Adult Social Care Activity and Finance Report, England, 2023-24 - NHS England Digital' (NHS England Digital2023) accessed 10 February 2025; LE Wales, 'Short to Medium Term Operational and Cost Pressures Affecting Social Care in Wales' (2020) <https://www.gov.wales/sites/default/files/publications/2021-04/short-to-medium-term-operational-and-cost-pressures-affecting-social-care-in-wales.pdf> – accessed 28 September 2024.

137 R Wittenberg, S Read, B Erens, et al., 'Who should pay for social care for older people in England? Results from surveys of public attitudes to the funding of social care' (2024) *Journal of Social Policy* 53, 1.

as a right for all. It would help to reduce inequalities in provision and encourage early intervention, thus saving scarce resources. Against this is the argument that it is not feasible during reduced public spending and would risk further rationing as public authorities struggle to meet increasing demand. Scotland provides free personal care if a person is assessed as needing it; this includes personal hygiene, assistance with eating, immobility needs, medication management, and well-being. Other forms of support, such as laundry, community-based provision, and shopping, are chargeable. In Wales, a person who exceeds the financial limits will pay a maximum of £100 per week for non-residential care. Who pays for social care is a longstanding debate which needs to be stripped of any party political toxicity and the avoidance of inflammatory language such as 'death tax' and 'dementia tax.' Some innovative thinking is required. Beresford et al. present a radical approach. They argue that a sustainable social care system should be free at the point of delivery and funded through general taxation on the same basis as the NHS. This would require a more progressive taxation system rather than the current regressive one. Good social care, they conclude, should be seen as an investment rather than a burden. Integration of health, social care, and other support services, such as housing, can only be achieved through consistent funding and principles.[138]

In 2011, Andrew Dilnot's Commission on Funding proposed a new way to fund social care.[139] It recommended limiting lifetime contributions made by people towards the cost of their social care. Dilnot suggested a cap of £35,000 beyond which the local authority would be responsible, subject to charging the person for some services. Many criticisms were levelled at the proposal, such as the bureaucracy involved – not least keeping track of what people pay for their care to identify when the cap is reached. It was a subject of political debate, ending with an amended version appearing in the CA 2014, which included a cap of £86,000.[140] However, as Clements points out, operating a cap on care costs could shift social care staff's focus from identifying and securing support to assessing financial entitlements, leading to a loss of morale and skill among social workers. This could result in their training being disregarded in favour of performing an auditing role.[141] Additionally, most people being assessed will not receive any financial benefit from the proposal. In her statement to the Westminster Parliament, the Labour government Chancellor announced that 'it will not be possible to take forward these charging reforms.' This follows the previous government's decision not to implement an £86,000 cap.[142] Although social care is devolved to Wales, any progress

138 P Beresford, C Slasberg, and L Clements, 'From dementia tax to a solution for social care' (2018) *Soundings* 68(68) 78.

139 A Dilnot, *Fairer Care Funding: The Report of the Commission on Funding of Care and Support. Vol. 1.* (HMSO, 2011).

140 CA 2014 Sections 15 and 16.

141 L Clements, *Administering a cap on costs (*Rhydian, 2024) <https://www.lukeclements.co.uk/administering-a-cap-on-costs/> – accessed 28 September 2024.

142 HM Treasury, 'Chancellor statement on public spending inheritance' (29 July 2024) <https://www.gov.uk/government/speeches/chancellor-statement-on-public-spending-inheritance> – accessed

on reform of its funding is, to some extent, dependent upon reform in England. However, as part of its disbanded Co-operation Agreement with Plaid Cymru, the Welsh Government established an expert group to explore a 'shared ambition to create a National Care Service, free at the point of need, and continuing as a public service.' The Expert Group's recommendations include moving towards a system where most non-residential care is free and where care costs in residential care, excluding accommodation costs, are also free. Following consultation the National Office for Care and Support was established. Its overall phased delivery plan will go beyond 2029.[143] Recently announced plans by the Westminster government are similarly longer term and include the third indpendent commission in the last thirty years. Baroness Casey's commission on social care will report in 2028.[144] For many older people, both initiatives will be too late.

In its report on the CA 2014, the Adult Social Care Committee of the House of Lords found that 'ageism is alive and well.' Older persons are seen negatively as passive, frail, vulnerable, and dependent, and as a problem to be fixed. Advertising and the media reinforce this stereotypical and ageist image. The negative portrayal perpetuates intergenerational conflict and affects how services are designed and delivered. The Committee referred to a belief that older persons and persons with disabilities are a burden and should have a more restricted life, with a lower value compared to others placed on them in the expectation that they will accept this. It challenged this assumption. Everybody has the opportunity to live a fulfilling life, regardless of their age or disability. Rather than focusing on providing minimal care to meet the basic needs of older persons and persons with disabilities, social care should challenge discriminatory perceptions and enable them to live a life of their choice.[145] The Committee's chilling conclusion is that,

> (T)he Care Act 2014 is a supreme example of policy which has failed its purpose, with the right principles and expectations lost in time. This needs to be put right immediately and the legislation that has been introduced must be made to work.[146]

The review of the SSWA 2014 suggested that

---

30 July 2024; Millie Cooke, 'Labour has "failed another generation of families" with cancellation of social care reforms, Dilnot says' *Independent* C (London, 31 July 2024): C Needham and P Hall, *Social care in the UK's four nations: Between two paradigms* (Policy Press, 2023) 79.

143 Welsh Government, *Towards a National Care and Support Service: initial implementation plan* (2023) 5-6 and 18–19 https://www.gov.wales/sites/default/files/publications/2023-12/Towards%20a%20National%20Care%20and%20Support%20Service%20initial%20implementation%20plan.pdf – accessed 28 September 2024.

144 Samuel, M. (2025). Commission on adult social care reform announced by government - Community Care. [online] Community Care. Available at: https://www.communitycare.co.uk/2025/01/03/commission-on-adult-social-care-reform-announced-by-government/ [Accessed 12 Mar. 2025]

145 House of Lords Adult Social Care Committee, 'A "gloriously ordinary life": spotlight on adult social care' Report of Session 2022-23, 8 December 2022 – HL Paper 99, paras 84–104.

146 ibid para 447.

> there remains therefore a distance between the highly aspirational rhetoric of individual agency under the Act and the extremely complex and, often, imperfect matter of enacting this in individual cases which can create frustration and stress. This is particularly acute where people in need of services seek to obtain them and find that provision is unavailable or not delivered in a manner that they feel maximises their well-being and is unsuitable for them.[147]

Such criticisms must be placed in the context of the hard work and commitment of many social care practitioners and those in the third sector who strive to deliver the aspirations of the legislation against evidence of the rationing of social care. Local authorities struggle to meet growing demand against a background of reduced funding. The Association of Directors of Adult Social Services, in its 2022 Autumn Survey Report, reveals that 94% of adult social services directors in England, when asked, disagree or strongly disagree that there is sufficient funding or workforce to meet the care costs of older persons and persons with disabilities in their areas.[148] In effect, reduced funding for local authorities has led to rationing social care to those in greatest need. The Local Government and Social Care Ombudsman in England notes an increase in cases where local authorities use cost to justify failing to provide social care.[149]

In its 2023 report on reforming adult social care in England, the National Audit Office highlighted the challenges for the adult social care sector. These had to be seen against increased service demand and uncertain funding. The report highlights several challenges, including concerns over quality, workforce shortages, financial sustainability of local authorities, provider stability, and high care costs for self-funders who often cross-subsidise local authority provision.[150] These are common challenges across England and Wales. Unless addressed, they undermine the intentions behind the 2014 legislation. Older persons and other users will suffer as a consequence. Tarrant's report on social care in Wales argues that a radical rethink of social care is required. She concludes,

> social care in its current format is not meeting the needs of those who use it. We need to re-think what social care needs to achieve in Wales, and how it

147 M Llewellyn, F Verity, S Wallace, et al., *From act to impact? final report of the evaluation of the Social Services and Well-being (Wales) Act 2014'* (University of South Wales, 2023) para 6.61 <https://pure.southwales.ac.uk/en/publications/from-act-to-impact-final-report-of-the-evaluation-of-the-social-s> – accessed 28 September 2024.

148 Association of Directors of Adult Social Services, *Autumn survey report 2022* (Association of Directors of Adult Social Services, 2022).

149 Local Government and Social Care Ombudsman, *Annual review of adult social care adult social care complaints 2021–22* (Local Government and Social Care Ombudsman, 2022) 1.

150 Department of Health and Social Care, *Reforming adult social care in England*. Session 2023–24 10 November 2023 HC 184 (Department of Health and Social Care, 2023).

can support those who use it to lead full lives. This work should be led by people who use social care.[151]

She argues that many politicians in Wales are committed to human rights, and this provides an opportunity for social care reform that prioritises social justice over the rhetoric of financial burdens and promotes innovative policies. Given that no significant social care reform took place between 1948 and 2014, the mindset in both national governments may regrettably be that further reform is premature.

Bibliography

Abdi S, Spann A, Borilovic J, et al. 'Understanding the care and support needs of older people: A scoping review and categorisation using the WHO International Classification of Functioning, disability and Health Framework (ICF)' (2019) *BMC Geriatrics* 19(1) 1.

Age Cymru, 'Older people in Wales: Fact and figures' (Swansea University, 2021) https://www.agecymru.wales/siteassets/documents/policy/age-cymru---older-people-in-wales---facts-and-statistics-2021.pdf?e=MDBX0q – accessed 28 September 2024.

Age Cymru, 'Why are we waiting? Delays in care assessments in Wales' (2024) https://www.agecymru.wales /siteassets /documents /why -are -we -still -waiting /why -are -we -still -waiting .pdf - accessed 28 September 2024.

Age UK, 'New Age UK research finds the numbers of UK over age 65s caring unpaid nearly double during the pandemic to more than 4 million' (2021) https://www.ageuk.org.uk/latest-press/articles/2021/new-age-uk-research-finds-the-numbers-of-uk-over-65s-caring-unpaid-nearly-double-during-the-pandemic-to-more-than-4-million/ - accessed 28 September 2024.

Age UK, 'Why can't I get care? Older people's experiences of care and support' (2022) https://www.ageuk.org.uk/globalassets/age-uk/documents/campaigns/care-in-crisis/why-cant-i-get-care-report.pdf - accessed 28 September 2024.

Allen K and Glasby J, '"The billion dollar question": Embedding prevention in older people's services - Ten "high-impact" changes' (2013) *The British Journal of Social Work* 43(5) 904.

Aronson L, *Elderhood* (Bloomsbury Publishing, 2021).

Association of Directors of Adult Social Services, 'Autumn survey report 2022' (2022) https://www.adass.org.uk/wp-content/uploads/2024/06/ADASS_Autumn_Survey_Report_Publication_15_November_2022-1.pdf - accessed 28 September 2024.

Audit Wales, 'Direct payments for adult social care' (2022) https://www.audit.wales/blog/audit-wales/2022/6/15/direct-payments-wales - accessed 28 September 2024.

Beresford P, Slasberg C, and Clements L, 'From dementia tax to a solution for social care' (2018) 68 *Soundings* 78.

Care Inspectorate Wales, 'Care InspectorateWales, 'Chief Inspector's Annual Report 2022–23' (2023) .https://www .careinspectorate.wales /sites /default /files /2023 -10 /261020 -CI -Report -22 -23 -en .pdf#:~ :text =Chief %20Inspector %E2%80 %99s %20Annual %20Report %202022 -23. %20Overview %20of %20our–accessed 28 September2028.'

CarersUK, 'Poverty and financial hardship of unpaid carers in the UK: A WPI economics report for carers UK' (2024) https://www .carersuk .org /media /dnxerxqv /poverty financial hardship uk_web .pdf- accessed 28 September 2024.

Cavallaro F, Grimm F, Allen L, et al. 'Why are delayed discharges from hospital increasing? Seeing the bigger picture' (The Health Foundation, 2003) https://www.health.org.uk/

151 A Tarrant, *Adult social care reform in Wales* (Wales Governance Centre, 2021) 14.

publications/long-reads/why-are-delayed-discharges-from-hospital-increasing-seeing-the-bigger#:~:text=Social%20care%20is%20often%20seen,without%20the%20care%20they%20need- accessed 28 September 2024.
Clements L, 'Administering a cap on costs' (*Rhydian*, 2024) https://www.lukeclements.co.uk/administering-a-cap-on-costs/ - accessed 28 September 2024.
Clements L, 'The Social Services & Well-being (Wales) Act 2014: An overview' (*Rhydian*, 29 November 2023) https://www.lukeclements.co.uk/rhydian-social-welfare-law-in-wales/an-overview-briefing-social-care-law-in-wales/ - accessed 28 September 2024.
D'Amen B, Socci M, and Santini S, 'Intergenerational caring: A systematic literature review on young and young adult caregivers of older people' (2021) *BMC Geriatrics* 21(1) 1.
Dalingwater L, 'Inequity in supply of health care?: The case of continuing health care in England' (2018) *The International Journal of Health, Wellness and Society* 8(4) 43.
De Benito Gellner M, 'The Declining Profitability of UK Care Homes - Healthcare Business International' (Healthcare Business International17 November 2023) accessed https://www.healthcarebusinessinternational.com/the-declining-profitability-of-uk-care-homes/ 5 February 2025.
Department of Health, 'Caring for people: Community care in the next decade and beyond' (1989) Cm. 849 https://archive.org/details/communitycareinn0000grea/page/n1/mode/2up - accessed 28 September 2024.
Department of Health and Social Care, 'Care and support statutory guidance. ' (2023) https://www.gov.uk/government/publications/care-act-statutory-guidance/care-and-support-statutory-guidance - accessed 28 September 2024.
Department of Health and Social Care, 'Guidance: Principles for maintaining continuity of care when moving across borders within the United Kingdom' (2015) https://www.gov .uk /government /publications /continuity -of -care -when -moving -across-borders -within -uk /principles -for -maintaining -continuity -of -care -when -moving -across -borders-within -the -united -kingdom#:~ :text =The %20aims %20of %20the %20principles ,day %20of %20the%20move %20and - accessed 28 September 2024.
Department of Health and Social Care, 'National Framework for NHS Continuing Healthcare and NHS- Incorporating the NHS Continuing Healthcare Practice Guidance' (2022) https://assets.publishing.service.gov.uk/media/64b0f7cdc033c100108062f9/National-Framework-for-NHS-Continuing-Healthcare-and-NHS-funded-Nursing-Care_July-2022-revised_corrected-July-2023.pdf - accessed 28 September 2028.
Department of Health and Social Care, 'Reforming adult social care in England' (Session 2023-24, 10 November 2023) HC 184.
Dilnot A, 'Fairer care funding; The report of the Commission on Funding of Care and Support', vol. 1 (2011). https://webarchive.nationalarchives.gov.uk/ukgwa/20130221130239/https://www.wp.dh.gov.uk/carecommission/files/2011/07/Fairer-Care-Funding-Report.pdf - accessed 28 September 2024.
Donoghue J and Taylor C, 'Over the rainbow: Direct payments and social inclusion' (2010) *Australian Health Review* 34(1) 127.
Ferguson I, 'Increasing user choice or privatizing risk? The antinomies of personalization' (2007) *The British Journal of Social Work* 37(3) 387.
Gee NR, Rodriguez KE, Fine AH, et al. 'Dogs supporting human health and well-being: A biopsychosocial approach' (2021) *Frontiers in Veterinary Science* 8, 630465.
Glasby J, Zhang Y, Bennett MR, et al. 'A lost decade? A renewed case for adult social care reform in England' (2021) *Journal of Social Policy* 50(2) 406.
Griffiths R, *Community care; agenda for action* (HMSO, 1988).
Ham C, Heenan D, Longley M, et al. 'Integrated care in Northern Ireland, Scotland and Wales: Lessons for England' (The King's Fund, 2013).
Hanratty B, Stow D, Collingridge Moore D, et al. 'Loneliness as a risk factor for care home admission in the English Longitudinal Study of Ageing' (2028) *Age and Ageing* 47(6) 896.

Hellström I, '"I'm his wife not his carer!" – Dignity and couplehood in dementia', in Hydén LC, Lindemann H, and Brockmeier J (eds) *Beyond loss: Dementia, identity, personhood* (online edn, Oxford Academic, 18 December 2014) https://doi.org/10.1093/acprof:oso/9780199969265.003.0005 - accessed 28 September 2024.

Holt A and Birchall J, '"Their mum messed up and gran can't afford to": Violence towards grandparent kinship carers and the implications for social work' (2022) *The British Journal of Social Work* 52(3) 1231.

House of Lords Adult Social Care Committee, A 'gloriously ordinary life'': Spotlight on adult social care, Report of Session 2022-23 (8 December 2022) HL Paper 99, paras 84-104.

Hudson B, 'Commissioning for change: A new model for commissioning adult social care in England' (2019) *Critical Social Policy* 39(3) 413.

Hughes MJ, Verreynne ML, Harpur P, et al. 'Companion animals and health in older populations: A systematic review' (2020) *Clinical Gerontologist* 43(4) 365.

James A and Clements L, 'What matters to carers? 'Is a "what matters" conversation an assessment?' (Rhydian: Wales Social Welfare Law Online, 2017) https://www.lukeclements.co.uk/rhydian-social-welfare-law-in-wales/assessments-eligibility-criteria/#_edn, 1 - accessed 28 September 2024.

Knapp M, Chua KC, Broadbent M, et al. 'Predictors of care home and hospital admissions and their costs for older people with Alzheimer's disease: Findings from a large London case register' (2016) *BMJ Open* 6(11) e013591.

Krause-Parello CA, Gulick EE, and Basin B, 'Loneliness, depression, and physical activity in older adults: The therapeutic role of human-animal interactions' (2019) *Anthrozoös* 32(2) 239.

Law Commission, 'Adult Social Care' (Law Com No 326, 2011).

Law Commission, 'Adult Social Care: A consultation paper' (Law Com No 192, 2011).

LE Wales, 'Short to medium term operational and cost pressures affecting social care in Wales' (2020) https://www .gov .wales/sites /default /files /publications /2021 -04 /short -to -medium -term -operational -and -cost -pressures-affecting -social -care -in -wales .pdf - accessed 28 September 2024.

Llewellyn M, Verity F, Wallace S, et al. 'From act to impact? Final report of the evaluation of the Social Services and Well-being (Wales) Act 2014' (University of South Wales, 2023) https://pure.southwales.ac.uk/en/publications/from-act-to-impact-final-report-of-the-evaluation-of-the-social-s - accessed 28 September 2024.

Local Government and Social Care Ombudsman, 'Annual review of adult social care complaints 2021-22' (2022) - https://www.lgo.org.uk/assets/attach/6312/ASC-Review-2021-22-FINAL.pdf - accessed 28 September 2024.

Local Government Association, 'Further urgent investment needed in social care - LGA on King's Fund Report' (LGA, 14 February 2024) https://www.local.gov.uk/about/news/further-urgent-investment-needed-social-care-lga-kings-fund-report - accessed 28 September 2024

Locke P, and West K, 'Direct payments for older adults in an age of austerity' (2018) *Ethics and Social Welfare* 12(3) 216.

Milsom SG, 'The benefits of independent older people's representation and why its development should be supported' (2023) *Working with Older People* 27(4) 304.

Naqvi D, Malik A, Al-Zubaidy M, et al. 'The general practice perspective on barriers to integration between primary and social care: A London, United Kingdom-based qualitative interview study' (2019) *BMJ Open* 9(8) e029702.

Needham C, Allen K, Burn E, et al. 'How do you shape a market? Explaining local state practices in adult social care' (2023) *Journal of Social Policy* 52(3) 640.

Needham C and Hall P, *Social care in the UK's four nations: Between two paradigms* (Policy Press, 2023).

NHS Wales, Welsh Government, 'Continuing NHS Healthcare: The national framework of implementation in Wales' (2021) https://www.gov.wales/sites/default/files/publications/2022-03/continuing-nhs-healthcare-the-national-framework-for--implementation.pdf - accessed 28 September 2024.

Office for National Statistics, 'Unpaid care by age, sex and deprivation, England and Wales: Census 2021' (13 February 2023) https://www.ons.gov.uk/peoplepopulationandcommunity/healthandsocialcare/socialcare/articles/unpaidcarebyagesexanddeprivationenglandandwales/census2021#unpaiCAmded-care-by-age-sex-and-geography-2021 - accessed 28 September 2024.

Oliver D, 'Rationing care by delaying decisions' (2019) *British Medical Journal* 367.

Petrillo M and Bennett MR, 'Valuing carers 2021: England and Wales' (2023) https://centreforcare.ac.uk/wp-content/uploads/2023/05/Valuing_Carers_WEB2.pdf - accessed 28 September 2024.

Prison Reform Trust, 'Doing time: The experiences and needs of older people in prison' (2010) https://prisonreformtrust.org.uk/wp-content/uploads/old_files/Documents/Doing%20Time%20the%20experiences%20and%20needs%20of%20older%20people%20in%20prison.pdf - accessed 28 September 2024.

Rasmussen J and Langerman H, 'Alzheimer's disease - Why we need early diagnosis' (2019) *Degenerative Neurological and Neuromuscular Disease* 9, 123.

Samuel, M. (2025). Commission on adult social care reform announced by government - Community Care. [online] Community Care.: https://www.communitycare.co.uk/2025/01/03/commission-on-adult-social-care-reform-announced-by-government/ [Accessed 12 Mar. 2025].

Sandel MJ, *What money can't buy: The moral limits of markets* (Macmillan, 2012).

Scourfield P, 'Caretelization revisited and the lessons of Southern Cross' (2012) *Critical Social Policy* 32(1) 137.

Social Care Wales, 'Making rights work for older people: Guidelines for Health and Social Care' (undated) https://www.gov.wales/sites/default/files/publications/2022-05/making-rights-work-for-older-people-guidelines-for-health-and-social-care.pdf - accessed 28 September 2024.

Spann A, Vicente J, Allard C, et al. 'Challenges of combining work and unpaid care, and solutions: A scoping review' (2020) *Health & Social Care in the Community* 28(3) 699.

Tarrant A, 'Adult social care reform in Wales' (Wales Governance Centre, 2021).

Tew J, Duggal S, Carret S, et al. 'Implementing the Care Act 2014: Building social resources to prevent, reduce or delay needs for care and support in adult social care in England' (University of Birmingham, 2019).

The King's Fund, 'Social care 360' (2024) https://assets .kingsfund .org .uk /f /256914 /x /10453129ad /social care 360 2024 .pdf - accessed 28 September 2024.

Wachman R, 'Southern Cross's incurably flawed business model let down the vulnerable' (*Guardian*, 16 July 2011).

We Own It, 'Care belongs in public ownership' (2021) https://weownit.org.uk/public-ownership/care-work- accessed 28 September 2024.

Welsh Government, 'Health and Social Care Regional Integration Fund' (2022) https://www.gov.wales/sites/default/files/publications/2022-02/health-and-social-care-regional-integration-fund-revenue-guidance-2022-2027.pdf - accessed 28 September 2024.

Welsh Government, 'Hospital discharge guidance' (December 2023) https://www.gov.wales/sites/default/files/publications/2023-12/hospital-discharge-guidance-december-2023.pdf - accessed 28 September 2024.

Welsh Government, 'Social Services and Well-being (Wales) Act 2014: Part 2 Code of Practice (General Functions)' (2015) https://www.gov.wales/sites/default/files/publications/2024-07/part-2-code-of-practice-general-social-care-functions-2024-version.pdf - accessed 28 September 2024.

Welsh Government, 'Social Services and Well-being (Wales) Act 2014: Part 3 Code of Practice (assessing the needs of individuals)' (2015) https://www.gov.wales/sites/default/files/publications/2019-05/part-3-code-of-practice-assessing-the-needs-of-individuals.pdf - accessed 28 September 2024.

Welsh Government, 'Social Services and Well-being (Wales) Act 2014: Part 11 Code of Practice (Miscellaneous and General') (Cardiff, 2015) https://www.gov.wales/sites/default/files/publications/2019-05/part-11-code-of-practice-miscellaneous-and-general.pdf - accessed 28 September 2024.

Welsh Government, 'Social Services Codes of Practice' (2022) https://www.gov.wales/social-services-codes-practice#Codesofpractice - accessed 28 September 2024.

Welsh Government, 'Towards a national care and support service for Wales: Initial implementation plan' (2023) https://www.gov.wales/sites/default/files/publications/2023-12/Towards%20a%20National%20Care%20and%20Support%20Service%20initial%20implementation%20plan.pdf - accessed 28 September 2024.

Welsh Local Government Association, 'A question of priorities: Social care in the context of the impact of austerity, rising demand, and the pandemic' (2023) https://www.dataunitwales.gov.uk/SharedFiles/Download.aspx?pageid=30&mid=64&fileid=410#:~:text=presents%20a%20summary%20analysis%20of%20the%20greatest%20current,range%20of%20priorities%20over%20the%20coming%20five%20years -.accessed 28 September 2024.

Williams J, 'Fifty-the new sixty? The health and social care of older prisoners' (2010) *Quality in Ageing and Older Adults* 11(3) 16.

Williams J, 'Social care and older prisoners' (2013) *Journal of Social Work* 13(5) 47.

Wittenberg R, Read S, Erens B, et al. 'Who should pay for social care for older people in England? Results from surveys of public attitudes to the funding of social care' (2024) *Journal of Social Policy* 53, 1.

Woolham J, Daly G, Sparks T, et al. 'Do direct payments improve outcomes for older people who receive social care? Differences in outcome between people aged 75+ who have a managed personal budget or a direct payment' (2017) *Ageing & Society* 37(5) 961.

6 Older persons

Abuse and neglect

Introduction

Elder abuse and neglect have a long history. The King James Bible warns against abusing and neglecting elders; it enjoins us to 'hearken unto thy father that begat thee, and despise not thy mother when she is old.'[1] King Lear is a play about the manipulative abuse of a father by his daughters to whom he entrusted his kingdom. Lear reflects on his treatment.

> Ingratitude, thou marble-hearted fiend,
> More hideous, when thou show'st thee in a child,
> Than the sea-monster![2]

Many ballads pick up the theme of parents being abandoned by ungrateful children who have benefitted from their property and wealth. For example, the seventeenth-century ballad, *The old man's complaint against his wretched son, who did undo himself to advance his marriage*, tells the tale of an older couple in great need who went to their son for support and their pleas were rejected.

> And humbly now me intreat
> our dear and loving Son,
> That thou wilt do for us in our age,
> as we for you have done:
> Now nay not so, he said,
> your suit is all in vain,
> 'Tis best for you I tell you true,
> to get you home again:
> The worlds not now as when I was born,
> all things are grown more dear,
> My charge of children likewise is great,
> as plainly doth appear,

1 Proverbs 23:22.
2 Shakespeare W, 'King Lear|: Open Source Shakespeare' (Opensourceshakespeare.org2015) accessed 12 February 2025 Act 1, Scene 4.

DOI: 10.4324/9780203798058-7

The best that I can do,
will hardly them maintain,
Therefore I say, he packing away,
and get you hame again.[3]

Thane records a cautionary medieval European tale in which a man becomes tired of caring for his father. In response, he carves a trough from which the father is to eat. However, the man is warned by his own son that a similar trough will be carved for him when he is old.[4]

It is relatively recently that elder abuse and neglect have been a matter of interest and concern for lawyers and other disciplines. As with the history of domestic abuse of women, there was denial that it happened. If it did, it was, in some distorted way of thinking, justified or confined to particular groups in society. The 'for better or for worse' argument was often used to dismiss the domestic abuse of women within marriage as being somehow justified. Writing about violence towards women in the 1960s, Erin Pizzey summed up the attitude towards domestic abuse.

> It would probably take a Charles Dickens to do full justice to the labyrinth of indifference, red tape, callousness, and simple incompetence between people in need and so many of the agencies meant to help them[5]

She refers to 'hands being washed in all directions' by those charged with protecting women at risk. Pizzey's work in campaigning and setting up the refuge in Chiswick raised awareness that women across all social groups experienced domestic abuse and were suffering in silence. Her work culminated in practical, procedural, and ongoing legal change, the most recent being the Domestic Abuse Act 2021 (DAA 2021). It is misleading to suggest that these changes have ended domestic abuse; they have not. The causes of domestic abuse go deeper than the law can fully address, but the law has a role to play. The changes that have been made have had some effect, although there is much more to do. Thankfully, many myths surrounding domestic abuse, such as the right of a husband to beat his wife[6] or rape her,[7] have been exposed for what they are.

Similar myths surround the abuse and neglect of older persons. For example, financial abuse by children is often 'justified' because they will get it all when their parents die; they might as well have it now. For those older persons living with dementia, there is a belief that it is a return to childhood which leads to them

3 University of Oxford, 'A ballad intituled, "The old mans complaint against his wretched son, who to advance his marriage, did undo himself"' (Oxford Text Archive 2009) <https://quod.lib.umich.edu/e/eebo/B01861.0001.001/1:1?rgn=div1;view=fulltext> – accessed 28 September 2024.

4 P Thane, 'The age of old age' in Pat Thane (ed), *The Long Hstory of Old SAge* (1st edn, Thames and Hudson, 2005) 10.

5 E Pizzey and A Forbes, *Scream Quietly or the neighbours will hear* (Penguin, 1974) 91.

6 Hale records that the Law allows a man to beat his wife with a stick no wider than his finger.

7 See *R v R* [1992] 1 AC 599.

being infantilised rather than being treated as adults. More generally, older persons may be victims of the 'unsound body equals an unsound mind' myth.[8] These are disempowering, leading others to make decisions on their behalf, such as in finance and healthcare. This may leave them without a voice and their wishes and feelings being ignored.[9] It may also result in them being abused or neglected. There is a failure to recognise that older persons are vulnerable to all forms of abuse and neglect. For example, it is often assumed that older persons are not sexually abused; 'how can they be victims of sexual abuse' is an unwritten and unspoken assumption. Research tends to concentrate on the sexual abuse of adolescents and younger adults; older persons are absent.[10] Research on sexual assaults against older persons in hospitals questioned whether allegations or suspicions are dealt with consistently. It was found that most cases do not lead to a crime being recorded or any internal NHS disciplinary processes being used.[11] It is the same internationally, where sexual violence has been weaponised in armed conflict.[12] There are many more myths; as with all myths about older persons, they are ageist, abusive, and disempowering.

LGBTQ+ older persons experience additional difficulties due to the lack of suitable support. Westwood points to the lack of research in this area and the need to explore the 'readiness (or not) of specialist agencies to meet their needs.' Disciplinary silos must be dismantled, and the experience of older LGBTQ+ must not be marginalised.[13] American research found that they may be reluctant to report abuse, particularly to the police. There is a compelling need for an intersectional approach to understand and address the abuse of older LGBTQ+ persons fully. Age, gender, and sex interact, affecting older LGBTQ+ persons. Elder abuse, including homo/transphobic abuse, should be understood within broader frameworks of

8 DH Powell, *The nine myths of aging: Maximizing the quality of later life* (W H Freeman and Co, 1998) 53–68.

9 D Brady, A Clifton, V Burr et al. 'The infantilisation of older people: Is it a problem?' (2014) *Mental Health Nursing (Online)* 34(5) 22.

10 B Fileborn and C Barrett, 'Sexual violence against older women: Documenting the practices of aged care service providers' in H Bows (ed) *Violence against older women, Volume II* (Palgrave, 2019) 101; H Bows, 'Introduction' in H Bows (ed) *Violence against older women, Volume II* (Palgrave, 2019) 4.

11 A Warburton-Wynn, 'Sexual Assault of Older People by Hospital Staff in England' (2022) 24 The Journal of Adult Protection 54 <https://wearehourglass.org/sites/default/files/inline-files/Sexual%20Violence%20and%20Assault%20against%20older%20people%20in%20hospitals%20in%20England%202021.pdf> accessed 28 September 2024.

12 Sleap B, 'No One Is Spared' (Human Rights Watch23 February 2022) <https://www.hrw.org/report/2022/02/23/no-one-spared/abuses-against-older-people-armed-conflict accessed 11 February 2025; RA Sitkin, BX Lee, and G Lee, 'To destroy a people: Sexual violence as a form of genocide in the conflicts of Bosnia, Rwanda, and Chile' (2019) *Aggression and Violent Behavior* 46, 219.

13 S Westwood, 'Abuse and older lesbian, gay bisexual, and trans (LGBT) people: A commentary and research agenda' (2019) *Journal of Elder Abuse and Neglect* 31(2) 97, 110.

unequal power relations.[14] There is a lack of age and LGBTQ+-friendly shelters and a risk that if one partner enters a care home, they will be reluctant to disclose their sexuality.[15]

The extent of abuse and neglect of older persons

The absence of an agreed definition of elder abuse and neglect has hampered reliable data collection. Ogg and Bennett conducted an early systematic study in 1992, which tentatively concluded that the rates of abuse of older persons known to health and social care practitioners were higher than for the general population.[16] A 2007 study by O'Keefe et al. looked at people aged sixty-six years and above living in private households in the community.[17] It did not include people living in care homes, hospitals, sheltered accommodation, or older persons lacking mental capacity. For these reasons, it is a conservative estimate. The study found that 2.6% of older persons disclosed mistreatment by a family member, friend, or carer. This translated to about 227,000 people or roughly one in forty. When mistreatment by neighbours and acquaintances is included, the prevalence rate jumps to 4% or approximately 342,000 people. Neglect was the most common form of mistreatment, reported by 1.1% of older persons, followed by financial abuse at 0.7%, and psychological and physical abuse at 0.4%. Women were more likely to report mistreatment compared to men, with rates of 3.8% and 1.1%, respectively. Mistreatment was found to be more prevalent among those experiencing declining health, depression, and loneliness. In their 2008 systematic review of studies measuring the prevalence of the abuse and neglect of older persons, Cooper et al. in their literature review found that 6% of the general older population and 25% of vulnerable older persons are at risk of abuse. Only a small proportion of the abuse and neglect of older persons was known to the protective services.[18] Hourglass's research in 2020 found that 22% of persons surveyed had personal experience of an

14 EM Bloemen, T Rosen, M LoFaso et al., 'Lesbian, gay, bisexual, and transgender older adults' experiences with elder abuse and neglect' (2019) *Journal of the American Geriatrics Society* 67(11) 2338.

15 J Hillman, 'Intimate partner violence among older LGBT adults: Unique risk factors, issues in reporting and treatment, and recommendations for research, practice, and policy' in B Russell (ed) *Intimate partner violence and the LGBT+ community: Understanding power dynamics* (Springer 2020) 237.

16 J Ogg and G Bennett, 'Elder Abuse in Britain' (1992) 305 *British Medical Journal* 998. For earlier studies of prevalence, see B Penhale, 'Elder abuse and adult safeguarding in UK' (2020) *International Handbook of Elder Abuse and Mistreatment* 311, 315–317.

17 O'Keefe M, Hills A and Doyle M, 'UK Study of Abuse and Neglect of Older People Prevalence Survey Report' (ResearchGate2007) <https://www.researchgate.net/publication/242099186_UK_Study_of_Abuse_and_Neglect_of_Older_People_Prevalence_Survey_Report#fullTextFileContent> accessed 11 February 2025 37.

18 Cl Cooper, A Selwood and G Livingston, 'The prevalence of elder abuse and neglect: A systematic review' (2008) 37 *Age and Ageing* 151.

older person who had been abused. It also reveals a distrubing lack of understanding of what constitutes abuse.[19]

Older persons experience abuse and neglect in many settings by a range of perpetrators. As with all generations, older persons have the right to live their lives free from violence and intimidation. The Human Rights Act 1998 (HRA 1998) requires public authorities to act in accordance with the European Convention on Human Rights (ECHR), which includes the rights to have life protected, not to be subjected to inhuman or degrading treatment, access to justice, and private life.[20] The law can help ensure older persons live safely and free of abuse and neglect, but it is not a panacea. We have had laws to protect children since the 1880s. However, the names Maria Colwell, Jasmine Beckford, Victoria Climbié, Peter Evans, Logan Mwangi and Charlie Roberts remind us that children still suffer horrendous abuse because the system does not prevent it or respond to it appropriately.[21] The history of child protection is one of lessons learned, changes made, and lessons forgotten until the next time.

It is necessary in adult safeguarding, as well as in child protection, to identify and address the root causes. When discussing the politics of child protection, Parton argues,

> there is a real danger in always discussing the nature of child maltreatment and developing public policy responses through the lens of scandal, blame and failure. We can almost be seen to be promulgating the view that child maltreatment is caused by the failures of child protection professionals and systems. The scandal-driven politics of child protection encourages a narrow view of what is at stake in trying to address the social problem of child maltreatment. Discussions of how public policy should be reformed are largely disconnected from any wider appreciation of what harms children, how their welfare and wellbeing might be improved and how such issues are related to wider social and economic factors and structures.[22]

This applies in equal measure to the abuse and neglect of older persons. The state may fail to protect, respond inadequately when harm occurs, and apportion blame and responsibility. Yet this must not divert us from asking why older persons are abused and neglected. The risk factors are many and varied, including disability, living arrangements, dependence, relationships, social and cultural norms,

19 Hourglass (2020). 'What does growing old in the UK look like?' [online] Hourglass. <'https://wearehourglass.org/sites/default/files/inline-files/SAFER%20AGEING%E2%80%93%20what%20does%20growing%20old%20in%20the%20UK%20look%20like__Layout%201.pdf> - accessed 28 Sep. 2024].

20 See Chapter 2.

21 See, for example, R Jones, *The story of baby P: Setting the record straight* (Policy Press, 2014).

22 N Parton, 'The contemporary politics of child protection: Part two (the BASPCAN Founder's Lecture 2015)' (2016) *Child Abuse Review* 25(1) 9.

and tolerance of violence in some institutions.[23] Why is it that there are those in society who feel empowered to abuse and neglect? Ageism is at the heart of the answer to these questions. Older persons are less valued and marginalised. If they are abused or neglected, it does not matter. It is a sad reflection on society that despite the excellent care provided for older persons by large numbers of practitioners and families, others feel empowered to abuse. Elder abuse and neglect are complicated and multifactorial.[24] Deprivation, vulnerability, environmental factors, stress, mental health, lack of resources to care, poor training, failing health, family dynamics, greed, and pure sadism, along with many other factors, need to be addressed if abuse and neglect are to end. Knight and Hester's research shows a strong link between dementia and the abuse of older persons, which makes them more susceptible to being victimised. In addition to this, pre-existing health conditions can further increase vulnerability to abuse. Unfortunately, those who experience such abuse often face difficulty in accessing the necessary care and support they need.[25] Dixon et al. identify some tensions between the Convention on the Rights of Persons with Disabilities approach to supported decision-making and the approach of the Mental Capacity Act 2005 (MCA 2005). Despite the uncertainties, much can be done to help persons living with dementia through adult safeguarding procedures. These include accessible information on safeguarding, the choice of location, and the timing of safeguarding meetings.[26] Elder law must play a significant part in addressing abuse and neglect, but the broader societal problems must also be tackled.

A short history of adult safeguarding law

Sally Greengross's seminal work The Law and Vulnerable Elderly People, published in 1986, identified gaps in the legal protection of vulnerable older persons, particularly when compared to children. In making this comparison, she was alert to the need to avoid infantilising older persons. She was writing at a time when legal protection for vulnerable older persons, and vulnerable adults in general, depended upon legislation designed for other purposes, such as the National Assitance Act 1948. With commendable foresight, she identified the nub of a still ongoing debate.

23 D Sethi, S Wood, F Mitis et al., (eds), *European report on preventing elder maltreatment* (World Health Organisation, 2011) https://iris.who.int/handle/10665/107293#:~:text=This%20report%20highlights%20the%20biological%2C%20social%2C%20cultural%2C%20economic,the%20protective%20factors%20that%20can%20help%20prevent%20it. accessed 28 September 2024..

24 F Gholipour, Z Khalili, and M Abbasian, 'Definitions and theories of elder abuse' (2020) *Elderly Health Journal* 6(2) 140.

25 L Knight and M Hester, 'Domestic violence and mental health in older adults' (2016) *International Review of Psychiatry* 28(5) 464.

26 J Dixon, J, S Donnelly, J Campbell et al., 'Safeguarding people living with dementia: How social workers can use supported decision-making strategies to support the human rights of individuals during adult safeguarding enquiries' (2014) *The British Journal of Social Work* 52(3)130.

> If people are to be protected despite themselves, what are the minimal acceptable infringements of their right to self-determination, which society believes are necessary for their own well-being? Does the state have the right to make such an assessment of need, and, if so, how much will it be influenced by available resources and priorities? To what extent are vulnerable `old people further disadvantaged by the paucity of legislation designed specifically to meet their needs? Should they be treated differently from other disadvantaged groups?[27]

In this key paragraph, she identified the need to respect autonomy, the responsibility of the state to protect, resource implications, and whether older persons should be treated differently. The tension between autonomy and protection is heightened in safeguarding cases. Resolving it is not simplistic and needs to be placed in a person-centred context, considering the older person's sense of self, emotional well-being, the nature of their relationships, and attachment to their existing home.[28] An older person who may appear to have made a poor decision or lacks cognitive ability may be acting to protect their own priorities as best they can.[29] The tensions were at the core of the debate in Scotland, Wales, and England as they framed their safeguarding laws. Northern Ireland is currently debating adult safeguarding laws.

In England and Wales, the Law Commission's 1995 report, Mental Incapacity, proposed reforming adult safeguarding law.[30] Recommendations included a duty on local authorities to investigate when they had reason to believe that a vulnerable adult was suffering or likely to suffer significant harm or serious exploitation.[31] The lack of any duty was a major weakness which was not addressed until the Care Act 2014 (CA 2014) in England and the Social Services and Well-being (Wales) Act 2014 (SSWA 2014) in Wales. Other recommendations included powers of entry, entry warrants, assessment orders, and temporary protection orders. These would not be available if a person had mental capacity and objected.[32] Although the proposals mainly related to mental capacity, the definition of 'vulnerable person' had a broader focus.

> We recommend that a 'vulnerable person' should mean any person of 16 or over who (1) is or may be in need of community care services by reason of mental or other disability, age or illness and who (2) is or may be unable to

27 S Greengross, *The Law and Vulnerable Elderly People* (Age Concern England, 1986) para 6.4.

28 K Mackay, 'Choosing to live with harm? A presentation of two case studies to explore the perspective of those who experienced adult safeguarding interventions' (2017) *Ethics and Social Welfare* 11(1) 33.

29 JM Martinez, DC Homeier, C Fowler et al., 'Conceptualizing person-centered care in elder mistreatment intervention: Use of a well-being framework' (2003) *The Gerontologist* 63(6) 973.

30 Law Commission, *Mental Incapacity* (Law Com No 231, 1995).

31 ibid paras 9.15–16.

32 ibid paras 9.19, 9.21–23, 9.24–26, 9.28–34.

take care of himself or herself, or unable to protect himself or herself against significant harm or serious exploitation.[33]

The government promptly rejected the other recommendations. In a statement, the Lord Chancellor argued that powers already existed in this area and there was no pressing need for reform; what those existing powers were is unclear.[34] Presumably, they included the limited jurisdiction of the old Court of Protection, the moribund Section 47 National Assistance Act 1948, the Mental Health Act 1983, and the National Health Service and Community Care Act 1990. These fell far short of a comprehensive and coherent set of powers and duties. Section 47 National Assistance Act 1948 allowed for the removal to a place of safety under a court order of a person suffering from 'grave chronic disease, or being aged, infirm or physically incapacitated' living in 'insanitary conditions' in circumstances where they are 'unable to devote to themselves' and not receiving proper care. An emergency procedure was available under the National Assistance (Amendment) Act 1951.[35] This legislation was designed to tackle poor post-war housing and not safeguarding and was repealed by the 2014 legislation, mainly because it was not human rights compliant.[36]

The constitutional changes in the late 1990s, particularly the HRA 1998 and devolution for Northern Ireland, Scotland, and Wales, changed the law reform landscape. Devolved powers incorporated health and social care, including adult safeguarding; however, policing and criminal justice were not devolved to Wales. The Scottish Parliament used its devolved powers to pass the Adult Support and Protection (Scotland) Act 2007 (ASPA 2007). England and Wales took a different approach, with each nation issuing statutory guidance outlining procedures for responding to suspected abuse and neglect cases.[37] As statutory guidance issued under Section 7 Local Authority Social Services Act 1970 local authorities were bound to follow it other than in exceptional circumstances.[38] Although the guidance did a reasonable job, reviews of the English and the Welsh guidance recognised that they were no longer fit for purpose.[39] The case for having legislation was grow-

33 ibid paras 9.6 and Draft Bill clause 36(2)

34 Lord Chancellor's Department, *Who decides: Making decisions on behalf of mentally incapacitated adults* (1997) Hansard, House of Lords Debates 18 November 1997 col 157.

35 D Hewitt, 'The strange deaths of section 47' (2012) 14 *Journal of Adult Protection* 39.

36 See CA 2014 s 46 and SSWA 2014 s.129. It was also repealed in Scotland by Schedule 2 Adult Support and Protection (Scotland) Act 2017.

37 Department of Health and Home Office, 'No Secrets: Guidance on Developing and Implementing Multi-Agency Policies and Procedures to Protect Vulnerable Adults from Abuse' (2000) <https://assets.publishing.service.gov.uk/government/uploads/system/uploads/attachment_data/file/194272/No_secrets__guidance_on_developing_and_implementing_multi-agency_policies_and_procedures_to_protect_vulnerable_adults_from_abuse.pdf accessed 12 February 2025; National Assembly for Wales, 'In Safe Hands: Implementing Adult Protection Procedures in Wales' (2000) <https://cysur.wales/media/xxybbuuj/in-safe-hands.pdfaccessed> - 12 February 2025.

38 See Sedley J in *R. v Islington LBC Ex p. Rixon* [1996] 3 WLUK 251.

39 Department of Health, 'Safeguarding Adults: Report on the review of "No Secrets"' (2009); J Magill, V Yeates and M Longley, *Review of In Safe Hands* (Welsh Institute for Health and Social Care University of Glamorgan, 2010).

ing stronger, as was the awareness of the extent of the abuse and neglect of older persons and others.[40] Thus far, the Westminster government had resisted proposals for adult safeguarding legislation based partly on a fear that it would interfere with personal autonomy. However, the Law Commission's 2011 review, Adult Social Care, included consideration of adult safeguarding. The gist of its recommendation was that there should be a new adult social care law, but whether it should consist of compulsory safeguarding powers and duties, as in the Scottish legislation, was a matter for each of the two governments.[41]

Placing adult safeguarding on a statutory basis

Both the CA 2014 and the SSWA 2014 chose to include adult safeguarding and place it on a statutory basis for the first time. However, as discussed below, the approaches were slightly different. Both rejected incorporating the extensive powers in the Scottish ASPA 2007. In developing a law, the first question is to ask to whom it will apply. Is the legislation to apply only to older persons, or is it of more general application? Some states in America have laws specifically designed to protect older persons or elders from abuse and neglect. For example, California Penal Code 368 PC makes it a crime to inflict physical or emotional abuse on anyone sixty-five or older. Other states, such as Florida, Georgia, Massachusetts, and Missouri, include vulnerable adults, incapacitated adults, disabled adults, impaired adults, and dependent adults in their safeguarding laws. Bows points to the risks of having older person-specific laws; they contribute to ageist attitudes and result in paternalism.[42] Neither England nor Wales adopted an older person-only remit for their safeguarding law.

The previous statutory guidance in both nations referred to 'vulnerable adults.' In its 2011 report, the Law Commission identified concerns over using 'vulnerable adults.' Consultees criticised it as 'stigmatising, dated, negative and disempowering.' They argued that it concentrated on social needs, which may exclude health needs.[43] The Commission recommended the term' adult at risk.' 'Adults at risk' is now used in England and Wales, although the wording is only used in Welsh legislation. England uses the term in its Guidance. Using similar but not identical language, the two pieces of legislation define an 'adult at risk' as a person who,

1. Has needs for care and support (whether or not the authority is meeting any of those needs).
2. Is experiencing, or is at risk of, abuse or neglect.

40 J Williams, 'State responsibility and the abuse of vulnerable older people: Is there a case for a public law to protect vulnerable older people from abuse?' in J Bridgeman, C Lind and H Keating (eds), *Responsibility, Law and Family* (Ashgate, 2008); J Williams, 'Public Law Protection of Vulnerable Adults' (2002) 2 Journal of Social Work 293.

41 Law Commission, *Adult Social Care* (Law Com No 326, 2011) rec 41.

42 See Chapter 1, pp 17-18.

43 Law Commission Adult Social Care (n41) 9.20–21.

3. Because of those needs is unable to protect himself or herself against the abuse or neglect or the risk of it.

See Section 42 CA 2014 and Section 126(1) SSWA 2014.

This does not follow the Law Commission's recommendation that it should be 'health or social care needs' and 'harm' instead of 'abuse.'[44] The definition has been criticised because the inability to protect in 3. must arise from the need for care and support identified under 1. This excludes, for example, an older person experiencing domestic abuse who does not have care and support needs but cannot protect themselves because they are being coerced or threatened. It also excludes those whose care and support needs arise from their inability to protect themselves from harm. The Older People's Commissioner for Wales put it this way in her evidence to the Health and Social Care Committee of the National Assembly For Wales; the proposed definition, she argued,

> currently reads that because a person has care and support needs they cannot protect themselves from harm; whereas the true situation is that because a person cannot protect themselves from harm they have care and support needs.[45]

The Committee's report highlighted concerns about the definition from a number of third-sector bodies.[46] However, both Acts included the link between the need for care and support and the inability to protect oneself. Pritchard-Jones argues that this definition does not remove the idea that the older person is somehow responsible for the abuse or neglect.

> Within both pieces of legislation [CA 2014 and SSWA 2014] and their supporting documents and instruments, the first conceptual criticism of vulnerability – the idea that the inability to protect oneself from abuse because of a need, which is generated by an impairment or a disability – therefore remains, despite the terminological shift to 'adult at risk'. Moreover, the fact that the adult has a disability or impairment which generates needs, which then means they are unable to protect themselves, does nothing to remove the idea that the adult themselves is 'to blame' for their abuse, which...was a key concern of the terminology 'vulnerable adult.'[47]

44 ibid 9.51

45 Evidence presented by the Older People's Commission for Wales to the National Assembly for Wales Health and Social Care Committee, 'Social Services and Well-Being (Wales) Bill: Consultation Responses' (2013) para 7.

46 National Assembly for Wales Health and Social Care Committee (2013). Social Services and Well-being (Wales) Bill: Stage 1 Committee Report. [online] Cardiff: National Assembly for Wales. <https://senedd.wales/media/r0rer5fy/cr-ld9418-e-english.pdf> - accessed 12 Feb. 2025]. 38–44.

47 L Pritchard-Jones, 'Adults at risk: "Vulnerability" by any other name?' (2018) 20 *The Journal of Adult Protection* 47, 54.

In reality, the language change is not one of substance; in Pritchard-Jones' words, it is 'merely etymological and illusory.' The definition may exclude an older person experiencing abuse or neglect. Spreadbury and Hubbard identify some groups that are regularly thought of as not meeting the criteria under the CA 2014, including homeless persons and those with addictions.[48] They argue that this may be driven by beliefs about lifestyle choices that disguise the true nature of the inability to protect oneself. The unspoken rationale for this restrictive definition is that it limits access to, or rations, safeguarding and thus saves money. By comparison, in Scotland, Section 3(1) ASPA 2007 requires the inability to safeguard well-being or property or other interests, being at risk of harm, and because of a disability, 'they are more vulnerable to being harmed' than other adults. The decision by Scotland not to include the need for care and support was based on consultation responses, which argued it was discriminatory and emphasised vulnerability.[49]

The CA 2014 and the SSWA 2014 refer to the risk of harm. This resonates with the duties in each Act relating to promoting well-being.[50] In defining 'well-being,' protection from abuse and neglect is included.[51] In Wales, a range of services are required to prevent people from suffering abuse and neglect. The CA 2014 refers more generally to services that prevent the development of the need for care and support.[52] The Care Act Guidance identifies six key principles underpinning adult safeguarding work: Empowerment, Prevention, Proportionality, Protection, Partnership, and Accountability.[53] When assessing abuse or neglect of adults at risk, the Welsh Guidance identifies factors to be considered. These include the adult's frailty or vulnerability, the extent and frequency of the abuse or neglect, its duration and impact, and the risk of further abuse involving the person or other adults at risk.[54] Uniquely, Wales includes an overarching duty to have due regard to the United Nations Principles for Older Persons, which contain the principle that '(O)lder persons should be able to live in dignity and free of exploitation and physical or mental abuse.'[55] Due regard is not the most robust legal duty; however, the duty must be performed in substance and is not just a tick-box exercise. It is a

48 K Spreadbury and R Hubbard, 'Definitions in adult safeguarding' in K Spreadbury and R Hubbard (eds) *The adult safeguarding practice handbook* (Policy Press, 2020) 93.

49 K Mackay and M Notman, 'Adult support and protection (scotland) act 2007: Reflections on developing practice and present day challenges' (2017) 19 *The Journal of Adult Protection* 187,189–190.

50 CA 2014 s.1 and SSWA 2014 s.5.

51 CA 2014 s.1(2)(c) and SSWA 2007 s.2(2)(b).

52 CA 2014 s.2 and SSWA 2014 s.15(2)(e).

53 Department of Health and Social Care, 'Care and support statutory guidance' (*Gov.UK*, revised 2025) <u></u>https://www.gov.uk/government/publications/care-act-statutory-guidance/care-and-support-statutory-guidance–accessed 13 March 2025.

54 Welsh Government, 'Social Services and Well-Being (Wales) Act 2014 Working Together to Safeguard People Volume I -Introduction and Overview Guidance on Safeguarding' (Welsh Government, 2016) https://www.gov.wales/sites/default/files/publications/2019-05/working-together-to-safeguard-people-volume-i-introduction-and-overview.pdf - acccessed 28 September 2024, para 25.

55 United Nations. United Nations Principles for Older Persons GA Res 46/91 (19 December 1991).

calculation that must be undertaken before a safeguarding decision is taken, not as an ex post facto justification.[56]

Defining 'abuse'

The label 'elder abuse' is problematic as it risks redefining what is, in many instances, criminal behaviour, such as assault, theft, and rape, into something which risks being regarded as less serious. It risks decriminalising it in public perception. For example, an assault on an older person by a spouse, family member, or practitioner is criminal behaviour. The risk and vulnerability factors behind the types of abuse may be different, which may make it difficult to identify. Each type of elder abuse has its own vulnerability and risk factors. For example, Dominguez et al. suggest that there were fewer vulnerability and risk factors in financial abuse-only cases when compared with co-occurring forms of abuse such as neglect or psychological.[57] Brammer and Biggs argue that the term 'elder abuse' must be approached cautiously as it risks being categorised as something apart from violence against other age cohorts. Assault is assault, regardless of the victim's age, the location, or the perpetrator. The term 'elder abuse' has helped raise awareness about the abuse and neglect experienced by many older persons. It is a marked improvement on the previously used term 'granny battering.' However, its continued use risks identifying older persons as different from other victims of crime. What matters is that the adult safeguarding law ensures that older persons have equal protection with others and that responses are based on them as individuals and not on ageist stereotypes.

Quite rightly, the CA 2014 and the SSWA 2014 resisted the idea of elder abuse-specific law. Abuse is a term used in the English and Welsh Acts. The CA 2014 does not define abuse, relying on it being an ordinary word that does not require a definition. The exception is financial abuse, which includes theft of money or property, fraud, being put under pressure concerning money or property, or having it misused.[58] However, the English Guidance is more detailed in describing abuse; in addition to physical abuse, it includes domestic violence, sexual abuse, psychological abuse, financial or material abuse, modern slavery, discriminatory abuse, and organisational abuse. Exploitation is identified as a common theme. Also included are neglect and acts of omission, such as withholding the necessities of life and self-neglect.[59] Although this is a comprehensive definition, the person must be within the meaning of an adult at risk as defined under the legislation, particularly the need for care and support, which is why they cannot protect themselves. In Wales Section 197(1) SSWA 2014 defines abuse as physical, sexual, psychological, emotional, or financial abuse. It applies to abuse in any setting – a

56 *R (Brown) v Secretary of State for Work and Pensions* [2008] EWHC 3158 (Admin), [2008] 12 WLUK 546.

57 S Fraga Dominguez, B Ozguler, JE Storey et al., 'Elder abuse vulnerability and risk factors: Is financial abuse different from other subtypes?' (2022) *Journal of Applied Gerontology* 41(4) 928.

58 CA 2014 s.42(3).

59 Care Act Guidance (n53) 14.17–19

private home, institution, or other place. A more detailed definition of financial abuse is included, as in the CA 2014. The 2023 Wales Safeguarding Procedures provides indicators of possible abuse and neglect.[60] In addition to physical, sexual, financial, and psychological abuse, it covers indicators of domestic violence and modern slavery. But again, this only applies to people within the definition of an adult at risk. Scotland's ASPA 2007 uses the word harm rather than abuse, as the Law Commission's 2011 report on reform in England and Wales recommended. This is a broader concept than abuse; in particular, it includes accidental harm because of self-neglect, neglect by a carer, and attempted suicide.[61]

At all times, consideration must be given to the possibility that the older person is subject to coercive or controlling behaviour. What they say may not be what they think or want; somebody controls them. In particular, an older person may refuse to cooperate with statutory enquiries; this may be because of coercive or controlling behaviour, which may have been a long-term feature of the relationship with the perpetrator. It is a common feature of all abusive relationships, but it is often not recognised in older person relationships.[62] It can be missed by an approach that equates abuse with particular and recent acts of violence, what Stark refers to as the violent incident model.[63] This gauges the severity of the injury inflicted or threatened. So, a statutory enquiry under the CA 2014 or the SSWA 2014 may focus on recent abusive acts and implement safeguarding measures, such as respite care for the perpetrator. However, in some cases, this may reinforce the environment in which coercive or controlling behaviour occurs. Looking at the history of the relationship may disclose long-term coercion and control, which needs to be addressed. Coercive or controlling behaviour may also be a feature in self-neglect cases. Coercive or controlling behaviour was made a crime by Section 76 Serious Crime Act 2015 as amended by the DAA 2021. The 2021 Act defines 'abuse' as physical or sexual abuse, violent or threatening behaviour, economic abuse, psychological abuse, and controlling or coercive behaviour. This brings it within the remit of the Act, which provides for a presumption that the victim is eligible for special measures in any criminal proceedings and the possible protection of Domestic Abuse Protection Notices and Domestic Abuse Protection Orders under the Act. For these provisions to apply, the perpetrator and victim must be

60 Welsh Government, 'Wales Safeguarding Procedures' (2023) <https://safeguarding.wales/en/adu-i/> – accessed 28 September 2024.

61 Scottish Government, 'Adult Support and Protection (Scotland) Act 2007: Code of Practice' (2014) 21 <https://www.pkc.gov.uk/media/25785/ASAP-Scottish-Government-Code-Of-Practice/pdf/Adult_Support_And_Protection_-_Scottish_Govenment_Code_Of_Practice.pdf?m=636099846743570000> accessed 18 April 2023; see also F Johnson, 'Problems with the Term and Concept of 'Abuse': Critical Reflections on the Scottish Adult Support and Protection Study' (2012) The British Journal of Social Work Volume 42(5) 833, 850

62 S Wydall, A Clarke, J Williams et al., 'Domestic abuse and elder abuse in Wales: A tale of two initiatives' (2018) *The British Journal of Social Work* 48(4) 962.

63 E Stark, *Coercive Control: The entrapment of women in personal life* (OUP 2009); E Stark 'Looking Beyond Domestic Violence: Policing Coercive Control' (2012) Journal of Police Crisis Negotiations 12(2)199.

'personally connected.' Personally connected is defined by Section 2 of the 2021 Act (which is also incorporated into s.76 Serious Crime Act 20215) as follows:

a) They are or have been married to each other.
b) They are or have been civil partners of each other.
c) They have agreed to marry one another (whether or not the agreement has been terminated).
d) They have entered into a civil partnership agreement (whether or not it has been terminated).
e) They are or have been in an intimate personal relationship with each other.
f) They each have, or there has been a time when they each have had a parental relationship concerning the same child.
g) They are relatives.[64]

Defining 'neglect'

Many older persons experience neglect. Data from England shows that over 40% of the enquiries completed by local authorities involved neglect or omission.[65] A similar picture emerges in Wales. In 2021–22, neglect was the highest in reports received by local authorities under the safeguarding provisions of the SSWA 2014. It ranged from approximately one-third of those aged sixty-five to seventy-four to about 45% of those aged eighty-five and over.[66] The most common location for neglect is the person's home. Neglect presupposes a duty to care. The duty is clear for those working in public sector health and social care and independent and third-sector providers of services; they have a legal duty of care. For others who provide care, there must be an undertaking to care for another who cannot care for themselves. For example, as a general rule, adult children have no legal requirement to care for their parents or relatives. However, in R v Instan, a niece lived with her seventy-three-year-old aunt; the aunt maintained the niece. A few weeks before her death, she was in good health but then got gangrene in her leg, preventing her from caring for herself. Only the niece knew of this but did not attempt to tell a doctor or anyone else. She continued to live at the aunt's expense. The aunt died due to gangrene, accelerated by neglect, lack of food, and a lack of nursing and medical care. These needs could have been met if others had known about the aunt's condition. The jury had to decide whether, in the circumstances of the living arrangements, the defendant impliedly undertook to either care for the aunt or let

64 See also p 195 and Serious Crimes Act 2015 s.76.
65 NHS Digital, 'Safeguarding Adults, England 2021–22' (2022) <https://digital.nhs.uk/data-and-information/publications/statistical/safeguarding-adults/2021–22> – accessed 28 September 2024.
66 StatsWales, 'Number of reports received during the collection year, by local authority, category of abuse and age group' (2022) <https://statswales.gov.wales/Catalogue/Health-and-Social-Care/Social-Services/social-services-performance-and-improvement-framework/adults/adult-safeguarding/numberofreportsreceivedduringthecollectionyear-by-localauthority-categoryofabuse-age> – accessed 28 September 2024.

others know that she needed care; it found that she did and was, therefore, guilty of manslaughter. Lord Coleridge CJ said,

> It is not correct to say that every moral obligation is a legal duty, but every legal duty is founded upon a moral obligation. In this case, as in most cases, the legal duty can be nothing else than the taking upon oneself the performance of the moral obligation. There is no question whatever that it was this woman's clear duty to impart to the deceased so much of that food, which was taken into the house for both, and paid for by the deceased, as was necessary to sustain her life. The deceased could not get it for herself; she could only get it through the prisoner. It was the prisoner's clear duty at common law to supply it to the deceased, and that duty she did not perform.[67]

In the later case of R v Stone, a sister came to live with her brother and his partner. She was found dead due to infected bed sores and prolonged immobilisation. They argued that they had not assumed a duty of care. On the evidence, the court found that they had. It was stressed that the duty of care could be discharged by providing necessary care or summoning help.[68] If the person rejects help, it will not be an unlawful killing.[69] Although these are criminal cases, they illustrate the need for a duty to care to prove neglect.

The CA 2014 says that neglect can be an act or omission. Examples are given in the Guidance.

- Ignoring medical, emotional, or physical care needs.
- Failure to provide access to appropriate health care, and support or educational services.
- The withholding of life's necessities, such as medication, adequate nutrition, and heating.[70]

Section 197(1) SSWA 2014 provides the following definition.

> neglect ('esgeulustod') means a failure to meet a person's basic physical, emotional, social, or psychological needs, which is likely to result in an impairment of the person's well-being (for example, an impairment of the person's health

Similar examples to those in the CA 2014 are given.[71]

67 [1893] 1 QB 450, 453–4.
68 [1977] 2 All ER 341.
69 *R (on the application of Jenkins) v HM Coroner for Portsmouth and South East Hampshire* [2009] EWHC 3229 (Admin), [2009] All ER (D) 103 (Dec).
70 Care Act Guidance (n53) 14.17
71 Welsh Guidance (n54) para25.

Self-neglect

BrayeStodolska et al. emphasise the importance of distinguishing between neglect and self-neglect. When a caregiver fulfils all their duties, but the older person refuses to accept help, this is considered self-neglect. It means the older person denies themselves or fails to provide proper food, clothing, personal hygiene, medication, or a safe living environment. The challenge is to meet the basic needs of the older person while ensuring that they can still make decisions about themselves consciously, even if some of these decisions may lead to self-harm.[72] Self-neglect involves the lack of self-care to the point where it threatens personal health, safety, and possibly that of others. The neglecting behaviour can be non-intentional or passive, caused by a physical or mental condition; alternatively, it can be intentional or active, which involves a choice by the person. It can manifest in many ways, including poor personal hygiene, unkemptness, poor diet, malnutrition, poor household cleanliness, and animal collecting. Possible causes are many. A traumatic life event may trigger self-neglecting behaviour, as might brain injury, dementia, physical illness, and mental health issues.[73] Pavlou and Lachs suggest that self-neglect is a 'geriatric syndrome', pointing out that two other geriatric syndromes are risk factors for self-neglect: cognitive impairment and depression.[74] Braye found that it 'makes plain that self-neglect is overwhelmingly seen as a problem of older adults.'[75]

Hoarding is a particular type of self-neglect which has come to public attention through media coverage.[76] This is sometimes called Diogenes syndrome after the Greek philosopher who threw his cloak into an empty wine casket outside Cybele's temple, calling it home. At the same time, he went around in daylight, 'looking for an honest man.'[77] Hoarding disorder is recognised by the Diagnostic and Statistical Manual of Mental Disorders (DSM-5) published by the American Psychiatric Association.[78] It has a number of causes including behavioural manisfestations of an organic disorder, schizophrenia, depressive disorder, or an obsessive compulsive disorder. For some older persons it may be a reaction to stress or trauma. These

72 A Stodolska, A Parnicka, B Tobiasz-Adamczyk et al., 'Defining elder neglect–a new proposal towards uniformity' (2024) *Ageing International* 1-42.

73 Braye S, Orr D and Preston-Shoot M, 'Self-Neglect and Adult Safeguarding: Findings from Research' (2011) <https://www.buckssafeguarding.org.uk/adultsboard/wp-content/uploads/sites/3/2020/08/SCIE-Report-46.pdf> - accessed 12 February 2025

74 MP Pavlou and MS Lachs, 'Could self-neglect in older adults be a geriatric syndrome?' (2006) 54 *Journal of the American Geriatrics Society* 831.

75 Braye (n73) para 2.5.

76 S Robehmed, 'The rise of hoarding' (*BBC News*, 23 December 2011) <https://www.bbc.co.uk/news/magazine-16299670> - accessed 28 September 2024..

77 JJ Mark, *The life of diogenes of sinope in diogenes laertius* (Ancient History Encyclopaedia, 2014) https://www.ancient.eu/article/740/the-life-of-diogenes-of-sinope-in-diogenes-laertiu/.- accessed 28 September 2024.

78 American Psychiatric Association, *Diagnostic and statistical manual of mental disorders* (5th edn, 2013) 132–133 <https://doi.org/10.1176/appi.books.9780890425787> - accessed 28 September 2024..

are complex matters and suggest caution in believing that a 'deep clean' response will, in itself, be an appropriate response. Homelessness often leads to self-neglect, and there is evidence of a failure to recognise the needs of homeless persons.[79] Although those who are homeless or rough sleeping are predominately younger persons, Age UK estimated that in 2019 in England, 9–12% of rough sleepers were fifty-five years and older, over 2,500 people sixty years and above were officially homeless, and around 4,000 older persons are estimated to be in hostels in any one night.[80] Rowlands and Williams noted an increasing prevalence of persons over fifty years in Wales sleeping out, albeit on a limited survey.[81] According to a recent Australian study, moving into a purpose-built care home can improve the mental well-being and overall quality of life for older persons who were previously homeless. Residents who participated in the study reported positive experiences and an enhanced quality of life after moving into the care home. The dignified living environment positively impacted their sense of purpose and psychological health. Most residents were referred to the home from hospitals due to declining health, and the care home primarily focused on providing high care and palliative care needs for homeless older persons. The staff found the work challenging but rewarding.[82]

How should the law respond to self-neglect? Should the law get involved with what some may consider lifestyle choices? It is argued that intervening in somebody's life, which may be based on a value judgement, is wrong. Under the MCA 2005, people can make decisions others consider unwise. This thinking led to the repeal of the power in Section 47 National Assistance Act 1948 to remove people living in insanitary conditions; people had the right to choose how they lived. However, Section 47 had its supporters. Some consultees to the Law Commission's proposal on adult social care argued that its repeal would leave certain groups unprotected whose lifestyle creates a significant risk to themselves and others.[83] Braye et al., drawing on the findings of serious case reviews and safeguarding adult reviews, point out that self-neglect highlights the ethical dilemma between respecting an older person's autonomy and exercising a protective duty of care. Autonomy may often prevail, closing down the prospect of any intervention. They propose a more nuanced, situated, and relational approach to understanding better the ethics

79 S Martineau and J Manthorpe, 'Safeguarding adults reviews and homelessness: Making the connections' (2020) *The Journal of Adult Protection* 22(4) 181.

80 Age UK, 'Older Homelessness (England), Policy Position Paper' (2019) <https://www.ageuk.org.uk/globalassets/age-uk/documents/policy-positions/housing-and-homes/ppp_older_homelessness_england.pdf> - accessed 28 September 2024.

81 B Rowland and J Williams, *National rough sleeper count questionnaires, local authorities housing network* (Local Authorities Housing Networks, February 2019) <https://www.wlga.wales/SharedFiles/Download.aspx?pageid=62&mid=665&fileid=2182>.-accessed 28 September 2024.

82 C Preti, CJ Poulos, RJ Poulos et al., 'Specialised residential care for older people subject to homelessness: Experiences of residents and staff of a new aged care home in Australia' (2024) *BMC Geriatrics* 24(1) 249.

83 Law Commission Adult Social Care (n41) 9.69.

of professional decision-making.[84] A flexible approach is required rather than a formulaic one; care and support must be tailored to the unique history and needs of the older person and seek to understand the person beyond their self-neglect.

A fundamental question about self-neglect is whether it is a safeguarding matter or a social care issue. If it is the former, then the safeguarding duties under the CA 2014 and the SSWA 2014 are engaged; if it is the latter, the social care powers and duties may be employed. Although self-neglect is not explicitly referred to in the definition of abuse and neglect, nothing suggests that it is not within it. The absence of a perpetrator does not take it outside the definition of an adult at risk in either piece of legislation. Self-neglect is not referred to in the CA 2014 in England but is included in the Guidance, which notes that it may not always prompt a safeguarding enquiry. Assessments should be made on a case-by-case basis and depend upon the person's ability to protect themselves by controlling their behaviour. There may come a point when they cannot do this without external support.[85] Initially, Wales was less committed to including self-neglect. The Senedd's Health and Social Care Committee report on the draft bill questioned whether its inclusion would adversely affect people's lifestyle choices.[86] However, the Procedures accompanying the SSWA 2014 now refer to self-neglect in their Possible Abuse and Neglect Indicators.[87] The decision on which route to take in self-neglect cases should be taken after considering all the evidence, including the history and possible causes of the neglect and the views of the older person. A proportionate response is necessary as self-neglect is a spectrum rather than an all-or-nothing phenomenon.[88] Any initial assessment should be revisited in the light of any additional information. Intervention (or non-intervention) must be flexible and designed to fit individual circumstances; this can take time. Research and the findings of reviews stress that inter-agency working and sharing information is a prerequisite to achieving a holistic response.[89] There is some concern that there may be delays in cases of self-neglect being brought to the attention of safeguarding teams, leading to a crisis response rather than a measured and longer-term approach. Owen et al. point out that self-neglect rarely arises suddenly and emphasise the need for early identification by safeguarding and other community services.[90] It is also necessary to consider the possibility that another person's behaviour may be causing the older person to self-neglect. For example, financial abuse often results in the older person being unable to provide the basics of living.

84 S Braye, D Orr, and M Preston-Shoot, 'Autonomy and protection in self-neglect work: The ethical complexity of decision-making' (2017) *Ethics and Social Welfare* 11(4) 320.

85 Care Act Guidance (n53) 14.17.

86 Health and Social Care Committee Report (n46) 40–1.

87 Welsh Safeguarding Procedures, 2023 (n60).

88 J Dawson, 'The conundrum of self-neglect' (2020) *British Journal of General Practice* 70(698) 453.

89 S Braye, D Orr, and M Preston-Shoot, 'Serious Case Review findings on the challenges of self-neglect: indicators for good practice' (2015) *The Journal of Adult Protection* 17(2) 75.

90 J Owen, J Woolham, J Manthorpe et al. 'Adult safeguarding managers' understandings of self-neglect and hoarding' (2022) *Health & Social Care in the Community* 30(6), e4405–e4415, 5.1.

Safeguarding duties

Duty to make enquiries: The significant achievement of both pieces of legislation is that adult safeguarding was placed on a statutory basis. The CA 2014 builds on the Section 42 definition of an adult at risk. If a local authority has 'reasonable cause to suspect that an adult in its area' is an adult at risk, regardless of whether they are ordinarily resident there, s.42(2) requires it to,

> make (or cause to be made) whatever enquiries it thinks necessary to enable it to decide whether any action should be taken in the adult's case (whether under this Part or otherwise) and, if so, what and by whom.
>
> (Section 42(2) CA 2014)

Section 126(1) and (2) SSWW 2014 adopts the same approach in a slightly different format. The threshold for triggering these duties to make enquiries is also based on a 'reasonable cause to suspect,' which is not an exceptionally high bar. It comes nowhere near the criminal standard of beyond all reasonable doubt. Certainty is not required. Information must be available to satisfy an objective observer that the facts underlying the concern may exist. A practitioner should summarise the information underlying the assessment, explain why they consider objectively that it meets the threshold for intervention, and prepare a brief statement of the possible risks for the adult if nothing is done.

The duty is to make enquiries; it is not a duty to investigate, although it may lead to a formal investigation. Enquiries are designed to gather information rather than investigate in detail. Both pieces of legislation provide for others, such as NHS bodies, to undertake an enquiry at the local authority's request. However, the authority remains responsible for ensuring the duty to make enquiries is fulfilled. An adult suspected of being at risk may refuse to cooperate with the enquiry; this does not relieve the local authority of its duty but does compromise the enquiry. If there is a refusal to cooperate, practitioners must be alert to the possibility of coercive control by another person, preventing the older person from deciding freely. Where the older person lacks the necessary capacity, the MCA 2005 provisions apply. Advocacy, which involves supporting and representing the views of the adult at risk, should be available when required. The outcome of an enquiry is a report identifying whether the adult is an adult at risk and, if so, to put in place an action plan. A plan should be linked to any social care plan for the adult.

Duty to cooperate: A recurring theme in adult safeguarding is the failure of public authorities to cooperate. Good working across different agencies and a willingness to share information are central to ethical adult safeguarding. No Secrets and In Safe Hands emphasised agencies working together and, importantly, sharing information, but it was only guidance. A legal duty to do so was necessary.[91] As

91 S Donnelly, and M O'Brien, 'Adult safeguarding legislation—the key to addressing dualism of agency and structure? An exploration of how Irish social workers protect adults at risk in the absence of adult safeguarding legislation' (2022) *The British Journal of Social Work 52*(6) 3677.

discussed in Chapter 5, the CA 2014 and the SSWA 2014 require 'relevant partners' to cooperate, including cooperating on adult safeguarding.[92]

Sharing information: Another recurring safeguarding theme is the failure of agencies and practitioners to share information. Information shared at an early stage may prevent abuse and neglect from escalating. The rationale for sharing information is that those involved obtain a broadly based and multi-agency assessment of the situation. It is also valuable because small snippets of information, which in isolation may appear unimportant, may identify a risk when put alongside information from others. The CA 2014 Guidance is unequivocal in emphasising the need to share.

> (N)o professional should assume that someone else will pass on information which they think may be critical to the safety and wellbeing of the adult. If a professional has concerns about the adult's welfare and believes they are suffering or likely to suffer abuse or neglect, then they should share the information with the local authority and, or, the police if they believe or suspect that a crime has been committed.[93]

Safeguarding is everybody's business. The assumption that others will report is dangerous and undermines the practitioner's duty to protect. The Welsh legislation requires a relevant partner to inform a local authority if they think an adult in its area is at risk; where the adult is in another authority's area, it must inform that authority.[94] The guidance reminds practitioners that they must share information following data protection law and the duty of confidentiality. These are not to be used indiscriminately as reasons not to share.[95] Information sharing must always be necessary, lawful, and proportionate.

Practitioners in health and social care may witness abuse and neglect in the person's home, care home, hospital, or wherever. These may be isolated and not reflect the standard of care provided. In other instances, there may be significant concerns about the conduct of a provider. Reporting procedures exist and must be used. Professional bodies also have procedures for reporting concerns about practitioners. However, organisational cultures and fear of personal consequences may deter people from using those procedures. There are significant disincentives to whistleblowing when reported concerns are ignored by those responsible. Higgins and Reitz neatly sum up the dilemma,

> Whistleblowing is a high-stakes activity, which rarely ends well for an individual. Its framing as a solitary activity ignores the social and relational

92 SSWA 2014 s.164

93 Care Act Guidance (n53) 14.43.2 and 14.180–95.

94 SSWA 2014 s.128.

95 Welsh Guidance (n54) 28.

consequences, pitting the lone individual against the weight of multiple professional bodies and relentless procedural scrutiny.[96]

The unpleasant personal experience of one whistleblower in a care home setting is captured in Chubb's book Beyond the Façade.[97]

The Public Interest Disclosure Act 1998 partly arose from the Piper Alpha oil rig disaster and the sinking of the Herald of Free Enterprise; in both cases, workers were aware of the dangers but could not speak out. The Act protects employees, freelancers, agency staff and directors if they make a 'protected disclosure.' A protected disclosure requires a reasonable belief that a wrongdoing has occurred; this includes a criminal offence, danger to the health and safety of an individual, and any attempt to conceal these deliberately. There must also be a reasonable belief that disclosure is in the public interest. The disclosure of abuse and neglect of an older person in a care home, hospital, or their home would be in the public interest. The whistleblower has the right not to be subjected to any detriment by their employer on the ground that they made a protected disclosure. Disclosures must be made following the law which means it must be made to the employer or the responsible person, a person on the 'Prescribed Persons' list, or more widely. The level of protection the Act provides depends upon which of these forms of disclosure is used. Raising concerns within the organisation is the first option, followed by reporting to a person on the Prescribed Person list. The Older People's Commissioner for Wales is on the list, as are the Care Quality Commission, Social Care Wales, the Equality and Human Rights Commission, the General Medical Council, and the Healthcare Inspectorate Wales.[98] Justifying a wider disclosure, for example, to the media, involves a stricter legal test, including the need to show that the concern is exceptionally serious. Unfortunately, the environment is not always conducive to sharing concerns within organisations. Many older persons who experience abuse or neglect will be isolated and dependent upon others to speak up for them. Fostering a culture where people can express concerns freely will allow organisations to take appropriate actions instead of relying on whistleblowing. Jones and Kelly refer to practitioners facing a whistleblowing or silence dichotomy and how this ignores the spectrum of alternatives that concerned employees may adopt to identify and prevent wrongdoing.[99] Openness and the ability to speak out without fear help improve practice.[100] A whistleblowing procedure is necessary,

96 J Higgins, and M Reitz, 'If whistleblowing is the answer, ask a better question' (2019) *Journal of the Royal Society of Medicine* 112(11) 453, 454.

97 E Chubb, *Beyond the façade* (Chipmunkapublishing 2008).

98 For a list of Prescribed Persons see Department for Business and Trade, 'Whistleblowing: List of Prescribed People and Bodies' (GOV.UK25 January 2025) <https://www.gov.uk/government/publications/blowing-the-whistle-list-of-prescribed-people-and-bodies--2/whistleblowing-list-of-prescribed-people-and-bodies> accessed 12 February 2025.

99 A Jones, and D Kelly, 'Whistle-blowing and workplace culture in older peoples' care: Qualitative insights from the healthcare and social care workforce' (2014) *Sociology of Health & Illness* 36(7), 986.

100 See M Syed, *Black box Thinking* (Penguin, 2015).

but its effect on those who use it is often devastating for emotional and personal well-being and career prospects.[101]

Forty-two states in America seek to overcome underreporting of the abuse or neglect of older persons by introducing mandatory reporting laws which impose a legal obligation on professionals and others to report possible cases. Moskowitz[102] raises three issues about mandatory reporting. First, what is the threshold for reporting; this is important for the creation of the duty, as failure to report may lead to a criminal conviction. Second, how to identify the holders of the duty. As Moskowitz points out, practice across the states does vary. Groups such as the clergy are included in some states; in others, the duty falls on 'any person having reasonable cause to believe' that a vulnerable adult is being abused.[103] Third, is mandatory reporting a breach of the older person's private life? Does it risk infantilising the older person and reducing their ability to control their own life?[104] Whether mandatory reporting should be introduced in England and Wales is a matter for discussion. In relation to children, proposed Westminster legislation will require professionals, such as social workers and teachers, to report instances of child sexual abuse. Failure to report or concealment will result in professional and criminal penalties. As well as Moskowitz's three issues, how practical would mandatory reporting in adult safeguarding be? Donnelly points out that there may be unintended consequences, including the risk of creating a culture of reporting rather than acting. It may also impinge on the confidential relationship between the person with the duty and the older person.[105]

Safeguarding powers

Whether a new legal framework should include safeguarding powers was a contentious matter during the debate on the new legislation in England and Wales. Of particular interest was whether there was a need for a power of entry when necessary access to a suspected adult at risk was frustrated by the refusal of the adult or third person.[106] The rights to private life and home life are protected by the HRA 1998 and the ECHR. These are qualified rights, and the question was whether legal

101 K Peters, L Luck, M Hutchinson et al., 'The emotional sequelae of whistleblowing: Findings from a qualitative study' (2011) *Journal of Clinical Nursing* 20(19–20) 2907.

102 S Moskowitz, 'Saving granny from the wolf: Elder abuse and neglect - the legal framework' (1998) 31 *Connecticut Law Review* 77.

103 Miss. Code Ann. § 43–47-7

104 LR Faulkner, 'Mandating the reporting of suspected cases of elder abuse: An inappropriate, ineffective and ageist response to the abuse of the older adults' (1983) *Family Law Quarterly* 16, 69.

105 S Donnelly, 'Mandatory reporting and adult safeguarding: A rapid realist review' (2019) *The Journal of Adult Protection* 21(5) 241.

106 For an account of the debates in Westminster, see J Manthorpe, S Martineau, C Norrie et al., 'Parliamentary arguments on powers of access–the Care Bill debates' (2016) *The Journal of Adult Protection* 18(6) 318; M Stevens, S Martineau, J Manthorpe et al., 'Social workers' power of entry in adult safeguarding concerns: Debates over autonomy, privacy and protection' (2017) *The Journal of Adult Protection* 19(6) 312.

powers of entry and access should be available if all else fails or whether that was an unjustified interference with autonomy. Any such powers would be a last resort. Social workers and others have developed extensive skills in negotiating access under challenging circumstances. Patience and perseverance are needed, as well as working across agencies. In most cases, these are effective, although they take time. It is the residue of cases where, despite the best efforts of social workers, access is denied, and the risk is unacceptable.[107] Limited powers of entry are available under Section 135 MHA 1983, although it is not a general power but limited to people with mental disorders. A warrant from a justice of the peace is necessary.[108] Before the CA 2014, a Department of Health consultation exercise sought to ascertain attitudes towards legal powers for England. It found that the public was against the powers (18% for and 77% against). Health professionals were 90% in favour and 0% against. Local authorities respondents were 72% for and 12% against. Others (third sector, police) were 60% for and 23% against. Intriguingly, the Westminster Government concluded that based on the views expressed, the consultation did not provide a compelling case for powers of entry. Public opinion and the fear of unintended consequences, such as jeopardising social worker and client relationships, were influential. No powers are included in the CA 2014.

The debate in Wales went in a different direction, although the same concerns about autonomy and private life were rehearsed. The Welsh Government included a modest power in the Bill to enter premises with a court order to speak privately to a person suspected of being an adult at risk. Other powers, such as those in the Scottish ASPA 2007, were not included; this was criticised by Age Cymru and the Older People's Commissioner for Wales, both of whom advocated the inclusion of additional powers of intervention, such as an assessment order and injunctions.[109] Section 127 SSWA 2014 introduced Adult Protection and Support Orders (APSO). An 'authorised officer' of a local authority may apply to a justice of the peace for an APSO concerning any person living on premises within the authority's area. Premises are defined broadly in the Guidance and include domestic premises, care and nursing homes, hospitals, or other places where the person may live.[110] What are the grounds for making an APSO? These are found in Section 127(4) SSWA 2014. A justice of the peace must be satisfied that,

1) The Authorised Officer has reasonable cause to suspect that a person is an adult at risk.
2) It is necessary for the Authorised Officer to gain access to the person to assess whether they are an adult at risk and to decide on what action should be taken.

107 S Martineau, and C Norrie, 'Practice perspectives and theoretical debates about social workers' legal powers to protect adults' (2020) *Journal of Social Work* 20(1) 3.

108 See p 242

109 Health and Social Care Committee Report (n46) 110.

110 Welsh Government, *Social Services and Well-being (Wales) Act 2014: Working Together to Safeguard People - Volume 4 Adult Protection and Support Orders* (2016) para 1.13

3) Making an order is necessary to fulfil the purposes of an APSO.
4) Exercising the power of entry will not put the person at greater risk of abuse or neglect.

Under Section 127(2) SSWA 2014, the purposes of an APSO are,

1) To enable the Authorised Officer and any other person accompanying the officer to speak privately with a person suspected of being an adult at risk.
2) To enable the Authorised Officer to find out whether that person is making decisions freely.
3) To enable the Authorised Officer to assess whether the person is an adult at risk, and to decide what, if any, action should be taken.

Conditions may be attached to the APSO, such as restricting the time it may be exercised. The Authorised Officer may be accompanied by a police officer and a person specified in the order who may be able to assist with communication and make any necessary assessments. These may include speech therapists and mental capacity and mental health specialists. The role of the police officer goes beyond gaining entry; they can assist in ensuring that the purposes of the APSO are achieved.[111] It is unclear whether an APSO allows multiple entries as the SSWA 2014 does not explicitly refer to the possibility. However, a favourable interpretation is that multiple entries are permitted, but only up to the point that they are necessary to achieve the purposes of the APSO. One thing the APSO does not allow is an open-ended power of access.[112]

There are two principal difficulties in the APSO procedure. First, the need for the Authorised Officer and the justice of the peace to be satisfied that making the order will not place the person at greater risk of abuse or neglect. If little is known about the suspected adult at risk and perpetrator, that is a tough judgement. That links with the second difficulty. If, upon obtaining access to the person, the Authorised Officer is satisfied that they are an adult at risk, what can be done? No further legal powers are available under the SSWA 2014. In the worst-case scenario, the adult at risk may now be in greater danger as the perpetrator may seek revenge. Clements points out that,

> (T)he [SSWA 2014] has taken a middle way – between the English Act, which provides no new safeguarding powers, and the Scottish Act which contains (in addition to a power of entry) a power of removal. There is a fear that the Welsh option may be the worst of both worlds – since it provides no

111 SSWA 2014 Section.127(3).

112 J Williams, 'Adult safeguarding in Wales: One step in the right direction' (2017) The Journal of Adult Protection 19(4) 175, 181.

power to do anything if the person is found to be 'at risk' and it repealed the power of removal under National Assistance Act 1948.[113]

Police powers may be available if appropriate, but as policing is not devolved to Wales, their use in a devolved issue may be problematic. For whatever reason, APSOs are rarely used, although the fact they are available means practitioners can refer to the power when access to a possible at-risk adult is denied.

Safeguarding boards

Under Section 43 CA 2014, each local authority must establish a Safeguarding Adults Board for their area. There are three primary responsibilities associated with this role. First, it involves developing and publishing a strategic plan outlining how the Board's objectives will be achieved and how members and partner agencies will contribute to the process. Second, an annual report must be published to evaluate the effectiveness of the work completed. Finally, the Board is responsible for commissioning safeguarding adult reviews. The membership consists of the local authority, the clinical commissioning group for the area, and the chief officer of the police, in addition to any others who may be appointed.

Section 134 SSWA 2014 establishes local Safeguarding Boards. Unlike England, Wales adopted a single social care system for children and adults; this does not include child protection, which remains under the Children Act 1989. Separate safeguarding Boards for adults and children must be established; however, there is an optional power to merge the two boards into a single Safeguarding Board.[114] Whether this is desirable is uncertain. Although child protection and adult safeguarding have the same overall objective, namely keeping people safe, the practicalities differ. Membership of the adult Safeguarding Boards includes the local authorities in the Boards area, the local Health Board, NHS Trusts, and the chief officer of police. Safeguarding Boards are required by Section 135 SSWA 2014 to protect adults within its areas who—

1. have needs for care and support (whether or not a local authority is meeting any of those needs), and
2. are experiencing, or are at risk of, abuse or neglect, and
3. to prevent those adults within its area mentioned in paragraph (i) from becoming at risk of abuse or neglect.

Safeguarding Boards must seek to achieve their objectives by coordinating and ensuring the effectiveness of what is done by each person or body represented on

113 See L Clements, 'The Social Services & Well-being(Wales) Act 2014: an overview' (Clements, 2022) <https://www.lukeclements.co.uk/wp-content/uploads/2023/09/Wales-SS-Well-being-Act-35-2022.pdf> - accesssed 28 September 2024.

114 SSWA 2014 Section.140 .

the Board. In addition to local Boards, Section 132 SSWA 2014 establishes the National Independent Safeguarding Board, whose role is to provide advice and support to local Safeguarding Boards, report on the effectiveness of safeguarding in Wales, and make recommendations to the government.

Safeguarding Adult Reviews in England and Practice Reviews in Wales are components of the process of learning and improving effective partnership working. They are not about apportioning blame but instead identifying areas for improvement and lessons learnt. The Safeguarding Boards in England are responsible for reviewing cases involving adults who have care and support needs when there is reasonable cause for concern about the effectiveness of collaborative efforts to protect them. One of two further conditions must be satisfied. First, if the person has died and there is reason to believe that their death was caused by abuse or neglect, a review will take place, regardless of whether the local authority was aware of the circumstances prior to the death. Second, if the person is still alive and there are suspicions of serious abuse or neglect that they have experienced, a review is also required. Furthermore, the Board has the authority to review other cases involving adults with care and support needs, regardless of whether the local authority was involved in addressing those needs. Each member of the SAB is required to cooperate and contribute to these reviews to identify valuable lessons from each case, which can then be applied to future situations.[115]

In Wales, the recently introduced Single Unified Safeguarding Review (SUSR) aims to streamline and enhance the safeguarding review process. Its primary goal is to merge existing review processes—such as Domestic Homicide Reviews, Child Practice Reviews, Adult Practice Reviews, Mental Health Homicide Reviews, and Offensive Weapons Homicide Reviews—into a single framework. This will eliminate overlapping reviews and promote a more efficient and collaborative safeguarding environment. The SUSR emphasises learning and improvement by identifying and analysing serious incidents to improve future safeguarding practices. It aims to ensure that lessons learned are recognised and acted upon through a comprehensive Action Plan. Additionally, the SUSR seeks to reduce the trauma experienced by those involved, including the subject of the review and their families, by conducting a single review instead of multiple potentially distressing ones, thus minimising the emotional burden. The SUSR promotes a collaborative, multi-agency approach, integrating practitioners, managers, and senior officers from various organisations to consider all relevant perspectives. This will help achieve an understanding of events within a reasonable timeframe, typically within 12 months, allowing for prompt dissemination and implementation of learning. Furthermore, the SUSR aims to promote a culture of accountability and transparency, ensuring that findings and review recommendations are widely shared and acted upon. The Wales Safeguarding Repository will support these efforts by enabling the storage and analysis of review reports The Safeguarding Boards play a key role in the SUSR process. They oversee SUSRs, ensure they are completed

115 CA 2014 Sections.44 (1)-(4).

within 12 months, and notify the Welsh Government about new reviews through the SUSR Co-ordination Hub. They approve and publish the final report and action plan, which are submitted to the Wales Safeguarding Repository. The Boards work with Community Safety Partnerships on Domestic Homicides and align findings with Well-being Plan priorities.[116]

SUSRs recognises that the death of, or serious harm to, an older person may be within the remit of more than one type of review. One case could previously be considered by two or more reviews, for example, a practice review and a domestic homicide review, leading to the duplication of work and information collection. Duplication was time-consuming for those involved in reviews and is distressing for families. Lessons learnt often go beyond the precise remit of the review and be relevant in other areas of practice. Robinson et al., in their analysis of domestic homicide, mental health, and adult practice reviews, emphasise this point by pointing out that the previous approach failed to look holistically at the lessons learned from multiple individual reviews.

> each review is commissioned and held separately, as specific to that context, situation, team or setting. This arrangement does not encourage or facilitate the spread of knowledge across local authorities and disciplines. Multiple, separate reviewing processes inhibit the learning and 'reading across' these incidents. This reinforces the divides between professional groups, almost as if they inhabit different 'planets'..., rather than allowing practitioners to make connections across their different practice settings.[117]

Asymetry across the United Kingdom

Although this book concentrates on England and Wales, placing the debate on safeguarding older persons within a United Kingdom context is helpful. Devolution allows each of the four nations to develop its own approach.[118] As discussed above, England and Wales have a similar procedure, although Wales has limited power through the APSO. Mention has been made of the Scottish ASPA 2007.[119] This contains a wide range of duties and powers including a duty to make enquiries, visits, assessment orders, removal orders, and banning orders. Built into these are

116 Welsh Government, 'Single Unified Safeguarding Review Statutory Guidance' (2024) <https://www.gov.wales/sites/default/files/publications/2024-12/single-unified-safeguarding-review-susr-statutory-guidance.pdf> - accessed 11 February 2025

117 AL Robinson, A Rees, and R Dehaghani, 'Making connections: A multi-disciplinary analysis of domestic homicide, mental health homicide and adult practice reviews' (2019) The Journal of Adult Protection, 21(1), 16.

118 J Williams, 'Safeguarding adults at risk: an asymmetrical approach to reform across the four nations' (2015) Elder Law Journal 5(4) 343; L Montgomery, J Anand, K Mackay, B Taylor, KC Pearson, and CM Harper, 'Implications of divergences in adult protection legislation' (2016) The Journal of Adult Protection 18(3) 149.

119 K Mackay, 'The Scottish adult support and protection legal framework' (2008) The Journal of Adult Protection 10(4) 25.

safeguards against the misuse of the powers. What difference have the powers in Scotland made? Are the powers in the ASPA 2007 used regularly? They are not a panacea, law rarely is. Mackay et al. emphasised the importance of a holistic approach.

> There was a wide range of aspects that made up a protection plan, and these can be grouped around legal orders, monitoring activities, and then emotional, practical, personal, financial, housing and relational support. Also, some people, due to physical or cognitive impairments, had been receiving or would receive personal and practical care.[120]

The fear expressed in England and Wales about the introduction of powers and their effect on autonomy and the right of persons to decide for themselves has not been realised in Scotland. Preston-Shoot and Cornish emphasise the importance of the principle of proportionality in adult safeguarding in Scotland. The possible tensions between autonomy and protection are recognised, but beneficial outcomes can, in some instances, be gained from using protection orders.[121] This is confirmed by McKay and Notman's review of the working of ASPA 2007 in one local authority. Their conclusions are informative for those who advocate stronger powers in England and Wales, and for Northern Ireland as it contemplates legislation. Giving social workers powers does not mean they will use them indiscriminately; rather, they develop proportionate ways of using them. Protection orders are a relatively small part of the response to safeguarding; they are to be used where all else has failed. Their research identifies a need to move away from the belief that nothing can be done if a person does not consent. ASPA 2007 is more nuanced than that as practitioners can undertake enquiries and investigate in other ways. Practitioners and agencies 'need to avoid ill-informed, one-off decisions that might overlook the emotional and relational aspects of the ability to make a choice and then to action it.'[122]

Northern Ireland is considering introducing adult safeguarding legislation. It currently relies on its 2015 Adult Safeguarding Prevention and Protection in Partnership policy.[123] In his Home Truths investigation, the Commissioner for

120 K Mackay, C McLaughlan, S Rossi et al. *Exploring How Practitioners Support and Protect Adults at Risk of Harm in the Light of the Adult Support and Protection (Scotland) Act 2007* para 9.9 (University of Sterling Research Repository, 9 December 2011) <https://storre.stir.ac.uk/handle/1893/3524> – accessed 28 September 2024.

121 M Preston-Shoot and S Cornish, 'Paternalism or Proportionality? Experiences and Outcomes of the Adult Support and Protection (Scotland) Act 2007' (2014) The Journal of Adult Protection 16(1) 5.

122 K Mackay and M Notman, 'Adult Support and Protection (Scotland) Act 2007: Reflections on Developing Practice and Present Day Challenges' (2017) The Journal of Adult Protection 19(4) 187, 189–90

123 The Department of Health, Social Services and Public Safety and the Department of Justice, 'Social Services and Public Safety and Department of Justice 'Adult Safeguarding Prevention and Protection in Partnership' (2015) <https://www.health-ni.gov.uk/sites/default/files/publications/dhssps/adult-safeguarding-policy.pdf?> – accessed 1 July 2024.

Older People Northern Ireland recognises that the 2015 policy has much to commend but it needs to be underpinned by a legislative framework.[124] The Republic of Ireland is also considering safeguarding legislation. A recent report by the Law Reform Commission for Ireland emphasises the need for a comprehensive statutory legal framework for adult safeguarding in Ireland. Amongst its many recommendations is the need for a set of guiding principles based on human rights. They include empowerment, protection, prevention, proportionality, integration, cooperation and accountability. It proposes that 'an adult at risk of harm' should be defined as,

> as an adult who by reason of their physical or mental condition or other particular personal characteristic or family or life circumstance (whether permanent or otherwise) needs support to protect themself from harm at a particular time.[125]

England, Scotland, and Wales provide different models, namely the minimalist approach in England, the maxi approach in Scotland, and, for want of a better term, the toe-in-the-water approach in Wales.[126] It will be interesting to see the debate's outcome in Northern Ireland.

Older persons and domestic abuse

Section 1 DAA 2021 defines domestic abuse as,

> Behaviour of a person ('A') towards another person ('B') is 'domestic abuse' if—
>
> (a) A and B are each aged 16 or over and are personally connected to each other, and
>
> (b) the behaviour is abusive.

Behaviour may be treated as 'towards' A if the conduct is directed at another person, for example, a grandchild. As discussed above, personally connected' refers to people who fall under one or more of the following categories: people who are or have been married to each other, those who are or have been civil partners, those who have agreed to marry (whether or not the agreement has ended), those who have entered into a civil partnership agreement (whether or not it has ended), those who are or have been in an intimate personal relationship with each other,

124 Commissioner for Older People Northern Ireland, 'Home Truths: A Report on the Commissioner's Investigation into Dunmurry Manor Care Home' (COPNI, 2018) 25.

125 Law Reform Commission, 'A Regulatory Framework for Adult Safeguarding' (2024) <https://www.lawreform.ie/news/the-law-reform-commission-publishes-report-on-a-regulatory-framework-for-adult-safeguarding.1141.html> – accessed 28 September 2024.

126 See Williams (n118).

those who have or had a parental relationship with the same child, or those who are related.[127]

Under the DAA 2021, the Secretary of State must appoint a Domestic Abuse Commissioner. Nicole Jacobs is the current Commissioner. The Commissioner is responsible for promoting good practices that help prevent domestic abuse. She also has a duty to ensure that the perpetrators of domestic abuse are identified, as well as the victims of such abuse and affected children. The Commissioner must also ensure that the people affected by domestic abuse are protected and supported. To carry out this duty, the Commissioner may assess and monitor the services provided to those affected by domestic abuse, make recommendations to public authorities, undertake research, provide information and training, increase public awareness, consult with public authorities and organisations, and cooperate with them. Much of the DAA 2021 applies to England and Wales, although the Commissioner cannot act concerning a Welsh-devolved area. A policy report published by the Commissioner identified some specific issues facing older persons who experience domestic abuse. According to the Commissioner's focus groups, older people face difficulties in accessing help when faced with domestic abuse. Her focus groups revealed that older victims and survivors are more likely to be socially isolated due to a lack of support networks, physical and/or mental health issues, and the constant presence of their abuser after retirement. They also have less access to online information and may struggle with telephone communication due to age-related hearing loss. Accommodation-based services can also be unsettling for older victims, especially when it is shared with younger people.[128]

In 2015, the Welsh Senedd passed the Violence Against Women, Domestic Abuse and Sexual Violence Act, which aims to improve measures designed to prevent gender-based violence, domestic abuse, and sexual violence. It focuses on safeguarding victims, providing better assistance to those affected, and appointing a National Adviser on gender-based violence, domestic abuse, and sexual violence. The Welsh Government has published a strategy designed to tackle violence against women, domestic abuse, and sexual violence for the years 2022 to 2026.[129] It builds on progress already made and explores new approaches. The strategy recognises that cooperation across government, non-devolved bodies, public and private sectors, and Welsh society is a prerequisite to achieving its goals. A National Partnership Board has been established to provide a framework for collaboration and ensure that all participants are accountable. Concerns that older persons were not fully included are addressed by the Strategy, which concedes that the needs of

127 See also p 180 and Serious Crimes Act 2015 Section.76.

128 Domestic Abuse Commissioner, 'A Patchwork of Provision: How to meet the needs of victims and survivors across England and Wales' (2022) 49 <https://domesticabusecommissioner.uk/wp-content/uploads/2022/11/DAC_Mapping-Abuse-Suvivors_Long-Policy-Report_Nov2022_FA.pdf> – accessed 28 September 2024.

129 Welsh Government, 'Violence against women, domestic abuse and sexual violence: strategy 2022 to 2026' (2022) <https://www.gov.wales/violence-against-women-domestic-abuse-and-sexual-violence-strategy-2022-2026-html> – accessed 28 September 2024.

older persons and children have not been adequately recognised.[130] One of the subgroups established under the strategy covers older people's and children's needs, recognising its whole life span approach.

Domestic abuse among older people is not uncommon and can take different forms, such as physical, sexual, emotional, or economic abuse. They may face challenges in seeking support due to a lack of awareness among professionals, dependence on the abuser, and a range of other factors such as disability, ethnicity, and LGBTQ+ status. As people age, they are equally vulnerable to abuse from their adult children or grandchildren as they are to their partner or spouse. Older persons who experience domestic abuse often have a health condition or disability, which often makes them dependent on their abuser for care and support.[131] Penhale discusses elder abuse in the context of domestic abuse.

> Elder abuse is thus viewed as a problem with its own distinctive characteristics, which set it apart from other forms of violence, instead of looking at the evident correspondences between the abuse of older women and violence towards younger women and developing responses in conjunction with these.[132]

A survey by the charity Hourglass showed that 34% of the UK population did not believe that acts of domestic violence directed at an older person were abuse.[133]

The findings of a 2016 study conducted by SafeLives on domestic abuse and older persons are disturbing. It found that persons aged sixty-one and older are at a higher risk of experiencing abuse from adult family members compared to younger persons. Additionally, they are more likely to experience abuse from a current intimate partner while also being less likely to attempt to leave a violent relationship.[134] Domestic abuse of older persons tends to fall into one of three categories. The first is domestic abuse that has grown older – it starts early in a relationship and continues into older age. The second is domestic abuse involving a perpetrator who is a new spouse or intimate partner. Third, stresses and strains may cause late-onset domestic abuse in later life, including illness, dependency, and retirement.[135] The

130 See Wydall et al. (n62),

131 Age UK, 'New data on domestic abuse in older people' (2022) <https://www.ageuk.org.uk/discover/2022/december/new-data-on-domestic-abuse-in-older-people/> – accessed 28 September 2024.

132 B Penhale 'Older women, domestic violence, and elder abuse: A review of commonalities, differences, and shared approaches' (2008) 15 *Journal of Elder Abuse & Neglect* 178.

133 Hourglass, 'Building a UK-Wide picture of the abuse of older people: Domestic abuse of older people' (2021) <https://wearehourglass.org/sites/default/files/inline-files/Domestic%20Abuse%20Of%20Older%20People%20_Layout%201_0.pdf> – accessed 1 July 2024.

134 SafeLives, 'Older people and domestic abuse' (2016) <https://safelives.org.uk/sites/default/files/resources/Safe%20Later%20Lives%20-%20Older%20people%20and%20domestic%20abuse.pdf>– accessed 28 September 2024.

135 EP Cramer, and SR Brady, 'Competing values in serving older and vulnerable adults: Adult protective services, mandated reporting, and domestic violence programs'(2013) *Journal of Elder Abuse & Neglect* 25(5) 453.

Table 6.1 Percentage of people aged sixteen years and over who were victims of domestic abuse as defined by the DAA 2021 – March 2023[a]

Age group	*Women*	*Men*
16 to 19	9.0	7.0
20 to 24	6.3	5.6
25 to 34	6.8	3.1
35 to 44	7.0	3.6
45 to 54	5.0	3.4
55 to 59	6.6	2.2
60 to 74	4.2	2.1
75 years and over	2.0	0.8

[a] Office for National Statistics, 'Domestic abuse victim characteristics, England and Wales: year ending March 2023' (24 November 2023) <https://www.ons.gov.uk/peoplepopulationandcommunity/crimeandjustice/articles/domesticabusevictimcharacteristicsenglandandwales/yearendingmarch2023#age> – accessed 28 September 2024. (The ONS includes the following caveat – 'Data for the year ending March 2023 are not badged as National Statistics. They are based on eight months of data collection because of an error in the survey, which resulted in missing data.')

dynamics of domestic abuse and older persons are complex. Myths around ageing, dementia, and carer stress need to be addressed. Studies have shown a strong link between dementia and the abuse of older persons, which makes them more susceptible to being victimised whilst facing difficulties accessing care and support.[136] It is also necessary to recognise that older persons, as well as being victims, may be perpetrators.[137]

The Office for National Statistics collects data on domestic abuse, which now includes people aged seventy-five and above. The 2023–23 data shows that more women are victim–survivors of domestic abuse across all age ranges(see Table 6.1). Although younger people, especially those aged sixteen to nineteen, are more likely to experience domestic abuse, a significant number of older persons are also victim–survivors. In very rough terms, the figures point to over one-third of a million older people experiencing domestic abuse in England and Wales.

In some instances, domestic abuse of an older person may be treated as a safeguarding matter and require local authorities to make enquiries. However, safeguarding procedures presuppose that the older person is an adult at risk. Not all

136 Knight and Hester (n25).

137 SM Benbow, S Bhattacharyya and P Kingston, 'Older adults and violence: An analysis of domestic homicide reviews in England involving adults over 60 years of age' (2019) *Ageing & Society* 39(6) 1097, 1117.

victim-survivors will be regarded as such. Although it is increasingly recognised that older persons experience domestic abuse, cases will often be diverted away from the criminal law and the civil law options available for victims of domestic abuse.[138] This reaction denies the older person justice and leads to exclusively welfarist responses, which may involve them moving out of their home into residential care whilst the perpetrator remains in the home.[139] Welfare-based responses are necessary, but so is the older person's ability to access the criminal and civil justice processes if appropriate. There are protective measures in place to support and provide protection for victims–survivors of domestic abuse. A narrow welfare approach may deny the older person the ability to access these, leading to a justice deficit.

Wydall highlights ageism in policy and practice responses to older persons who survive domestic abuse. Incorrect assumptions may be made about an older person's ability to make choices about accessing justice and protecting their human rights. Although policymakers and practitioners have given some recognition, she advocates a more transformative response that addresses older survivors' rights and entitlement.[140] It is important to discuss civil law options with older persons who are victim–survivors of elder abuse. In their study of access to justice, Clarke et al. identified only four cases out of a pilot study of 131 older persons where a civil remedy was sought; successful outcomes were achieved in three cases. They conclude,

> Awareness of the civil law and how to access advice and support needs to be raised amongst practitioners to ensure that, where appropriate, civil justice is pursued. If victims are not at least aware of the options, then they have effectively been disempowered. In cases involving incapacity, the [Independent Mental Capacity Advocate] is well placed to make a valuable contribution to the discussion on whether or not to use the civil law.[141]

Several civil law options can be pursued in cases of domestic abuse. Whilst these may not be totally effective, and accessing legal advice may be difficult, they are an option and should not be denied to older persons. Domestic abuse is as devastating for an older person as it is for all generations. For some older persons, domestic abuse may have been a part of their lives for decades. The use of civil law options may help them restructure their lives and break away from a violent past. The main civil law remedies are outlined in Table 6.2.

138 H Bows and N Westmarland, 'Rape of older people in the united kingdom: challenging the "real-rape" stereotype' (2017) *The British Journal of Criminology* 57(1) 1.

139 A Clarke, S Wydall, J Williams et al., *An evaluation of the "Access to Justice" Pilot Project* (Welsh Government, 2012) <https://www.gov.wales/sites/default/files/statistics-and-research/2019-08/121220accesstojusticeen.pdf>– accessed 128 September 2024.

140 Wydall, S. 'Intimate partner violence: Transforming the response to older victim-survivors in later life' in J Devaney, C Bradbury Jones, RJ Macy, C Øverlien, and S Holt, (eds) *The Routledge international handbook of domestic violence and abuse* (Routledge, 2021) 184.

141 Clarke et al. (n139) 43.

Table 6.2 Domestic abuse – civil law options

Legislation	*Power*
Non-molestation orders. Sections 42–42A Family Law Act 1996 (FLA 1996).	The court may grant an order if a person associated with the respondent applies for it, either in other family proceedings or separately, and the court believes that the order would benefit any other party involved in the family proceedings or a relevant child, even if no application has been made. The court must consider all circumstances, including the need to ensure the health, safety, and well-being of the applicant or, if issued, the person benefiting from the order; and any relevant child. It is an offence to breach an order (Section 42A) FLA 1996
Occupation orders, Sections 33–41 Family Law Act 1996.	An occupation order regulates property occupation and is only granted in serious cases. It can prevent someone from living in the property they own jointly or solely. Three requirements must be met: the applicant must have a legal or contractual benefit in the property or a right to occupy it; the property must have been or be intended to be both parties' home; the parties must be 'associated' (see Sections 62–63 FLA 1996). The Court applies the balance of harm test and weighs the harm the applicant or any child will suffer if no order is made against the harm the respondent will suffer if granted. If the applicant will suffer significant harm without the order, it will be granted unless the respondent will suffer greater harm. The Court may also issue an order at its discretion. The court will consider housing needs, financial resources, the impact of the order, and the conduct of all parties when deciding whether to grant an order of occupation.
Stalking Protection Orders. Section 1 Stalking Protection Act 2019.	The police may apply to a magistrates' court for a stalking protection order in respect of a person (D) if it appears to the chief officer that D has carried out acts associated with stalking and poses a risk associated with stalking to another person. The order prevents D from carrying out acts associated with stalking. There must be a reasonable cause to believe the order is necessary to protect another person from risk regardless of whether they were the victim of the stalking. It prohibits D from doing anything described in the order or requires D to do anything described in the order.

(*Continued*)

Table 6.2 (Continued)

Legislation	*Power*
Domestic Abuse Protection Notice. Sections 22–26 Domestic Abuse Act 2021. These provisions are not yet fully in force but as of 24 September 2024 they are being piloted in Greater Manchester, and the London Boroughs of Croyden, Sutton and Bromley. It is anticipated the pilot will run for two years and then be evaluated. When in force, they will replace domestic violence protection orders under Sections 24–26 Crime and Security Act 2010.	A police inspector can issue a Domestic Abuse Protection Notice (DAPN) to prevent someone from being abusive towards a person aged sixteen or older with whom they have a personal connection. The notice applies throughout the United Kingdom and can include provisions such as prohibiting the recipient from contacting the protected person or entering their premises. A DAPN cannot be issued to anyone under eighteen, and before issuing a DAPN, the officer must consider several factors, including the well-being of any person under eighteen and the opinion of the protected person. A police officer can arrest the recipient without a warrant if there are reasonable grounds for believing they are in breach of the notice. The notice remains valid until the application for a domestic abuse protection order is decided upon
Domestic Abuse Protection Order. Domestic Abuse Act 2021. These provisions are not yet fully in force but as of 24 September 2024 they are being piloted in Greater Manchester, and the London Boroughs of Croyden, Sutton and Bromley. It is anticipated the pilot will run for two years and then be evaluated. When fully in force, they will replace domestic violence protection orders under Sections 27–33 of the Crime and Security Act 2010.	A Domestic Abuse Protection Order (DAPO) is an order of the court designed to prevent P from being abusive towards a person aged sixteen and above who is personally connected to them. The order can either prohibit or require specific actions. A DAPO can be made on the application of a person seeking protection from domestic abuse, the appropriate chief officer of police, a person specified in regulations made by the Secretary of State, or any other person with leave of the court. The court can also make a DAPO of its own accord in cases where the accused person has been convicted of an offence or has been acquitted. Two conditions must be satisfied. First, on a balance of probabilities, P has been abusive to a person aged sixteen or over who is personally connected to them. Second, the DAPO is necessary and proportionate to safeguard the victim from domestic abuse, or the risk of it, carried out by P. The court must consider several factors, including the welfare of any person under eighteen years whose well-being is relevant to the order and the opinion of the person seeking the order for their protection. The court can issue a DAPO without prior notice. However, it must provide P with an opportunity to respond to the application as soon as it is convenient. A person who breaches the terms of a DAPO without reasonable excuse commits an offence for which the maximum sentence on conviction is five years imprisonment.

Identifying the level of risk to an older person who is a victim-survivor of domestic abuse is key to determining how to respond. The Domestic Abuse, Stalking, and Honour-Based Violence tool (DASH) is used by practitioners to assess the risk to victim-survivors of domestic abuse by helping identify the level of risk for the victim and any children involved. The risk is categorised as standard, medium, or high. A high-risk assessment meets the threshold for referral to a Multi-Agency Risk Assessment Conference (MARAC). To be considered high-risk, the victim–survivor needs to answer 'yes' to fourteen or more criteria on the DASH. MARACs are held regularly between agencies to share information on high-risk domestic abuse cases and ensure a coordinated and proactive approach to safeguard those at risk. They assess the risk level, develop safety plans, and coordinate support and interventions to protect the victim–survivor and any children affected. MARAC aims to prevent further incidents of abuse, reduce the risk of harm, and hold perpetrators accountable for their actions. Meetings involve representatives from agencies involved in responding to domestic abuse cases. Some of the typical participants include the police, health (for example, GPs and mental health), housing authorities, social services, probation, education, victim support, children's services, substance misuse, and independent domestic violence advisors. MARACs must address the particular needs of older victim-survivors of domestic abuse, including access to targeted services tailored to their needs, such as mental health support, care, and assistance with daily living activities. Cases involving older persons should be approached with sensitivity and empathy to provide meaningful support. It is necessary to create an environment that inspires trust and encourages older persons to come forward, especially since they may face unique challenges, such as cultural norms that discourage seeking help or feelings of shame and fear. A well-coordinated response is required to address the intricacies of domestic abuse involving older persons. MARACs provide a platform for professionals from diverse fields to collaborate and offer holistic solutions to meet the needs of older persons. By providing personalised support, identifying vulnerabilities, fostering sensitivity, and streamlining responses across agencies, MARACs can play a prominent role in ensuring older victim–survivors' safety and well-being.

Further innovative thinking is needed to enhance the effectiveness of the MARAC system. The lack of standard IT systems for all agencies has hindered information sharing. More attention and resources are needed to support perpetrators in multi-agency settings. There is also a need to address the issue of assessing risk dynamics. Understanding the factors that affect the implementation of innovative multi-agency initiatives to address domestic abuse is crucial. Further research is needed involving families and perpetrators using professional experience as a valuable source of evidence in improving the policing of domestic abuse.[142] MARACs

142 P Davies, C Barlow, and R Fish, 'The hard and complex work of implementing new multi-agency risk assessment approaches to policing domestic abuse' (2023) *Crime Prevention and Community Safety* 25(2)

have an important role to play in addressing domestic abuse in high-risk cases. It is important to note that not all cases of domestic abuse involving older persons are high-risk. Therefore, there must be coordinated community responses in place that can support all older victim-survivors, whether they are deemed high-risk through the MARAC model or at standard risk. This is to ensure early intervention by the various agencies to minimise escalation.

The Criminal Law

There are a limited number of criminal offences specifically aimed at the abuse and neglect of vulnerable persons. These include ill-treatment or neglect under Section 44 MCA 2005 in the case of incapacity and Section 127 MHA 1983 regarding patients under the Act. Additionally, Sections 20–25 Criminal Justice and Courts Act 2015 create two offences of ill-treatment or willful neglect, one by a care worker and the other by a care provider. However, most forms of abuse and neglect will be a general criminal offence. These include criminal damage, theft, actual bodily harm, false imprisonment, harassment, property offences, rape and other sexual offences, misuse of medication, domestic abuse, blackmail, and murder. Older people are also susceptible to fraud and spams. Ongoing research seeks to establish why spammers often target older persons. Cognitive ability, trust, internet experience, and tactics employed by spammers may increase the risk of internet fraud among older persons. However, there is still no consensus on the precise causes of this susceptibility.[143]

In deciding to prosecute a crime against an older person, the Crown Prosecution Service (CPS) should not rely on pre-conceived or stereotypical norms about older persons; each case should be assessed individually. Regard must be had to the diversity of older persons.[144] The CPS applies the two-stage Full Code Test to decide whether to prosecute.[145] The first stage is the evidential test – is there enough evidence to provide a realistic prospect of conviction? Assumptions such as older persons are forgetful and confused and will make poor witnesses must be avoided. The second part of the test is whether prosecution is needed in the public interest. A prosecution is more likely if the accused is in a position of trust, the victim is vulnerable, there is a possible repetition of offending, and the importance of maintaining public confidence. It is less likely where it will negatively affect the victim's physical or mental health.

In some criminal cases, special measures are available under Part 2 of the Youth Justice and Criminal Evidence Act 1999. They require adjustments to the court

143 Y Shang, Z Wu, X Du, X et al., 'The psychology of the internet fraud victimization of older adults: A systematic review' (2022) *Frontiers in Psychology* 13, 912242.

144 Crown Prosecution Service, 'Guidance on prosecuting crimes against older people' (2009) <https://www.cps.gov.uk/legal-guidance/older-people-prosecuting-crimes-against>. – accessed 1 July 2024.

145 Crown Prosecution Service, The Code for Crown Prosecutors (2018) <https://www.cps.gov.uk/publication/code-crown-prosecutors> – accessed 28 september 2024.

proceedings designed to assist vulnerable and intimidated victims and witnesses. An older person may be eligible for special measures to help give evidence as a victim or a witness. Special measures include screening the witness from the accused, a support person, communication aids, giving evidence via live-link or in private if the court determines that the witness may be intimidated, or video-recording their evidence, thus reducing the need to attend the trial in person.[146] The Domestic Abuse Act 2021 extends the availability of special measures to witnesses in cases involving offences where it is alleged that the behaviour of the accused amounts to domestic abuse as defined in Section 1 DAA 2021. This provision is partially in force. Special measures are also made available in family proceedings and civil proceedings where domestic abuse has been or is alleged.[147]

A welfareist approach to the abuse of older persons may encourage a view that not prosecuting cases is in the 'public interest' because it avoids exposing older persons to the criminal justice system. However, older persons have the same right to access criminal and civil justice options as younger people.[148] An exclusively welfareist approach violates the Article 5 ECHR right. It is the case that prosecutions for the abuse and neglect of older persons are the exception, often due to underreporting by victims who are afraid, embarrassed, or unable to report. Many choose not to report the crimes to avoid criminalising their families, who may be the perpetrators.[149] Although older persons' fear of crime may be exaggerated, the impact of being a victim on well-being is severe. Several factors make older persons more vulnerable to the impact of crime, including heightened fear of crime, a higher prevalence of physical and mental impairments or disabilities, a greater likelihood of living alone, a lack of support networks, and higher levels of insecurity. Supporting older victims and witnesses throughout the investigative process, trial, and post-conviction or acquittal is crucial.

Conclusion

Do existing laws and procedures in England and in Wales safeguard older persons who experience or are at risk of abuse and neglect? The answer is a yes and a no. Many examples of good practices that are preventative, person-centred, and rights-based exist. However, we know that things go wrong and that some older persons' lives are destroyed by unimaginable abuse and neglect in care homes, hospitals,

146 LC Hoyano, 'Striking a balance between the rights of defendants and vulnerable witnesses: Will special measures directions contravene guarantees of a fair trial?' (2001) *Criminal Law Review* 948; A Clarke, J Williams and S Wydall, 'Access to justice for victims/survivors of elder abuse: A qualitative study' (2016) *Social Policy and Society* 15(2) 207; .Williams, J., Wydall, S. and Clarke, A. 'Protecting older victims of abuse who lack capacity: the role of the Independent Mental Capacity Advocate'. Elder Law Journal, (2013), pp.167–74.

147 DAA 2021 Section.62–64.

148 A Clarke et al. (n146)

149 S Wydall, and R Zerk, 'Domestic abuse and older people: Factors influencing help-seeking' (2017) *The Journal of Adult Protection* 19(5) 247.

the community, and their own homes. Are further powers required? There is a strong case for saying England and Wales should have gone further in their legislation. In some ways, the Welsh approach is the worst of both worlds – intervention is too limited and risks worsening the situation. In considering its approach, Northern Ireland could look at a model that goes further than England and Wales but not quite as far as Scotland. That is an option. Some parts of the ASPA 2007 may appeal; others may not. Perhaps the biggest challenge to achieving effective safeguarding is the effect that austerity and the failure to 'fix' social care will have on the ability of practitioners to engage in preventative work and to respond appropriately when support is needed. In addition, ageist assumptions about older persons who experience abuse and neglect must be challenged. Most importantly, the underlying causes of older abuse must be addressed.

Bibliography

Age UK, 'New data on domestic abuse in older people' (2022) https://www .ageuk .org .uk /discover/2022 /december /new -data -on -domestic -abuse -in -older -people/ | Discover | Age UK - accessed 28 September 2024.

Age UK, 'Older homelessness (England), policy position paper' (2019) <https://www .ageuk.org.uk/globalassets/age-uk/documents/policy-positions/housing-and-homes/ppp _older_homelessness_england.pdf> - accessed 28 Septembmer 2024

American Psychiatric Association, *Diagnostic and statistical manual of mental disorders* (5th ed, 2013) <https://doi.org/10.1176/appi.books.9780890425787>, 132–133.

Benbow SM, Bhattacharyya S, and Kingston P, 'Older adults and violence: An analysis of domestic homicide reviews in England involving adults over 60 years of age' (2019) *Ageing & Society* 39(6) 1097, 1117.

Bloemen EM, Rosen T, LoFaso M, et al. 'Lesbian, gay, bisexual, and transgender older adults' experiences with elder abuse and neglect' (2019) *Journal of the American Geriatrics Society* 67(11) 2338.

Bows H, 'Introduction' in Bows H (ed.) *Violence against older women, volume II* (Palgrave, 2019) 4.

Bows H and Westmarland M, 'Rape of older people in the United Kingdom: Challenging the "real-rape" stereotype' (2017) *The British Journal of Criminology* 57(1) 1.

Brady D, Clifton A, Burr V, et al. 'The infantilisation of older people: Is it a problem?' (2014) *Mental Health Nursing* 34(5) 22.

Braye S, Orr D, and Preston-Shoot M, 'Autonomy and protection in self-neglect work: The ethical complexity of decision-making' (2017) *Ethics and Social Welfare* 11(4) 320.

Braye S, Orr D and Preston-Shoot M, 'Self-Neglect and Adult Safeguarding: Findings from Research' (2011) <https://www.buckssafeguarding.org.uk/adultsboard/wp-content/ uploads/sites/3/2020/08/SCIE-Report-46.pdf> - accessed 12 February 2025.

Braye S, Orr D, and Preston-Shoot M, 'Serious case review findings on the challenges of self-neglect: Indicators for good practice' (2015) *The Journal of Adult Protection* 17(2) 75.

Chubb E, *Beyond the façade* (Chipmunkapublishing, 2008).

Clarke A, Williams J, and Wydall S, 'Access to justice for victims/survivors of elder abuse: A qualitative study' (2016) *Social Policy and Society* 15(2) 207.

Clarke A, Wydall S, Williams J, et al. 'An evaluation of the "Access to Justice" Pilot Project' (Welsh Government, 2012) 121220accesstojusticeen.pdf (gov.wales). - accessed 1 July 2024.

Clements L, 'The Social Services & Well-Being (Wales) Act 2014: An overview' (Clements, 2022) https://www.lukeclements.co.uk/wp-content/uploads/2023/09/Wales-SS-Well-being-Act-35-2022.pdf.

Commissioner for Older People Northern Ireland, 'Home truths: A report on the commissioner's investigation into dunmurry manor care home' (COPNI, 2018) 25.

Cooper CI, Selwood A, and Livingston G, 'The prevalence of elder abuse and neglect: A systematic review' (2008) *Age and Ageing* 37, 151.

Cramer EP and Brady SR, 'Competing values in serving older and vulnerable adults: Adult protective services, mandated reporting, and domestic violence programs' (2013) *Journal of Elder Abuse & Neglect* 25(5) 453.

Crown Prosecution Service, 'The Code for Crown Prosecutors' (2018) https://www.cps.gov.uk/publication/code-crown-prosecutors - accessed 128 September 2024.

Crown Prosecution Service, 'Guidance on prosecuting crimes against older people' (2009) https://www.cps.gov.uk/legal-guidance/older-people-prosecuting-crimes-against. - accessed 28 September 2024.

Davies P, Barlow C, and Fish FR, 'The hard and complex work of implementing new multi-agency risk assessment approaches to policing domestic abuse' (2023) *Crime Prevention and Community Safety* 25(2) 148-65.

Dawson J, 'The conundrum of self-neglect' (2020) *British Journal of General Practice* 70(698) 453.

Department for Business and Trade, 'Whistleblowing: List of Prescribed People and Bodies' (GOV.UK25 January 2025) <https://www.gov.uk/government/publications/blowing-the-whistle-list-of-prescribed-people-and-bodies--2/whistleblowing-list-of-prescribed-people-and-bodies> accessed 12 February 2025

Department of Health, 'Safeguarding Adults : A Consultation on the Review of the "No Secrets" Guidance' (2009) <https://lx.iriss.org.uk/sites/default/files/resources/safeguarding%20adults.pdf> accessed 12 February 2025

Department of Health and Home Office, 'No Secrets: Guidance on Developing and Implementing Multi-Agency Policies and Procedures to Protect Vulnerable Adults from Abuse' (2000) <https://assets.publishing.service.gov.uk/government/uploads/system/uploads/attachment_data/file/194272/No_secrets__guidance_on_developing_and_implementing_multi-agency_policies_and_procedures_to_protect_vulnerable_adults_from_abuse.pdf> accessed 12 February 2025.

Department of Health and Social Care, 'Care and Support Statutory Guidance. Health and social care' (Gov.UK, revised 2023) https://www.gov.uk/government/publications/care-act-statutory-guidance/care-and-support-statutory-guidance - accessed 1 July 2024.

Department of Health, Social Services and Public Safety and the Department of Justice, 'Adult safeguarding prevention and protection in partnership' (2015) https://www.health-ni.gov.uk/sites/default/files/publications/dhssps/adult-safeguarding-policy.pdf - accessed 28 September 2024.

Dixon J, Donnelly JS, Campbell J, et al. 'Safeguarding people living with dementia: How social workers can use supported decision-making strategies to support the human rights of individuals during adult safeguarding enquiries' (2014) *The British Journal of Social Work* 52(3) 130.

Domestic Abuse Commissioner, 'A patchwork of provision: How to meet the needs of victims and survivors across England and Wales' (2022) 49 DAC_Mapping-Abuse-Suvivors_Long-Policy-Report_Nov2022_FA.pdf (domesticabusecommissioner.uk) - accessed 128 September 2024.

Donnelly S, 'Mandatory reporting and adult safeguarding: A rapid realist review' (2019) *The Journal of Adult Protection* 21(5) 241.

Donnelly S and O'Brien M, 'Adult safeguarding legislation - The key to addressing dualism of agency and structure? An exploration of how Irish social workers protect adults at risk in the absence of adult safeguarding legislation' (2022) *The British Journal of Social Work* 52(6) 3677.

Faulkner LR, 'Mandating the reporting of suspected cases of elder abuse: An inappropriate, ineffective and ageist response to the abuse of the older adults' (1983) *Family Law Quarterly* 16, 69.

Fileborn B and Barrett C, 'Sexual violence against older women: Documenting the practices of aged care service providers' in Bows H (ed.) *Violence against older women, volume II* (Palgrave, 2019) 101.

Fraga Dominguez S, Ozguler B, Storey JE, et al. 'Elder abuse vulnerability and risk factors: Is financial abuse different from other subtypes?' (2022) *Journal of Applied Gerontology* 41(4) 928.

Gholipour F, Khalili Z, and Abbasian M, 'Definitions and theories of elder abuse' (2020) *Elderly Health Journal* 6(2) 140.

Greengross S, *The law and vulnerable elderly people* (Age Concern England, 1986).

Hewitt D, 'The strange deaths of Section 47' (2012) *Journal of Adult Protection* 14, 39.

Higgins J and Reitz M, 'If whistleblowing is the answer, ask a better question' (2019) *Journal of the Royal Society of Medicine* 112(11) 453, 454.

Hillman J, 'Intimate partner violence among older LGBT adults: Unique risk factors, issues in reporting and treatment, and recommendations for research, practice, and policy' in Russell B (ed.) *Intimate partner violence and the LGBT+ community: Understanding power dynamics* (Springer, 2020) 237.

Hourglass (2020). What does growing old in the UK look like? [online] Hourglass. https://wearehourglass.org/sites/default/files/inline-files/SAFER%20AGEING%E2%80%93%20what%20does%20growing%20old%20in%20the%20UK%20look%20like__Layout%201.pdf- accessed 28 September 2024.

Hourglass, 'Building a UK-Wide picture of the abuse of older people: Domestic abuse of older people' (2021) https://wearehourglass.org/sites/default/files/inline-files/Domestic%20Abuse%20Of%20Older%20People%20_Layout%201_0.pdf- accessed 28 September 2024.

Hoyano LC, 'Striking a balance between the rights of defendants and vulnerable witnesses: Will special measures directions contravene guarantees of a fair trial?' (2001) *Criminal Law Review* 948 969.

Sleap B, 'No One Is Spared' (Human Rights Watch23 February 2022) <https://www.hrw.org/report/2022/02/23/no-one-spared/abuses-against-older-people-armed-conflict> accessed 11 February 2025.

Johnson F, 'Problems with the term and concept of 'abuse': Critical reflections on the Scottish Adult Support and Protection Study' (2012) *The British Journal of Social Work Volume* 42(5) 833, 850.

Jones A and Kelly D, 'Whistle-blowing and workplace culture in older peoples' care: Qualitative insights from the healthcare and social care workforce' (2014) *Sociology of Health & Illness* 36(7) 986.

Jones R, *The story of Baby P: Setting the record straight* (Policy Press, 2014).

Knight L and HesterM, 'Domestic violence and mental health in older adults' (2016) *International Review of Psychiatry* 28(5) 464.

Law Commission, 'Mental Incapacity' (Law Com No 231, 1995).

Law Reform Commission, 'A regulatory framework for adult safeguarding' (2024) https://www.lawreform.ie/news/the-law-reform-commission-publishes-report-on-a-regulatory-framework-for-adult-safeguarding.1141.html - accessed 28 September 2024.

Lord Chancellor's Department, 'Who decides: Making decisions on behalf of mentally incapacitated adults' (Hansard, HL Deb 18 November 1997) col 157.

Mackay K, 'Choosing to live with harm? A presentation of two case studies to explore the perspective of those who experienced adult safeguarding interventions' (2017) *Ethics and Social Welfare* 11(1) 33.

Mackay K, 'The Scottish adult support and protection legal framework' (2008) *The Journal of Adult Protection* 10(4) 25.

K Mackay, C McLaughlan, S Rossi et al. *Exploring How Practitioners Support and Protect Adults at Risk of Harm in the Light of the Adult Support and Protection (Scotland) Act 2007* (University of Sterling Research Repository, 9 December 2011) https://storre .stir .ac .uk /handle /1893 /3524 – accessed 28 September 2024.

Mackay K and Notman M, 'Adult Support and Protection (Scotland) Act 2007: Reflections on developing practice and present day challenges' (2017) *The Journal of Adult Protection* 19(4) 187, 189–190.

Magill J, Yeates V, and Longley M, 'Review of in safe hands' (Welsh Institute for Health and Social Care, University of Glamorgan, 2010).

Manthorpe J, Martineau S, Norrie C, et al. 'Parliamentary arguments on powers of access - The Care Bill debates' (2016) *The Journal of Adult Protection* 18(6) 318.

Mark JJ, 'The life of Diogenes of Sinope in Diogenes Laertius' (Ancient History Encyclopaedia, 2014) https://www.ancient.eu/article/740/the-life-of-diogenes-of-sinope -in-diogenes-laertiu/.- accessed 28 September 2024.

Martineau S and Manthorpe J, 'Safeguarding adults reviews and homelessness: Making the connections' (2020) *The Journal of Adult Protection* 22(4) 181.

Martineau S and Norrie C, 'Practice perspectives and theoretical debates about social workers' legal powers to protect adults' (2020) *Journal of Social Work* 20(1) 3.

Martinez JM, Homeier, DC, Fowler C, et al. 'Conceptualizing person-centered care in elder mistreatment intervention: Use of a well-being framework' (2003) *The Gerontologist* 63(6) 973.

Montgomery L, Anand J, Mackay K, et al. 'Implications of divergences in adult protection legislation' (2016) *The Journal of Adult Protection* 18(3) 149.

Moskowitz S, 'Saving Granny from the wolf: Elder abuse and neglect - The legal framework' (1998) *Connecticut Law Review* 31, 77.

National Assembly for Wales Health and Social Care Committee (2013). Social Services and Well-being (Wales) Bill: Stage 1 Committee Report. Cardiff: National Assembly for Wales. <https://senedd.wales/media/r0rer5fy/cr-ld9418-e-english.pdf> -accessed 12 Feb. 2025.

National Assembly for Wales, 'In Safe Hands: Implementing Adult Protection Procedures in Wales' (2000) <https://cysur.wales/media/xxybbuuj/in-safe-hands.pdf> accessed 12 February 2025

NHS Digital, 'Safeguarding Adults, England 2021–22' (2022) https://digital .nhs .uk /data -and -information /publications /statistical /safeguarding -adults /2021–22 – accessed 28 September 2024

Office for National Statistics, 'Domestic abuse victim characteristics, England and Wales: year ending March 2023' (24 November 2023) https://www .ons .gov.uk /peo plep opul atio nand community /crimeandjustice /articles /dom esti cabu sevi ctim char acte rist icse ngla ndandwales /yearendingmarch2023 #age – accessed 28 September 2024.

Ogg J and Bennett G, 'Elder abuse in Britain' (1992) *British Medical Journal* 305, 998.

O'Keefe M, Hills A and Doyle M, '(PDF) UK Study of Abuse and Neglect of Older People Prevalence Survey Report' (Research Gate2007).

Older Peoples Commissioner for Wales, ' Consultation on the Social Services and Wellbeing (Wales) Bill' (2013) <http://seneddtest.assemblywales.org/documents/s16727/SSW %2031%20Older%20Peoples%20Commissioner%20for%20Wales.pdf> accessed 12 February 2025.

Owen J, Woolham J, Manthorpe J, et al. 'Adult safeguarding managers' understandings of self-neglect and hoarding' (2022) *Health & Social Care in the Community* 30(6) e4405–e4415, 5.1.

Parton N, 'The contemporary politics of child protection: Part Two (the BASPCAN Founder's Lecture 2015)' (2016) *Child Abuse Review* 25(1) 9.

Pavlou MP and Lachs MS, ‘Could self-neglect in older adults be a geriatric syndrome?’ (2006) *Journal of the American Geriatrics Society* 54 831.

Penhale, B. 'Elder Abuse and Adult Safeguarding in UK'. in: Shankardass, M. (eds) *International Handbook of Elder Abuse and Mistreatment.* (2020, Springer, Singapore) https://doi.org/10.1007/978-981-13-8610-7_18 311-31.

Penhale B, ‘Older women, domestic violence, and elder abuse: A review of commonalities, differences, and shared approaches’ (2008) *Journal of Elder Abuse & Neglect* 15, 178.

Peters K, Luck L, Hutchinson M, et al. ‘The emotional sequelae of whistleblowing: Findings from a qualitative study’ (2011) *Journal of Clinical Nursing* 20(19–20) 2907.

Pizzey E and Forbes A, *Scream quietly or the neighbours will hear* (Penguin, 1974).

Powell DH, *The nine myths of aging: Maximizing the quality of later life* (W H Freeman and Co, 1998).

Preston-Shoot M and Cornish S, ‘Paternalism or proportionality? Experiences and outcomes of the Adult Support and Protection (Scotland) Act 2007’ (2014) *The Journal of Adult Protection* 16(1) 5.

Preti C, Poulos CJ, Rpoulos RJ, et al. ‘Specialised residential care for older people subject to homelessness: Experiences of residents and staff of a new aged care home in Australia’ (2024) *BMC Geriatrics* 24(1) 249.

Pritchard-Jones L, ‘“Adults at risk”: “Vulnerability” by any other name?’ (2018) 20 *The Journal of Adult Protection* 47, 54.

Robehmed S, ‘The rise of hoarding’ (*BBC News*, 23 December 2011) https://www.bbc.co.uk/news/magazine-16299670.

Robinson AL, Rees A, and Dehaghani R, ‘Making connections: A multi-disciplinary analysis of domestic homicide, mental health homicide and adult practice reviews’ (2019) *The Journal of Adult Protection* 21(1) 16.

Rowland B and Williams J, ‘National rough sleeper count questionnaires, local authorities housing network’ https://www .wlga .wales /Shared-Files /Download .aspx ?pageid =62 &mid =665 &fileid =2182.-accessed 28 September 2024.

SafeLives, ‘Older people and domestic abuse’ (2016) https://safelives.org.uk/sites/default/files/resources/Safe%20Later%20Lives%20-%20Older%20people%20and%20domestic%20abuse.pdf. - accessed 28 September 2024.

Scottish Government, ‘Adult Support and Protection (Scotland) Act 2007: Code of practice’ (2014) 21 https://www.pkc.gov.uk/media/25785/ASAP-Scottish-Government-Code-Of-Practice/pdf/Adult_Support_And_Protection_-_Scottish_Govenment_Code_Of_Practice.pdf?m=636099846743570000 - accessed 18 April 2023.

Sethi D, Wood S, Mitis F, et al. (eds) ‘European report on preventing elder maltreatment’ (World Health Organization 2011) - <https://iris.who.int/handle/10665/107293#:~:text=This%20report%20highlights%20the%20biological%2C%20social%2C%20cultural%2C%20economic,the%20protective%20factors%20that%20can%20help%20prevent%20it.> accessed 28 September 2024..

Shakespeare W, ‘King Lear|: Open Source Shakespeare’ (Opensourceshakespeare.org2015) accessed 12 February 2025 Act 1, Scene 4’.

Shang Y, Wu Z, Du X, et al. ‘The psychology of the internet fraud victimization of older adults: A systematic review’ (2022) *Frontiers in Psychology* 13, 912242.

Sitkin RA, Lee BX, and Lee G, ‘To destroy a people: Sexual violence as a form of genocide in the conflicts of Bosnia, Rwanda, and Chile’ (2019) *Aggression and Violent Behavior* 46, 219.

Spreadbury K and Hubbard R, ‘Definitions in adult safeguarding’ in Spreadbury K and Hubbard R (eds) *The adult safeguarding practice handbook* (Policy Press, 2020) 93.

Stark E, *Coercive control: The entrapment of women in personal life* (OUP, 2007).

Stark E, ‘Looking beyond domestic violence: Policing coercive control’ (2012) *Journal of Police Crisis Negotiations* 12(2) 199.

StatsWales, 'Number of reports received during the collection year, by local authority, category of abuse and age group' (2022) https://statswales.gov.wales/Catalogue/Health-and-Social-Care/Social-Services/social-services-performance-and-improvement-framework/adults/adult-safeguarding/numberofreportsreceivedduringthecollectionyear-by-localauthority-categoryofabuse-age – accessed 28 September 2024.

Stevens M, Martineau S, Manthorpe J, et al. 'Social workers' power of entry in adult safeguarding concerns: Debates over autonomy, privacy and protection' (2017) *The Journal of Adult Protection* 19(6) 312.

Stodolska A, Parnicka A, Tobiasz-Adamczyk B, et al. 'Defining elder neglect - A new proposal towards uniformity' (2024) *Ageing International 1-42.*

Syed M, *Black box thinking* (Penguin, 2015).

Thane P, 'The age of old age' in Thane P (ed.) *The long history of old age* (1st edn, Thames and Hudson, 2005) 10.

UNGA, United Nations principles for older persons, Res 46/91 (19 December 1991).

University of Oxford, 'A ballad intituled, "The old mans complaint against his wretched son, who to advance his marriage, did undo himself" (Oxford Text Archive, 2009) https://quod.lib.umich.edu/e/eebo/B01861.0001.001/1:1?rgn=div1;view=fulltext – accessed 28 September 2024.

Warburton-Wynn A, 'Sexual violence and assault against older people in hospitals in England: Research paper' (Hourglass, 2012).

Welsh Government, 'Single Unified Safeguarding Review (SUSR) draft statutory guidance' (2023) https://www.gov.wales/single-unified-safeguarding-review-statutory-guidance – accessed 28 September 2024.

Welsh Government, 'Social Services and Well-Being (Wales) Act 2014 Working Together to Safeguard People Volume I -Introduction and Overview Guidance on Safeguarding' (2016) <https://www.gov.wales/sites/default/files/publications/2019-05/working-together-to-safeguard-people-volume-i-introduction-and-overview.pdf> accessed 12 February 2025.

Welsh Government, 'Working Together to Safeguard People Volume 4 -Adult Protection and Support Orders Social Services and Well-Being (Wales) Act 2014 Guidance on Safeguarding' (2016) <https://www.gov.wales/sites/default/files/publications/2019-05/working-together-to-safeguard-people-volume-4-adult-protection-and-support-orders.pdf> accessed 12 February 2025.

Welsh Government, 'Violence against women, domestic abuse and sexual violence: strategy 2022 to 2026' (2022) https://www .gov .wales /violence -against -women -domestic -abuse -and -sexual-violence -strategy -2022 -2026 -html – accessed 28 September 2024.

Welsh Government, 'Wales safeguarding procedures' (2023) https://safeguarding.wales/en/adu-i/ – accessed 28 September 2024.

Welsh Government, 'Single Unified Safeguarding Review Statutory Guidance October 2024 2 Single Unified Safeguarding Review: Statutory Guidance' (2024) https://www.gov.wales/sites/default/files/publications/2024-12/single-unified-safeguarding-review-susr-statutory-guidance.pdf -accessed 11 February 2025.

Westwood S, 'Abuse and older lesbian, gay bisexual, and trans (LGBT) people: A commentary and research agenda' (2019) *Journal of Elder Abuse and Neglect* 31(2) 97.

Williams J, 'Adult safeguarding in Wales: One step in the right direction' (2017) *The Journal of Adult Protection* 19(4) 175, 181.

Williams J, 'Public law protection of vulnerable adults' (2002) *Journal of Social Work* 2, 293.

Williams J, 'Safeguarding adults at risk: An asymmetrical approach to reform across the four nations' (2015) *Elder Law Journal* 5(4) 343.

Williams J, 'State responsibility and the abuse of vulnerable older people: Is there a case for a public law to protect vulnerable older people from abuse?' in Bridgeman J, Lind C, and Keating H (eds), *Responsibility, law and family* (Ashgate 2008).81-102.

Wydall S, 'Intimate partner violence: Transforming the response to older victim-survivors in later life' in Devaney J, Bradbury Jones C, Macy RJ, Øverlien C, and Holt S (eds) *The Routledge international handbook of domestic violence and abuse* (Routledge, 2021) 184.

Wydall S, Clarke A, Williams J, et al. 'Domestic abuse and elder abuse in Wales: A tale of two initiatives' (2018) *The British Journal of Social Work* 48(4) 962.

Wydall S and Zerk R, 'Domestic abuse and older people: Factors influencing help-seeking' (2017) *The Journal of Adult Protection* 19(5) 247.

7 Older persons and liberty

Introduction

Older age is not a reason for taking away liberty. However, there may be situations where it is necessary to restrict or deny an older person their full liberty to protect them from unacceptable risks and ensure they have treatment and care. However, this is not a freestanding power to be used arbitrarily. The relevant human right is in Article 5 European Convention on Human Rights (ECHR). For current purposes, it states,

> 5.(1) Everyone has the right to liberty and security of person. No one shall be deprived of his liberty save in the following cases and in accordance with a procedure prescribed by law:
>
> (a) – (d) …
>
> (e) the lawful detention…of persons of unsound mind…;
>
> (f) …
>
> 2. Everyone who is arrested shall be informed promptly, in a language he understands, of the reasons for his arrest and any charge against him.
>
> 4. Everyone who is deprived of his liberty by arrest or detention shall be entitled to take proceedings by which the lawfulness of his detention shall be decided speedily by a court and his release ordered if the detention is not lawful…

A person can only be deprived of liberty on the grounds of an 'unsound mind' if three minimum conditions identified by the European Court of Human Rights (ECtHR) in Winterwerp v Netherlands are met.

1. The person must be reliably shown, by objective medical evidence, to be of unsound mind.
2. the person's mental disorder must be of a kind to warrant compulsory confinement. The deprivation of liberty must be shown to have been necessary in the circumstances.
3. the mental disorder, verified by objective medical evidence, must persist throughout the period of detention.

DOI: 10.4324/9780203798058-8

In Winterwerp, the ECtHR declined to define 'unsound mind,' arguing that the term was 'continually evolving' due to shifting attitudes and understanding of mental health. In Stockport MBC v KB and Ors the judge said,

> these words have no mystical powers; they are not an 'open sesame' giving access to the Article 5 cave. They refer to a mental disorder. It is for the court to be satisfied that P is of unsound mind on the basis of the evidence before it.[1]

Under Article 5 ECHR, the deprivation must be effected by a procedure prescribed by law to avoid arbitrary decisions based on discriminatory assumptions. The article's implications were considered in the 1981 case of X v United Kingdom.[2] Under the Mental Health Act 1959, a Mental Health Tribunal did not have the authority to release a detained patient; it could only provide a recommendation. This was held to be insufficient to meet the requirements of Article 5(4) of the ECHR, which stipulates the need for an appropriate procedure to challenge detention and to secure release if detention is unlawful.

Article 5 was central in R v Bournewood Community and Mental Health NHS Trust Ex p. L, where the issue was whether a non-objecting patient requiring treatment for his mental health could be an informal patient rather than be formally admitted under the Mental Health Act 1983 (MHA 1983). It was agreed that he lacked mental capacity. The hospital argued that he was not being detained as he had not chosen to leave and was compliant. Alternatively, if he was detained, the common law doctrine of necessity could authorise detention and treatment. The Court of Appeal held that he should be detained under the MHA 1983 as he was, based on the facts, deprived of his liberty.[3] He would be prevented if he tried to leave. The common law doctrine of necessity could not be used to authorise keeping him in hospital. The potential implications of the Court of Appeal's approach were far-reaching as many older persons in hospitals or nursing homes living with dementia would have to be detained under the MHA 1983.[4] Although this caused fear among the government and local authorities, the decision adhered to the well-established principle that the common law could only be used in situations not covered by a statute. Nevertheless, the House of Lords reversed the Court of Appeal's decision and held that he was not deprived of his liberty as he was not in a locked ward and had made no attempt to leave.[5] The hospital was entitled to treat and care for him under the common law doctrine of necessity. Thus, it was unnecessary to detain older persons living with dementia in care homes and hospitals under the

1 Stockport Metropolitan Borough Council v KB & Or [2023] EWCOP 58, [2023] 12 WLUK 407 [20].
2 App no 7215/75 (ECtHR 5, November 1981).
3 [1998] 2 WLR 764.
4 See, for example, R Jacoby, 'Old age psychiatry and the law' (2002) *The British Journal of Psychiatry* 180(2) 116; C Parker, 'Ability to leave?' (1998) *Elderly Client Advisor* 3, 3–5; D Brahams, 'Incapable patients must be treated "formally"' (1998) *Medico-Legal Journal* 66, 36.
5 [1999] 1 AC 458.

MHA 1983; the Court of Appeal's approach was considered incorrect by the House of Lords.[6]

The House of Lords decision failed to protect many older persons from being unlawfully deprived of their liberty in care homes, nursing homes, and hospitals. Subsequently, the case was taken to the ECtHR as HL v United Kingdom.[7] In his application, HL argued that articles 5(1) and (4) ECHR had been violated. The ECtHR agreed, arguing that the fact HL did not resist the detention was irrelevant since the right to liberty is too significant to be lost for that reason alone. In deciding whether there was a deprivation of liberty, the starting point must be to look at the concrete situation and consider a number of factors. So, for example, the duration must be considered, as is how any restrictions are implemented. In addition, the ECtHR found the common law doctrine of necessity was inadequate in providing legal grounds for his detention. It lacked procedural rules and safeguards, did not allow review, and relied on clinical judgement. Although judicial review and habeas corpus were available, they did not meet the Article 5(1) requirements of being a procedure prescribed by law. This lacuna in the law, known as the Bournewood gap, resulted in many thousands of older persons in care homes, hospitals and nursing homes being unlawfully detained in violation of their ECHR rights. In response to the ECtHR's decision, the Mental Health Act 2007 amended the Mental Capacity Act 2005 (MCA 2005) and introduced the Deprivation of Liberty Safeguards (DoLS).[8] DoLS aims to ensure that deprivations of liberty in care homes or hospitals of persons who do not have capacity comply with Article 5(1) ECHR, thus bridging the gap identified in the Bournewood case.

Deprivation of Liberty Safeguards (DoLS)

Obtaining a DoLS authorisation

Section 4A(1) MCA 2005 clarifies that depriving someone of their liberty is not permitted other than in two situations. First, it is lawful to deprive a person of their liberty if it is by a decision made by the Court of Protection under Section 16(2)(a) MCA 2005 regarding a personal welfare matter.[9] Second, a person may be deprived of liberty in a care home or hospital if authorised by Schedule A1 MCA 2005, namely DoLS.[10] However, Section 4B MCA 2005 permits deprivation where it involves providing life-sustaining treatment or carrying out a vital act while the court is deciding any relevant issue, and there is a question about whether there is authority to detain under Section 4A. It is a temporary measure and not an ongoing

6 G Ritchie, 'The Bournewood Fright' (1999) *Amicus Curiae* 14, 21.

7 App no 45508/99 (ECtHR, 5 October 2004).

8 See MCA 2005 ss 4A, 4B and Sch A1.

9 See Chapter 3.

10 MCA 2005 Section.4A(3)-(5). Section 4A has been amended prospectively by the Mental Capacity (Amendment) Act 2019, which is yet to be implemented.

authority to deprive whenever a concern about a person's safety arises.[11] A vital act is one in which whoever is doing it reasonably believes it to be necessary to prevent a serious deterioration in the person's condition.[12]

DoLS aim to protect those who are deprived of their liberty. Under Section 64(5) MCA 2005, a reference to the deprivation of a person's liberty has the same meaning as in Article 5(1) ECHR, which, on its own, is not very helpful, although it points us in the direction of the ECtHR jurisprudence. In Storck v Germany, the Court identified three elements of a deprivation, namely an objective element, which is the person's confinement in a restricted space for a not negligible length of time; a subjective element that the person has not validly consented to the confinement which may be due to lack of mental capacity; and the attribution of responsibility for the confinement to the State.[13] The courts in the United Kingdom have adopted this approach.[14] The person subject to DoLS is known as the relevant person (RP). DoLS cannot authorise medical treatment, which must be consented to by the RP. If the person lacks the capacity to consent to medical treatment, the best interests test is used. DoLS is monitored by the Care Quality Commission in England and the Healthcare Inspectorate Wales and Care Inspectorate Wales, but they cannot investigate individual cases.

The procedure for obtaining standard and urgent DoLS authorisations is described in Schedule A1 MCA 2005. DoLS only applies to persons in care homes or hospitals and not, for example, in their homes. If family members are responsible for arranging care or treatment for self-funders deprived of their liberty in care homes or hospitals, they could be considered outside Article 5(1) ECHR as the State is not directly involved. However, the Code clarifies that DoLS applies to care or treatment arranged publicly and privately in care homes or hospitals.[15] The care home or hospital is referred to as the managing authority and must apply for a DoLS if they believe there is a deprivation of liberty or one is about to take place. The application is made to the supervisory body. Where a DoLS is applied to a person in a hospital in England, the responsible supervisory body will be the relevant Primary Care Trust, the Welsh Ministers or the Local Health Board if they commission the care and treatment, or the Primary Care Trust for the area in which the hospital is located. In Wales, the supervisory body will be the Welsh Ministers or a Local Health Board unless a Primary Care Trust commissions the relevant care and

11 See *Havering London Borough Council v AEL* [2021] EWCOP 9 [48], [2021] 1 WLUK 375.

12 MCA 2005 Section.4B. As with Section.4A, this section is amended prospectively by the Mental Capacity (Amendment) Act 2019, which is yet to be implemented.

13 App no 61603/00 (ECtHR, 16 September 2005).

14 See, for example, *JE v DE and Surrey County Council* [2006] EWHC 3459 (Fam), [2007] 2 F.L.R. 1150; *A Local Authority v EBY and others* [2023] EWHC 2494 (Fam), [2023] 10 WLUK 66); *A local authority v KK and others* [2020] EWCOP 68 | [2020] 12 WLUK 355; *R (on the application of Dowsett) v Secretary of State for Justice* [2013] EWHC 687 (Admin), [2013] 3 WLUK 773.

15 Ministry of Justice, 'Mental Capacity Act 2005: Deprivation of Liberty Safeguards' (2008) <https://www.cqc.org.uk/sites/default/files/Deprivation%20of%20liberty%20safeguards%20code%20of%20practice.pdf>– accessed 28 September 2024 para 1.21; see also MCA 2005 64(6) .

treatment, in which case it will act in that capacity. Where the DoLS is applied to a person in a care home, whether in England or Wales, the supervisory body will be the local authority for the area where the person is ordinarily resident. However, if the person is not ordinarily resident in the area of any local authority, such as a person of no fixed abode, the supervisory body will be the local authority for the area where the care home is situated.[16] Assessments for standard authorisations must be completed within twenty-one days. The DoLS duration can be for up to twelve months. This is a maximum, and shorter periods should be used if appropriate; they can be renewed for further periods if the criteria continue to be met. In urgent cases, the managing authority can immediately deprive a person of their liberty for up to seven days using an urgent authorisation. However, it must simultaneously apply for a standard authorisation with an expectation that the criteria will be met. An urgent application can be extended once if the assessment is not completed.

The DoLS Code provides guidance. All decisions must be made and reviewed in a structured manner, and the reasons for decisions must be recorded. The established best practices for care planning must be followed, and a proper assessment must be carried out to determine if the person lacks the capacity to make decisions regarding the proposed care or treatment following the principles of the MCA 2005. Decision-makers should evaluate if the combination of all the restrictions imposed constitutes a deprivation of liberty, even if each restriction on its own would not. Care plans should be regularly reviewed, involving an advocacy service. Under the DoLS Code, decision-makers must consider all the circumstances, including the measures taken, their duration, and the impact of any restraints or restrictions. They must also explain the necessity and purpose of the measures. Steps should be taken to help the person maintain contact with their family, friends, and carers. The opinions of the person receiving care and their family or caregivers should be considered, including any objections they may have. It is necessary to consider how restraints and restrictions are implemented to minimise the chances of causing deprivation, but if a deprivation does occur, efforts should be made to find a less restrictive way of providing care or treatment. If appropriate, the managing authority should explore reducing deprivation to a restriction by lessening its intensity. Minor changes to the care plan might eliminate the need for a deprivation.[17]

DoLS requires six assessments to be undertaken on behalf of the supervisory body:

Age assessment: The RP meets the age requirement if they have reached eighteen years.

The mental capacity assessment: The RP meets the mental capacity requirement if they lack the capacity to decide whether they should be accommodated in the hospital or care home for care or treatment.

16 Ibid para 3.3
17 ibid para 2.6–2.8.

Mental health assessment: The RP meets the mental health requirement if they suffer from a mental disorder within the MHA 1983. This assessment must be undertaken by a doctor approved under Section12 MHA 1983 or a doctor with experience in diagnosing mental disorders.

Best interest assessment: The RP meets the best interests requirement if the following conditions are met.

1) The RP is, or is to be, deprived of their liberty.
2) It is in the best interests of the RP to be deprived of their liberty.
3) To prevent harm to the RP, depriving them of their liberty is necessary.
4) It is a proportionate response to the likelihood of the RP suffering harm and the seriousness of that harm.

No refusals assessment: There is a refusal if,

i. The RP has made a valid advance decision which applies to some or all of the relevant treatments.
ii. A DoLS would conflict with a valid decision of a donee or deputy for the RP to be accommodated in the hospital or care home to receive some or all of the relevant care or treatment in circumstances which amount to deprivation of the person's liberty or at all.

The eligibility requirement: The RP will be ineligible if detained under the MHA 1983, subject to conditions under the MHA1983 which would be inconsistent with a DoLS, or objects to treatment or detention for mental disorder.

At least two assessors are needed because different practitioners must undertake the mental health and best interest assessments, although it is desirable to avoid the involvement of too many assessors.

Who is involved in the DoLS procedure?

A key person in the DoLS process is the Best Interests Assessor (BIA), who is qualified and experienced in mental health, social work, nursing, occupational therapy, or psychology. Their role is to assess whether a deprivation of liberty is in the best interests of the RP, is necessary to keep them safe from harm, and is proportionate based on the likelihood and severity of potential harm. During the assessment, the BIA should involve the RP as much as possible and provide support as needed.[18] They must also consider the views of those whom the RP has named for consultation, any caregivers or people interested in RP's welfare (such as family and friends), an attorney under an Enduring or Lasting Power of Attorney, or a Court of Protection deputy. The BIA should consider whether conditions need to be attached to a DoLS. Any conditions should be the minimum necessary and not

18 Reg 5 The Mental Capacity (Deprivation of Liberty: Standard Authorisations, Assessments and Ordinary Residence) Regulations 2008. SI 2008/1858.

be a substitute for a good care plan. In recommending conditions to the supervisory authority, BIAs should aim for the minimum necessary constraints so that they do not unnecessarily prevent or inhibit the hospital or care home staff from responding appropriately to the person's needs, whether they remain the same or vary over time. The BIA should discuss any proposed conditions to be attached to the DoLS with the care home or hospital staff. BIAs must state in their report if changes to any recommended conditions would significantly affect their conclusions. Conditions may cover contact, cultural considerations, or other factors affecting the person's best interests.[19]

A Relevant Person's Representative (RPR) must be appointed to assist and support a person within the DoLS process. This should be done at the time of authorisation or as soon as possible and practical.[20] Rather like the nearest relative under the MHA 1983, the role acknowledges the right of the person at risk of losing liberty to have somebody speak up on their behalf. The RPR must understand the effect of the authorisation, how it can be reviewed or challenged, and how to request the support of an Independent Mental Capacity Advocate (IMCA). The choice of RPR can be based on a recommendation by the BIA and is usually a relative or friend, but it can be a paid role if no appropriate person is available. They maintain contact with the RP, represent them, and offer support. Additionally, they may request a review of the DoLS, initiate a complaint, or apply to the Court of Protection. If the RPR becomes unable or unwilling to continue in the role and the DoLS is still in effect, the supervisory body should appoint a new representative.[21]

The MCA 2005 involves three types of IMCA in the DoLS process, namely, Section 39A IMCA, Section 39C IMCA, and Section 39D IMCA. Each role is different but designed to support the RP and RPR. If a person is subject to Schedule A1 MCA 2005 and the managing authority cannot find a suitable person (other than somebody providing care or treatment professionally or for payment) to consult about the person's best interests, a Section 39A MCA 2005 IMCA should be appointed. The managing authority must notify the supervisory body of the need for an IMCA; the supervisory body must then appoint an IMCA. A person is subject to Schedule A1 in one of the following situations:

1. If an urgent authorisation is given.
2. When the following three conditions are met:
   i. A standard authorisation has been requested.
   ii. No urgent authorisation was given before the request for a standard authorisation was made.
   iii. The requested standard authorisation will not be in force on, before, or immediately after the expiry of an existing one.

19 DoLS Code (n15) paras 4.74-75.
20 Ibid para 7.1.
21 MCA 2005 Schedule A1, Pt 10.

iv. When the supervisory body appoints a person to assess whether there is a deprivation of liberty in response to a request by a third party to consider the necessity for an authorisation of detention.

The role of the Section 39A IMCA will end upon authorisation unless they are exercising their right to apply to the Court of Protection to challenge the DoLS. This extends to making the application and supporting the RP in applying to the Court.

The supervisory body must instruct a Section 39C IMCA upon notification by the managing authority that the following Section 39C conditions apply.

1. A standard or urgent authorisation is in force.
2. The appointment of an RPR ends.
3. There is no appropriate person to consult (other than one engaged in providing care or treatment for P in a professional capacity or for payment) about the person's best interests.

The appointment of a Section 39C IMCA ends when a new RPR is appointed; they have the same powers as the RPR, including the right to request a review and access the Court of Protection.

The supervisory body must instruct a Section 39D IMCA if a standard or urgent DoLS is in force and the RPR is unpaid. Instruction must take place in any one of three situations:

1. Where the RP requests an advocate.
2. Where the RPR requests an advocate.
3. When the supervisory body has reason to believe that, without an IMCA, neither the RP nor the RPR would be able to exercise relevant rights, have failed to exercise them, or are unlikely to exercise them when it would be reasonable to do so.

The rationale is that an unpaid RPR may need help understanding the role and assistance in, for example, making a complaint. The RP and unpaid RPR must be made aware that support from Section 39D IMCA is available. The involvement of Section 39D IMCA is not ongoing, and a decision should be made on whether their continued involvement is necessary, especially if there are no active formal proceedings, such as an application to the Court of Protection.

During the authorisation period, the care home or hospital may remove some or all of the restrictions causing the deprivation of liberty, effectively ending the basis for the DoLS authorisation. In such a case, they must apply to the supervisory body to formally end the authorisation. Either an RPR or an IMCA can request a review at any time. Depending on the circumstances, the supervisory body will decide which requirements must be reassessed. The RP, RPR, and IMCA must be informed of the review's outcome in writing. Where a person's capacity fluctuates over time, the Code recommends that a qualified professional should assess whether there is any indication that the person may regain capacity in the longer term. If it is likely that the person will only regain capacity on a short-term basis, the authorisation should remain in place, but the situation should be reviewed.[22]

What is a deprivation of liberty?

One of the leading authorities on deprivations of liberty is the case of Cheshire West, which went to the Supreme Court via the Court of Appeal. This joint appeal involved two cases involving Cheshire West and Surrey councils. The first case involved a thirty-eight-year-old man referred to as P, who had cerebral palsy and Downs syndrome and required twenty-four-hour care. P lived in a spacious bungalow with a pleasant atmosphere; it was not a care home or hospital. He needed help with all activities of daily living. Occasionally, P put pieces of his incontinence pad into his mouth. He wore a body suit to prevent this, and his mouth was regularly cleaned to remove any material. P also exhibited challenging behaviour, requiring regular intervention. The second case involved two teenage sisters, referred to as MIG and MEG, who had a history of being neglected and abused; they were placed in foster care by the local authority. At the time of the first court hearing, MIG lived with her foster mother. She did not attempt to leave, and her bedroom door was not locked. She also attended local education facilities and went on trips with her foster mother. She was content with the arrangements. However, if she had tried to leave home, her foster mother would have restrained her. MEG's behaviour was more challenging, and she was living in a small specialist home for adolescents, which was not a care home or hospital and, therefore, outside the scope of DoLS. She had behavioural problems requiring staff intervention, and carers accompanied her wherever she went. She also received tranquillising medication. MEG had never tried to leave the unit. Were P, MIG, and MEG deprived of their liberty? Although the cases involved younger persons, the general issues are familiar to practitioners working with older persons. The Supreme Court considered the three Storck components 'common ground.'[23]

The objective element

The ECtHR in Guzzardi v Italy emphasised that the right to liberty in Article 5 ECHR aims to ensure that nobody should be arbitrarily deprived of liberty. It is not concerned with restriction but with deprivations, the difference being degree or intensity and not nature or substance. The ECtHR continued,

22 DoLS Code (n15) paras 8.22–24.
23 *P (by his litigation friend the Official Solicitor) v Cheshire West and Chester Council and another; P and Q (by their litigation friend the Official Solicitor) v Surrey County Council* [2014] UKSC 19, [37], [2014] AC 986.

> In order to determine whether someone has been 'deprived of his liberty' within the meaning of Article 5 , the starting point must be his concrete situation and account must be taken of a whole range of criteria such as the type, duration, effects and manner of implementation of the measure in question.[24]

Using the Storck criteria, the Supreme Court in Cheshire West had to decide whether P, MIG, and MEG were confined in a restricted space for a non-negligible length of time. What is a non-negligible length of time? Understandably, there is no fixed definition. It will vary according to the individual circumstances and the nature and consequences of any restrictions imposed. For example, a nineteen-year-old young man who was severely autistic and epileptic was placed in leg restraints and confined in the back of a police van for forty minutes; this was a deprivation.[25] A wait of thirteen hours in a hospital for an MHA 1983 assessment was unlawful, although a wait of up to eight hours would probably not be.[26] The context and degree of intensity must be taken into consideration.

In Cheshire West, Lady Hale, in the Supreme Court, adopted the 'acid test' to decide whether there has been a deprivation of liberty. First, is the person subject to continuous supervision and control? Second, is the person free to leave? What does constant supervision and control entail? The Code of Practice identifies factors that the courts consider important.

1. Restraint, including sedation, is used to admit a person to an institution where that person resists admission.
2. Staff exercise complete and effective control over a person's care and movement for a significant period.
3. Staff exercise control over assessments, treatment, contacts, and residence.
4. The institution has decided that the person will only be released into the care of others or permitted to live elsewhere if the institution's staff consider it appropriate.
5. A request by carers for a person to be discharged to their care is refused.
6. The person cannot maintain social contact because of restrictions placed on their access to other persons.
7. The person loses autonomy because they are under continuous supervision and control.[27]

This is a partial list. Continuous and complete supervision does not necessarily require 24/7 monitoring or constant accompaniment; it may involve a lighter touch. The key is the level of monitoring or accompaniment. [28]

24 *Guzzardi v Italy* App no 7367/76 (ECtHR, 6 November 1980); ibid Lady Hale [20].
25 *ZH v Commissioner of the Police for the Metropolis* [2013] EWCA Civ 69; [2013] 1 W.L.R. 3021.
26 *R (Sessay) v South London and Maudsley NHS Foundation Trust* [2011] EWHC 2617 (QB,[2012] Q.B. 760.
27 DoLS Code (n15) para 2.5.
28 *Stanev v. Bulgaria* Application no. 36760/06 (ECtHR, 17 January 2012).

What if an older person living with dementia in a care home has some freedom within the home to walk around and go out into the garden?[29] In JE v DE and Surrey County Council,[30] DE had suffered a stroke, had visual impairment, and was living with dementia. He probably lacked the capacity to decide where he lived. Within the home, he had a substantial amount of freedom and also outside contact. Any restrictions imposed were less extensive than those in HL v UK.[31] However, as with HL, he was not free to leave. The restrictions were intended to be indefinite. The local authority said the police would be informed if an attempt was made to leave. Whether the person is in locked or open conditions is not determinative. Munby J said,

> The simple reality is that DE will be permitted to leave the institution in which [the local authority] has placed him and be released to the care of [his wife] only as and when, – if ever; probably never, – [the local authority] considers it appropriate. [The local authority's] motives may be the purest, but in my judgment, [it] has been and is continuing to deprive DE of his liberty.[32]

Lord Kerr in Cheshire West said liberty refers to freedom from external constraints; it does not depend on the ability to 'exploit one's freedom.' Freedom to leave is different from the ability to leave. Contentment with the conditions does not determine whether a person has been deprived of their liberty.[33] In R (Ferreira) v HM Senior Coroner for Inner South London and others,[34] the patient was in an ICU and died after she dislodged a tube with her hands. The Court of Appeal had to decide whether she died in 'state detention' for the Coroners and Justice Act 2009. In this situation, it was held that Cheshire West did not apply as it did not provide guidance on Article 5's relevance in urgent or intensive care cases. Arden LJ stated that any deprivation of liberty she experienced fell within the category of 'commonly occurring restrictions on movement' recognised by the ECtHR in the police kettling case of Austin v UK.[35] The patient was not deprived of her liberty because her treatment for her physical illness would have been provided to anyone regardless of their mental capacity. Any limitations on her movements were due to her physical condition and treatment. Therefore, the State was not responsible for any loss of liberty as the root cause was her physical condition. However, the patient would have been free to leave if the acid test were applicable. If she attempted to leave, the doctors would try to persuade her not to, but there was no evidence to suggest they would prevent her from going. Although there was continuous supervision and control, the patient did not lack the freedom to leave despite the difficulty or

29 DoLS Code (n.15) para 2.18–2.24.
30 [2006] EWHC 3459 (Fam), [2006] 12 WLUK 635. |
31 *HL case* (n7).
32 *JE v DE case* (n14) [126].
33 *Cheshire West case* (n23) [76].
34 [2017] EWCA Civ 31, [2018] Q.B. 487.
35 *Austin v United Kingdom* App no 39692/09 (ECtHR, 14 September 2011).

impossibility of doing so.[36] The fact that the surroundings may be agreeable and appropriate does not matter if the person is prevented from leaving. Lady Hale put it this way,

> the fact that my living arrangements are comfortable, and indeed make my life as enjoyable as it could possibly be, should make no difference. A gilded cage is still a cage.[37]

Thus, older persons living in a warm, comfortable, and friendly care home may still be deprived of their liberty despite the agreeable surroundings. The critical question is whether they are free to leave. Older persons who lack capacity must have safeguards and reviews in place, regardless of where they live, to ensure that their living arrangements are in their best interests.

In Cheshire West, the Court of Appeal adopted the idea of relative normality as the comparator when deciding if a deprivation had occurred. It argued that P's care plan did not involve depriving him of his liberty, and he was living a life that was as normal as possible when compared to another person with similar disabilities. Normality was a relative concept. This decision had worrying consequences for older persons living in care homes, hospitals, or other settings who needed a heavily restrictive care package due to advanced dementia or similar. The Court of Appeal considered them not to be deprived of their liberty as this intensity of care is normal for someone in their situation. This undermines the rationale behind DoLS and is discriminatory, as many people needing safeguards would not receive them – an uncomfortable decision. The Supreme Court took a completely different approach. People living with dementia and other disabilities have the same human rights as anybody else. There may be a need to limit or restrict those rights because of their disability, but the starting point should be the same as for everyone else. The comparator is the same regardless of the person's disability. This is consistent with the duty under the Convention on the Rights of Persons with Disabilities to cater for the special needs of those with disabilities.[38] The Supreme Court found that P was deprived of his liberty.

MIG's situation was different from P's. The Court of Appeal felt that she was not deprived of her liberty given the relative normality of the arrangements, which were no more intrusive than required to protect her. As noted above, the Supreme Court rejected the relative normality approach. Even though MIG lived in a normal

36 C Stevenson, 'Deprivation of liberty and intensive care units: The Queen (on the application of Ferreira) v HM Senior Coroner for Inner South London and others' (2017) *Elder Law Journal* 141; B Troke, 'Cheshire West and acute hospitals' (2017) *Local Government Lawyer* 23 February 2017.

37 Cheshire West (n23) [46].

38 On the applicability of the Convention on the Rights of Persons with Disabilities, see *Stanev v Bulgaria* App no 36760/06 (ECtHR, 17 January 2012) and *DD v Lithuania* App no 13469/06 (ECtHR, 9 July 2012). See also, C Slobogin, 'Eliminating mental disability as a legal criterion in deprivation of liberty cases: The impact of the Convention on the Rights of Persons with Disabilities on the insanity defense, civil commitment, and competency law' (2015) *International Journal of Law and Psychiatry* 40, 36.

family home, she was under the complete supervision of those caring for her. The Supreme Court found by a majority that she was deprived of her liberty. MEG's regime was more intrusive than MIGs. Again, the Supreme Court disagreed with the Court of Appeal and found that she was deprived of her liberty. For both MIG and MEG, as with P, a central component of the decision was that they were not free to leave. What was significant about the P, MIG, and MEG cases was that they were not deprived of their liberty in a care home or hospital and thus fell outside the DoLS procedure. Lords Carnwarth, Hodge, and Clarke dissented, arguing that MIG and MEG, who lived happily in domestic settings, could not be considered deprived of their liberty. The majority disagreed; the deprivation was the State's responsibility, which distinguished it from, in their case, normal domestic restrictions imposed by parents on their children. Although this was long recognised as a problem, particularly for those older persons deprived of liberty in their homes for their safety, it was now clear that a post-Bournewood gap had received judicial recognition. No safeguards equivalent to DoLS were available for older persons deprived of their liberty outside of care homes or hospitals. To legitimise such deprivations, the only course of action was the apply to the Court of Protection. This is discussed further below.

The subjective element – no valid consent to the deprivation

The second Storck element is that the person has not consented to the deprivation. A lack of objection must not be interpreted as indicating consent. The person must have the capacity to form an intention to leave or to remain. Compliance requires capacity under the MCA 2005. A person's consent to being deprived of their liberty is only valid under Article 5 if substantial and credible evidence establishes their mental capacity to consent through a fair and proper process. All necessary information regarding the placement and any intended treatment must be provided when giving consent.[39] In A Primary Care Trust v LDV, the test was whether the person could understand, retain, use, and weigh the necessary information. The courts should not identify in advance the precise information that a person must understand, retain, use, and weigh to decide whether to consent to a placement that will result in a deprivation of liberty. A better approach is for the doctor to consider the concrete situation and assess the level of the person's understanding of their situation. Based on the clinician's assessment and all other relevant evidence, the court will then consider whether practical measures were taken to assist the patient in making their decision. If such actions were taken, the court would decide, on the balance of probabilities, whether the person lacked the capacity to make the decision. In the instant case, the court felt that her ability to retain, use, and weigh the following information was relevant.

1. She was there for mental disorder care and treatment.

39 *M v Ukraine* App no 2452/04 (ECtHR, 19 April 2012).

2. Treatment would include supervision, medication, and physical restraint.
3. Hospital staff could conduct property and personal searches.
4. She needed permission to leave and could only leave under supervision.
5. If she left without permission and supervision, staff would search for and return her, possibly involving the police.

However, it emphasised that although they were relevant in this case, they were not intended to be a precedent.[40]

The deprivation must be attributable to the State.

The deprivation must be attributable to the State, which may include its direct involvement through a public body such as a local authority or indirect. Indirect imputability involves states' positive obligation under Article 5(1) ECHR to protect people against deprivations of liberty by a private person. The Court of Protection in Staffordshire County Council v SRK discussed this point.[41] Following a road accident, SRK was awarded compensation by the court, which was used to purchase an adapted bungalow and fund his care. He required continuous supervision and control and was not free to leave. He lacked the capacity to consent to the care arrangements. His care was coordinated by a specialised brain injury case manager and delivered by private caregivers with the costs being privately financed and managed by a financial deputy of the Court of Protection. The local authority was not involved. A question arose whether this deprivation was attributable to the State, either directly or indirectly. Charles J stated that the local authority's investigation into an alleged deprivation of liberty or actions taken by the Care Quality Commission does not automatically make the State directly responsible as it is part of the supervision and regulation of private care providers. It is not direct participation by the State in SRK's private deprivation of liberty within Article 5. However, when a civil court awards damages or the Court of Protection appoints a deputy, or when trustees or attorneys under a lasting power of attorney receive a damages award and must make decisions on behalf of the person, they should be aware that a care and treatment plan can result in a deprivation of liberty. The court, Court of Protection, deputies, trustees, or attorney should take appropriate measures to ensure the local authority is aware of the situation and can thus fulfil their duty to investigate, support, and, where necessary, apply to the Court of Protection. Financial deputies should report any care arrangements that may deprive a person of their liberty, including privately funded care at home, as this requires authorisation. If a welfare order is not made in such cases, it would breach the State's positive obligations under Article 5 and its responsibility for the deprivation of liberty.

40 *A Primary Care Trust v LDV (by her litigation friend the Official Solicitor),* [2013] EWHC 272 (Fam), 2013] 2 WLUK 453.

41 *Staffordshire County Council v SRK (by his litigation friend SK), RK, Irwin Mitchell Trust Corporation, The Secretary of State for Justice* [2016] EWCA Civ 1317, [2017] Fam. 278.

When a referral is made, the State gains knowledge of the situation, which leads to an indirect responsibility for the deprivation of liberty. Charles J was reluctant to make the order, saying that an independent check by the Court of Protection would add unnecessary expense and divert resources from care. However, following Cheshire West's cautious approach, he concluded that a welfare order and supporting evidence help those involved focus and reduce the risk of mistakes. It promotes better decision-making, reviews, investigation, supervision, and regulation.

Many older persons receive care in their own homes, supported living, extra care facilities, or other services provided by private providers, where they may be deprived of their liberty. These arrangements may involve input from a public authority, such as occasional or regular visits from a social worker or healthcare professional or direct payments. The level of involvement will depend on the older person's circumstances. In some cases, the input may be significant enough for the State to be directly responsible for the deprivation of liberty. For example, where the local authority funded the placement, provided the family with information on providers and determined what was in the person's best interests under the MCA 2005, it was held to be directly imputable to the State.[42] In contrast, in others, the level and nature of the involvement may trigger a positive obligation since it is the State's indirect responsibility.[43]

The Supreme Court in Cheshire West identified the legal lacunae that many older persons are experiencing outside of care homes or hospitals. Their care regime effectively deprived them of their liberty, and no supervisory or review procedure existed. Lady Hale made it clear that in the case of vulnerable people, we should err on the side of caution as to what constitutes deprivation. An older person may be deprived of their liberty in their own home in the context of receiving care and treatment, and for this deprivation of liberty to be attributable to the State. How can protection be provided given the unavailability of DoLS? In such cases, an application must be made to the Court of Protection to protect the person's rights. In Re X, Munby PFD suggested a 'streamlined' process for these applications. He identified twenty-five questions to be considered but did not deal specifically with the individual cases before him. He emphasised that a judge, not a court officer, must issue Court of Protection authorisation for a deprivation. He suggested that an initial application for authorisation does not necessarily require an oral hearing as a paper application is acceptable, provided there is a clear right to request a timely review at an oral hearing. Article 5, he argued, does not require joining the person as a party to an application; however, they must be able to 'participate' in a manner that allows them to present their cases properly and satisfactorily. In principle,

42 *London Borough of Haringey v R (by his litigation friend, the Official Solicitor) and others* [2016] EWCOP 12, [2016] All ER (D) 78.

43 *Staffordshire case* (n41).

a person alleged to lack mental capacity can participate in and be represented in proceedings without being joined as a party.[44]

The Court of Appeal held that it could not entertain an appeal against the Munby PFD decision as the issues he addressed were hypothetical and not directly related to the cases in question, even though a definitive answer might be helpful. [45] Although it lacked jurisdiction, Black LJ made the obiter dicta point that the person needed to be joined as a party.

> (H)ad I been in a position to determine the issue in these proceedings, I would have held that in order that deprivations of liberty are reliably subjected to thorough scrutiny, and effective procedural safeguards are provided against arbitrary detention in practice, it is presently necessary for P to be a party in the relevant proceedings.[46]

An Article 5 ECHR-compatible procedure for considering increased deprivation applications following Cheshire West was needed. This was introduced by the Court of Protection Practice Direction 11A – Deprivation of Liberty Applications. Part 1 of the Direction covers the procedure for standard and urgent DoLS applications in care homes and hospitals.[47] Part 2 covers the application procedure for a deprivation outside the formal DoLS process under Section 16(2)(a) MCA 2005. Applications are made on Form COPDOL11. Paragraph 35 of the Directions outlines the provision for involving the subject of an application under Section 16(2)(a) MCA 2005. Before lodging an application with the court, the subject of the application must be consulted. The applicant must inform the person of several matters, including the nature of the application, the proposed arrangements, the person's right to express their views, wishes and feelings, and their right to seek to participate in the proceedings by being joined as a party or otherwise. Additionally, the applicant should inform them that they can seek advice and assistance if they disagree with the proposed arrangements in the application. Provision is made for a streamlined paper-only application and an oral hearing, depending on the judge's assessment of which procedure is more suitable. In the longer term, the gap identified in Cheshire West for people not living in care homes or hospitals is intended to be addressed by the Liberty Protection Safeguards, discussed below.

The Mental Health Act 1983

Older persons and mental health

The MHA 1983, as amended by the Mental Health Act 2007, is the primary source of mental health law, with civil admissions covered in Part II and patients

44 In re X and others (Court of Protection: Deprivation of Liberty) (Nos 1 and 2) [2014] EWCOP 25, [2015] 1 W.L.R. 2454.

45 [2015] EWCA Civ 599, [2016] 1 W.L.R. 227.

46 ibid [108] Black LJ.

47 MCA 2005 Section.21A and Schedule 1A.

in criminal proceedings or under sentence in Part III. While much of the legislation is devolved to Wales as a health function, Part III powers are reserved to the Westminster Government as part of the criminal justice system, including the treatment, detention, and release of patients. This Chapter focuses specifically on civil admissions. The two nations share this single piece of legislation. However, Wales has used its devolved powers to give the MHA 1983 a Welsh flavour while retaining its basic provisions. Wales has its own Code, statutory forms, regulations, and Mental Health Review Tribunal. Furthermore, the Mental Health (Wales) Measure 2010 initiative applies to Wales.

Older persons experience mental ill-health in the same way as other generations. Although younger persons are more likely to be detained under the MHA 1983, many older persons are also detained. In 2022–23 in England, 135.9 per 100,000 in the age group eighteen to thirty-four were detained. For those aged sixty-five and over, the figure is 83.8 per 100,000.[48] Older persons may have longstanding conditions or ones brought on later in life. As always, stereotypical assumptions about the mental health of older persons must be challenged. Sadly, the term 'senile' still creeps into use to describe an older person who may recall and process information more slowly than previously but who can function very effectively. Their intellectual function is in good shape, albeit processing speed is reduced. Dementia is perhaps the best-known form of mental disorder for older persons, and the data shows that it affects a significant number. A diagnosis of a form of dementia is not in itself a reason for detention under the MHA 1983; other conditions must be satisfied. Many older persons living with dementia also experience mental health issues such as depression, anxiety, bipolar disorder, schizophrenia, and psychosis. These comorbidities are frequently underdiagnosed. Professionals with specialised skills and knowledge should be involved when using the MHA 1983 for persons living with dementia.[49] Practitioners involved in the admission process should have a sufficient understanding of dementia and undertake a thorough clinical assessment and diagnosis using validated tools to help ensure the best care. Older persons will also experience schizophrenia, bipolar disorders, depressive disorders, personality disorders, and feeding and eating disorders, as well as others. These must never routinely be written off as an inevitable part of the ageing process. Nor should a person with mental ill-health be redefined by health and social care as an

48 NHS Digital, 'Mental health act statistics, annual figures England, 2023-24' (12 September, 2024) – <https://digital.nhs.uk/data-and-information/publications/statistical/mental-health-act-statistics-annual-figures/2023-24-annual-figures> - accessed 12 February 2025..

49 Department of Health, *Mental Health Act 1983: Code of Pactice* (2015) <https://assets.publishing.service.gov.uk/media/5a80a774e5274a2e87dbb0f0/MHA_Code_of_Practice.PDF> - accessed 28 September 2024 paras 14.123–14.125; Welsh Government, 'Mental Health Act Code of Practice for Wales' (2016). <https://www.gov.wales/sites/default/files/publications/2019-03/mental-health-act-1983-code-of-practice-mental-health-act-1983-for-wales-review-revised-2016.pdf> accessed 28 September 2024 paras 14.113-116; Mental Health Foundation, 'The Interface between Dementia and Mental Health an Evidence Review' (2016) <https://www.mentalhealth.org.uk/sites/default/files/2022-09/MHF-dementia-mental-health.pdf> - accessed 13 February 2025.

older person and those needs dispaced at (say) sixty-five by more generic older person's services. It is necessary to get past age and see them as a person. COVID-19 harmed the mental health of many older persons. Isolation, inability to access face-to-face support, and the fear of infection were not conducive to good mental health. Social isolation is linked to depression, anxiety, and cognitive decline. It also reduces resilience factors such as self-worth, purpose, and feeling valued.[50] During COVID-19, older persons with disabilities fared even worse, with more of them having clinically significant symptoms of depression than those without a disability.[51] In many respects, the pandemic was a perfect storm for older people's mental health. [52] Nevertheless, it is necessary to recognise that COVID-19 accentuated what was already a health and social care problem, namely the difficulty some older persons experience in accessing mental health services. Ageism may contribute to poorer access to mental health services and result in depression and anxiety.[53] It also harms the self-esteem of older persons, leading to self-directed ageism, whereby ageist attitudes are manifested in an older person's self-perception.[54] COVID-19 also had a disproportionate impact on BAME populations with increased infection rates, severity, and mortality; research has highlighted their increased mental health needs, health inequalities, comorbidities, and socioeconomic inequities. Further work on understanding the impact of COVID-19 on the mental health of older BAME populations is necessary due to their underrepresentation in existing studies.[55]

Previous research in Australia identified poor mental health literacy amongst older persons. This may be for several reasons. Messages about mental health awareness may be delivered through media less frequently accessed by older persons. Education programmes are crucial in promoting mental health literacy amongst younger people, but for many older persons, such programmes did not exist when they were of school age. Awareness-raising campaigns may not target older persons, and in later life, they may avoid learning more about mental health

50 A Novotney, 'The risks of social isolation' (2019) *American Psychological Association* 50(5) 32.

51 A Steptoe and G Di Gessa, 'Mental health and social interactions of older people with physical disabilities in England during the COVID-19 pandemic: a longitudinal cohort study' (2021) *The Lancet Public Health* 6(6) e365.

52 L Webb, 'Covid-19 lockdown: a perfect storm for older people's mental health' (2021) *Journal of Psychiatric and Mental Health Nursing* 28(2) 300.

53 H Kang Kim, 'Ageism and Psychological Well-being among Older Adults: A Systematic Review' (2022) *Gerontology and Geriatric Medicine* 8, 1-22.

54 L Ayalon, (2022). 'Ageism towards oneself vs. Ageism towards others in the context of views of aging' in Y Palgi, A Shrira, and M Diehl, (eds) *Subjective views of aging. International perspectives on aging* (Cham: Springer, 2022); Centre for Ageing Better, 'Ageism: What's the harm?' (2023) https://ageing-better.org.uk/resources/ageism-whats-harm – accessed 28 September 2024.

55 Z Khan, K Israel-McLeish, C Ballard, et al., 'Levels of loneliness and mental health in older adults across ethnic groups during the COVID-19 pandemic in the UK' (2023) *Journal of the American Medical Directors Association* 24(5) 710.

due to social stigma.[56] Mental health literacy differs by age and mental disorder type and should be reflected in awareness-raising initiatives. Greater self-awareness and understanding of mental health encourage help-seeking behaviour by older persons. In addition, focused and age-appropriate information about mental health will help address stigma and misconceptions.

One area of mental health success is that people with learning disabilities live longer and into older age. Better social care and treatment have contributed to this, and so has the support given by parents, families, and others to encourage independent living, which often involves care and support. A care deficit arises as carers, particularly parents, get older and can no longer care in the same way.[57] People with learning disabilities are at a higher risk of developing dementia and may experience a faster decline in cognitive abilities than those without the disability. However, symptoms of dementia may not be as noticeable for people with more complex learning disabilities, particularly in the early stages.[58] To support older persons with learning disabilities, policies aimed at older persons in general should include those with learning disabilities. Learning disability practitioners and policymakers should be familiar with the broader policy agenda for older persons and take advantage of appropriate older-person initiatives.

Principles

The MHA 1983, rather like DoLS, allows the State to deprive people of their liberty or restrict their freedom in the community if their mental health requires it for their safety or that of others. As with DoLS, the MHA 1983 is designed to include safeguards for those at risk of admission or who have been admitted. Although the MHA 1983 covers England and Wales, there are some differences in how it operates in the two nations. Each nation has its own Code of Practice issued under s.118 MHA 1983.[59] The section requires that the codes include a statement of principles informing decision-making under the MHA 1983.[60] These are captured in the two Codes-see Table 7.1.

Both Codes emphasise that each principle is of equal importance.[61] Under the Welsh Code, staff must follow age-appropriate best practices when intervening where older patients display challenging behaviours. Hospitals must prioritise staff training with a specialised programme for working with vulnerable older persons.

56 L Farrer, L Leach, KM Griffiths et al., 'Age differences in mental health literacy' (2008) *BMC Public Health* 8, 1.

57 C Walker, 'Ageing and people with learning disabilities: In search of evidence' (2015) *British Journal of Learning Disabilities* 43(4), 246.

58 Alzheimer's Society, 'Learning disabilities and dementia: Factsheet 430' (November 2022) <https://www.alzheimers.org.uk/sites/default/files/2022-10/430LP-learning-disabilities-and-dementia.pdf> – accessed 28 September 2024.

59 MHA Codes (English and Welsh) (n49).

60 MHA 1983 Section.118(2A) and (2B).

61 MHA Codes (English and Welsh) (n49) paras 1.23 and 1.30.

Table 7.1 Mental Health Act Code Principles – England and Wales

English Code – paras 1.1 – 1.22	*Welsh Code paras 1.1 – 1.29*
The least restrictive option and maximising independence.	Dignity and respect.
Empowerment and involvement.	The least restrictive option and maximising independence.
Respect and dignity.	Fairness, equality and equity.
Purpose and effectiveness.	Empowerment and involvement.
Efficiency and equity.	Keeping people safe.
	Effectiveness and efficiency.

In particular, staff using necessary restrictive interventions must receive training on properly using such measures involving older persons. They should have the knowledge and skills to adapt manual restraint techniques to accommodate age, frailty, and the heightened risk of fractures.[62] The English Code recognises the opportunities for specialised services to help older persons receive age-appropriate care. It is essential to prioritise participation and proportionality when providing healthcare to older patients.[63] Placements of older persons in secure units also require sensitivity. Age balance in secure services is a factor, as is respect for older person's agency.[64] As with the Welsh Code, it emphasises the need to minimise risks associated with restrictive interventions and the importance of taking into consideration individual vulnerabilities and unique needs related to, for example, older age, disability, poor physical health, and any history of traumatic abuse.[65]

The definition of mental disorder in the original MHA 1983 was amended by the Mental Health Act 2007. Section 1(1) MHA 1983 defines mental disorder as 'any disorder or disability of the mind.' An older person with learning disabilities generally does not fall within the definition unless their disability is 'associated with abnormally aggressive or seriously irresponsible conduct' on their part. Learning disability is 'a state of arrested or incomplete development of the mind,' including significant impairment of intelligence and social functioning. Dependence on drugs or alcohol is not considered to be a mental disorder.[66]

Who is involved in the MHA 1983 procedures?

Many people are involved in a patient's admission and treatment under the MHA 1983. An Approved Mental Health Professional (AMHP) can make an application for admission. Where a local authority has reason to think that an application

62 Welsh Code (n49) paras 26.59 – 26.61.
63 English Code (n49) para 34.20
64 R Claasje Visser, D MacInnes, J Parrott et al., 'Growing older in secure mental health care: The user experience' (2021) *Journal of Mental Health* 30(1) 51.
65 English Code (n49) para 26.7
66 MHA 1983 ss.1(1) (2) (2A)(3) and (4).

should be made, it must make arrangements for an AMHP to consider the case. An AMHP can be a social worker, occupational therapist, or nurse specially trained in mental health practice, including the MHA 1983. Doctors cannot be AMHPs. AMHPs are responsible for evaluating all available information, including medical recommendations, to decide if a person should be detained and to coordinate the care of those who are detained. The views of family and friends may be helpful. AMHPs help ensure that people undergoing mental health emergencies receive the necessary care and support. They collaborate closely with other healthcare professionals to ensure their patients' needs are met and their rights safeguarded. Section 115 MHA 1983 provides that an AMHP may at all reasonable times enter and inspect premises (other than a hospital) in which a 'mentally disordered person' is living if there is reasonable cause to believe the person is not under 'proper care.' Authenticated proof of the AMHP status must be shown if requested.

'Nearest relative' refers to a family member with responsibilities for those subject to the MHA 1983. They can apply to detain a person or to place them under guardianship, object to the person being sectioned or placed under guardianship, discharge the patient, and apply to the Mental Health Tribunal. They can also ask for an independent advocate to support the person. Section 26 MHA 1983 defines the nearest relative. The term nearest relative has a specific legal meaning, and they may not always be the same person as the next of kin. The following list determines the order of priority of relatives: husband, wife, or civil partner (including a cohabitee for more than six months); son or daughter; father or mother; brother or sister; grandparent; grandchild; uncle or aunt; and niece or nephew. Since the 2007 amendments to the MHA 1983, civil partners have had equal status to a husband or wife when determining the nearest relative. Typically, the person highest on the list is the nearest relative. However, when determining the nearest relative of a patient who ordinarily resides with or is looked after by one or more of their relatives or who was cared for by one or more relatives before being admitted to a hospital, priority should be given to those relatives over others. If there is more than one relative of the same description, priority is given to those of the whole blood over those of the same description of the half-blood. The older or eldest of two or more relatives of the same description is preferred to younger ones, regardless of sex. A person who has lived with the patient for at least five years is considered equivalent to a relative but ranks last in the hierarchy. They cannot be the nearest relative if the patient is married or in a civil partnership unless the spouse or partner is excluded. If a patient's spouse or civil partner is permanently separated from them, either by agreement, court order, or has deserted or been deserted by the patient, they will be treated as if they were deceased and therefore excluded. Additionally, if the nearest relative is under 18 and not the spouse or parent, they are considered deceased for this purpose. The county court has the power to appoint an acting nearest relative if there is no one to assume the role or the person is incapable of performing it. If a nearest relative unreasonably objects to a patient being detained under Section 3 MHA 1983 or guardianship, they may be removed through an application to the county court. Similarly, if they unreasonably object to an application or have exercised their powers without regard for the patient's welfare or the public interest.

These are known as displacement proceedings. Finally, they may be replaced if they are unsuitable to act as the nearest relative.[67]

Applications for admission under Sections 2 and 3 MHA 1983 must include two medical recommendations by doctors who must have jointly or separately personally examined the patient.[68] In the case of separate examinations, a maximum of five days can elapse between each examination. One medical recommendation must be by a doctor approved under Section 12 MHA 1983 – the 'Section 12 doctor.' If practicable, one of the doctors should have had previous acquaintance with the patient. Their recommendations are part of the information the AMHP will consider in deciding whether the patient should be admitted to a hospital.

An approved clinician is a mental health professional approved by the Secretary of State, the Welsh Ministers in Wales, or a person or body authorised to exercise this function. The MHA 1983 specifies that only approved clinicians can make certain decisions. The responsible clinician is the approved clinician in charge of the patient's care and treatment when detained under the MHA 1983. Their responsibilities include treatment decisions, reviewing detentions, granting leave of absence, and discharge power. Approved clinicians may be doctors, psychologists, nurses, occupational therapists, and social workers. It is not a requirement that the responsible clinician is a doctor.

An Independent Mental Health Advocate (IMHA) may be appointed under Part X MHA 1983 to assist patients in understanding their rights, their treatment, any conditions imposed on them, and the legal authority under which they are detained. In England, patients who meet the criteria are eligible for support from an IMHA and are known as qualifying patients. Qualifying patients include those detained under the MHA 1983, those liable to be detained even if not currently detained, and patients subject to guardianship or a Community Treatment Order (CTO). People detained under the Section 4 MHA 1983 emergency application, Section 5 holding powers, and in a place of safety under Sections 135 or 136 are not qualifying patients. A Welsh-qualifying patient is one who is currently detained or liable to be detained under the MHA 1983. This includes patients on leave of absence, under guardianship, or on a CTO. Patients detained under a Section 4 MHA 1983 emergency application or the Section 5 holding powers are also eligible for the support of an IMHA. However, the right does not apply to anybody taken to a place of safety under Section 135 or 136 MHA 1983. In England and Wales, informal patients (patients receiving in-patient treatment in a hospital voluntarily) are qualifying patients if they are under consideration for Section 57 MHA 1983 treatment. or if they are under eighteen, for ECT or other treatment to which Section 58A applies. The forms of detention and the treatment provisions are discussed below.

67 MHA 1983 Sections.26, 29 and 30.

68 On 'personally examined' see *Devon Partnership NHS Trust v Secretary of State for Health and Social Care* [2021] EWHC 101 (Admin), [2021] 1 W.L.R. 2945; J Williams, 'Mental Health Act 1983 assessments: The use of video technology'(2022) *Medico-Legal Journal* 90(3)134.

Civil law admission under the MHA 1983

Under the MHA 1983, four civil law procedures exist for hospital admission. Section 2 MHA 1983 allows for the detention for a maximum of twenty-eight days of a person who has a mental disorder in a hospital for assessment, or for assessment followed by treatment, of their mental disorder. The grounds are that the patient's mental disorder is of a nature or degree that warrants detention in hospital for assessment or assessment followed by medical treatment for a limited period. The detention must be necessary for their health or safety or the protection of others. Applications must be based on the written medical recommendations in the prescribed form of two registered medical practitioners, each of whom must state their opinion that the conditions set out in Section 2 are met. An AMHP or the nearest relative can make the application, although applications by the latter are rare.

Applications under Section 3 MHA 1983 follow a similar pattern to Section 2, albeit there are differences in the grounds. It allows detention in a hospital for treatment of a mental disorder and is often referred to as a treatment order. A patient can be admitted to a hospital and detained for up to six months, which may be extended by a further six months and after that for periods of twelve months, provided the criteria for detention still apply. The application must be based on the two written recommendations, in the prescribed form, from two registered medical practitioners, each including a statement that, in their opinion, the conditions for detention are complied with. These include that the patient has a mental disorder of a nature or degree that makes it appropriate for them to receive medical treatment in a hospital, that it is necessary for the health or safety of the patient or the protection of other persons that they should receive such treatment, and that it cannot be provided unless they are detained. Appropriate medical treatment must be available for the patient. The term 'appropriate medical treatment' refers to medical treatment that is appropriate considering the nature and severity of the disorder and all other circumstances. 'Medical treatment' must be for the purpose of alleviating or preventing the worsening of a mental disorder or its symptoms and manifestations. It includes nursing, psychological interventions, specialist mental health habilitation, rehabilitation, and care. This broad definition replaces the old treatability test, which focused on the intervention's outcome. Appropriate medical treatment does not require anybody to state what is likely to happen.[69] Applications are made by the AMPH or, in rare cases, by the nearest relative.

Section 4 MHA 1983 provides that an emergency application may be made where there is an urgent necessity for the person to be detained under Section 2. A written recommendation must be obtained from a registered medical practitioner who has recently seen the patient where obtaining a second opinion would cause delays. An AMHP or the nearest relative may apply. A Section 4 MHA 1983 admission may be converted into a Section 2 admission if the second medical

69 MHA 1983 ss 3(4), 145(1AB) and (4); T Branton and G Brookes, 'Definitions and criteria: The 2007 amendments to the Mental Health Act 1983' (2010) *Advances in Psychiatric Treatment* 16(3) 161, 165.

recommendation is forthcoming upon arrival at the hospital; otherwise, the patient can be detained for a maximum of seventy-two hours.

Under Section 5(2) MHA 1983, a doctor or an approved clinician can hold an in-patient in hospital when the registered medical practitioner or approved clinician in charge of the treatment believes the patient might meet the admission criteria under the MHA 1983. They must provide a written report to the hospital managers. Once submitted, the patient can be detained in the hospital for seventy-two hours starting from the submission of the report. The section applies regardless of whether the patient was admitted for a mental disorder or a physical condition. Section 5(2) should only be used when it is impractical or unsafe to make an application without detaining the patient. It should not be employed as a substitute for an application, even for detaining a patient for seventy-two hours or less. Section 5(4) MHA 1983 applies to patients already being treated for a mental disorder as an in-patient in a hospital where a nurse of the prescribed class concludes the patient has a mental disorder, making it necessary for their health, safety, or the protection of others to be immediately restrained from leaving and the immediate attendance of a practitioner or clinician to provide a report is not possible. In that case, the nurse must record that in writing. The hospital then has the authority to detain the patient for up to six hours. These short-term procedures should give time for the patient to be assessed under the MHA 1983.[70]

Besides detention in hospital, guardianship under Section 7 MHA 1983 provides a community-based structure. To meet the criteria for guardianship, the patient must have a mental disorder of a nature or degree that warrants being placed under guardianship for their welfare or the safety of others. Two medical recommendations confirming that the patient meets the criteria must support an application. The recommendations should state the reasons for the opinions and why it is necessary to obtain guardianship. An AMHP or the nearest relative can make applications for guardianship. The appointed guardian may be a local social services authority or any other person. It can require the patient to live at a specific location and attend specified places and times for medical treatment, education, occupation, or training. Additionally, there is a power to require access to the patient by a registered medical practitioner, AMPH, or other specified person at any place where the patient lives. There is no power to require the patient to undergo medical treatment.[71] Section 18(7) MHA 1983 includes the power to convey the patient to a hospital or other place as required under the guardianship or to be returned to that place if necessary. The use of guardianship is in decline. In England, in 2023-24, there were only forty new cases, with 120 continuing cases.[72]

70 English and Welsh Codes (n49) paras 18.3-18.21 and 18.2-18.18; paras 18.22-18.36 and 18.19-18.27.

71 MHA 1983 Sections. 7 and 8.

72 NHS Digital, 'Guardianship under the Mental Health Act 1983, England - 2021–22, 2022–23 & 2023–24' (22 August 2024) <https://www.gov.uk/government/statistics/guardianship-under-the-mental-health-act-1983-england-2021-22-2022-23-2023-24> – accessed 28 September 2024.

Under Section 17 MHA 1983, the responsible clinician may grant a detained patient leave of absence from the hospital subject to any conditions they deem necessary for the patient's well-being or the safety of others. The primary purpose of Section 17 MHA 1983 is to allow the patient to be temporarily absent to enable, for example, family visits or to trial independent living. Leave is given for a specified period or indefinitely; it can be extended while the patient is on leave. For extended Section 17 leave (more than seven consecutive days) to be lawful, there must be ongoing hospital treatment, although hospital and treatment are given broad interpretations. Where the responsible clinician considers that keeping a patient on leave of absence in custody is necessary for their well-being or the safety of others, they may require them to stay in the hospital during their leave of absence. The patient may be kept in the custody of any hospital staff officer or any other person authorised in writing by the managers of the hospital. If the patient is required under the conditions of the leave to be placed in another hospital during their leave, they will be placed in the custody of an officer of that hospital. The responsible clinician may recall the patient back to the hospital by giving notice in writing to the patient or the person in charge of the patient. This applies if the clinician believes recall is necessary for the patient's health or safety or to protect others. However, if the patient is no longer subject to detention, there is no power of recall.[73] Before granting longer-term leave, the responsible clinician must consider whether it would be better for the patient to be subject to a Community Treatment Order (CTO) under Section 17A MHA 1983. Paragraphs 31.7 of the English and Welsh Codes provide pointers on deciding what is more appropriate.

The responsible clinician may discharge a detained patient from the hospital under a CTO, which makes them liable to recall.[74] For people sixty-five and over, the rate for CTOs is 5.9 per 100,000 population; this is lower than other age groups.[75] The AMHP must agree that the criteria for a CTO are met and that it is appropriate to make the order which lasts for six months but can be renewed for a further six and then for twelve months by the responsible clinician. Consultation with those involved in the patient's care, including family and friends, is desirable.[76] Conditions may be attached to a CTO, which the patient must follow. These include living in a particular place and attending appointments for treatment, although in Welsh Ministers v PJ,[77] the Supreme Court held that imposing conditions that amount to a deprivation of the patient's liberty is not permissible. PJ was discharged from hospital to a care home under a CTO with specific conditions that were deemed to be a deprivation of liberty under Article 5 ECHR. The Court emphasised that the lack of enforcement of the CTO conditions did not negate the deprivation of liberty. The judgment highlighted the necessity of practical and

73 MHA 1983 Section.17; English and Welsh Codes (n49) Chapter 7 and Chapter 27.
74 MHA 1983 Section.17A-G.
75 NHS Digital (n48).
76 English and Welsh Codes (n49) paras 29.10 and 29.28.
77 [2018] UKSC 66, [2020] A.C. 757.

effective protection of ECHR rights, focusing on the patient's actual situation. If the CTO patient is deprived of their liberty in a care home or elsewhere, a DoLS or Court of Protection order under the MCA 2005 must be obtained. A DoLS can exist alongside a CTO (and also alongside guardianship or leave of absence), provided that it does not conflict with the conditions of the CTO or leave set by the RC.[78] Section 17E MHA 1983 allows the responsible clinician to recall a CTO patient if they believe the patient needs medical treatment for a mental disorder and there is a risk of harm to the patient or others if not recalled. The clinician can also recall patients if they fail to comply with any CTO conditions. The recall notice must be given to the patient in writing. Hospital managers have the authority to detain the recalled patient under the MHA 1983. Varying or suspending a CTO should be discussed with family and friends. The patient has the right to support from an Independent Mental Health Advocate (IMHA). The nearest relative has rights regarding their care and treatment, such as the right to access information about the patient.[79]

Patients are discharged from hospital or a CTO when the authorised period of detention ends unless it is renewed, but the responsible clinician can discharge if they conclude that the conditions for detention no longer exist; there is no need to wait until the end of the formal period. A patient detained under Sections 2 or 3 MHA 1983 or subject to a CTO can request a review of their detention by the hospital managers under Section 23 to decide whether they can be discharged. The hospital managers must also review a decision to renew detention or a CTO. Typically, this responsibility is assigned to a panel of laypersons with appropriate training. A request for a review can be made at any time, although some restrictions may be imposed in the case of multiple applications. The managers receive written reports from medical, nursing, and social care staff. During the hearing, the managers, the responsible clinician, a nurse, and a social worker may be present, and the nearest relative may attend if the patient wishes. The patient and/or their advocate may also participate.

The Mental Health Review Tribunal in England and the Mental Health Review Tribunal for Wales (MHRT) hear applications for discharging patients subject to the MHA 1983. Patients detained under Sections 2, 3, and 7 guardianship and CTOs may be discharged by the MHRT. An application for a patient detained under Section 2 MHA 1983 may be made within the first fourteen days after being detained. An application for discharge from Section 3 MHA 1983 can be made at any time during the first six months of detention. If the detention is renewed after the first six months, an application can be made once during the second six-month period and following any further renewals once every twelve months. If an application is not made, the patient is automatically referred to the MHRT in the second six months of detention and again after three years. For patients under Section 7 MHA 1983 guardianship, an application may be made once during the first six

78 MHA 1983 ss.17 – 17G.

79 English and Welsh Codes (n49) paras 31.8-31.11 and 31.8-31.11 respectively.

months. If it is renewed again, one application may be made in the next six months. After that, applications can be made once every twelve months.

Treatment provisions

Section 56 MHA 1983 applies the Part IV treatment provisions to detained patients. with some exceptions. It also covers informal patients, giving them the same rights as detained patients regarding Section 57 MHA 1983 treatments requiring consent and a second opinion. The exceptions are patients detained under an emergency application with no second medical recommendation, in-patients detained under Section 5 MHA 1983 holding powers, and those removed to a place of safety under Sections 135 or 136 as discussed below. The treatment provisions relate to treatments for a mental disorder. A patient with mental capacity has the right to refuse treatment for a physical health condition unless the condition is a symptom or underlying cause of their mental ill-health. The treatment provisions are outlined in Table 7.2 below.

Section 63 MHA 1983 allows 'medical treatment' to be given to a patient with a mental disorder, even without their consent, if it is carried out by or under the guidance of an approved clinician. This applies to treatment other than under Sections 57, 58, or 58A MHA 1983. Section 145(4) MHA 1983 defines medical treatment as a treatment intended to alleviate or prevent a worsening of the disorder or its symptoms. Medical treatment includes treating the disorder's symptoms ancillary to the core treatment. For example, nasogastric feeding, a blood transfusion and force-feeding have been held to be medical treatments for mental disorders.[80] These cases demonstrate the broad application of the section in addressing various aspects of mental disorders, including ancillary treatments. If there is uncertainty about whether the medical treatment falls within the remit of Section 63 MHA 1983, an application to the court is necessary. However, where there is no uncertainty, the framework under the Act should be applied; no court application is necessary.[81]

The treatment provisions for CTO patients who have not been recalled to hospital under Section 17E MHA 1983 are contained in Part 4A. Treatment falls under Part 4A MHA 1983 if it is 'relevant treatment,' which is defined by Section 64A as treatment 'for the mental disorder from which the patient is suffering' and does not come within Section 57 treatment (surgical operation for destroying brain tissue or for destroying the functioning of brain tissue). Relevant treatment cannot be given unless there is authority and, in the case of Section 58 (consent or second opinion) and Section 58A MHA 1983 (ECT), the certificate requirement must be

80 B v Croydon Health Authority [1995] Fam 133, [1995] 1 All ER 683; Nottinghamshire Healthcare NHS Trust v RC [2014] EWHC 1317 (COP), [2014] All ER (D) 28 (May); R (B) v Ashworth Hospital Authority [2005] UKHL 20, [2005] 2 AC 278.

81 North Tees and Hartlepool NHS Foundation Trust and another v KAG (a protected party, by her litigation friend the Official Solicitor) and others [2024] EWCOP 38. See also Williams J 'Hunger-strikes: a prisoner's right or a "wicked folly"?' *The Howard Journal of Criminal Justice* (2001) 40(3) 285.

Table 7.2 Part 4 MHA 1983: Treatment provisions for Sections 2 and 3 patients

MHA section	*Type of treatment*	*Authorisation to treat*
Treatment requiring consent and a second opinion – Section 57 MHA 1983	*Any surgical operation for destroying brain tissue or for destroying the functioning of brain tissue' ('neurosurgery' or 'psychosurgery'); and the surgical implantation of hormones to reduce male sex drive.*	*The patient consents; and the patient's consent and capacity to consent is certified in writing by a Second Opinion Appointed Doctor (SOAD) and two other appointed people; and the SOAD certifies in writing that it is appropriate for the treatment to be given.*
Treatment requiring consent or a second opinion – Section 58 MHA 1983	The administration of medication for a mental disorder where three months have passed from the day on which any form of medication for the disorder was first administered during the current period in which the patient is liable to detention (s.58(1)(b) MHA 1983.	The patient consents, and the appropriate clinician (AC) or SOAD has certified that the patient consents and has capacity to consent; or a SOAD certifies that it is appropriate for the treatment to be given despite either the patient (a) refusing to consent or (b) lacking capacity to consent.
Electro-convulsive therapy – Section58AMHA 1983.	Electroconvulsive therapy (ECT) is a procedure that uses small electric currents to trigger a brief seizure in the brain. The procedure is done under general anaesthesia.	If a patient with capacity consents, the AC in charge of the treatment or a SOAD must certify that the patient has capacity and consents. If a patient lacks capacity, a SOAD must certify that the patient lacks capacity (i.e., is not capable of understanding the nature, purpose, and likely effects of the treatment), that the treatment is appropriate, and that it would not conflict with an advance decision or decision of a donee, deputy, or Court of Protection. The SOAD must consult two other persons who have been professionally concerned with the patient's medical treatment (one must be a nurse; registered medical practitioners, the responsible clinician, or an approved clinician in charge of the treatment are excluded).
Urgent treatment – Section 62 MHA 1983.	When any of conditions (a) to (d) below are met, Sections 57 and 58 are not applicable. Where either (a) or (b) is met, Section 58A is not applicable. Urgent treatment: (a) which is immediately necessary to save the patient's life; or (b) which (not being irreversible) is immediately necessary to prevent a serious deterioration of the patient's condition; or (c) which (not being irreversible or hazardous) is immediately necessary to alleviate serious suffering by the patient; or (d) which (not being irreversible or hazardous) is immediately necessary and represents the minimum interference necessary to prevent the patient from behaving violently or being a danger to self or to others.	

met. However, the certificate requirement does not apply if the treatment is Section 64G treatment (emergency treatment for patients lacking capacity) or the treatment is immediately necessary and the patient or, if appropriate, a donee, deputy, or the Court of Protection consent. In addition, the certificate requirement does not apply where the administration of medicine during the first month of the CTO is Section 58(1)(b) MHA 1983 type treatment. Authority to treat may arise from the consent of a patient with capacity; under this Part, patients with capacity cannot be given treatment unless they consent. If the patient lacks capacity, a donee of an LPA, a deputy of the Court of Protection, or the Court itself may give authority. Treatment may also be authorised under Section 64D MHA 1983 (treatment of patient's lacking capacity) or Section 64G. The certificate requirement is fulfilled if a registered medical practitioner appointed under Part 4 MHA 1983 certifies in writing that the treatment is appropriate to be given or that the treatment must be given subject to certain conditions that must be followed; such a certificate cannot be provided by the responsible clinician or the person in charge of the treatment. However, if authority is given through the consent of a patient with capacity, the certificate requirement is fulfilled if the responsible clinician in charge of the treatment certifies in writing that the patient has capacity and has consented. Special provision is made in Section 64D for CTO patients who lack capacity. There are five conditions for a valid authorisation.

1. Before giving the treatment, the person giving the treatment takes reasonable steps to establish whether the patient lacks capacity to consent to the treatment.
2. When giving the treatment, the person reasonably believes the patient lacks capacity to consent.
3. The person has no reason to believe the patient objects to being given the treatment, or if they have reason to believe that the patient objects, it is unnecessary to use force to provide the treatment. The reasonableness or unreasonableness of any objection is irrelevant.
4. The person giving the treatment is in charge of the treatment and an approved clinician, or the treatment is provided under the direction of that clinician.
5. Giving the treatment does not conflict with a valid and applicable advance decision or a decision of a donee or deputy or of the Court of Protection.

Emergency treatment may be given under Section 64G MHA 1983 to a CTO patient who lacks capacity. When providing the treatment, the person must reasonably believe the patient lacks capacity to consent and that it is immediately necessary. If it is necessary to use force against the patient, the treatment must be necessary to prevent harm, and the force must be proportionate to the likelihood of the patient's suffering harm and the seriousness of that harm. Treatment is immediately necessary if it is immediately necessary for one of the following reasons: to save the patient's life; to prevent a serious deterioration of the patient's condition that is not irreversible; to alleviate serious suffering by the patient and it is not irreversible or hazardous; or if it represents the minimum interference necessary to prevent the patient from behaving violently or being a danger to himself or others and it is not irreversible or hazardous. Where the treatment is ECT under Section 58A MHA 1983, it is immediately necessary if it falls within one of the first two of these conditions. Where treatment is immediately necessary, it can be given even if it conflicts with an advance decision or the decision of someone who has the authority under the MCA 2005 to refuse it on the patient's behalf.[82]

Care following discharge

Patients detained under Section 3 MHA 1983 have the right to aftercare under Section 117 upon leaving the hospital once they are discharged. Under this provision, health and social services are responsible for providing or making arrangements for after-care services in collaboration with voluntary agencies. This responsibility continues until the health and local social services are satisfied that the person no longer needs the services other than where the patient is under a CTO. A wide range of services fall under Section 117 MHA 1983, including healthcare, social care, supported or independent accommodation, and social, cultural, and spiritual assistance. Local authorities can offer direct payments for Section 117 services to those who have the capacity to request them. These payments can also be made to a suitable person acting on their behalf. Before making direct payments, the local authority must be satisfied that the person, or anyone acting on their behalf, can manage the payments and that direct payments are the appropriate way of addressing their care and support needs.[83] A recent Supreme Court decision, R (on the application of Worcestershire CC) v Secretary of State for Health and Social Care,[84] clarified that the Section 117 duty ends if the patient is detained for a second time. In this case, the patient was ordinarily resident in authority W when discharged from hospital but was then moved to a residential setting in authority S. Whilst there, she was detained for a second time, at which point the Section 117 duty on W ended. Upon discharge from the second detention, the local authority S had the duty to provide the care as that was her place of ordinary residence when detained. She could not be deemed ordinarily resident in W [85]

In 2012, the National Assembly For Wales (now the Senedd) enacted the Mental Health (Wales) Measure 2010. The National Assembly For Wales was a previous incarnation of what is now the Senedd, the Welsh Parliament. Under the cumbersome law-making process at the time, the Assembly could pass Measures which, for practical purposes, have the same effect as Acts. The Measure has a rights-based focus and addresses people's needs.[86] It consists of four parts. The first part concerns the provision of local primary mental health support services. This encompasses joint initiatives to deliver primary mental health support services, the

82 See English and Welsh Codes (n49) paras 24.14-24.28 and 24.11-24.26, respectively.

83 See pp 155-57

84 *R (Worcestershire County Council) v SSHSC* [2023] UKSC 31, [2023] 1 W.L.R. 2790.

85 See pp 134-35

86 See Welsh Code (n49) Chapter 34.

obligation to provide local primary mental health support services, and duties to conduct primary mental health assessments. Doctors in primary care should have more services available for patient referrals. The second part deals with coordinating and planning care for those using secondary mental health services. This includes appointing and outlining the functions of care coordinators and the duty to coordinate mental health service provision. A care coordinator should be a qualified social worker, mental health or learning disability nurse, occupational therapist, psychologist, doctor, dietician, physiotherapist, or speech and language therapist.[87] The third part concerns assessing former secondary mental health service users. It includes arrangements for assessing them, their entitlement to assessment, and the purpose of the assessment. It enables patients to return to the mental health services that previously cared for them without needing a GP referral. Lastly, part four relates to mental health advocacy, including independent mental health advocates, their powers, and duties.[88] A 2022 report by MIND Cymru identified some of the successes of the Measure and areas where more needs to be done.

> The Measure has had a positive impact on mental health services in Wales. It has delivered clear benefits, including improving access to primary care with hundreds of thousands of people receiving an assessment and support for their mental health. Similarly, the expansion of inpatient advocacy deserves recognition. However, the Measure's impact has been uneven. It has proved more effective in some areas than others. Ultimately, there remains much to be done to deliver its aims.[89]

In 2024 the Welsh Government published a Draft Mental Health and Wellbeing Strategy (2024–34) for Wales. The draft strategy focuses on community empowerment, reducing stigma, person-centred care, equitable access, and preventing suicide and self-harm. It recognises that mental health encompasses a range of conditions impacting emotions, thinking, and behaviour, influenced by factors such as relationships, physical health, traumatic experiences, substance misuse, financial status, and community environment. The draft strategy emphasises the importance of engaging in activities to protect and improve mental health. These activities include participating in leisure activities, connecting with others, being physically active, engaging with nature, learning new things, helping others, finding time to relax, and getting good quality sleep. It also emphasises the importance of community assets such as parks, community centres, cultural institutions, and recreational facilities in promoting mental health and overall well-being. The point is made that community assets include physical activity services for older persons.

87 Welsh Government, *Code of Practice to Parts 2 and 3 of the Mental Health Act Measure 2010* (Welsh Government, 2012) para 3.26.

88 See National Assembly for Wales, *Post-legislative Scrutiny of the Mental Health (Wales) Measure 2010* (Health and Social Care Committee, January 2015).

89 MIND Cymru, *The Mental Health Measure ten years on* (2022) 7 https://www.mind.org.uk/media/13351/thementalhealthmeasure_tenyearson.pdf – accessed 28 September 2024.

Additionally, it stresses the need for a connected system for mental health and well-being services, involving various sectors such as health, social care, substance misuse, housing, education, and the justice system working together to provide support. There is a link between the draft strategy and the Age Friendly Wales Strategy for an Ageing Society, which emphasises harnessing the potential of older persons. It is designed to be a strategy for all age groups, encompassing children, young people, adults, and older persons; the challenge, when implemented, is how it will ensure equality across all age groups.[90]

Warrants, removal, and places of safety

Under Section 135 MHA 1983, where a justice of the peace receives information on oath from an AMHP and has reasonable grounds to suspect that a person with a mental disorder is being ill-treated, neglected, or not under proper control, or is unable to care for themselves while living alone, the justice may issue a warrant authorising a constable to enter the premises where the person is believed to be. The constable can use force if necessary to obtain entry and may remove the person to a place of safety to allow for an MHA 1983 assessment or make other care arrangements. 'Place of safety' may include local authority residential accommodations, hospitals, police stations, independent hospitals, mental health care homes, or other suitable places. However, if the person is already in a place of safety, the constable may prevent the person from leaving pending an assessment or other care arrangements. If it appears to a constable that a person has a mental disorder and requires immediate care or control, the constable may under Section 136 MHA 1983 remove the person to a place of safety, or if the person is already in such a place, keep them there or move them to another place of safety. The constable must consider it necessary in the person's best interests or to protect others. The person can be in any place other than a house, flat, or room where the person or anybody else lives or a connected garden, garage or outhouse unless it has shared access. Force may be used to enter any place where the power is exercisable, if necessary. Before deciding to exercise the power, the constable must, if practicable, consult with a registered medical practitioner, a registered nurse, an AMPH, or a person specified in the regulations. In exercising either of these powers, the constable has, subject to conditions, the power to search the person if there are reasonable grounds for believing they may be a danger to themselves or others, or they are concealing an item that could cause physical injury.[91]

The Mental Health Act 1983 (Places of Safety) Regulations 2017 state that a police station can only be used as a place of safety for a person if their behaviour

90 Welsh Government, 'Welsh Government Draft Mental Health and Wellbeing & Suicide and Self-harm Prevention Strategies (2024-2034)' (11 March 2024) <https://www.powysmentalhealth.org.uk/news/welsh-government-draft-mental-health-and-wellbeing-suicide-and-self-harm-prevention-strategies-2024-2034/> – accessed 28 September 2024.

91 MHA 1983 Section.136C.

presents an imminent risk of serious injury or death, there is no other suitable place of safety in the police area, and they will have access to a healthcare professional while detained. Regular checks and reviews are also required during their detention at the police station. Before deciding to use a police station, the officer must, if reasonably practicable, consult with a registered medical practitioner, a registered nurse, an AMPH, an occupational therapist or a paramedic.[92] The person may be detained at a place of safety to be examined by a registered medical practitioner and interviewed by an AMPH; detention should not normally exceed twenty-four hours, starting upon arrival at the place of safety or the commencement of the person's detention at their original place of safety. Before the period of detention ends, a constable, an AMHP, or an authorised person may take the detained person to one or more other places of safety where they may be detained for a period ending no later than the original permitted detention period. A registered medical practitioner can extend the detention of a person detained under Section 135 or 136 for a further period not exceeding twelve hours if they believe it is necessary due to the person's condition. This extension is permissible if assessing the person within the initial twenty-four-hour period is impracticable. If the person is detained at a police station, the authorisation for extension can only be given if approved by an officer of the rank of superintendent or above.[93]

The MCA 2005 and MHA 1983 interface

An older person cannot be detained under MHA 1983 at the same time as being subject to a DoLS authorisation. The MHA 1983 allows for compulsory detention and treatment of people with mental disorders relying on diagnostic and risk criteria outlined in the Act. It does not consider capacity or best interests, unlike the MCA 2005, where these are the key factors to be considered. The MCA 2005 applies to decisions on care and treatment for those without capacity. This includes patients with mental disorders, except where treatment falls within the treatment provisions of the MHA 1983. However, there are situations where a decision must be made on which legislation to use. The Code gives guidance on which to use if the patient has a mental disorder under the MHA 1983.[94] Both Codes provide a helpful summary of when the MHA 1983 and DoLS are available – this is reproduced in table 7.3 below.

Guidance is given on patient objection. In some cases, the patient may be able to express an objection, whereas in others, the patient's wishes, feelings, past and present views and values should be considered if they can be ascertained. In cases of doubt, decision-makers should err on the side of caution and treat the patient as objecting. The perceived reasonableness of the objection is not the issue.[95]

92 The Mental Health Act 1983 (Places of Safety) Regulations 2017 SI 2017/ 1036.
93 MHA 1983 Section,136B.
94 English and Welsh Codes (n49) paras 13.58 – 13.61 and 13.33—49 respectively.
95 ibid paras 13.49 – 13.51 and 13.33 repectively.

Table 7.3 Interface between the MHA 1983 and the MCA 2005

	P objects to the proposed accommodation in hospital for care and/or treatment; or to any of the treatment they will receive there for the mental disorder	*P does not object to the proposed accommodation in a hospital for care and/ or treatment; or to any of the treatment they will receive there for the mental disorder.*
P has the capacity to consent to being accommodated in hospital for care and/or treatment.	Only the MHA 1983 is available.	MHA 1983 is available. Informal admission might be appropriate. Neither DoLS nor a Court of Protection order is available.
P lacks the capacity to consent to being accommodated in the hospital for care and/or treatment.	Only the MHA 1983 is available.	The MHA 1983 is available. DoLS is available and potentially a Court of Protection order.

In AM v South London and Maudsley NHS Trust and Secretary of State for Health,[96] Charles J, the presiding judge, held that DoLS may be an alternative to the MHA 1983 in some situations. AMPHs should consider this option and not view the MHA 1983 as the default; the decision is case-specific and must be informed by the need for the least restrictive intervention. Factors to be considered include the risk posed to others, fluctuating capacity, restraint use, and treatment types. DoLS may be less restrictive than the MHA 1983, although a less restrictive regime for one person may not be less restrictive for another. It is, however, worth remembering that the MHA 1983 Code states that if 'the [MCA2005] can be used safely and effectively to assess or treat a patient, it is likely to be difficult to demonstrate that the criteria for detaining the patient under the MHA 1983 are met.'[97]

Conclusion – reform

Cheshire West tested the law on the deprivation of liberty. One consequence of the Supreme Court's decision is the backlog and unacceptable delays in responding to deprivations as public authorities struggle to find the necessary resources to ensure that human rights are respected.[98] In 2018, the Care Quality Commission highlighted long procedural delays in assessing requests for DoLS to authorise patients to stay in the hospital, in particular wards providing care for older persons, many living with dementia. Consequently, staff have increasingly relied on the

96 [2013] UKUT 365 (AAC), [2013] 8 WLUK 60 |

97 English Code (n49) para 14.23.

98 C Carter, 'Watchdog uncovers delays of up to six years in handling DoLS cases because of council triage system' (2021) <https://www.communitycare.co.uk/2021/02/16/watchdog-uncovers-delays-six-years-handling-dols-cases-council-triage-system/> – accessed 28 September 2024.

MHA 1983 to authorise the deprivation. Staff also mentioned that in the past, such patients would have been less likely to be subject to the MHA 1983 or any other legislative framework. The report further noted that a ward manager attributed the noticeable increase in detention under the MHA 1983 of those aged sixty-five and older to the Cheshire West effect. In some areas, all older patients in older persons' wards were detained under the MHA 1983,[99] although there was no suggestion that those detentions did not meet the admission criteria.

The Law Commission undertook a review of DoLS.[100] It followed a report by the House of Lords Select Committee on the MCA 2005, which concluded,

> (T)he level and breadth of criticism of the Deprivation of Liberty Safeguards, including from the judiciary, demonstrates that the legislation is not fit for purpose. Better implementation would not be sufficient to address the fundamental problems identified.[101]

The Law Commission found that local authorities failed to seek authorisations for deprivations of liberty in cases not involving care homes or hospitals, despite the Cheshire West's recognition of the need for protection. It highlighted concerns about the bureaucratic burden imposed on already hard-pressed public bodies and Cheshire West's practical and financial implications. DoLS were also considered disconnected from the empowering ethos of the MCA 2005, and its terminology carried negative connotations. It recommended that DoLS be replaced, as a matter of pressing urgency, by the Liberty Protection Safeguards (LPS). In response, the Westminster Government introduced the Mental Capacity (Amendment) Act 2019, which will introduce the LPS when and if implemented.[102] Under the LPS scheme, care providers will have a 'responsible body' to manage tests and assessments for any deprivation of liberty. This responsible body could be either a hospital trust or a local authority adult social care service. Their role is to communicate with the person and their loved ones and to authorise any deprivation of liberty in specific settings. In NHS hospitals, the hospital manager is responsible for the hospital's operations. The local Clinical Commissioning Group will be the responsible body for continuing health providers outside of hospital settings, while the

99 Care Quality Commission. 'Mental Health Act: The rise in the use of the MHA to detain people in England' (12 May 2022) <https://www.cqc.org.uk/publications/themed-work/mental-health-act-rise-mha-detain-england#:~:text=people%20in%20England-,Mental%20Health%20Act%20%E2%80%93%20The%20rise%20in%20the%20use%20of%20the,to%20detain%20people%20in%20England&text=This%20report%20looks%20at%20causes,to%20treat%20people%20in%20hospitals> – accessed 28 September 2024.

100 Law Commission, *Mental Capacity and Deprivation of Liberty* (Law Commission 372, 2017).

101 Select Committee on the Mental Capacity Act 2005, *Mental Capacity Act 2005: Post-legislative Scrutiny* (HL Paper 139) para 32.

102 See Department for Education, Department of Health and Social Care, Ministry of Justice, and Welsh Government, *Changes to the MCA Code of Practice and implementation of the LPS: Consultation Document* (2022) <https://www.gov.uk/government/consultations/changes-to-the-mca-code-of-practice-and-implementation-of-the-lps/changes-to-the-mca-code-of-practice-and-implementation-of-the-lps-consultation-document> – accessed 28 September 2024.

local authority will be responsible in all other cases. Three assessments will be conducted to authorise an LPS, which will be integrated into existing care planning and assessments if deemed appropriate. The responsible body will organise the assessments and ensure the evidence supports a deprivation of liberty. It will conduct regular reviews, and the person under the LPS will have the right to an appropriate representative to safeguard their interests. The Court of Protection will determine any disputes or appeals. Initially, an LPS can be renewed for up to one year and then up to three years.

The assessments will determine whether the person has a mental disorder, whether their condition is severe enough to mean they lack the capacity to consent to their care and treatment, and whether the care and treatment proposed are necessary and proportionate to the risk of harm they will likely suffer without this care. Caregivers and other interested parties must be consulted before any deprivation, and a family member or somebody close to the person will have the opportunity to represent and support them during the process and raise any concerns about an LPS. A special safeguard is included when it is reasonable to believe the person would not want to live or receive treatment in a particular place. An Approved Mental Capacity Professional (AMCP) will review the information relied on by the responsible body and meet with the person if appropriate and practicable. The AMCP can consider other cases referred to them by the responsible body. An LPS includes people deprived of their liberty in domestic settings, such as their home, family home, shared living, supported living, care homes, and hospitals. For those deprived of their liberty outside care homes and hospitals, applying to the Court of Protection will no longer be necessary.

Harding emphasises that the effectiveness of LPS will depend on how it is used in everyday life. She hopes the implementation process will be mindful of this and 'proceed with disability, social justice, rather than procedural expediency in mind.'[103] Series is cautious about LPS and discusses its consequences for people in care homes, hospitals, and other settings.

> The LPS challenges, particularly around its provisions for representation, will provide safeguards that are currently entirely absent for people in settings such as supported living, and potentially improve access to justice… Yet people in care homes and hospitals will lose layers of protection that the DoLS deliver in theory (although often not in reality). The scheme is highly vulnerable to human rights renewals and appeals, unless creatively patched up by the Code and the courts, as the DoLS themselves were.[104]

103 R Harding, 'Safeguarding freedom? Liberty Protection Safeguards, social justice and the rule of law' (2021) *Current Legal Problems* 74(1) 329–359, 342.

104 L Series, (2019). 'On detaining 300,000 people: The Liberty Protection Safeguards' (2019) *International Journal of Mental Health and Capacity Law* 25(82) 122.

One benefit of LPS is streamlining procedures (three assessments rather than six), hopefully leading to a greater understanding of the process than is achievable under DoLS.[105]

Although initially intended to be implemented in 2020 and then in 2022, in April 2023, the Conservative government announced that LPS would be delayed until after the general election, ostensibly to allow it to concentrate on its plans for social care reform. Thus far, the newly elected government has not provided an implementation timetable, so, in all probability, it will be delayed beyond 2025. Meanwhile, older persons and others will remain unlawfully deprived of their liberty. One experienced practitioner and DoLS lead summed up the situation as follows.

> We battled with the scheme [DoLS], but backlogs grew, no one could find an easy solution. Then DoLS scheme was declared not fit for purpose and the new light of the Liberty Protection Safeguards began to be switched on, only now it's been switched off.[106]

Not much more can be said.

Mental health law has experienced a similar lack of political commitment to reform. The MHA 1983 requires sensitive reform rather than repeating the over-politicised changes made by the 2007 amendments. A Draft Mental Health Bill was published by the government in 2022, which aimed to bring mental health law up to date and provide better protection for those with learning disabilities and autism. Sir Simon Wessely's 2018 independent review influenced the Bill. His approach is encapsulated in the title of the report, 'Modernising Mental Health: Increasing Choice, Reducing Compulsion.'[107] Among the changes advocated by Wessely was new legislation setting out a purpose and set of principles on the face of the legislation. The principles proposed are choice and autonomy, least restriction, therapeutic benefit, and treating the person as an individual. Professionals would be required to record how the principles are taken into consideration.[108] Each of the principles is discussed in the Report. The Conservative government published a white paper, 'Reforming the Mental Health Act,' in response to the Wessely report.[109] It aimed

105 EJ Shortis, AJ Newton-Clarke, A Verma, DE Allen, E Viola, and NH Metcalfe, 'Reforming DoLS: Liberty Protection Safeguards' (2023) *Postgraduate Medical Journal* 99(1173) 788.

106 L Currie, 'I wouldn't start from here' (*Mental Capacity Law and Policy*, 4 November 2023) <https://www.mentalcapacitylawandpolicy.org.uk/guest-post-by-lorraine-currie-i-wouldnt-start-from-here-a-blog-about-the-deprivation-of-liberty-safeguards/> – accessed 28 September 2024.

107 S Wessely, *Modernising the Mental Health Act: increasing choice, reducing compulsion Gov UK* (Independent Review of the Mental Health Act 1983, December 2018) <https://assets.publishing.service.gov.uk/media/5c6596a7ed915d045f37798c/Modernising_the_Mental_Health_Act_-_increasing_choice__reducing_compulsion.pdf> – accessed 28 September 2024.

108 ibid p 68.

109 Department of Health and Social Care, 'Reforming the Mental Health Act' (2021) https://www.gov.uk/government/consultations/reforming-the-mental-health-act/reforming-the-mental-health-act - accessed 28 September 2024.

to modernise the MHA 1983 and introduce policy and practice reforms to enhance the experience of patients receiving treatment and detention. In 2021, the government conducted a public consultation on its proposals. A joint House of Commons and House of Lords committee reviewed the draft bill.[110] Although the Committee broadly supported the bill, they expressed concerns about its implementation, the availability of community-based treatment alternatives to hospitalisation, and the possibility of unintended consequences. They suggested several improvements and favoured establishing a statutory Mental Health Commissioner. The incoming Labour government in 2024 committed in the King's Speech to legislate to modernise the Mental Health Act to make it fit for the twenty-first century. No reference was made to the reform of DoLS.

A private members bill, the Mental Health Standards of Care (Wales) Bill, was introduced in the Senedd Cymru in December 2024 by James Evans MS. Under the proposal, patients could be detained if they pose a genuine risk of serious harm to themselves or others. In addition, there must be a reasonable prospect of therapeutic benefit for the patient, ensuring that the detention is justified and constructive. Additionally, the nearest relative's role will be replaced by the Nominated Person role, allowing patients to select someone to represent them. However, since its introduction, the Westminster government has agreed to new legislation which may lead to the Bill being withdrawn in favour of a combined England and Wales approach.

Northern Ireland adopted a radical approach to law reform, and the Mental Capacity Act (Northern Ireland) 2016 adopts an innovative approach. It is based in part on the Bamford review of mental health and learning disability. Rather than separate legislation for mental health and mental capacity, it follows Bamford's proposal and adopts a fused approach.

> Government should adopt a coherent and coordinated approach to legislative provision. This should be through the introduction of comprehensive provisions for all people who require substitute decision-making. A single legislative Framework is proposed for interventions in all aspects of the needs of people requiring substitute decision-making, including mental health, physical health, welfare or financial needs.[111]

The Act replaces the need for separate mental health and mental capacity legislation with fused legislation covering all medical and social care. Involuntary treatment is permitted only when decision-making capacity is impaired and the

110 Joint Committee on the Draft Mental Health Bill, *Draft Mental Health Bill* (HC 2022-23, 696 and HL 2022-23 Paper 128) <https://committees.parliament.uk/publications/33599/documents/182904/default/> - accessed 12 February 2025

111 D Bamford, 'The Bamford Reiew of Mental Health and Learning Disability (Northern Ireland): A comprehensive legislative framework' (2007) <https://www.health-ni.gov.uk/sites/default/files/publications/dhssps/legal-issue-comprehensive-framework.pdf> - accessed 28 September 2024 para 8.7.

intervention is in the person's best interest. The pros and cons of replacing traditional mental health laws with capacity-based laws have been extensively debated. It is acknowledged that not having separate mental health legislation that makes decisions about involuntary treatment based on diagnosis and risk necessitates a change in practice for professionals working in mental health in Northern Ireland. Lynch et al. point out that such,

> (F)usion legislation…is a radical change in the approach to involuntary psychiatric treatment. It is an exciting and innovative development, and there are substantial potential benefits, including the reduction of stigma, the protection of patient autonomy, and the removal of confusing parallel mental health and mental capacity legislation.[112]

This resonates with Article 12(2) of the Convention on the Rights of Persons with Disabilities, which requires that state parties recognise the legal capacity of persons with disabilities to the same degree as others in all aspects of life. The 'fusion approach' of integrating mental health and incapacity legislation aims to reduce discrimination, provide a comprehensive legal framework, prioritise autonomy and rights, involve stakeholders, and allow for gradual implementation. It can improve the legal landscape surrounding mental capacity in Northern Ireland but will face challenges related to consistent application, practitioner training, and adequate resources.[113]

As with other age groups, the MCA 2005 and MHA 1983 fail to offer comprehensive protection for older persons when deprived of their liberty. Despite the Cheshire West case and other concerns, the law has not been updated adequately. LPS and Mental Health Act reform are delayed. Due to austerity, all aspects of health and social care are struggling. Many older persons grappling with mental ill-health face ageism and the stigma surrounding mental health, along with the belief that mental health inevitably deteriorates with age. This can be challenging for the older person and their families, friends, and dedicated practitioners. One of the Lancet Commission's key messages is,

> Stigma and discrimination contravene basic human rights and have severe, toxic effects on people with mental health conditions that exacerbate marginalisation and social exclusion…[114]

112 G Lynch, C Taggart, and P Campbell, 'Mental Capacity Act' (Northern Ireland) 2016' (2017) *BJPsych Bulletin* 41(6) 353, 357.

113 See G Davidson M Daly, M Harper et al 'The Fusion Approach to Mental Capacity Law in Northern Ireland: Possibilities and Challenges' in C Kong, J Coggin and M Daly (eds), Queen's University Belfast (Bristol University Press 2023) <https://pure.qub.ac.uk/en/publications/the-fusion-approach-to-mental-capacity-law-in-northern-ireland-po accessed> 19 February 2025, 46.

114 G Thornicroft, C Sunkel, AA Aliev et al., 'The Lancet Commission on ending stigma and discrimination in mental health' (2022) *The Lancet* 400(10361) 1438.

Endless reports, academic literature, and anecdotal evidence from older service users and practitioners highlight the problems. In response, promises are made, and promises are often forgotten.

Bibliography

Alzheimer's Society, 'Learning disabilities and dementia: Factsheet 430' (November 2022) https://www.alzheimers.org.uk/sites/default/files/2022-10/430LP-learning-disabilities-and-dementia.pdf - accessed 28 September 2024.

Ayalon L, 'Ageism towards oneself vs. ageism towards others in the context of views of aging' in Palgi Y, Shrira A, and Diehl M (eds) *Subjective views of aging. International perspectives on aging* (Springer, 2022) 41-58.

Bamford D, 'The Bamford Review of Mental Health and Learning Disability (Northern Ireland): A comprehensive legislative framework' (2007) <https://www.health-ni.gov.uk/sites/default/files/publications/dhssps/legal-issue-comprehensive-framework.pdf>- accessed 28 September 2024.

Brahams D, 'Incapable patients must be treated "formally"' (1998) *Medico-Legal Journal* 66, 36.

Branton T and Brookes G, 'Definitions and criteria: The 2007 amendments to the Mental Health Act 1983' (2010) *Advances in Psychiatric Treatment* 16(3) 161.

Care Quality Commission, 'Mental Health Act: The rise in the use of the MHA to detain people in England' (12 May 2022) https://www .cqc .org .uk /publications /themed -work /mental -health-act -rise -mha -detain -england#:~ :text =people %20in %20England-,Mental %20Health %20Act%20 %E2 %80 %93 %20The %20rise %20in %20the %20use 20of %20the ,to %20detain %20people%20in %20England &text= This%20 rep ort %2 0look s %20a t %20c auses ,to %2 0trea t %20p eople%20in %20ho spita ls - accessed 28 September 2024.

Carter C, 'Watchdog uncovers delays of up to six years in handling DoLS cases because of council triage system' (2021) https://www .communitycare .co .uk /2021 /02 /16 / watchdog -uncovers -delays-six -years -handling -dols -cases -council -triage -system/ - accessed 28 September 2024.

Centre for Ageing Better, 'Ageism: What's the harm?' (2023) https://ageing-better.org.uk/resources/ageism-whats-harm - accessed 28 September 2024.

Claasje Visser R, MacInnes D, Parrott J, et al. 'Growing older in secure mental health care: The user experience' (2021) *Journal of Mental Health* 30(1) 51.

Currie L, 'I wouldn't start from here' (Mental Capacity Law and Policy, 4 November 2023) https://www.mentalcapacitylawandpolicy.org.uk/guest-post-by-lorraine-currie-i-wouldnt-start-from-here-a-blog-about-the-deprivation-of-liberty-safeguards/ - accessed 28 September 2024.

Davidson G, Daly M, Harper M et al'The Fusion Approach to Mental Capacity Law in Northern Ireland: Possibilities and Challenges' in C Kong, J Coggin and M Daly (eds), Queen's University Belfast (Bristol University Press 2023) <https://pure.qub.ac.uk/en/publications/the-fusion-approach-to-mental-capacity-law-in-northern-ireland-po> - accessed 19 February 2025.

Department of Education, Department of Health and Social Care, Ministry of Justice, and Welsh Government, 'Changes to the MCA code of practice and implementation of the LPS: Consultation document' (2022) https://www.gov.uk/government/consultations/changes-to-the-mca-code-of-practice-and-implementation-of-the-lps/changes-to-the-mca-code-of-practice-and-implementation-of-the-lps-consultation-document - accessed 28 September 2024.

Department of Health 'Mental Health Act 1983: Code of Practice' (2015) <https://assets.publishing.service.gov.uk/media/5a80a774e5274a2e87dbb0f0/MHA_Code_of_Practice.PDF> -accessed 12 February 2025

Department of Health and Social Care, 'Reforming the Mental Health Act' (2021) https://www.gov.uk/government/consultations/reforming-the-mental-health-act/reforming-the-mental-health-act - accessed 28 September 2024.

Farrer L, Leach L, Griffiths KM, et al. 'Age differences in mental health literacy' (2008) *BMC Public Health* 8, 1.

Harding R, 'Safeguarding freedom? Liberty Protection Safeguards, social justice and the rule of law' (2021) *Current Legal Problems* 74(1) 329.

House of Lords Select Committee on the Mental Capacity Act 2005, 'Mental Capacity Act 2005: Post-legislative scrutiny' (HL Paper 139, 2005).

Jacoby R, 'Old age psychiatry and the law' (2002) *The British Journal of Psychiatry* 180(2) 116.

Joint Committee on the Draft Mental Health Bill, *Draft Mental Health Bill* (HC 2022-23, 696 and HL 2022-23 Paper 128) <https://committees.parliament.uk/publications/33599/documents/182904/default/> - accessed 12 February 2024.

Kang H and Kim H, 'Ageism and psychological well-being among older adults: A systematic review' (2022) *Gerontology and Geriatric Medicine* 8, 1-22.

Khan Z, Israel-McLeish K, Ballard C, et al. 'Levels of loneliness and mental health in older adults across ethnic groups during the COVID-19 pandemic in the UK' (2023) *Journal of the American Medical Directors Association* 24(5) 710.

Law Commission, 'Mental Capacity and Deprivation of Liberty' (Law Com 372, 2017).

Thornicroft G, Sunkel NSC, Aliev AA et al. 'The Lancet Commission on Ending Stigma and Discrimination in Mental Health' (2022) 400 The Lancet 1438 <https://www.thelancet.com/journals/lancet/article/PIIS0140-6736(22)01470-2/fulltext> - accessed 19 February 2025

Lynch G, Taggart C, and Campbell P, 'Mental Capacity Act (Northern Ireland) 2016' (2017) *BJPsych Bulletin* 41(6) 353.

Mental Health Foundation, 'The Interface between Dementia and Mental Health : An Evidence Review' (2016) <https://www.mentalhealth.org.uk/sites/default/files/2022-09/MHF-dementia-mental-health.pdf accessed> 13 February 2025.

Mind Cymru, 'The Mental Health Measure Ten YearsOn' (2022) https://www.mind.org.uk/media/13351/thementalhealthmeasure_tenyearson.pdf - accessed 28 September 2024.

Ministry of Justice, 'Mental Capacity Act 2005: Deprivation of liberty safeguards' (2008) <https://www.cqc.org.uk/sites/default/files/Deprivation%20of%20liberty%20safeguards%20code%20of%20practice.pdf> - accessed 28 September 2024.

National Assembly for Wales, 'Post-legislative scrutiny of the Mental Health (Wales) Measure 2010' (Health and Social Care Committee, January 2015).

NHS Digital, 'Guardianship under the Mental Health Act 1983, England - 2021-22, 2022-23 & 2023-24' (22 August 2024) https://www .gov .uk /government /statistics /guardianship -under -the-mental -health -act -1983 -england -2021 -22 -2022 -23 -2023 -24- accessed 28 September 2024.

NHS Digital, 'Mental Health Act statistics, annual figures England, 2023-24 (12 September 2024) - <https://digital.nhs.uk/data-and-information/publications/statistical/mental-health-act-statistics-annual-figures/2023-24-annual-figures> -accessed 12 February 2025. .

Novotney A, 'The risks of social isolation' (2019) *American Psychological Association* 50(5) 32.

Parker C, 'Ability to leave?' (1998) *Elderly Client Advisor* 3, 3–5.

Ritchie G, 'The Bournewood Fright' (1999) *Amicus Curiae* 14. 21.

Series L, 'On detaining 300,000 people: The Liberty Protection Safeguards' (2019) *International Journal of Mental Health and Capacity Law* 25, 82.

Shortis EJ, Newton-Clarke AJ, Verma A, et al. 'Reforming DoLS: Liberty Protection Safeguards' (2023) *Postgraduate Medical Journal* 99(1173) 788.

Slobogin C, 'Eliminating mental disability as a legal criterion in deprivation of liberty cases: The impact of the Convention on the Rights of Persons with Disabilities on the insanity defense, civil commitment, and competency law' (2015) *International Journal of Law and Psychiatry* 40, 36.

Stevenson C, 'Deprivation of liberty and intensive care units: The Queen (on the application of Ferreira) v HM Senior Coroner for Inner South London and others' (2017) *Elder Law Journal* 141.

Thornicroft G, Sunkel C, Aliev AA, et al. 'The Lancet Commission on ending stigma and discrimination in mental health' (2022) *The Lancet* 400(10361) 1438.

Troke B, 'Cheshire West and acute hospitals' (*Local Government Lawyer*, 23 February 2017).

Troke B, 'The death of Deprivation of Liberty Safeguards (DOLS)?' (2012) *Social Care and Neurodisability* 3(2) 56.

Walker C, 'Ageing and people with learning disabilities: In search of evidence' (2015) *British Journal of Learning Disabilities* 43(4) 246.

Webb L, 'Covid-19 lockdown: A perfect storm for older people's mental health' (2021) *Journal of Psychiatric and Mental Health Nursing* 28(2) 300.

Welsh Government, 'Code of Practice to Parts 2 and 3 of the Mental Health Act Measure 2010' (2012) - <https://www.bing.com/search?q=code+of+practice+mental+health+act+measure&gs_lcrp=EgRlZGdlKgcIBhBFGMIDMgcIABBFGMIDMgcIARBFGMIDMgcIAhBFGMIDMgcIAxBFGMIDMgcIBBBFGMIDMgcIBRBFGMIDMgcIBhBFGMIDMgcIBxBFGMID0gEKNTUwMTk3ajBqNKgCCLACAQ&FORM=ANAB01&PC=ACTS> - accesssed 28 September 2024.

Welsh Government, 'Mental Health 1983 Code of Practice for Wales' (2016) <https://www.gov.wales/sites/default/files/publications/2019-03/mental-health-act-1983-code-of-practice-mental-health-act-1983-for-wales-review-revised-2016.pdf> accessed 12 February 2025.

Welsh Government, 'Welsh Government Draft Mental Health and Wellbeing Strategy (2024-2034)' (11 March 2024) <https://www.gov.wales/draft-mental-health-and-wellbeing-strategy> – accessed 28 September 2024.

Wessely S (2018) 'Modernising the Mental Health Act increasing choice, reducing compulsion ' (Independent Review of the Mental Health Act 1983, December 2018) <https://assets.publishing.service.gov.uk/media/5c6596a7ed915d045f37798c/Modernising_the_Mental_Health_Act_-_increasing_choice__reducing_compulsion.pdf> – accessed 28 September 2024.

Williams J, 'Hunger-strikes: A prisoner's right or a "wicked folly"?' (2001) *The Howard Journal of Criminal Justice* 40(3) 285.

Williams J, 'Mental Health Act 1983 assessments: The use of video technology' (2022) *Medico-Legal Journal* 90(3) 134.

8 Older persons and international law

Introduction

Global population ageing is both a remarkable achievement and an enormous challenge.[1] The global age composition has changed, and this is predicted to continue. Figure 8.1 plots the changes in population by age groups from 1950 projected to 2100.

HelpAge International reports that nearly 66% of the 868 million people over sixty live in developing nations; this number is expected to rise to 80% by 2050. Africa, Latin America, the Caribbean, and Asia will probably grow their older populations rapidly.[2] This will present many challenges globally and within these countries, including ensuring access to health care in later life, adequate social pensions, and addressing human rights deficits. There will be changes to what is known as the dependency ratio, which measures the ratio of 'dependents,' namely children fifteen and younger and adults sixty-five and over. Figures compiled by Our World in Data show variations in the ratio.[3] The United Kingdom has a ratio of 57.81%, France 62.%, Nigeria 80.25%, and China 44.73%. Across Africa, it is 75.49%, but the large number of younger people explains this. In Asia, the ratio is 48.80%, and in Europe 55.24%. The measure has some value; however, it assumes that all sixty-five and above are dependent, whereas they are not. The 'fundamental fallacy' is the word 'dependent.'[4] Older persons worldwide continue to contribute directly and indirectly to economic development, society, and care. Desai and Tye, in their study on the Asian perspective on ageing, state that

> (T)he economic contribution of older people in developing countries is not well understood. There is no doubt, however, that there are high rates of

1 World Health Organization, *Active ageing: A policy framework* (WHO Organization 2002) 6 <https://iris.who.int/handle/10665/67215> – accessed 28 September 2024.

2 Help Age International, *Developing countries face ageing revolution* (Help Age International, 2015) <https://www.helpage.org/news/developing-countries-face-ageing-revolution/> – accessed 28 September 2024.

3 H Ritchie and M Roser, 'Age structure' (Updated 2024, Published online at OurWorldInData .org)'https://ourworldindata .org /age -structure> – accessed 28 September 2024

4 NE Cutler, 'The Twenty-first Century "Dependency Ratio" – Older People vs. Older Workers' (2013) *Journal of Financial Service Professionals* 67(6) 19-24.

DOI: 10.4324/9780203798058-9

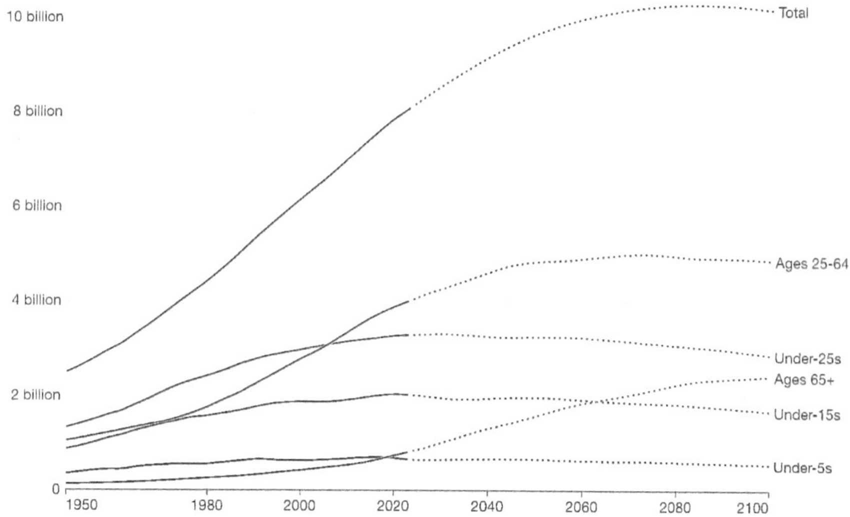

Figure 8.1 Population by age group, World Historic estimates from 1950 to 2021, and projected to 2100 based on the UN medium scenario – Our World in Data.

H Ritchie and M Roser, 'Age structure' (Updated 2024, Published online at OurWorldInData.org) 'https://ourworldindata.org/age-structure> – accessed 28 September 2024.

> economic participation by older men and women. Greater still is their contribution made to the informal economy. Older people have naturally assumed roles such as tending to childcare, cooking and other household tasks and taking on many part-time jobs in the informal sector. Younger adults are 'released' for employment purposes and the cumulative effect is beneficial to the whole household unit.[5]

Older persons do not automatically become 'dependent' at sixty-five. Many older persons work past their sixty-fifth birthday out of choice or necessity – their economic contributions continue. Contributions are also made through supporting their families and communities. The ratio also ignores the sad fact that in some countries, many children work rather than be in education, often driven by family poverty and exploitative multinational corporations. The old-age dependency ratio (the number of people older than sixty-four relative to the fifteen to sixty-four age group) is higher in higher-income countries, mainly Europe, North America, and East Asia. For example, the 2021 comparative figures are 31.2% in Europe and 6.3% in Africa. In its current form, the old-age dependency ratio is misleading as a fixed chronological age approach assumes a steady state in life expectancy and

5 V Desai and M Tye, 'Critically understanding Asian perspectives on ageing' (2009) *Third World Quarterly* 30 1007, 1016.

health in later life.[6] An alternative dependency ratio is the Labor Force Dependency Ratio, which seeks to measure participation in the workforce. Again, this assumes participation and contributions are measured solely by involvement in the labour force; older persons participate in many other ways to the economic and social fabric. The worldwide average median age is 30.4 years, which hides some variation. In Japan, it is 49, New Zealand 37.3, Malaysia 30.5, Lebanon 28.6, and Nigeria 17.9.[7] There is a move from a young to an ageing population. In higher-income countries, lower birth rates and increased life expectancy meant the crossover point has been reached, whereas, for many countries, that point is yet to come. Growing awareness of an ageing population has generated international interest in older persons at national, regional, and worldwide levels.[8]

International collaboration is essential for addressing the challenges related to the ageing global population. In particular, international law can play a central role in promoting and protecting the rights and interests of older persons. One obstacle to this is the need for disaggregated data about older persons. Collecting better disaggregated worldwide data is needed to measure the health and well-being of older persons, poverty in older age, and abuse and neglect. There have been calls for governments, United Nations agencies, and other international bodies to publish more disaggregated data, including separate data for men and women in ten-year age brackets rather than one cohort aged sixty years and over. As is often the case for older persons, age-disaggregated data was in short supply during COVID-19. Lloyd-Sherlock et al. highlight the gap in high-quality mortality data arising from COVID-19. Despite the pandemic's disproportionate impact on older persons, excess mortality data disaggregated by age group is only available in some high-income countries. Such data is necessary to ensure fair treatment for older persons and that policies are not based on ageist attitudes. It will allow ageism to be challenged by highlighting its consequences.[9] A similar point is made in the BMJ Opinion section. The authors cite the 2015 United Nations Sustainable Development Goals, which committed, by 2020, to leaving nobody behind and strengthening the capacity to report disaggregated data. They conclude by saying,

> Data collection is political: an act of deciding *what* and *who* is worth counting—and identifying who is left behind. While effective health surveillance systems will not intrinsically help to create better health, they can enable more equitable targeting of policies and programmes. Such data also provide

6 WC Sanderson and S Scherbov, 'Remeasuring aging' (2010) *Science* 329(5997) 1287.

7 Ritchie and Rosser (n3).

8 See, for example, A Mooney and A Cotter, *Just a number: An international legal analysis on age discrimination* (Ashgate, 2008).

9 P Lloyd-Sherlock, L Sempe, M McKee, and A Guntupalli, 'Problems of data availability and quality for COVID-19 and older people in low-and middle-income countries' (2021) *The Gerontologist* 61(2) 141, 143.

a means to hold governments accountable for their promises to leave no one behind.[10]

Reliable data collection needs to be improved, not only in health and care. Little detailed data exists on older persons regarding employment, savings and debts, gender, and socio-cultural and economic factors that may deny them access to services. Older people are left behind; they must be counted if governments are committed to identifying and addressing inequality based on age.[11]

Abuse of older persons' human rights – a worldwide perspective

The rights guaranteed to all people by instruments such as the Universal Declaration of Human Rights (UDHR) do not appear to be applied universally across all age groups. A lack of awareness of the needs of older persons and the exclusion of older persons from programmes addressing health, poverty, and social care demonstrates that ageism transcends national and regional boundaries and is truly worldwide. Practices continue regarding older persons that would rightly attract condemnation if applied to children, although much more needs to be done to protect children. Age awareness, particularly older age, must be embedded when implementing international human rights instruments to ensure they do not exclude people based on age. Many older persons are denied fundamental human rights and do not have an effective remedy for those breaches. Some examples will be considered.

Elder abuse

The World Health Organisation (WHO) predict elder abuse cases will increase as the world population ages. It estimates the worldwide number of victims will grow to approximately 320 million by 2050. In 2021, one in six people aged sixty and over experienced abuse in a community setting. Within institutional settings, the prevalence of abuse is high. The COVID-19 pandemic exacerbated this. Poor data prevents an accurate assessment of the levels of elder abuse.[12] A 2017 study across twenty-eight countries, including low and middle-income countries, reported the following prevalence estimate of older persons experiencing different kinds of abuse: psychological abuse, 11.6%; financial abuse, 6.8%; neglect, 4.2%; physical

10 United Nations, 'Transforming our world: The 2030 Agenda for sustainable development' (2015) <https://sustainabledevelopment.un.org/content/documents/21252030%20Agenda%20for%20Sustainable%20Development%20web.pdf> – accessed 28 September 2024.

11 K Buse, A Gautam, U Hussain, and V Olarewaju, 'The dearth of disaggregated health data: a political rather than a technical challenge' (2023) BMJ 381 http://dx.doi.org/10.1136/bmj1254.

12 Y Yon, M Ramiro-Gonzalez, CR Mikton et al., 'The prevalence of elder abuse in institutional settings: A systematic review and meta-analysis' (2019) *European Journal of Public Health* 29(1) 58; World Health Organization, 'Abuse of older people' (2022) <https://www.who.int/news-room/fact-sheets/detail/abuse-of-older-people> – accessed 28 September 2024.

abuse, 2.6%; and sexual abuse, 0.9%.[13] The WHO in 2022 pointed out that despite significant numbers of older persons experiencing abuse, it remains a low worldwide priority for several reasons. The complexity of elder abuse is one reason. Abuse takes many different forms. Ageism leads to low worldwide awareness and is a significant risk factor. The WHO highlights the consensus that most forms of intervention have been shown not to work. The first two of its five priorities are combating ageism and better data on prevalence, risk, and protective factors. Addressing ageism necessitates seeing how it intersects with other forms of prejudice and discrimination. How does ageism intersect with, for example, sexism, racism, homophobia, transphobia, and ableism? The lack of data on prevalence is particularly acute in low and middle-income countries, making it difficult to assess the scale of abuse.[14]

There is limited research on violence against older women compared to younger women. A better understanding of violence against older women is needed to ensure that the response by the international and national communities is appropriate and effective. Meyer et al. point out violence's significant impact on older women's physical and mental well-being. Her qualitative literature review confirmed that older women are abused, and the abuse shares characteristics with the abuse of younger women but may be exacerbated by partner retirement or conditions such as dementia. The study concludes,

> (O)lder women described being strongly influenced by social norms that dictate a sense of duty to stay in a relationship with an abusive partner, a desire to protect children, and shame and silence surrounding experiences of violence.[15]

A particular form of violence against older women is 'witch' killings. For example, in Tanzania, 17,220 women were abused between 1998 and 2001 due to witchcraft allegations and 10% were killed. Across the nine project districts where HelpAge International works, there were 444 'witch' killings between 1999 and 2004. Of these, all except nine were older women.[16] It is a matter of grave concern that, for some, the killing of somebody believed to be a witch is akin to self-defence justifying extrajudicial reprisals.[17] Reports of witch killing, mainly of older women,

13 United Nations. 'World Elder Abuse Awareness Day 15 June' (2023) <https://www.un.org/en/observances/elder-abuse-awareness-day/background> – accessed 28 September 2024.

14 World Health Organisation, 'Tackling abuse of older people: Five priorities for the United Nations Decade of Healthy Ageing (2021–2030)' (2022) <https://www.who.int/publications/i/item/9789240052550> – accessed 28 September 2024.

15 SR Meyer, ME Lasater, and C García-Moreno, 'Violence against older women: A systematic review of qualitative literature' (2020) *PLoS One* 15(9) e0239560, 37.

16 M Van Steenbergen, ' Witchcraft used as excuse for violence against older women in Tanzania' *The Guardian* (London, 1 October 2012).

17 R Solomon, 'Witch-killings and the law in Uganda' (2020) *Journal of Law and Religion* 35(2) 270; R Strating and B Edmondson, 'Beyond democratic tolerance: Witch killings in Timor-Leste' (2015) *Journal of Current Southeast Asian Affairs* 34(3) 37.

in an eastern province of the Democratic Republic of Congo suggest the attacks are driven by *bajakazi* – bogus preachers or self-described psychics who claim to be able to detect witches.[18] Another form of violence against older women is rape as a weapon of armed conflict. Rape is not confined to younger women and girls. Combatants use it to terrorise and send a 'man to man' message to show that those attacked cannot protect their women.[19] Human Rights Watch report that in the conflict in the Tigray region of Ethiopia and the Amhara and Afar regions, they found that healthcare providers treated rape survivors, including women between the ages of fifty and seventy. Similar reports come from South Sudan's war. These are not isolated incidents.[20]

The WHO notes that older women are abandoned in some traditional societies, and their property is seized.[21] Elder abuse cannot be eradicated unless the needs of older persons for shelter, food, security, and access to health care are met. The international community should be encouraged to create an environment that accepts ageing as a natural part of life, where older persons are given the right to live with dignity and participate fully in society. Access to health care and access to justice must be improved to support older persons experiencing abuse. At present, older persons' experience of abuse is intensified by an inadequate understanding of its prevalence, causes, and the barriers standing in the way of effective action. As in national systems, the international community has not yet responded with a sufficient commitment to this growing abuse of human rights.

AIDS and HIV

Approximately 1.5% of global deaths (630,000), are attributed to HIV/AIDS. There are wide national variations. In the United Kingdom, the figure is 0.4%, Brazil 1.1%, Guinea 3.56%, Tanzania 7.68%, and South Africa 27.53%.[22] Older persons living with HIV fall into two categories. First, those diagnosed when they were younger who, thanks to effective treatment programmes, have benefitted from antiretroviral therapy, meaning it is no longer life-limiting. They may, however, experience discrimination, for example, in residential care. The combination of ageism and HIV-related stigma may exclude people.[23] Second, older persons are

18 'Witch-hunt murders surge in Democratic Republic of Congo' *Guardian* (London, 28 September 2021).

19 N Danjibo and A Akinkuotu, 'Rape as a weapon of war against women and girls' (2019) *Gender and Behaviour* 17(2) 13161.

20 Human Rights Watch, 'No one is spared: Abuses against older people in armed conflict' (2022) <https://www.hrw.org/sites/default/files/media_2022/02/global_olderpeople0222_web.pdf> – accessed 28 September 2024.

21 ibid.

22 M Roser andH Ritchie, 'HIV/AIDS' (2023) *Our World in Data* <https://ourworldindata.org/hiv-aids#almost-1-million-people-die-from-hiv-aids-each-year-in-some-countries-it-s-the-leading-cause-of-death> – accessed 28 September 2024. .

23 MJ Brown and O Adeagbo, 'HIV and aging: Double stigma' (2021) *Current Epidemiology Reports* 8(2) 72.

first diagnosed later in life. Prevalence and incident infections of those over fifty are increasing faster than the general population. It is estimated that the number of people aged fifty and over with HIV increased globally from 5.4 million in 2015 to 8.1 million in 2020.[24] Schmid et al. note the surprisingly high prevalence and incidence of HIV amongst people fifty years and over, although it is often not recognised as an 'older person's illness.' Symptoms of HIV infection, such as fatigue, memory lapses, shortness of breath, poor sleep, and weight loss, may be dismissed as inevitable features of ageing. For older persons, there may be a shorter time from diagnosis to the onset of AIDS, partly because doctors fail to consider HIV, and there is a delayed diagnosis.[25] Ageist assumptions are made about older persons engaging in activities considered risk factors. Older persons, it is assumed, do not engage in sexual activity, and even if they do, it is with a single partner. Condoms may no longer be used once the fear of an unwanted pregnancy disappears. The need for sexual health education and counselling does not stop at a particular age.[26]

Most deaths from AIDS (83%) have occurred in Sub-Saharan Africa, although little is known about the epidemiology among older persons.[27] One scenario in this region is where a grandparent, who may themselves be HIV positive, becomes the primary care provider for grandchildren whose parents have died of AIDS – the so-called missing generation. Older persons may also be responsible for the care of two generations because of HIV/AIDS, and many fear being infected by the persons they care for.[28] HelpAge International found that up to half of the world's children orphaned by AIDS are cared for by an older person. Older persons may also provide care for adult children who are HIV-positive or have AIDS. The charity states,

> (O)ver the last decade, the HIV and AIDS epidemic has had a devastating impact on older people, yet this impact remains under-reported and has not been properly addressed. Older people's needs and concerns are often overlooked by HIV and AIDS programmes because of the erroneous assumption

24 The Lancet Healthy Longevity, 'Ageing with HIV' (2022) The Lancet 3 (3) - <https://www.thelancet.com/journals/lanhl/article/PIIS2666-7568(22)00041-1/fulltext> - accessed 19 February 2025. e119., L Tavoschi, JG Dias, A Pharris, D Schmid, A Sasse, D Van Beckhoven, et al., 'New HIV diagnoses among adults aged 50 years or older in 31 European countries, 2004–15: An analysis of surveillance data' (2017) *The Lancet HIV* 4(11) e514.

25 G Schmid B Williams, J Garcia-Calleja, et al. 'The unexplored story of HIV and ageing' (2009) *Bulletin World Health Organisation* 87(3) 162.

26 MMG Wilson, 'Sexually transmitted diseases in older adults' (2006) *Current Infectious Disease Reports* 8(2) 139; J Williams, 'Intimate relationships between older people in institutional settings: Ageism, protection or fear?' (2015) *Ethics, Medicine and Public Health* 1(2), 194–202.

27 Rosser and Ritchie (n22).

28 C Munthree, 'Growing old in the era of a high prevalence of HIV/AIDS: The impact of AIDS on older men and women in KwaZulu-Natal, South Africa' (2010) *Research on Aging* 32(2) 155.

> that older people are not affected. This must change urgently if a comprehensive response to the HIV and AIDS epidemic is to be delivered.[29]

AIDS/HIV may deprive older persons of their support, and they are left alone to care for grandchildren.[30] Older persons are affected directly and indirectly by HIV/AIDS.

In addition to the physical and mental strain of caring, older persons also experience discrimination. The stigma and irrational fear of mixing with anybody living in the same house as an HIV/AIDS person may lead to social isolation. There is also a financial loss as they may be unable to earn or sell their produce. Nhongo draws attention to the financial implications of caring and its impact on children's development. In a paper based on family development in Namibia, Nhongo concludes,

> Large numbers of older people simply do not have the resources to cover the cost of bringing up several grandchildren and meeting their own needs. The economic burden is not only a cause of concern for older people, but is also a source of dissatisfaction for some of the children in their care.[31]

Research in Tanzania highlights that some orphans feel they are not well supported and their grandparents do not meet their needs. Older persons echo these sentiments, saying that as they care for the sick and later strive to generate sufficient income to meet food and other basic needs, they cannot care for their grandchildren as they would like.[32]

Disaster relief

Reports of natural disasters are disturbing and not uncommon. It is necessary to exercise some caution when interpreting trends in reported natural disasters and identifying historical patterns.[33] Increases could partly result from improved reporting and data collection. For example, the increase in reported small and medium disasters does not necessarily indicate a significant rise in this type of disaster. However, the fact they are more likely to be recorded is essential as older persons may be significantly affected by them and require support. They are now less likely to be ignored. Reporting has improved. In 2023, the Turkey–Syria earthquake is

29 Help Age International, 'As heavy as a mountain rock: How HIV affects older people' (2009) *Help Age International* 3.

30 T Kautz, E Bendavid, J Bhattacharya et al 'AIDS and Declining Support for Dependent Elderly People in Africa: Retrospective Analysis Using Demographic and Health Surveys' BMJ 2010;340:c2841.

31 TM Nhongo, 'Impact of HIV/AIDS on generational roles and intergenerational relationships' (Workshop on HIV/AIDS and Family Well-being, Namibia, 28–30 January 2004) <http://www.un.org/esa/socdev/unyin/workshops/Windhoek-backgroundpaper2.pdf> – accessed 28 September 2024.

32 TM Nhongo, 'The changing role of older people in African households and the impact of ageing on African family structures' (2004) *African Conference on Ageing, Johannesburg, South Africa* 1.

33 H Ritchie and P Rosado, *Is the number of natural disasters increasing?* (Our World in Data, 2024) <https://ourworldindata.org/disaster-database-limitations> – accessed 28 September 2024.

estimated to have killed more than 55,000 people and injured a further 10,000. People saw their homes destroyed and possessions lost.[34] Many of those affected by such natural disasters are older people. Limited research exists into the impact of natural disasters on older people, and there is concern that the international community's responses to their needs and the contribution that they can make are lacking. A strategic approach to older people in natural disasters is required.[35] Duggan et al., in their study of older persons' perception of disaster relief, found that older persons who had experienced disaster relief expressed concern about protecting their rights and preventing loss of independence in responding and preparing for a disaster. There was a mistrust of governments. They also had concerns about the ability to access resources. In addition to the immediate effects of catastrophe, older persons may be experiencing poverty and long-standing health conditions.[36]

Interestingly, Rafiey et al., whilst highlighting the lack of research, conclude that older persons have higher positive mental health when caught up in natural disasters. They advocate using older persons' knowledge and experience and involving them in disaster planning. Older persons are also providers of emotional support to families and communities.[37] A contrary finding by Parker et al. suggests that older adults were 2.11 times more likely to experience symptoms of PTSD and 1.73 times more likely to develop adjustment disorder than younger adults.[38] Older persons have greater difficulty coping with the aftermath of a disaster. Following the earthquake in Newcastle, Australia, in 1989, older persons reported higher overall post-traumatic stress symptoms, with even higher levels reported amongst older women. Older persons may also underutilise support services.[39] The study concludes that 'the elderly should be the focus of extra assistance following disasters, preferably in the form of augmentation of existing services with which they are familiar.'[40] The need for older persons to be direct beneficiaries of relief is essential. HelpAge International, in its report on the effect of the Tsunami on older persons in Aceh, Indonesia, stated that,

34 British Red Cross, 'Six months on from the Turkiye-Syria earthquake, and mental health is a "ticking time bomb" (2023) <https://www.redcross.org.uk/stories/disasters-and-emergencies/world/psychosocial-support-after-the-turkey-syria-earthquake> – accessed 28 September 2024.

35 L Fernandez, D Byard C Lin et al., 'Frail elderly as disaster victims: Emergency management strategies' (2002) *Prehospital and Disaster Medicine* 17(2) 67.

36 S Duggan, P Deeny, R Spelman et al., 'Perceptions of older people on disaster response and preparedness' (2010) *International Journal of Older People Nursing* 5(1) 71.

37 H Rafiey, YA Momtaz, F Alipour, H Khankeh et al., 'Are older people more vulnerable to long-term impacts of disasters?' (2016) *Clinical Interventions in Aging* 1791.

38 KE Cherry, PD Allen, and S Galea, 'Older adults and natural disasters: Lessons learned from hurricanes Katrina and Rita' in P Dass-Brailsford (ed) *Crisis and disaster counselling: Lessons learned from Hurricane Katrina and other disasters* (SAGE, 2010) <https://deepblue.lib.umich.edu/bitstream/handle/2027.42/64028/Cherry_older?sequence=1&mod=article_inline> - accessed 28 September 2024; ML O'Donnell and D Forbes, 'Natural disaster, older adults, and mental health–a dangerous combination' (2016) *International Psychogeriatrics* 28(1) 9.

39 S Ticehurst R Webster, V Carr et al., 'The psychological impact of an earthquake on the elderly' (1996) *International Journal of Geriatric Psychiatry* 11, 943.

40 ibid 950.

> (O)lder people should be recognised as direct beneficiaries of relief aid and rehabilitation efforts. To date, a lot of interventions have focused on the household level. This is based on two assumptions: first, that older people are visible, so special efforts to identify them are not necessary; and second, that families and communities are caring for them. However, experience shows that targeting older people as direct beneficiaries is a very effective way to make older people's needs and capacities more visible, promote intergenerational solidarity and empower older people.[41]

Deeny et al. emphasise the contribution that older people can make to disaster relief. They warn of the danger of automatically assuming that older people are vulnerable and in need; they may be a vibrant resource that can be used to assist in the relief programme.[42] In its Aceh report, HelpAge International recognised the vital contribution that older persons make in many societies but found that 'these capabilities often remain unrecognised or under-utilised during emergency situations.'[43] In its Emergency Handbook, the United Nations Refugee Agency highlights three key points when responding to the needs of older persons during emergencies. They emphasise the need to identify older persons and not assume they are visible. Older persons should be consulted about their needs, capacities, and shortcomings in protection and assistance programmes. They should be consulted on the content of food and Core Relief packages, and steps must be taken to ensure that older persons can access distribution mechanisms.[44]

Poverty and older persons

There is a close link between older age and poverty in high, medium, and low-income countries. Retirement (forced or otherwise), failing health, caring responsibilities, and the inability to access financial services are significant contributors to global older age poverty. Poverty in older age is a risk factor for death by suicide. Suicide prevention programmes should recognise this.[45] In their research on poverty in developing nations, Barrientos et al. highlight several factors that must be addressed. One of the most important considerations is the need for older persons to have access to employment opportunities. This is essential from a poverty reduction and social inclusion perspective. While older persons tend to participate in the labour force at higher rates in low-income countries, the kind of work

41 HelpAge International, 'Older People in Aceh, Indonesia 18 Months after the Tsunami Issues and Recommendations' (2006) <https://www.helpage.org/silo/files/older-people-in-aceh-indonesia-18-months-after-the-tsunami-issues-and-recommendations.pdf> accessed 19 February 2025, 13..

42 Duggan et al (n36).

43 Aceh report (n41).

44 United Nations Refugee Agency, 'Emergency handbook: Older persons' (UNHCR, 2023). <https://emergency.unhcr.org/protection/persons-risk/older-persons>_- accessed 28 September 2024.

45 JW Choi, TH Kim, J Shin et al., 'Poverty and suicide risk in older adults: a retrospective longitudinal cohort study' (2019) *International Journal of Geriatric Psychiatry* 34(11) 1565.

available to them is predominantly informal and precarious. Another issue that contributes to poverty among older persons is the limited access to healthcare services. Unfortunately, healthcare priorities often neglect the needs of older people. Additionally, the lack of support from households and social networks can further exacerbate poverty among older persons.[46] The earnings of older persons in employment are invariably much lower than those of younger persons. The International Labour Organization estimates that 78% of older persons' employment is informal, which means lower pay, volatility, and few social protection benefits.[47] Older workers often work in sectors that suffered more during the COVID-19 pandemic, such as hospitality and tourism. Re-entering employment may be difficult and involve a decline in the job standards.[48]

The reason often given for poverty in older age is that older persons no longer can undertake employment and maintain themselves. Barrientos et al. argue,

> this view is based on the segmentation of lives into young, 'prime age' and old, with correlates of dependence and independence, and on a purely instrumental valuation of lives. …(D)eveloping an appropriate perspective on old age poverty, and relevant policy, requires focusing on whole lives, rather than segments, and adopting a perspective on the value of lives which includes both instrumental and intrinsic considerations. …Reducing poverty and vulnerability in later life requires acknowledging and facilitating older people's contribution to the development process.[49]

HelpAge International has suggested several measures to combat poverty in older age. These include enacting laws that protect older workers from discrimination and exploitation in formal and informal economies and implementing flexible economic policies that use their skills and experience. To ensure financial security for all older persons, non-contributory pensions should be provided, while free healthcare should be accessible to all by eliminating barriers such as user fees. Additionally, inclusive education and training programmes must be made available to people of all ages throughout their lives. Microfinance programmes, particularly microcredit schemes, should be made accessible to all older persons so they have equal access to financial resources as other age groups. Mandatory retirement laws should be repealed, and the retirement age should be flexible and voluntary. Furthermore, it is essential to research and disaggregate data on older workers in both formal and informal economies to recognise their contributions and needs.[50]

46 A Barrientos, M Gorman and A Heslop, 'Old age poverty in developing countries: Contributions and dependence in later life' (2003) *World Development* 31(3) 555.

47 International Labour Office, *Women and men in the informal economy: A statistical picture* (International Labour Office, 2018).

48 *OECD Employment Outlook 2020: Worker security and the COVID-19 crisis* (OECD Publishing, 2020).

49 Barrientos (n46) 568.

50 See M Gorman, A Livingstone, K Truelove et al., *Forgotten workforce: Older people and their right to decent work* (Help Age International, 2010) 44.

These and other measures require action by national governments, which is most effectively achieved through worldwide and regional collaboration.

Poverty manifests itself in income insecurity, malnutrition, poor health, unfit water and sanitation, and inadequate housing. Older persons may have to limit or stop working altogether because of retirement options, failing health, or family responsibilities. One way of tackling poverty in older age is through social pensions. Non-contributory social pensions are a better response to poverty in older age than contributory pensions, which, in addition to being difficult to administer in less developed countries, discriminate against older women. Contributory pensions do not address older age poverty in the world's poorer countries.[51] They account for one in three pensions worldwide and one in ten in low-income countries. The World Bank estimates that social pensions cover nearly 35% of the population aged sixty years and over in OECD countries and the European and Central Asia, East Asia and Pacific, Latin America and the Caribbean, and South Asia regions. These are seen as the most effective way of supporting older persons and people with a disability. Regrettably, the expansion of social pension schemes and other non-contributory benefits affects the level of pension that can be afforded. At a minimum, they should cover poverty gaps and provide sufficient resources to meet health and social care needs.[52]

International law

'Is international law law?' is a recurring question asked of undergraduate law students and, to a lesser extent, students of international relations. This question has exercised the minds of leading legal philosophers, and no clear answer has been forthcoming. Such recondite matters are beyond the scope of this book. Instead, some general points should be noted. International law is often effective and ensures that necessary standards are applied despite claims to the contrary. For example, the 1944 Chicago Convention on Civil Aviation provides an effective and safe air transport network whenever we fly in international airspace. Yes, there are failings of international law, such as acts of aggression, abuse of human rights, and environmental damage, but violations are also unwelcome features of national legal systems. International law helps identify violations of agreed-upon international standards. Sometimes, a state breaching international law may face sanctions or diplomatic isolation or be subject to a tribunal or court. Admittedly, some states may escape sanctions because of who they are or their transgressions are not investigated. Despite this, international law establishes standards that states and regional organisations can implement and enforce in their domestic or regional law.

51 S Harper and E Klien, 'Forty years of global action on ageing: What has been achieved?' (2022) *Journal of Population Ageing* 15(1) 13.

52 The World Bank, 'Understanding poverty: Pensions' (2023) <https://www.worldbank.org/en/topic/pensions#2> – accessed 28 September 2024.

International law and global collaboration are necessary to address issues of common interest; for example, no state has the answer to global warming and environmental damage. Similarly, nations must combine to agree on common standards and identify aspirations for older persons in our ageing world. Traditionally, the subjects of international law were sovereign states, as shown by the reference to the law of nations. Political aspiration for greater unity between nations led to the creation of international organisations, such as the League of Nations, which the United Nations replaced after World War II. Gradually, international organisations became accepted as subjects of international law. Ultimately, the law affects persons and increasingly, individuals are recognised as having standing in international law and have moved from being objects to subjects. For example, the European Convention on Human Rights enabled states to allow individuals to bring proceedings under the Convention. Human rights and international criminal law are two areas in which individuals are prominently featured.[53] The individual now has rights (and, in some instances, obligations) and is not always dependent on a state to intercede where their international law rights may have been violated. Non-governmental organisations (NGOs) are also increasingly recognised as subjects of international law, particularly in advocating for international agreements about their area of expertise. HelpAge International is an NGO promoting the rights of older persons worldwide through, for example, its participation in the United Nations Open-Ended Working Group on Ageing.[54]

How is international law made?[55] Article 38 of the Statute of the International Court of Justice identifies four principal sources of international law.

1. international conventions (treaties), whether general or particular, establishing rules expressly recognised by states through signature and ratification.
2. international custom, as evidence of a general practice accepted as law.
3. the general principles of law recognised by civilised nations.
4. subject to the provisions of Article 59, [i.e. that only the parties are bound by the decision in any particular case before the International Court of Justice] judicial decisions and the teachings of the most highly qualified publicists of the various nations, as subsidiary means for the determination of rules of law.

Examples of international conventions include the European Convention on Human Rights, the Convention on the Rights of Persons with Disabilities, and the Convention on the Elimination of All Forms of Discrimination Against Women. Customary international law may be based on United Nations General Assembly resolutions such as the United Nations Universal Declaration of Human Rights. The general principles are often used when a convention or custom is absent. An

53 C Giorgetti, 'Rethinking the individual in international law' (2018) *Lewis & Clark Law Review* 22, 1085.

54 See pp. 273-74

55 See V Lowe. (2007) *International law* (OUP, 2007) 11–18.

example of a general principle gleaned from national legal systems is the rules of natural justice, such as that nobody can be a judge in their cause. Finally, the residual or subsidiary sources of international law are judicial decisions and the teaching of 'highly qualified publicists' of various nations. Identifying highly qualified publicists is difficult, although research highlights who they might be.[56]

What does international law do for older persons? In many instances, it involves that category of law that applies to different age cohorts but requires the elder law lawyer to ask how it works for older persons. However, work is underway to develop a bespoke convention for older persons, as discussed below.

The United Nations

The United Nations was founded in response to the atrocities of the World War II. It consists of several bodies, including the General Assembly and the Economic and Social Council. The General Assembly, through its resolutions, is the principal policymaking body. General Assembly resolutions are not legally binding but may reflect state practice. Resolutions are persuasive and may morph into customary international law. The UN's functions are detailed in its Charter; its provisions bind signatory states. Article 55 of the Charter imposes a legal obligation on members to promote 'universal respect for, and observance of, human rights and fundamental freedoms for all without distinction as to race, sex, language or religion.' Under Article 56 of the Charter, Members pledge to take joint and separate action in cooperation with the UN to achieve this objective. The UDHR was approved by a resolution of the General Assembly in 1948.[57] It is a declaration of principles rather than a treaty and was intended to be aspirational and form the basis for regional and state initiatives. Some states have incorporated references to the UDHR in their constitutions. The primary significance of the UDHR is that it 'represents the only common ground when many states discuss human rights' and has contributed to the development of customary international law of human rights.[58] Hannum notes that 'it is impossible to ignore its political as well as its moral influence on the conduct of international relations.'[59] It has played a role in developing international, national and regional human rights instruments. Article 25 of the UDHR states that,

> Everyone has the right to a standard of living adequate for the health and well-being of himself and of his family, including food, clothing, housing and medical care and necessary social services, and the right to security in

56 ST Helmersen, 'Finding "the most highly qualified publicists": Lessons from the International Court of Justice' (2019) *European Journal of International Law* 30(2) 509.

57 UNGA Res 217(III) (10th December 1948).

58 H Hannum, 'The status of the Universal Declaration of Human Rights in national and international law' (1995) *Georgia Journal of International and Comparative Law* 25 287, 353.

59 H Hannum, 'The UDHR in national and international law' (1998) *Health and Human Rights* 144, 149.

> the event of unemployment, sickness, disability, widowhood, old age or other lack of livelihood in circumstances beyond his control.

Although Article 25 is a rare reference to older persons, the UDHR is an inclusive instrument. The Preamble refers to the 'equal and inalienable rights of all members of the human family', which must include older persons. Several examples from the UDHR reinforce the inclusive principle.

Article 1: 'All human beings are born free and equal in dignity and rights. They are endowed with reason and conscience and should act towards one another in a spirit of brotherhood.'
Article 2: 'Everyone is entitled to all the rights and freedoms set forth in this Declaration, without distinction of any kind, such as race, colour, sex, language, religion, political or other opinion, national or social origin, property, birth or other status.'
Article 3: 'Everyone has the right to life, liberty and security of person.'
Article 7: 'All are equal before the law and are entitled without any discrimination to equal protection of the law. All are entitled to equal protection against any discrimination in violation of this Declaration and against any incitement to such discrimination.'
Article 22 'Everyone, as a member of society, has the right to social security and is entitled to realisation, through national effort and international cooperation and in accordance with the organisation and resources of each State, of the economic, social and cultural rights indispensable for his dignity and the free development of his personality.'

'All' and 'everyone' can only be read as including older persons.

Arising out of the UDHR are nine human rights treaties binding in international law on signatories. They are,

1. The International Covenant on Civil and Political Rights and its Optional Protocol – 1966.
2. The International Covenant on Economic, Social and Cultural Rights and its Optional Protocol – 1966.
3. The Convention against Torture and Other Cruel, Inhuman or Degrading Treatment or Punishment – 1984.
4. The Convention on the Rights of the Child – 1989.
5. The International Convention on the Elimination of All Forms of Racial Discrimination – 1965.
6. The Convention on the Elimination of All Forms of Discrimination against Women – 1979.
7. The Convention on the Rights of Persons with Disabilities – 2006.
8. The International Convention on the Protection of the Rights of All Migrant Workers and Members of Their Families – 1990.
9. The International Convention for the Protection of All Persons from Enforced Disappearance – 2006.

The International Bill of Human Rights consists of the UDHR, the Covenant on Civil and Political Rights, the Covenant on Economic, Social and Cultural Rights, and their Optional Protocols. All nine treaties have an impact on the lives of older persons. Older persons have multiple characteristics, such as disability, sexual orientation, race, gender, employment status, and detention status. Intersectionality is an essential aspect of protecting and promoting the human rights of older persons, although it has tended to be overlooked.[60] An older person's life experience is shaped by age, ethnicity, race, social class, gender, identity, sexual orientation, and other aspects of social stratification. Older persons are not a homogeneous group defined only by age.[61]

The International Covenant on Civil and Political Rights[62] does not refer directly to older persons. However, the non-discrimination duty in Article 2(1) and the equal treatment before the law duty in Article 26 include the words 'or other status.' Even though the Covenant does not explicitly refer to older persons, they are included under 'other status.' The omission of a specific reference to older persons was likely due to a lack of awareness during the drafting process when demographic ageing was not fully understood[63]. It has not prevented the UN from embarking on a programme of action on ageing. The rights protected by the Convention include rights to life, liberty and security of person, freedom of movement, equality before the law, right to recognition as a person before the law, freedom from arbitrary interference, freedom of association and minority protection. These are designed to protect older persons as they protect other generations.

The International Covenant on Economic, Social and Cultural Rights follows a similar pattern, with Article 1 reaffirming that all people have the right to self-determination, be free to determine their political status, and freely pursue their economic, social, and cultural development. The Covenant protects the right to an adequate standard of living, education, social security, and work and fair treatment at work. Article 12 imposes a duty on signatory states to 'recognise the right of everyone to the enjoyment of the highest attainable standard of physical and mental health'. At its Thirteenth Session in 1995, the Committee on Economic, Social and Cultural Rights pointed out that as the Covenant applies to all members of society, older persons are entitled to enjoy the rights recognised in the Convention.[64]

In 1982, the UN adopted the Vienna International Plan of Action on Ageing, the first-ever international agreement on ageing. It includes over sixty recommendations on aspects of ageing, such as health, nutrition, housing, family, social

60 AS Gutterman, *Intersectionality and the rights of older persons* (AS Gutterman, 2023) SSRN 4339758.

61 ibid 4.

62 'International Covenant on Civil and Political Rights' GA Res 2200 (XXI) (16 December 1966).

63 See generally KL Tang and JJ Lee, 'Global social justice for older people: The case for an international conventionon the rights of older people' (2006) British Journal of Social Work 36, 1135.

64 Committee on Economic, Social and Cultural Rights, 'General comment No. 6, The economic, social and cultural rights of older persons' (Thirteenth Session, 1995), U.N. Doc. E/C.12/1995/16/ Rev 1.

welfare, income security, employment, and education. The Plan has five objectives, including increasing awareness of ageing issues, proposing educational and training programmes, and suggesting policy measures to ensure older persons' social and economic well-being.[65] The Plan identifies a crucial challenge in formulating an international response to an ageing worldwide population, namely the diverse nature of the global community. It states,

> The Plan of Action can only include proposals for broad guidelines and general principles as to the ways in which the international community, Governments, other institutions and society at large can meet the challenge of the progressive ageing of societies and the needs of the elderly all over the world. More specific approaches and policies must, by their nature, be conceived of and phrased in terms of the traditions, cultural values and practices of each country or ethnic community, and programmes of action must be adapted to the priorities and material capacities of each country or community.[66]

National governments have a prominent role in implementing the Vienna Plan, given the differences in ageing experiences across diverse societies. Within the broad guidelines and the general principles, states can consider the nature of their societies when shaping their responses. However, they are not given a free hand in implementing or adopting the plan. It refers to '...a number of basic considerations which reflect general and fundamental human values, independent of culture, religion, race or social status.' These cannot be diluted. Reference is made to the disparity of ageing worldwide. The existence of inequalities in medicine, public health, and poor economic infrastructures present barriers to achieving progress. The traditional family unit is changing, which has implications for societies where care structures often depend exclusively on the extended family. In rural areas, depopulation and poor transport are challenging.[67]

The Plan recommends that the structure for international cooperation be mirrored at the national level to ensure that older persons are involved in the implementation process.[68] It envisages achieving collaboration through the United Nations and its organs. Technical cooperation and exchanging information and experience are explicitly mentioned as collaboration areas. In addition, it recognises that the challenge is dynamic and that studies and reviews are necessary to assess the effectiveness of existing guidelines and to learn from experience.[69] At the regional level, the United Nations regional commissions periodically review regional plans.[70]

65 United Nations, 'Report of the World Assembly on Aging' A/Conf.113/31; GA Res 37/51 (1982)
66 ibid para 26.
67 ibid paras 35 and 37–39.
68 ibid para 87.
69 ibid para 112.
70 ibid para 113–114.

Alexandre and Asghar question the effectiveness of the Vienna Plan. Lack of resources in developing countries, low priority given to ageing in countries where the proportion of older persons is low, and lack of expertise within governments are cited as obstacles to implementation. They conclude,

> Despite all good intentions and thoughtful design, the [Vienna Plan] had serious shortcomings in its implementation: it had been seen as mostly relevant to demographically, and economically, advanced countries, while developing countries often omitted ageing from their policy agendas and channelling their limited resources towards other pressing priorities.[71]

The Madrid International Plan on Ageing, adopted at the Second World Assembly on Ageing in 2002, identified further areas of concern.[72] It placed greater emphasis on developing countries than the Vienna Plan.[73] It stressed the importance of nations incorporating older persons within their social and economic strategies. Older persons should also be protected during armed conflict and foreign occupation. In addition, the Madrid Plan recognises that older persons should be provided with universal and equal access to health care and services. Paragraph 13 captures the thinking behind the Madrid Plan. It states,

> The promotion and protection of all human rights and fundamental freedoms, including the right to development, is essential for the creation of an inclusive society for all ages in which older persons participate fully and without discrimination and on the basis of equality. Combating discrimination based on age and promoting the dignity of older persons is fundamental to ensuring the respect that older persons deserve. Promotion and protection of all human rights and fundamental freedoms is important in order to achieve a society for all ages.

To achieve this, it recognises the importance of intergenerational work. A reciprocal relationship between and among generations must be nurtured, emphasised, and encouraged through dialogue. Furthermore, it calls upon governments to continue their efforts to mainstream the concerns of older persons into their policy agendas.[74]

The Vienna and Madrid Plans were innovative and raised awareness of the many issues arising from global ageing.[75] They were helpful developments and encour-

71 S Alexandre, and Z Asghar, 'International policy frameworks on ageing: Assessing progress in reference to the Madrid International Plan of Action on Ageing' (2018) *Журнал исследований социальной политики* 16(1) 141.

72 United Nations, *Madrid International Plan of Action on Ageing* (Second World Assembly on Ageing, 2002) <https://www.un.org/esa/socdev/documents/ageing/MIPAA/political-declaration-en.pdf >– accessed 28 September 2024.

73 Alexandre and Asghar (n71) 142.

74 Madrid Plan (n72) para 13.

75 Patterson WR, 'Vienna International Plan of Action on Ageing', in D Gu and ME Dupre *Encyclopedia of Gerontology and Population Aging* (Springer Nature 2021) accessed 5 February 2025, 5369-5373.

aged national governments to respond to the challenge. However, despite advances, it is argued that the UN must assume full leadership and mobilise worldwide action on ageing.[76] The UN Secretary General's 2011 report to the General Assembly recognised that many challenges required national and international strategies. Highlighted areas of concern were discrimination and the toleration of ageism, poverty, violence and abuse, and the lack of specific measures and specialist services. In 1991, the General Assembly passed the United Nations Principles for Older Persons.[77] The Principles were designed to ensure that the world's nations would prioritise attention to older persons. They focused on independence, participation, care, self-fulfilment, and dignity. The Preamble to the Resolution sets the context within which it was drafted. The awareness of scientific research disproving many stereotypes about inevitable and irreversible declines with age is of particular significance. It also recognises the need to ensure that opportunities are provided for willing and capable older persons to participate in and contribute to the ongoing activities of society. Several first, second, and third-generation rights are identified in the Resolution. Under the heading of independence, it is recognised that older persons should be able to determine when and at what pace they withdraw from the labour force; have access to adequate food, water, shelter, clothing, and healthcare through the provision of income, family and community support and self-help; be able to live in environments that are safe and adaptable to personal preferences and changing capacities; and be able to reside at home for as long as possible. Participation entails remaining integrated in society and participating in policy formulation. Older persons are entitled to family, health, and social care appropriate to their society's cultural values, including ensuring access to social and legal services to enhance autonomy, protection, and care. They should be able to enjoy human rights and fundamental freedoms in any shelter, care or treatment facility; this includes full respect for dignity, beliefs, needs and privacy and the right to make decisions about care and quality of life. Self-fulfilment consists of accessing society's educational, cultural and spiritual resources. Of particular importance is the inclusion of dignity as one of the fundamental principles; they have the right to live in dignity and security and free of exploitation and abuse. The Principles were reaffirmed in the 1992 Proclamation of Ageing.[78] Wales and Northern Ireland have adopted the Principles into parts of their domestic law, including the remit of the older persons' Commissioners in each nation.[79] Other UN initiatives include the Decade of Healthy Ageing (2021–2030), the Year of Older Persons in 1999, and making 1 October the International Day of Older Persons. In 2013, the General Assembly established the mandate of the Independent Expert on the enjoyment of

76 H Kendig, N Lucas, and KJ Anstey, 'Thirty years of the United Nations and global ageing: An Australian perspective' (2013) *Australasian Journal on Ageing* 32(28) 32.

77 GA A/RES/46/91 (16 December, 1991).

78 GA A/RES/47/5 (16 October 1992).

79 See Section 7(1) Social Services and Well-being (Wales) Act 2014; Section25 Commissioner for Older People (Wales) Act 2006; Section2(3) Commissioner for Older People Act (Northern Ireland) 2011.

all human rights by older persons; it was renewed in 2019.[80] The mandate includes assessing the implementation of national, regional, and international standards relevant to older persons, identifying and promoting best practices, reporting on challenges and protection gaps, and making recommendations. The mandate holder presents an annual report to the Human Rights Council of the General Assembly.

In his 2021 report to the General Assembly, the UN Secretary-General likened the COVID-19 pandemic to a stress test on how prepared states were for an ageing society. The pandemic experience of older persons involved complex challenges compounded by structural inequality and disadvantages deeply rooted in ageism. He concludes,

> efforts must be made to explicitly and directly address the underlying structures, attitudes and practices that violate the rights of older persons and increase the risks and vulnerabilities they experience. Ensuring full and equal participation by older persons will be crucial. Their perspectives and expertise in identifying challenges, opportunities and solutions should inform and support recovery efforts. Building stronger legal frameworks at the national and international levels to protect the human rights of older persons, including accelerated efforts to develop proposals for an international legal instrument, will be the key to promoting and protecting the rights and dignity of older persons.[81]

This leads to a discussion on the possibility of an international convention on the human rights of older persons.

An international convention on the rights of older persons?

In 2010, the UN General Assembly established the Open-Ended Working Group on Ageing (OEWG).[82] Building on the Madrid Plan, the GA Resolution sets out the purpose of the OEWG. The General Assembly,

> (D)ecides to establish an open-ended working group, open to all States Members of the United Nations, for the purpose of strengthening the protection of the human rights of older persons by considering the existing international framework of the human rights of older persons and identifying possible gaps and how best to address them, including by considering, as appropriate, the feasibility of further instruments and measures, and requests the Secretary-General to provide all necessary support within existing resources for the duration of its mandate[83]

80 GA A/HRC/RES/24/20 (8 October 2013); GA A/HRC/RES/42/12 (4 October 2019).

81 'Report of the Secretary-General: Follow-up to the International Year of Older Persons: Second World Assembly on Ageing' GA A/76/156 (7 July 2022) paras 61–63.

82 GA A/Res/65/182 (21 December 2010).

83 ibid para 28.

The OEWG brought together member states, NGOs, National Human Rights Institutions, and UN agencies to discuss ways to enhance the human rights of older persons. NGOs and National Human Rights Institutions contribute to the deliberations and argue the case for a Convention. For the fourteenth session in May 2024, the two focus areas for discussion were accessibility, infrastructure and housing, and participation in public life and decision-making. The first area examined the laws and policies in different countries that safeguard the rights of older persons to access infrastructures and habitats, such as suitable housing and equal access to transportation, information, communication, and public facilities. It also considered the difficulties and challenges older persons face in realising their right to accessibility at national and international levels. Additionally, the session examined programmes and policies that support older persons in living independently and staying connected with their communities as they age. The second area sought to identify the laws and policies in countries that protect the rights of older persons. These rights include equal treatment without discrimination based on age in public life and decision-making; not experiencing ageism or age discrimination in laws and policies; freedom of speech and the ability to receive and share information; the right to peaceful assembly and association; the ability to participate in government; the ability to participate in public life and decision-making; and being supported if these rights are violated.[84]

During the fourteenth session, the European Union representative reiterated the EU's commitment to upholding the human rights of older persons and promoting their active engagement in communities. The European Union has discussed the obstacles older people face and expressed openness to discussing accessibility, infrastructure, living environment, and participation in public life. While recognising the necessity to address deficiencies in the international human rights framework, the European Union did not explicitly advocate for a new convention. It identified two key principles to guide efforts to promote the rights of older persons. First, its strategies for addressing discrimination and promoting equality are rooted in intersectionality. An approach that considers the intersection of factors such as sex, race, ethnicity, social origin, religion, political opinion, disability, sexual orientation, and gender identity is necessary. Age should be considered alongside other personal characteristics to challenge stereotypes, combat discrimination, and promote diversity and inclusion. Second, intergenerational solidarity and justice require policies and initiatives benefitting all generations, including housing, care, and participation in public life and decision-making. These include intergenerational living, community-based services and care, and intergenerational learning and dialogue opportunities.[85]

84 United Nations, *Open-ended Working Group on Ageing for the purpose of strengthening the protection of the human rights of older persons: Fourteenth session* (United Nations Office of the High Commissioner, 2024) <https://social.un.org/ageing-working-group/fourteenthsession.shtml> – accessed 28 September 2024.

85 MLA Marca, *EU statement – UN Open-ended Working Group on ageing: Opening* (European Union, 20 May 2024)<https://www.eeas.europa.eu/delegations/un-new-york/eu-statement-%E2%80%93-un-open-ended-working-group-ageing-opening_en?s=63> – accessed 28 September 2024.

The draft decision arising out of the fourteenth session recommends that UN member states address gaps in protecting the human rights of older persons. This can be done by considering various options, including creating an international legally binding convention to promote and protect the human rights of older persons, developing optional protocols to existing human rights treaties, addressing the human rights of older persons in relevant multilateral fora, and updating the international plan of action on ageing. Additionally, it emphasises the importance of collecting age-disaggregated data and strengthening cooperation with regional commissions and other relevant stakeholders to promote discussions on ageing. Furthermore, the decision highlights the need to address specific human rights issues older persons face in United Nations intergovernmental processes, combat ageism, and promote a positive public image of older persons and their contributions to society. In response, the General Assembly passed a resolution on 13 August 2024, which decided that the OEWG had completed the work specified in the 2010 resolution. It urges the relevant United Nations bodies to consider the recommendations made by the OEWG at its 2024 session. It also calls on the President of the General Assembly to arrange a 'high-level meeting' in the next session to promote an exchange of ideas and experiences relating to the recommendations. This meeting should address the challenges and opportunities associated with the rights and well-being of older persons fairly and inclusively and identify any future steps to address these issues.[86]

What is the case for an international convention? The immediate answer is that existing international law does not work. The generic international human rights provision, such as the UDHR, and the specific age-focused provisions have yet to work effectively for older persons. Although many worthy initiatives are underway under the auspices of, for example, the United Nations and the World Bank, development needs to be faster, and inequality remains. Aspirational soft law does not deliver. The international community must find a way to tackle the challenge of global ageing; a bespoke convention is one way of doing this. Comparisons can be made with the United Nations Convention on the Rights of the Child and the United Nations Convention on the Rights of Persons with Disabilities. These recognise that for children and persons with disabilities, a human rights deficit needs to be addressed through bespoke instruments. Provisions from both conventions have been used to inform and influence national laws.[87] The Rights of the Child Convention recognises the duty of society to enable children to develop their capacity and eventual autonomy, something not directly addressed in the generic provision. Fortin writes,

> The Convention recognises that children are active and creative and may need to struggle to shape their own lives. As such, they must be assisted to develop their independence and ability to take responsibility for their future...

86 GA A/Res/78/L.104/Rev 1 (13 August 2024).
87 See, for example, the Rights of Children and Young Persons (Wales) Measure 2011.

> In particular, they require the liberties essential to notions of autonomy if they are to develop their own capacity for autonomy and play an active part in society.[88]

Conscious of the need not to infantilise older persons, it is legitimate to point out that they are also entitled to shape their lives, continue to develop their independence and protect their autonomy; ageist attitudes and invisibility often deprive them of these.

Tang and Lee argue the case for a convention. Claims against violations of older persons' human rights are more substantial when encapsulated in law, hence the interest in what they refer to as a 'strategy of legality.'[89] A strategy of legality has negative connotations; anything can be justified, providing the law permits it. However, in this context, their argument is benign and based on the law providing a strength that transcends political and moral pressure. In 2010, a coalition of NGOs, including Age UK, the International Federation on Ageing, Global Action on Ageing and the International Association of Gerontology, argued in support of a convention.

> A UN Convention on the Rights of Older Persons is necessary to ensure that older women and men can realise their rights. With a new UN convention, and the assistance of a Special Rapporteur, governments can have an explicit legal framework, guidance and support that would enable them to ensure that older people's rights are realised in our increasingly ageing societies.[90]

As mentioned above, an Independent Expert has been appointed. The NGOs reported that in 2010, treaty bodies monitoring human rights rarely raised questions about the rights of older persons. For example, they refer to the United Nations Periodic Review system and how older persons are invisible in state reports.[91] This is a four-year review of the human rights record of all 192 members of the United Nations aimed at improving the human rights situation and addressing violations when they occur. More recently, Mikołajczyk, while pointing out the flaws in the Review system and its vulnerability to politicisation, recognises that in recent cycles, older persons' rights and dignity and the dangers of age discrimination have been more frequently raised. However, states rarely explicitly refer to the dangers of ageism in their recommendations to other states.[92]

In asking whether existing international and regional law is sufficient, the NGOs identify normative and implementation gaps. Normative gaps exist where existing

88 J Fortin, *Children's rights and the developing law* (2nd edn, Butterworths, 2003) 41.

89 Tang and Lee (n63).'

90 International Federation of Ageing et al., 'Strengthening older people's rights: Towards a UN Convention' <https://social.un.org/ageing-working-group/documents/Coalition%20to%20Strengthen%20the%20Rights%20of%20Older%20People.pdf> – accessed 28 September 2024.

91 For Periodic Reviews, see GA Res 60/251 (15 March 2006).

92 N Bambeni, *Social ageing challenges faced by older adults exposed to conditions of underdevelopment and extreme poverty* (IntechOpen, 2022).

provisions fail to address issues faced by older persons. They give examples of the lack of international standards on rights within the community, longer-term care settings for caregivers and those for whom they care, legal planning for older age, and mandatory retirement age. The International Council on Human Rights Policy define normative gaps as existing,

> when a recurrent event (or act or structural factor) deprives human beings of their dignity. Even when existing instruments provide protection in certain respects, in many cases a new or more comprehensive instrument is required to frame the rights of an affected group more clearly or in human rights terms. Such standards enable members of the group to protect their rights more effectively and clarify the duties of states at the same time.[93]

In the early years of the development of global human rights, 'foundation standards' that apply to all people were developed, including the UDHR. Gradually, these foundation standards were complemented by provisions designed to protect the rights of specific groups, such as the Convention on the Rights of the Child 1989, the International Convention on the Elimination of All Forms of Racial Discrimination 1965, the Convention on the Elimination of All Forms of Discrimination against Women 1979, and the Convention on the Rights of Persons with Disabilities 2006. These focused instruments concentrated on identifying principles common to the group, recognising new rights, and specifying state duties not clearly defined by the foundation standards.[94] The underlying principles for older persons include ageism and the discrimination it facilitates. New rights include social pensions, retirement, and health and social care access. The shortage of references to older age in earlier human rights instruments and the reliance on the words 'or other status' leads to the failure to recognise and consequently address the rights of older persons. These gaps deprive older persons of their dignity.

The current generic international provision does not recognise when an older person is deprived of their dignity, or when recognised, it is ignored. Older persons are overlooked.[95] COVID-19 provides a case study of how older persons are often forgotten. Although they are not at greater risk of contracting the virus, there is a higher risk of death if they do. It impacts older persons as carers and as somebody being cared for. Isolation, access to health care, and the added vulnerability of those living in residential settings significantly affected older persons during the pandemic. Amongst other things, the pandemic raised issues of equal access to health care, ageism and stereotyping of older persons, the integration of older

93 International Commission of Jurists and the International Service for Human Rights, *Human rights standards: Learning from experience* (International Council on Human Rights Policy, Switzerland, 2006) 7.

94 ibid.

95 MA Malek, and MA Razzak, 'Rights of the elderly: An emerging human rights discourse' (2017) *International Journal of Law and Management* 59(2) 284, 291.

persons into national responses to the pandemic, and the lack of disaggregated data.[96] An older persons' Convention would promote a more explicit focus on their rights in any future pandemic.

In addition to normative gaps, the NGOs identified implementation gaps in their 2010 report. Implementation is part of the Independent Expert's mandate, which refers to,

> the implementation of existing international instruments with regard to older persons while identifying both best practices in the implementation of existing law related to the promotion and protection of the rights of older persons and gaps in the implementation of existing law.[97]

An implementation gap includes rights in international law that individual state laws do not adopt or implement. Enforcement of international human rights standards is most effectively achieved through its adoption or incorporation into national law. The European Convention on Human Rights is an example of this principle. National courts can address violations of the ECHR and failures by governments to guarantee the rights of those within their jurisdiction. Implementation gaps arise because of failures to identify and enforce existing provisions. Doron and Apter highlight the weak and overburdened systems of accountability; furthermore, there are no effective sanctions. Although arguing strongly in favour of a convention, they note that there are 'genuine concerns' arising from past experiences of the working of international law.[98]

There are counterarguments to the case for a new convention. One is the potential distraction cost of getting political approval for a new convention and then agreeing on its content. The OEWG, during its fourteen years, has been hampered by a lack of universal buy-in. Does this detract from making existing provisions work for older persons? Fredvang and Biggs [99]discuss the opposing arguments. One such idea is that universalism is traditionally regarded as a fundamental feature of human rights. However, as Mégret argues, universalism ignores the development of a more fragmented approach to human rights, recognising that for groups such as children, persons with disabilities, Indigenous people, and migrant workers, there are subtle but significant differences in how their rights should be treated. Older

96 V Bílková, 'COVID-19 and older persons—in need of a comprehensive human rights approach' (2022) *Journal of Human Rights Practice* 14(1) 267. See also JE Ataguba, DE Bloom, and AJ Scott, 'A timely call to establish an International Convention on the Rights of Older People' (2021) *The Lancet Healthy Longevity* 2(9) e540–e542.

97 United Nations, 'Report of the Human Rights Council: The human rights of older persons', A/RES/67/143 (24 September 2013) 54.

98 I Doron and I Apter, 'The debate around the need for an international convention on the rights of older persons' (2010) *The Gerontologist* 50(5) 586-93, 590.

99 Fredvang M and Biggs S, 'The rights of older persons: Protection and gaps under human rights law'' (Brotherhood of St Laurence, 2012) <https://apo.org.au/node/31446> – accessed 28 September 2024

persons may be added to this list as the missing piece of the human rights jigsaw.[100] Mégret states that the '…fragmentation of the human rights project may be in line with a more post-modern sensitivity to rights, one more attuned to the diversity of human experience.' Of course, this trend invites discussion regarding the intelligibility and coherence of universal rights, a debate that needs to happen.[101] Fredvang and Biggs argue that the soft law approach, such as the UN Principles for Older Persons and the Madrid International Plan of Action on Ageing, is sufficient. The adoption of the UN Principles in Wales and Northern Ireland is an example of how it may be used as a basis for national law, although it does depend on state willingness. Again, implementation is a challenge. While it is important not to underestimate soft law's potential, it has thus far proved inadequate. They also refer to the cost of drafting and implementing a convention, which is undeniably a factor in the reluctance of some states to support the idea. The Convention on the Rights of Persons with Disabilities predated the worldwide economic downturn; today, governments may be less willing to commit resources. This might be particularly the case in those countries where older persons are the fastest-growing cohort.[102]

From the limited discussion above, it is apparent that older persons are still marginalised in the international community. Despite being mentioned only occasionally, older persons should enjoy the same universal human rights as all other generations. However, there is division among states regarding the need for a specialised convention for older persons. Many developed countries argue that existing laws (including soft law) are sufficient to protect their human rights. They cite reasons such as treaty fatigue, reporting burden, and costs. AGE Platform Europe identifies European countries as the most sceptical, with some being supportive, others cautious, and the majority not attending meetings of the OEWG. Only Portugal, Malta, Slovenia, and Austria support a Convention. As noted above, the European Union could be more supportive. Countries in Latin America and Africa are supportive of the convention.

Is it necessary to have an international agreement on the rights of older persons? The OEWG has done a commendable job highlighting the human rights violations experienced by older persons. The group has examined issues such as access to employment and the labour market, social security and welfare, abuse and violence, dignity, housing, social inclusion, health care and social care, and discrimination. AGE Platform Europe reports that while the OEWG was not drafting a new agreement, they identified potential issues that could be included in any future convention. Although there has been progress, more governments must support a convention before the drafting process can begin. The likelihood of a convention is

100 K Bluestone and K Hill, 'A UN Convention on the Rights of Older People: A missing piece of the human rights Jigsaw' (2015) *Elder Law Journal* 328.

101 F Mégret, 'The human rights of older persons: A growing challenge' (2011) *Human Rights Law Review* 11(1) 37, 39. See also A Langlois, 'Human rights: The globalisation and fragmentation of moral discourse' (2002) *Review of International Studies* 28(3) 479.

102 JD Sciubba, 'Securing rights in the twenty-first century: A comparison of the disability and older persons' rights conventions' (2016) *Journal of Human Rights* 15(4) 533.

minimal until a significant number of countries sign up. The issues are becoming increasingly apparent, but political will is required rather than mere rhetoric. How long should we wait for an agreement? At what point will those opposed recognise that this worldwide crisis will worsen as the population ages? Will it be too late? While we wait for any future agreement, campaigners must continue identifying and addressing normative gaps. The UN, regional organisations, states, NGOs, and National Human Rights Institutions must strengthen their monitoring and reporting mechanisms to ensure that the needs of older people are prominent in the rights discourse.

Regional protection of the rights of older persons

Significant developments have occurred at the regional level, particularly under the auspices of the Organisation of American States (OAS) and the Organisation of African Unity (OAU). The OAS approved the Inter-American Convention on Protecting the Human Rights of Older Persons in 2015.[103] It entered into force in 2017. The OAS began drafting the Convention in 2011 and completed the work within four years, thus demonstrating what can be achieved with state commitment.[104] The Preamble to the Convention recognises,

> the need to address matters of old age and ageing from a human rights perspective that recognises the valuable current and potential contributions of older persons to the common good, to cultural identity, to the diversity of their communities, to human, social, and economic development, and the eradication of poverty

According to the Convention's first article, the rights outlined within it should not interfere with any rights already established by international or national laws. If a participating state already has laws protecting Convention rights, they do not need to implement those provisions. The second article defines an 'older person' as someone sixty years old or older unless their country's laws have a different age limit, which cannot exceed sixty-five. Article 3 identifies fifteen principles that recognise older persons' vital societal contributions. They include upholding dignity and independence, encouraging participation and self-fulfilment, and ensuring judicial protection.

The Convention requires states to safeguard older persons' human rights and fundamental freedoms without discrimination. In doing so, they must comply with the duties in Article 4, which includes preventing and punishing any mistreatment of older persons, including neglect and insufficient care. Affirmative measures are

103 Organisation of American States. 'Inter-American Convention on Protecting the Human Rights of Older Persons. (A-70)' (2009) <.https://www.oas.org/en/sla/dil/inter_american_treaties_a-70_human_rights_older_persons.asp> accessed 5 February 2025.

104 D Rodriíguez-Pinzón, 'Inter-American Convention on Protecting the Human Rights of Older Persons' (2016) *International Legal Materials* 55(5) 985.

necessary to achieve equality, but such actions should not be discriminatory or long-term. Legislation, budgetary, and other measures should be strengthened to ensure equitable access to justice and preferential treatment, and resources should be available to achieve economic, social, and cultural rights. Civil society involvement and data gathering are necessary for policy implementation, as well as promoting public organisations that protect, promote, and raise awareness of the rights of older persons.

Chapter IV of the Convention provides a comprehensive set of rights for older persons. Given their potential use in any future international or regional convention, listing those rights is worthwhile.

Article	**Right**
5	Equality and non-discrimination for reasons of age
6	Right to life and dignity in old age
7	Right to independence and autonomy
8	Right to participation and community integration
9	Right to safety and a life free of violence of any kind
10	Right not to be subjected to torture or cruel, inhuman, or degrading treatment or punishment
11	Right to give free and informed consent on health matters
12	Rights of older persons receiving long term care
13	Right to personal liberty
14	Right to freedom of expression and opinion and access to information
15	Right to nationality and freedom of movement
16	Right to privacy and intimacy
17	Right to social security
18	Right to work
19	Right to health
20	Right to education
21	Right to culture
22	Right to recreation, leisure, and sports
23	Right to property
24	Right to housing
25	Right to a healthy environment
26	Right to accessibility and personal mobility
27	Political rights
28	Freedom of association and assembly
29	Situations of risk and humanitarian emergencies
30	Equal recognition before the law
31	Access to justice

Signatory states recognise the importance of educating society about the Convention and treating older persons with respect and dignity as part of the awareness-raising duty. They agree to promote a positive attitude towards ageing and to avoid stereotypes; programmes that sensitise the public should be developed and included in educational programmes. Older persons contribute wisdom and productivity to society, and recognition of their contributions must be promoted.[105] A follow-up mechanism comprises a Conference of States Parties and a Committee of Experts.[106] The Convention is an exciting and inspiring example of what can be achieved beyond soft law. It highlights the duty of states to ensure the human rights of older persons are fully enjoyed. It helps OAS members focus on rights and encourages signatories to align their national systems with international standards to protect the fundamental rights of older persons.[107]

The OAU Protocol on the Rights of Older Persons in Africa, a protocol to the African Charter on Human and Peoples' Rights, was adopted in 2016. Fifteen countries have ratified it so far,[108] the number required for it to come into force. The African Charter already has several protocols focusing on specific groups, such as children, women, and youth. Chirwa and Rushwaya challenge the view that older persons remain universally revered in African societies. Traditionally, older members of African communities held valuable knowledge about various topics, including medicine, agriculture, and customary laws, due to their lifelong dedication to the community. They also had power in their communities. This view is no longer as accurate as it was, although it remains in some remote parts and in indigenous groups.[109] The Protocol seeks to address this changed environment for older persons. An older person is defined in Article 1 as sixty and above. Parties to the Protocol must uphold the rights and freedoms contained in it and take legislative action to implement them. They should also incorporate the UN Principles for Older Persons into national laws to safeguard rights. The Protocol prohibits age discrimination against older persons and encourages the elimination of ageist stereotypes. It calls for corrective measures to end discrimination in law and practice at all levels.[110]

The range of rights covered is comprehensive and includes access to justice and equal protection, employment, social protection, conflicts and disasters, health services, education, participation, and recreation activities. One right worth highlighting is Article 12, which is the right to support older persons in caring for vulnerable children. States must implement measures supporting older persons who care for orphans and vulnerable children, particularly when financially struggling. Support should include financial assistance, material support, and other necessary

105 OAS Charter (n104) Article 32.

106 ibid Chapter VI.

107 Rodriíguez-Pinzón (n105) 987.

108 African Union, 'Protocol to the African charter on human and peoples' rights on the rights of older persons In Africa' (2016) <https://au.int/en/treaties/protocol-african-charter-human-and-peoples-rights-rights-older-persons> – accessed 28 September 2024; Help Age International (2024). A new era for older people in Africa: AU Protocol on Rights of Older Persons comes into force. https://www.helpage.org/news/a-new-era-for-older-people-in-africa-au-protocol-on-rights-of-older-persons-comes-into-force/ [Accessed 18 Mar. 2025].

109 DM Chirwa, and CI Rushwaya, 'Guarding the guardians: A critical appraisal of the protocol to the African Charter on the Rights of Older Persons in Africa' (2019) *Human Rights Law Review* 19(1) 53, 56.

110 African Union (n108) Article 3.

resources. Additionally, when children are cared for by older persons such as grandparents, social or other benefits intended for the children should be paid to the carer. A feature of the Protocol, also found in Article 29 of the African Charter, is the inclusion of duties for older persons. They have a responsibility to share their knowledge and experience with younger generations, encourage inter-generational dialogue and solidarity, and play a role in mediating and resolving conflicts.[111] Chirwa and Rushwaya recognised weaknesses in the Protocol, particularly choosing sixty as the single and absolute criterion for 'older person.' They also note the potential risk of undermining the African concept of non-state actors having human rights duties. Nevertheless, they conclude that the Protocol recognises the vulnerability of older persons and expands upon the African Charter's general provisions. It also interprets rights within the context of Africa's experiences, history, values, and traditions.

Conclusion

At the international level, there has been considerable activity in seeking to protect and promote the rights of older people. The Convention on the Rights of Older People initiative has followed the conventions on disability, children and women in moving from a universal approach which emphasises 'all' and 'everyone' enjoying shared fundamental rights to a system that, building on universal instruments, accommodates the specific needs and interests of groups. Progress on an older person's Convention has been a victim of state reticence to contemplate committing more resources to international human rights instruments. Currently, reliance is placed on soft law and non-binding declarations. There are concerns surrounding the use and development of international instruments that portray older persons as needing protection rather than as holders of rights. Recognising and upholding the rights of older people beyond issues such as guardianship and social security is necessary. In many respects, the OEWG and others have identified the problems. A comprehensive, right-centred approach is required to tackle the various challenges confronting older persons. Enforcement at the national level remains challenging. Time is running out; the challenges are not going to go away. Regional agreements may be the answer without a global consensus on a convention. However, whereas there may be a political willingness in some regions, such as the OAS, the same failure to commit at the international level may also inhibit regional initiatives. Older people deserve better. As American basketball player and coach John Wooden said, 'The greatest failure of all is the failure to act when action is needed.'

111 ibid Article 20.

Bibliography

African Union, 'Protocol to the African charter on human and peoples' rights on the rights of older persons In Africa' (2016) https://au.int/en/treaties/protocol-african-charter-human-and-peoples-rights-rights-older-persons - accessed 28 September 2024.

Agence France-Presse in Bukavu, 'Witch-hunt murders surge in Democratic Republic of Congo' (*Guardian*, 28 September 2021).

Alexandre S and Asghar Z, 'International policy frameworks on ageing: Assessing progress in reference to the Madrid International Plan of Action on Ageing' (2018) *Журнал исследований социальной политики* 16(1) 141.

Ataguba JE, Bloom DE, and Scott AJ, 'A timely call to establish an international convention on the rights of older people' (2021) *The Lancet Healthy Longevity 2*(9) e540–e542.

Bambeni N, 'Social ageing challenges faced by older adults exposed to conditions of underdevelopment and extreme poverty' (IntechOpen, 2022).

Barrientos A, Gorman M, and Heslop A, 'Old age poverty in developing countries: Contributions and dependence in later life' (2003) *World Development* 31(3) 555.

Bílková V, 'COVID-19 and older persons - In need of a comprehensive human rights approach' (2022) *Journal of Human Rights Practice* 14(1) 267–284.

Bluestone K and Hill K, 'A UN Convention on the rights of older people: A missing piece of the human rights jigsaw' (2015) *The Elder Law Journal* 328-332.

British Red Cross, 'Six months on from the Turkiye-Syria earthquake, and mental health is a "ticking time bomb"' (2023) https://www.redcross.org.uk/stories/disasters-and-emergencies/world/psychosocial-support-after-the-turkey-syria-earthquake - accessed 28 September 2024.

Brown MJ and Adeagbo O, 'HIV and aging: Double stigma' (2021) *Current Epidemiology Reports* 8, 72.

Buse K, Gautam A, Hussain U, et al. 'The dearth of disaggregated health data: A political rather than a technical challenge' (2023) BMJ 381 http://dx .doi .org /10 .1136 /bmj.1254. - accessed 28 September 2024.

Cherry KE, Allen PD, Galea S, et al. 'Older adults and natural disasters' in *Crisis and disaster counseling: Lessons learned from Hurricane Katrina and other disasters* (2009) <https://deepblue.lib.umich.edu/bitstream/handle/2027.42/64028/Cherry_older?sequence=1&mod=article_inline?> - accesssed 28 September 2028, 115-30.

Chirwa DM and Rushwaya CI, 'Guarding the guardians: A critical appraisal of the protocol to the African charter on the rights of older persons in Africa' (2019) *Human Rights Law Review* 19(1) 53.

Choi JW, Kim TH, Shin J, et al. 'Poverty and suicide risk in older adults: A retrospective longitudinal cohort study' (2019) *International Journal of Geriatric Psychiatry* 34(11) 1565.

Committee on Economic, Social and Cultural Rights, 'General Comment No. 6, The economic, social and cultural rights of older persons' (Thirteenth session, 1995), U.N. Doc. E/C.12/1995/16/Rev 1.

Cutler NE, 'The twenty-first century "dependency ratio" – Older people vs. Older Workers' (2013) *Journal of Financial Service Professionals* 67(6) 19-24.

Danjibo N and Akinkuotu A, 'Rape as a weapon of war against women and girls' (2019) *Gender and Behaviour* 17(2) 13161.

Desai V and Tye M, 'Critically understanding Asian perspectives on ageing' (2009) *Third World Quarterly* 30(5) 1007–1025.

Doron I and Apter I, 'The debate around the need for an international convention on the rights of older persons' (2010) *Gerontologist* 50(5) 586-93.

Duggan S, Deeny P, Spelman R, et al. 'Perceptions of older people on disaster response and preparedness' (2010) *International Journal of Older People Nursing* 5(1) 71.

Fernandez LS, Byard D, Lin CC, et al. 'Frail elderly as disaster victims: Emergency management strategies' (2002) *Prehospital and Disaster Medicine* 17(2) 67–74.

Fortin J, *Children's rights and the developing law* (2ed Butterworths, 2003) .
Fredvang M and Biggs S, 'The rights of older persons: Protection and gaps under human rights law' (Brotherhood of St Laurence, 2012) https://apo.org.au/sites/default/files/resource-files/2012-08/apo-nid31446.pdf
Giorgetti C, 'Rethinking the individual in international law' (2018) *Lewis & Clark Law Review* 22, 1085.
Gorman DM, Livingstone A, Truelove K, et al. *Forgotten workforce: Older people and their right to decent work* (HelpAge International, 2010).
Gutterman AS, 'Intersectionality and the rights of older persons' (2023)SSRN 4339758.
Hannum H, 'The status of the Universal Declaration of Human Rights in national and international law' (1995) *Georgia Journal of International & Comparative Law* 25, 287.
Hannum H, 'The UDHR in national and international law' (1998) *Health and Human Rights* 3, 144.
Harper S and Klien E, 'Forty years of global action on ageing: What has been achieved?' (2022) *Journal of Population Ageing* 15(1) 1.
Helmersen ST, 'Finding 'the most highly qualified publicists': Lessons from the International Court of Justice' (2019) *European Journal of International Law* 30(2) 509.
Help Age International, 'As heavy as a mountain rock: How HIV affects older people' (2009) *Help Age International* 3.
Help Age International, 'Developing countries face ageing revolution' (Help Age International, 2015) <https://www.helpage.org/news/developing-countries-face-ageing-revolution/> - accessed 28 September 2024.
HelpAge International, 'Older People in Aceh, Indonesia 18 Months after the Tsunami Issues and Recommendations ' (2006) 1-17 <https://www.helpage.org/silo/files/older-people-in-aceh-indonesia-18-months-after-the-tsunami-issues-and-recommendations.pdf> accessed 19 February 2025.
Human Rights Watch, 'No one is spared: Abuses against older people in armed conflict' (2022) https://www.hrw.org/sites/default/files/media_2022/02/global_olderpeople0222_web.pdf - accessed 28 September 2024.
Help Age International (2024). A new era for older people in Africa: AU Protocol on Rights of Older Persons comes into force. https://www.helpage.org/news/a-new-era-for-older-people-in-africa-au-protocol-on-rights-of-older-persons-comes-into-force/ - accessed 18 Mar. 2025.
International Commission of Jurists and the International Service for Human Rights, 'Human rights standards: Learning from rxperience' (International Council on Human Rights Policy, Switzerland, 2006).
'International Covenant on Civil and Political Rights' GA Res 2200 (XXI) (16 December 1966).
International Federation of Ageing, et al. 'Strengthening older people's rights: Towards a UN Convention' https://social.un.org/ageing-working-group/documents/Coalition%20to%20Strengthen%20the%20Rights%20of%20Older%20People.pdf - accessed 28 September 2024.
International Labour Office, 'Women and men in the informal economy: A statistical picture' (International Labour Office, 2018).
Kautz T, Bendavid E, Bhattachary J et al 'AIDS and Declining Support for Dependent Elderly People in Africa: Retrospective Analysis Using Demographic and Health Surveys': BMJ 2010;340:c2841
Kendig H, Lucas N, and Anstey KJ, 'Thirty years of the United Nations and global ageing: An Australian perspective' (2013) *Australasian Journal on Ageing* 32, 28–34.
Langlois AJ, 'Human rights: The globalisation and fragmentation of moral discourse' (2002) *Review of International Studies* 28(3) 479.

Lancet Healthy Longevity, 'Ageing with HIV' (2022) The Lancet 3 (3) <https://www.thelancet.com/journals/lanhl/article/PIIS2666-7568(22)00041-1/fulltext> - accessed 19 February 2025. e119.,

Lloyd-Sherlock P, Sempe L, McKee M, et al. 'Problems of data availability and quality for COVID-19 and older people in low-and middle-income countries' (2021) *The Gerontologist* 61(2) 141.

Lowe V, *International law* (OUP, 2007) 11.

Malek MA and Razzak MA, 'Rights of the elderly: An emerging human rights discourse' (2017) *International Journal of Law and Management* 59(2) 284–302.

Marca MLA, 'EU statement - UN open-ended working group on ageing: Opening' (European Union, 20 May 2024) https://www .eeas .europa .eu /delegations /un -new -york /eu -statement- %E2 %80 %93-un -open -ended -working -group -ageing -opening en ?s =63> - accessed 28 September 2024.

Mégret F, 'The human rights of older persons: A growing challenge' (2011) *Human Rights Law Review* 11(1) 37.

Meyer SR, Lasater ME, and García-Moreno C, 'Violence against older women: A systematic review of qualitative literature' (2020) *PLoS One* 15(9) e0239560.

Mooney Cotter A, *Just a number: An international legal analysis on age discrimination* (Ashgate, 2008).

Munthree C and Maharaj P, 'Growing old in the era of a high prevalence of HIV/AIDS: The impact of AIDS on older men and women in KwaZulu-Natal, South Africa' (2010) *Research on Aging* 32(2) 155.

Nhongo TM, 'The changing role of older people in African households and the impact of ageing on African family structures' in *African Conference on Ageing, Johannesburg, South Africa* (August 2004) 18.

Nhongo TM, 'Impact of HIV/AIDS on generational roles and intergenerational relationships' in *Proceedings of the workshop on HIV/AIDS and family well-being, Windhoek, Namibia* (January 2004) 28.

O'donnell ML and Forbes D, 'Natural disaster, older adults, and mental health - A dangerous combination' (2016) *International Psychogeriatrics* 28(1) 9.

OECD, *OECD employment outlook 2020: Worker security and the COVID-19 crisis* (OECD Publishing, 2020)

Organisation of American States 'Inter-American Convention on Protecting the Human Rights of Older Persons' (2009). <https://www.oas.org/en/sla/dil/inter_american_treaties_a-70_human_rights_older_persons.asp >- accessed 5 February 2025.

Rafiey H, Momtaz YA, Alipour F, et al. 'Are older people more vulnerable to long-term impacts of disasters?' (2016) *Clinical Interventions in Aging* 11, 1791.

Ritchie H and Rosado P, 'Is the number of natural disasters increasing?' (Our World in Data, 2024) https://ourworldindata.org/disaster-database-limitations - accessed 4 June 2024.

Ritchie H and Roser M, 'Age structure' (Our World in Data, 2024) https://ourworldindata.org/age-structure - accessed 28 September 2024.

Rodriíguez-Pinzón D, 'Inter-American convention on protecting the human rights of older persons' (2016) *International Legal Materials* 55(5) 985–1006.

Roser M and Ritchie H, 'HIV/AIDS' (Our World in Data, 2023) https://ourworldindata.org/hiv-aids#almost-1-million-people-die-from-hiv-aids-each-year-in-some-countries-it-s-the-leading-cause-of-death - accessed 28 September 2024.

Sanderson WC and Scherbov S, 'Remeasuring aging' (2010) *Science* 329(5997) 1287–1288.

Schmid GP, Williams BG, Garcia-Calleja JM, et al. 'The unexplored story of HIV and ageing' (2009) *Bulletin of the World Health Organization* 87, 162–162A.

Sciubba JD, 'Securing rights in the twenty-first century: A comparison of the disability and older persons' rights conventions' (2016) *Journal of Human Rights* 15(4) 533–549.

Solomon R, 'Witch-killings and the law in Uganda' (2020) *Journal of Law and Religion* 35(2) 270.

Strating R and Edmondson B, 'Beyond democratic tolerance: Witch killings in Timor-Leste' (2015) *Journal of Current Southeast Asian Affairs* 34(3) 37–64.

Tang KL and Lee JJ, 'Global social justice for older people: The case for an international convention on the rights of older people' (2006) *British Journal of Social Work* 36(7) 1135.

Tavoschi L, Dias JG, Pharris A, et al. 'New HIV diagnoses among adults aged 50 years or older in 31 European countries, 2004–15: An analysis of surveillance data' (2017) *The Lancet HIV* 4(11) e514–e521.

The World Bank, 'Understanding poverty: Pensions' (2023) https://www.worldbank.org/en/topic/pensions#2 - accessed 28 September 2024.

Ticehurst S, Webster RA, Carr VJ, et al. 'The psychosocial impact of an earthquake on the elderly' (1996) *International Journal of Geriatric Psychiatry* 11(11) 943.

UNGA Res 217(III) (10th December 1948).

United Nations, 'Madrid International Plan of Action on Ageing' (Second World Assembly on Ageing, 2002) <https://www.un.org/esa/socdev/documents/ageing/MIPAA/political-declaration-en.pdf> - accessed 28 September 2024.

United Nations, 'Open-ended Working Group on Ageing for the purpose of strengthening the protection of the human rights of older persons: Fourteenth Session' (United Nations Office of the High Commissioner, 2024) https://social .un .org /ageing -working -group / fourteenthsession .shtml>– accessed 28 September 2024.

United Nations, 'Report of the Human Rights Council: The human rights of older persons', A/RES/67/143 (24 September 2013) 54.

United Nations, 'Report of the secretary-general: Follow-up to the international year of older persons: Second world assembly on ageing' GA A/76/156 (7 July 2022).

United Nations, 'Report of the World Assembly on Aging' A/Conf.113/31; GA Res 37/51 (1982).

United Nations, 'Transforming our world: The 2030 agenda for sustainable development' (2015) https://sustainabledevelopment.un.org/content/documents/21252030%20Agenda%20for%20Sustainable%20Development%20web.pdf - accessed 28 September 2024.

United Nations, 'World elder abuse awareness day' (15 June 2023) https://www.un.org/en/observances/elder-abuse-awareness-day/background - accessed 28 September 2024.

United Nations Refugee Agency, 'Emergency handbook: Older persons' (UNHCR, 2023) <https://emergency.unhcr.org/protection/persons-risk/older-persons> - accessed 28 September 2024.

Van Steenbergen M, 'Witchcraft used as excuse for violence against older women in Tanzania' (*The Guardian*, 1 October 2012).

Williams J, 'Intimate relationships between older people in institutional settings: Ageism, protection or fear?' (2015) *Ethics, Medicine and Public Health* 1(2) 194.

Wilson MMG, 'Sexually transmitted diseases in older adults' (2006) *Current Infectious Disease Reports* 8(2) 139.

World Health Organization, 'Abuse of older people' (2022) https://www.who.int/news-room/fact-sheets/detail/abuse-of-older-people - accessed 28 September 2024.

World Health Organization, 'Ageing and health' (WHO, 2022) https://www.who.int/news-room/fact-sheets/detail/ageing-and-health - accessed 28 September 2024.

World Health Organization, 'Active ageing: A policy framework' (WHO Organization, 2002) https://iris.who.int/handle/10665/67215 - accessed 28 September 2024.

World Health Organization, 'Tackling abuse of older people: Five priorities for the United Nations Decade of Healthy Ageing (2021–2030)' (2022) https://www.who.int/publications/i/item/9789240052550.- accessed 28 September 2024.

WR Patterson WR, 'Vienna International Plan of Action on Ageing' in D Gu and ME Dupre (eds) *Encyclopedia of Gerontology and Population Aging* (Springer Nature 2021) https://link.springer.com/referenceworkentry/10.1007/978-3-030-22009-9_246#citeas> accessed 5 February 2025, 5369–5373.

Yon Y, Ramiro-Gonzalez M, Mikton CR, et al. 'The prevalence of elder abuse in institutional settings: A systematic review and meta-analysis' (2019) *European Journal of Public Health* 29(1) 58.

Index

FSC
www.fsc.org
MIX
Papier | Fördert gute Waldnutzung
FSC® C083411

Kolibri 360 GmbH
Ferdinand-Jühlke-Straße 7
99095 Erfurt, Deutschland
produktsicherheit@kolibri360.de